JOE McGINNISS

CRUEL DOUBT

POCKET STAR BOOKS

New York London Toronto Sydney Tokyo Singapore

A Pocket Star Book published by
POCKET BOOKS, a division of Simon & Schuster Inc.
1230 Avenue of the Americas, New York, NY 10020

ISBN: 0-671-77539-1

First Pocket Books printing June 1992

10 9 8 7 6 5 4 3 2 1

"Masterfully weaves together the tangled threads of the most shocking and grisly murder case in recent memory . . . SPELLBINDING."

—*Sacramento Union*

"McGinniss [is] the Alfred Hitchcock of the true-crime genre, a genre he often transcends."

—*Boston Globe*

"What McGinniss . . . does so superbly is to bring us just a little closer to the heart of darkness and make us understand that there is, in the end, no accounting for human behavior."

—*Detroit News*

"McGinniss again shows why he heads the ranks of true-crime authors—delivering a page-burner of shifting suspicions, macabre ironies, and reversals of field too extreme for fiction. . . ."

—*Kirkus Reviews*

"A lurid psychological thriller and a detective story with all the intriguing detail of a classic whodunit . . . We begin to perceive a purposeful spiraling as we draw closer and closer to the truth. . . . What is most impressive about *CRUEL DOUBT* is the author's ability to infuse a well-reported crime story with genuine suspense . . . plenty of shocks and surprises. McGinniss is also adept at evoking the colorful personalities and hothouse environment of the rural South. . . . A startlingly intimate profile of the Von Steins and the various miseries that seemed to build toward the Walpurgisnacht of Lieth's murder."

—*Los Angeles Times*

Books by Joe McGinniss

Cruel Doubt
Blind Faith
Fatal Vision
Going to Extremes
Heroes
The Dream Team
The Selling of the President

FOR MY FAMILY
WITH LOVE AND GRATITUDE

Acknowledgments

Early in 1990, when she wrote to Dr. Jean Spaulding and others, asking them to cooperate fully with me in the preparation of this book, Bonnie Von Stein said she wanted "one person to share everything I know with, good or bad," I was that person.

Neither Bonnie nor any member of her family nor anyone else who spoke with me or with my research assistant, Robyn Smith, received any form of financial compensation. Nor did anyone seek or receive the right ot review, approve, or in any way exercise control over my use of the information they so generously and candidly shared with me.

These days, that is a rare circumstance. It arose in large part, I believe, out of their respect for Bonnie's wishes, and from their admiration and affection for her. If she wanted the truth told, the truth—as they knew it—was what they would tell, even if aspects of it might not be consistent with Bonnie's point of view.

Thus, it seems appropriate to thank, first and foremost, Bonnie Von Stein. Because she is the central figure in this book, I'll not offer any capsule description of her here, but trust that the reader will come to know her in the pages that follow. I shall say only that never once—even when made uncomfortable by some of what came to interest me—did Bonnie pull back from her absolute and unflinching them pain. Some are portrayed in this book, some are not, but I am grateful to them all.

These include Andrew Arnold; Rene Bailey; Karen Barbour; George and Peggy Bates; Polly Bates; Vivian Bates; Elwood Blackmon; Donna Brady; Tom Brereton; Eric Caldwell; Kim Craft; Sylvia Craven; Washington, North Carolina, chief of police John Crone; Janie and Leesa Edwards; Vince Hamrick; Mary Ann Harris; Tiffany Heady; Anne Henderson; Neal Henderson; John Hubard; Dr. Page Hudson; Frank Johnston; Will Lang; Keith Mason; Stephanie Mercer; Mitchell Norton; Steven Outlaw; Bill Osteen, Sr. (now the Honorable William Osteen, United States District Judge for the Central District of North Carolina); Bill Osteen, Jr.; Joanne Osteen; Angela Pritchard; Chris Pritchard; Steve Pritchard; Sam and Ramona Ravan and their children, Julie and Joe; Laura Reynaud; Dr. Billy Royal; Wayland Sermons; Linda Sloane; Dave and Sue Smith; Wade Smith; Dr. Jean Spaulding; Lt. John Taylor of the Washington, North Carolina police department; Steve Tripp; Kenyatta Upchurch; Jim Vosburgh; Curtis and Barbara Wagoner; Jonathan Wagoner; Judge Thomas Watts; and Lewis Young.

(I should point out that Judge Watts, though extending great courtesy both to me and to Robyn Smith, made a special point of *not* commenting in any way, directly or indirectly, on or off the record, about any matters that came before him in court.)

Many of those listed above went far beyond the dictates of either professionalism or courtesy and provided invaluable assistance and often great hospitality as well. To them, I have much to repay.

If there are omissions above, they are inadvertent, and I apologize.

Among those mentioned, I must single out Bonnie's two children, Chris and Angela. Again, they are central characters in the story that follows, and readers, I hope, will come to some understanding of them in the context of their experiences. Here, I would like to say only that both squarely addressed even the most personal and probing of questions, and for that I respect them and am grateful.

ACKNOWLEDGMENTS

I also owe thanks to Teri Andrews, clerk of court in Beaufort County, North Carolina; to Bill Dowdy of the North Carolina State Bureau of Investigation and those other officials of the organization who granted Lewis Young permission to share with me the results of his investigation; to officials at the Polk Youth Correctional Institution in Raleigh, and at the state correctional facilities in Goldsboro, Lillington, and Asheville, who readily granted both Robyn Smith and me access for interviews with Chris Pritchard and Neal Henderson.

Special thanks are due Tammy Hensley, assistant to Dr. Jean Spaulding, who laboriously typed the transcripts of my tape-recorded discussions with Dr. Spaulding.

And appreciation, too, to Brookie Sterling, Roger Smith, and Jim Klepfer, who combined to introduce my family and me to the pleasures of a very special part of North Carolina—Bald Head Island.

For technical support during the writing, I thank James Plunkett, Emilia Seibold, and Geoff Chappell of Synectic Systems, East Dover, Vermont. They were always there (and sometimes here) when needed.

Traditionally authors thank their wives for emotional support, patience, fortitude, understanding, etc. Nancy is certainly due that, but also much more. Having worked professionally as a journalist and editor herself, she contributed in more ways than I can count to whatever quality this book may possess. From inception of the idea through final revision of the manuscript—where her relentless scrutiny and keen editorial perceptions proved especially beneficial—she has been invaluable.

I am also grateful to my son Matthew, whose ideas regarding structure and form proved helpful indeed.

But if any one person's contributions overshadowed those of all others, it is Robyn Smith's. In the past, I've occasionally relied on people for help with research, and I've never been disappointed in the result.

Robyn Smith, however, proved to be far more than what is traditionally thought of as a "research assistant." A former television journalist currently enrolled in the Graduate School of Journalism at Columbia University, Robyn con-commitment to give me unrestricted access to all information within her control, and to all people who could shed light on any part of this story, even if it illuminated corners disturbing to her. That, I think, is a rare form of courage.

In addition to Bonnie, I would like to express my deep appreciation to all those who were so generous with their insights, information, and time, even when—as was sometimes the case—they were discussing matters that caused tributed so much to this book, in so many ways, that in fairness she should almost be deemed a collaborator. Never before have I relied so heavily on someone else's help; but never before have I had available someone of Robyn Smith's caliber. She is an extraordinarily gifted and energetic journalist, and it was my great good fortune that the course of her life gave her the freedom, at a crucial time in the life of this project, to do the work I needed done.

She personally interviewed more than thirty people. In many cases, I'd already spoken to them at length, but even here Robyn obtained new and valuable information. In other instances—as with George and Peggy Bates, Donna Brady, Dr. Page Hudson, Frank Johnston, Keith Mason, Wayland Sermons, and Judge Watts—she did it all herself. In addition, Robyn conducted the sensitive and difficult June 1991 interviews with both Chris and Angela Pritchard, and I cannot imagine how anyone could have done a better job. However this book may be judged, it would have been a lesser work without her involvement.

To my agent, Mort Janklow, who has made such an enormous contribution to my professional life, goes a special word of thanks. And appreciation also to Bill Haber of the Creative Artists Agency.

Lastly, for their unwavering faith in, commitment to, and support of, my work, I would like to thank Richard E. Snyder, president of Simon & Schuster, and Michael V. Korda, editor in chief, and also editor of this book.

Contents

Doubts are more cruel than the worst of truths.

—Molière
Le Misanthrope

Introduction

In the middle of February 1990, I received a phone call from a lawyer in Raleigh, North Carolina, named Wade Smith. I'd met him in 1979, when he'd served as local counsel for Jeffrey MacDonald, a former Green Beret doctor convicted of murdering his wife and two children, about whom I had written in a book called *Fatal Vision*. MacDonald had not liked the book, but Wade and I had become friends in the years that followed.

He was chairman of Tharrington, Smith and Hargrove, a thirty-lawyer firm, which, in the years since I'd first met him, had grown into one of the most respected and prosperous in the South. Wade himself, at fifty-two, had advanced from being one of the most prominent criminal lawyers in North Carolina to being one of the state's most esteemed citizens. He'd served as chairman of the Democratic Party's state committee, his name still surfaced occasionally when possible candidates for governor were discussed, and he was about to become national president of the University of North Carolina's alumni association.

He said he had a client who'd just been through some difficult experiences, in the midst of which he'd given her a copy of *Fatal Vision*. Having read it, she had learned that Wade knew me, and she had asked him to contact me.

Although she'd shunned all publicity and valued her privacy highly, she remained so troubled by so much of what had happened to her that she wondered if I might want to write a book that could explore some of what she'd endured for eighteen months, and that might perhaps examine those aspects of her ordeal that, to her, still posed unanswered questions.

Another murder was the last thing I wanted, but Wade Smith is a persuasive man. After half an hour on the phone with him, I agreed that I'd fly to Raleigh and at least talk to the woman, whose name was Bonnie Von Stein.

I met her on Wednesday, February 21. She was forty-six years old, she wore a plain blue dress and thick glasses. Her brown hair, graying at the edges, was limp and straight. She looked frail and weary, and her face was devoid of expression. The very act of talking seemed painful for her. The air in the room where we spoke reeked of misery. She was everything I wanted no part of, yet I was there. And as she started to speak, I knew that one of two things would happen: either I'd start to care, which would be bad; or else I wouldn't, which might be worse.

It became clear quickly that she was not a person who simply craved the fifteen minutes of notoriety that attach themselves to anyone willing to titillate the public with his or her grief and complaints of injustice. To the contrary, she seemed almost disturbingly private.

She wasn't in it for the money, either. I told her I could not give her any money; that I wasn't interested in acquiring her "rights." Almost as if offended by the notion, she said she wouldn't even consider taking money.

I also explained that it was not my practice to write a person's "authorized" version of events. That there had never been a circumstance under which I'd given a subject the right to approve, or even to see before publication, what I had written. That did not surprise her, either. She said she'd never thought a serious writer would work otherwise.

If not for Wade, of course, I would not even have been in Raleigh. As it was, I could leave at any time. I could just stand up and tell her it had been nice to meet her and wish her well and walk out the door and spend an evening warmed by Wade's *joie de vivre* and then, in the morning, fly home. I didn't need Bonnie Von Stein or her pain.

But what I began to sense that first day, and felt even more strongly the next, was that what she wanted from me was something both more complex and harder to provide than money or celebrity.

I thought, and still think, that Bonnie was hoping that if she threw her whole life open to me, if she held back no secrets whatsoever—if she authorized and even urged lawyers and psychiatrists and children and other family members and anyone else she'd ever known to talk to me with absolute candor—I might somehow be able to illuminate for her the darkness that had come to fill her days.

She believed—or wanted very much to believe—that I might find explanations for the inexplicable; answers to unanswerable questions; solutions to insoluble problems. She wanted me, I think, to make comprehensible to her all that she had endured and all she would forever have to abide.

None of us, however, really wants to part with every secret. Perhaps certain darknesses are best left undisturbed. There is a danger, in sending forth someone to search for truth, that we might suddenly find ourselves confronted by aspects of it that we've had deep and compelling reason to deny.

Early on, Wade told me this about Bonnie: "There's no way you can hurt her. This is a woman with nothing left to lose."

It might have been one of the few times I've known him to be wrong.

PART ONE

A DEATH
IN THE
FAMILY

JULY 1988–JANUARY 1989

1

The fire was burning in a swamp just a few feet off the edge of the road. This was in Pitt County, North Carolina, one mile west of the Beaufort County line. It was four-thirty A.M., pitch-black, Monday, July 25, 1988.

Noel Lee had been loading hogs. That is a task that in North Carolina, in summer, is best done after midnight and before dawn. Otherwise, the hogs are too hot by the time they reach the slaughterhouse. You don't want them over-heated when you kill them. It spoils the meat. The hogs had moved good, loaded out fast. The truck had come in about three-thirty, and in not much more than an hour it was on its way again.

Lee was just starting home, the hog stink still heavy in the air, when he saw the flames burning in the darkness. It was odd, a fire in the swamp in the middle of the night. He was curious enough to take a closer look. But not so curious, when he got there, that he got out of his truck. He didn't know, he said later, what might be waiting for him behind the flames.

The fire was only a foot or two in diameter, the flames three or four feet high. What struck him most—other than the fact of the fire itself—was how strongly the flames burned in the damp, as if fueled by a flammable liquid.

There was no traffic, no one in sight. State Road 1565, known locally as Grimesland Bridge Road, off state highway 264, about ninety-five miles east of Raleigh, thirty miles inland from the coast, was not a major thoroughfare at any hour. At four-thirty A.M. on July 25, 1988, it was just a black line through farmland and darkness. The only light anywhere was the light from the mysterious fire. Noel Lee sat for a few moments in his truck, staring at it, wondering where it had come from, and why. Then he went home to bed, having no idea how many lives would be forever altered by his having noticed the flames.

Seven miles away, in Washington, North Carolina, Bonnie Von Stein, forty-four years old, lying on the floor of her bedroom, had finally reached the police dispatcher.

"This is an emergency," she said very softly.

"Can I help you?" asked the dispatcher, a young woman.

"Yes, this is an emergency."

"Well, what do you need, ma'am?" The dispatcher thought it was the crazy lady who often called in the middle of the night.

"I need the police and an ambulance."

"Well, where do you need 'em?"

"One ten Lawson Road."

"One ten, what road?"

"Lawson."

"One ten Lawson Road?"

"L-A-W-S-O-N." Very softly, Bonnie Von Stein spelled it out.

"I can't hear you, ma'am, could you speak up?"

"I'm sorry. The intruder may still be in the house."

"Okay, why do you need an ambulance?"

"My husband may be dying and I think I may be, too."

"Your husband did what?"

"My husband may be dying and I may be dying also." The dispatcher knew now. It wasn't the crazy lady. It was somebody else.

"Okay, what is your name, please?"

"Bonnie Von Stein." She was still speaking so softly she could barely be heard.

"Bonnie what?"

4

"Von Stein."

"Okay, Bonnie Von Stein. Bonnie, hold on just a minute and I'm getting an officer on the way. Okay? Don't hang up on me, all right?"

"Yes."

The dispatcher put out the call, then came back on the line. "Bonnie, are you still there?"

"Yes, I'm here."

"Okay. Is someone in your house?"

"I don't know if they are still here or not."

"Okay, did someone—why—where are you bleeding?"

"In the chest. I've been beaten and stabbed, I think."

"Okay. Is your husband—is he beaten and stabbed also?"

"Yes."

"Okay, I have an officer on the way and I want you to stay right there with me, okay? Don't hang up until the police get there."

"I don't know where my daughter is." She had a daughter, Angela, eighteen years old. She also had a son, Chris, who was nineteen and away at college.

The dispatcher spoke to the officers who were on their way to the scene. "She advised she and her husband have been beaten and stabbed. She advised her daughter is also in the house and she doesn't know where she's at."

"What's the address?" an officer asked.

"One ten Lawson. One ten Lawson," the dispatcher said.

"Please hurry," Bonnie Von Stein said.

"Okay," the dispatcher said. "They're getting there just as fast as they can, and I am going to stay with you, okay? Okay, you hear—I hear the sirens going out right now. You just hold on."

"I'll try."

"Can you stay on the phone while I call the rescue?"

"Uh-huh."

"Okay, you stay on there and don't hang up." The dispatcher then spoke to the officers. "I'm not taking any chances, I'm calling rescue."

"We're en route," an officer said. "Be just a minute."

The dispatcher spoke to fire and rescue. "Captain Lewis, we have a possible stabbing and beating, one ten Lawson Road. Bonnie Von . . . Stal-dine is the complainant. We have three officers on the way at this time. I can't give you any more than that right now because the lady can hardly talk."

"One ten Lawson Road?"

"One ten Lawson Road. There may be more than one person injured."

"Okay, we're rolling."

"Okay, thank you Captain Lewis." Then the dispatcher spoke to Bonnie Von Stein. "Okay, Bonnie, the rescue's on the way, too, okay?"

"Yes." The voice was still very faint.

"But I am not going to hang up until you hear 'em there with you."

"I don't hear my husband breathing as fast."

"Where is your husband, Bonnie?"

"In bed."

"Can you wake him?"

"I can't reach him. I'm on the floor."

"Okay, can you call him?"

"No."

"Okay. And you don't know about your daughter?"

"No."

"Is there anybody else that lives there with you?"

"They're not at home."

There was a pause. "Okay, Bonnie?" the dispatcher said.

"Huh?"

"You still with me?"

"Yes."

"Now, look, you hang in there. Don't—don't pass out on me, okay?"

"I'll try."

"Okay, 'cause you stay calm and cool like you're doing, you're going to help everybody. Where are you in the house?"

"I'm in the bedroom on the right."

"You're in the what? Bedroom on the right?"

"The bedrooms are upstairs." She was speaking even more softly now, as if the last of her breath were almost gone. "My daughter . . . is in bedroom on left."

"Your daughter is what, dear?"

"In the bedroom on the left."

The dispatcher spoke to the officers. "She advises she is in the bedroom on the right, her daughter's on the left."

"God, I hope this is a bad dream," Bonnie Von Stein said.

Two police cars reached the house. "Okay, do you hear them?" the dispatcher said.

"Think so."

"Okay, how can they get in?"

"I don't know."

"You don't know how they can get in?"

"No."

"Can you give—will you—"

"I don't know how they got in."

An officer spoke. "You advise which door was unlocked?"

"She says she doesn't know how they got in," the dispatcher said. "Stand by. I'm trying to get you more."

"That's the policemen," Bonnie Von Stein said. "I hear them."

"Yes," the dispatcher said. "There are four policemen there."

"Okay," an officer said. "I got the back door open. The back door's been forced open, I believe."

"The back door is open," the dispatcher said to Bonnie Von Stein. "The back door has been forced open and they are coming in."

"Oh, my God," Bonnie Von Stein said. Then she began to cry.

"You just—you just lay right there—look, don't get excited. Okay, Bonnie? You calm down . . . calm down, okay?"

"I have cats. Please, I don't want my cats hurt."

"Okay, Bonnie, you just calm down and think good thoughts . . . and I'm not going to hang up with you until Officer Sparrow comes in and talks with me. Okay?"

"Okay."

"When Officer—when officer comes in—Officer Sparrow is my husband, okay? So you ask for him . . ."

"Okay."

" . . . and tell him I'm on the phone and let me talk to him."

"Okay."

"Okay, can you call him?"

"The light's turned off."

"Okay, his name is David."

Bonnie Von Stein heard policemen in the hallway outside her room. "Uh, please come in," she said. "Please come in." They didn't seem to hear her. There was a pause. "Please come in!" she called, raising her voice for the first time. The door opened. "Yes . . . please," she said. "Turn the light on."

An officer named Tetterton did. And when he did, he cried out, *"Oh, my God in this world!"*

"Officer . . . Officer . . . Officer Sparrow," Bonnie Von Stein said.

Sparrow was there. "Yes, ma'am."

"Oh, it's not a dream."

Tetterton was on the radio to the dispatcher. "Dispatch rescue!" he was saying. "Call the rescue!"

"I hear," the dispatcher said. "I got 'em on the way."

"Is my—my daughter in the other bedroom?" Bonnie Von Stein said. She was sounding increasingly distraught. "I think I heard my daughter talk."

"Okay," the dispatcher said to the officers. "Please advise me if that subject's daughter is all right so I can calm her down."

A moment later, an officer named Edwards called out, "She's okay."

"Okay," the dispatcher said. "Bonnie, your daughter is fine."

"My husband must be bad . . . oh, God! . . . I see him!"

"Okay, don't look at him, Bonnie. Bonnie, don't look at him."

"He was trying to help me."

"Okay, do you remember seeing anybody?"

"Oh, it was dark, I don't know."

"Okay."

"I know he had a big club or a baseball bat . . . and a knife. I didn't hear anything. I'm sorry."

"We're gonna need an investigator," Edwards said.

"Bonnie?" the dispatcher said.

"Yes."

"Okay, now you hang in there with me."

"Don't let my daughter come in here."

"Okay," Tetterton said. He called to another officer, "Tell her not to come in here."

"Bonnie?" the dispatcher said.

"Yes."

"The rescue's coming, okay?"

"Yes."

"Okay, don't look at your husband."

Tetterton then took the phone from Bonnie Von Stein. "Hey," he said.

"Tetterton?"

"Yo."

"God," the dispatcher said.

"In bad shape, gal," Tetterton said. "We got to have a uh . . . uh . . . a rescue right quick."

"They're on the way," the dispatcher said.

Tetterton hung up the phone.

Hearing Bonnie call out repeatedly, "How is my daughter? . . . How is my daughter?" Patrolman Edwards had taken two or three steps down the hall and opened the first door he came to. He shined his high-powered police flashlight on the bed. He could see a figure lying there. Using a wall switch, he turned on the room light. He saw Angela, unharmed. Next to the bed, an electric fan was running.

Angela rolled over and asked calmly, "What is it?"

She recognized Edwards. She and her friends called him Danny the Dickhead because he used to chase them from the mall parking lot whenever they gathered there on weekend nights.

"Are you okay?" he asked.

"I'm fine. What's going on?" She seemed neither alarmed

nor even surprised to see a police officer in her bedroom at four-thirty A.M.

"You need to get up and put your clothes on," he told her.

Angela had been sleeping in a T-shirt and underpants. She got out of bed and pulled on a pair of jeans. She was about five two and maybe weighed a few pounds more than she would have liked, but was not an unattractive girl. She had reddish brown hair, a snub nose, and freckles.

Edwards noticed a dark brown stain on the jeans she'd put on.

"Is that blood?"

She looked at the stain. "No, that's just oil and saddle soap," she said. "I spent most of yesterday at the stables." Then she asked again, "What's going on?"

He did not answer immediately. Edwards didn't know whether any intruders were still in the house. He thought someone might have tried to flee through the attic upon hearing the arrival of the police.

"How do you get to the attic?" he asked.

Angela told him the only access was through a crawl space inside her closet. He opened the closet and immediately saw that it was packed full of clothes, leaving the crawl space inaccessible.

As he was checking the closet, Angela stepped out of her room, into the hallway, and seeing activity and hearing noise, walked to the doorway of the master bedroom.

The blood-drenched body of her stepfather lay sprawled across the double bed. He was wearing only a pair of briefs. It was quite obvious to Angela that he was dead. Her mother was lying on the floor, emergency medical technicians gathered around her.

She heard her mother ask, "Where's Angela?"

"I'm here, Mom," she said. "I'm fine."

Then someone shouted, "Get her out of here!"

Angela stood at the bedroom doorway, still staring inside.

Officer Sparrow told her to go downstairs and to wait in the living room and to be sure she did not touch anything.

She made no reply, but as instructed, walked downstairs.

"She didn't seem curious," Sparrow would later say. "She didn't appear to have any emotion."

Within minutes, Tetterton came down and spoke to her. "Your mother's been hurt," he said. "I don't know how bad." Then he said he thought that Lieth was dead.

Later, he would recall her reaction: "To her mother's situation, she was real calm. To her stepfather, it was slight tears in her eyes, but she was real calm."

He asked if she had heard or seen any of what had happened upstairs. She said no, she'd been sound asleep until Edwards had come into her room and turned on the light.

Tetterton then asked if, under the circumstances, there was someone—a family member or friend—whom she might want to call and ask to come over.

"Can I call my boyfriend?" she asked.

"Sure," Tetterton said, "go ahead."

As she walked toward the kitchen, Tetterton noticed the cats. There seemed to be cats everywhere, running all over the downstairs. Later, when they were all rounded up, there were thirteen. Thirteen cats and a rooster.

When police and rescue personnel had first arrived at the house, they found the cord that connected the kitchen telephone to its receiver disconnected. An emergency medical technician had plugged it back in, so he could call the hospital.

From that phone, Angela called a friend of hers named Andrew Arnold, who lived only about two miles away.

Awakened from a sound sleep himself, and surprised to be hearing from Angela at that hour, Arnold recalled her saying, "Mom and Lieth have just been stabbed and beaten. Can you come over?" He said he would come right away.

She also called her brother, Chris, who was attending summer session at North Carolina State University in Raleigh, about a hundred miles away. She told him essentially what she'd told Andrew Arnold. Then she went back and sat in the living room, amid the cats.

The stretcher bearing her mother was rushed down the stairs and out to the ambulance that waited in the driveway.

Angela watched in silence. Her detachment struck Officer Sparrow as so unusual that he referred to it in the report he wrote later that day: "The young lady seemed to be unemotional concerning the entire traumatic incident. She was never emotional or curious as to what had taken place."

When Andrew Arnold arrived, he went right to her, put his arm around her, and hugged her. He was her friend, but they did not have a romantic involvement.

Later, he would recall, "There might have been a few tears or a snuffly nose, but she did not cry."

A policeman said they wanted her to go to the station and make a statement. She walked out of the house without even putting on her shoes. She rode to the station in a patrol car, with Andrew following.

All she could tell them was that she didn't know anything because she'd been asleep the whole time. She wasn't sure how long the detective talked to her. Maybe half an hour. When he was done, Andrew gave her a ride to the hospital. Still barefoot, she walked into the emergency room, looking for her mother.

Bonnie was conscious, with doctors working over her. She told Angela to go back to the house and make sure she gathered up the cats.

When the phone rang, just before five A.M., in room 611B of Lee Dorm on the campus of North Carolina State University in Raleigh, nobody answered immediately.

Chris Pritchard had been up until three-thirty, drinking beer and playing cards. He'd drunk too much beer. The phone rang and rang, until his roommate, who'd drunk less and who'd gone to bed earlier, finally answered it. He fell back to sleep as soon as he handed Chris the phone.

Angela was calling. Chris listened in silence to what she said. As soon as he hung up, he began thrashing around the room, throwing clothes and chair cushions into the air, and shouting that he couldn't find his car keys.

He dashed out the door and ran down six flights of stairs to the street. Fifty yards from the dorm entrance stood a campus police telephone booth, illuminated by a blue light.

Chris sprinted to the phone, picked it up, and started to babble.

He was shouting so hysterically that the dispatcher couldn't even make out his name. But there was something about a stabbing or killing in some place that sounded like Washington. And car keys: over and over, he kept yelling that he couldn't find his car keys.

The dispatcher put out a call at 5:17 A.M., asking a car to go to the blue-light phone on Dan Allen Drive, near Sullivan. She said a person on the line was talking loudly. To campus police at NC State, this was no big deal. More than ten thousand students were on campus for summer session, and the campus itself—as it was all year—was saturated with alcohol and illegal drugs. A middle-of-the-night call on an emergency phone from someone screaming hysterically was not an unprecedented occurrence.

Two officers reached the phone at 5:19. Chris Pritchard, who'd been slumped against a lamppost on the sidewalk, jumped up and ran toward them, waving his hands frantically in the air.

"I lost my keys! I can't find my fucking car keys! My mother and father have been beaten and stabbed. In Washington. In Beaufort County. I've got to get down there! But I can't find my keys!"

Chris was five nine and weighed only 150 pounds. He was wearing a baseball cap, sweatshirt, and shorts and looked too young to be in college. To the officers, who had some experience in such matters, he seemed either drunk or high on drugs. He wouldn't shut up. He just kept babbling the same thing. They couldn't tell if it was a hoax or not, so they took him to campus police headquarters and called the Washington, North Carolina, police from there.

It was no hoax. And at a few minutes past six A.M., with Chris lying down on the backseat, a campus police car set off on the two-hour drive to Little Washington. He fell asleep almost immediately and slept almost all the way home, until they reached the outskirts of Washington and had to wake him to ask directions to his house.

2

John Taylor was twenty-six years old, a slender and dark-haired man with a neatly trimmed mustache who spent most of his waking hours with a toothpick in his mouth. His real name was Haskell Taylor, Jr., but he'd been called John almost all his life, nicknamed after the Jimmy Dean song "Big Bad John."

Born in California, he had moved to eastern North Carolina at the age of twelve. He'd worked as an electrician and then for Texas Gulf, before joining the Washington police department in 1984. For the past two years, he'd been a detective. He liked to think he knew the town, knew who was who among its residents. But as he stood in Lieth Von Stein's bedroom, taking pictures of the bloody body on the bed, he had to admit that the name was not one with which he was familiar.

Taylor had seen crime scenes more gross, but none that seemed such a personal intrusion. Whoever he had been, Von Stein had met a terrible end. Clubbed and stabbed to death in his own bed, after having apparently been awakened from sleep for just a startling, savage moment.

Taylor moved to his right, stepped over a stack of *Wall Street Journals* that lay on the floor beneath a personal computer, and bent down to take another photograph. The poor bastard. Whoever had done it hadn't taken any chances. Taylor leaned over the blood-soaked mattress and took a picture from directly above.

Von Stein. Von Stein. John Taylor was certain: it was not a name he'd ever heard before. Guy didn't look old. Maybe early forties, a little overweight. Kind of balding on top, there where he'd been smacked with the club. Had a little beard that might have looked reddish in color if it hadn't been for all the blood.

The wife had been taken out before Taylor arrived. Rushed to the hospital, still alive, but unconscious and bleeding heavily from the chest.

Taylor backed up against a wall and tried a shot that would show the body's position on the bed. *Christ, there was a lot of blood.* It was six A.M., just starting to get light. It would be another very hot and humid day: one of the sad facts of life in North Carolina in July.

As he continued to photograph the body, John Taylor decided he might be more comfortable if the bedroom were just a little bit cooler, so he stepped to the thermostat and turned up the air-conditioning.

He spent about another twenty minutes in the bedroom, then brought his camera downstairs, where one of the other officers told him they'd finally collected all the cats.

Strangest thing he'd ever seen: thirteen cats at a murder scene. Thirteen cats and a *rooster*. When Taylor had first arrived, terrified cats were running all over the house. It had taken three officers, plus the daughter and a couple of her friends, to round them up and put them in carrying cases so they could be taken to a veterinarian's office. The daughter said her mother was a member of the Beaufort County Humane Society. She also said the rooster was a pet.

Taylor walked through the kitchen and into an enclosed porch area that led to the backyard. There, he photographed a green, canvas, Army-style knapsack that lay on the floor, near the door. The knapsack appeared empty.

He also photographed the only signs of damage he could see. A hole had been smashed in a large, double-paned plate-glass window adjacent to the back door. Shards of glass lay on the floor, near the knapsack and door. Stepping through the open doorway, Taylor saw that a screen outside the plate-glass window had been slashed twice, each cut about twelve inches long.

Inside the house, except for the contents of a purse scattered across a kitchen counter, nothing appeared to be disturbed.

To John Taylor, it didn't look like a burglary. It looked as if someone had come to the house to murder Lieth Von Stein.

At the hospital, Bonnie drifted in and out of consciousness. She was as pale as the sheets on which she lay. A tube was in her chest where a lung had collapsed, and through another, in her arm, she was receiving a blood transfusion, and through another, intravenous fluids. Her hair was matted with blood, her eyes were glazed from sedatives, and there were gashes in her forehead where she'd been struck by a club.

By four-fifty A.M., when she'd arrived at the emergency room, her blood pressure had dropped to ninety over sixty. A pair of inflatable antishock trousers had been placed on her legs in an attempt to stabilize her blood pressure.

The two-inch-long stab wound in her chest had punctured her right lung, causing such severe internal bleeding that she required an immediate two-pint blood transfusion. When a tube was first inserted into the collapsed lung, more than five hundred cubic centimeters of bloody fluid were sucked out.

In addition to the stab wound, she had a large bruise on the right side of her chest. She'd also been hit three times on the forehead with a blunt object, each blow producing both a bruise and a cut severe enough to require suturing. She also had a fractured thumb.

Had she not managed to call the police, she might easily have slipped into shock and died from blood loss, or other complications of her punctured lung. By seven A.M., however, the doctor who examined her was able to write that she was "alert and conscious and responding well to stimuli." He termed her condition "stable," which was not to say she had not been very badly hurt, or that she was yet out of danger.

By shortly after noon, she had improved to the point where not only was her physical condition termed "stable," but a doctor who examined her wrote that she was "emotionally controlled, pleasant, and cooperative."

Within hours, in various quarters of Little Washington,

this demeanor would come to be described as being not at all what one would expect from a woman whose husband had been brutally murdered in the middle of the night, and who herself had been seriously injured—unless, of course, the event was just what she'd been hoping for, and what she might even have managed to arrange.

Chris reached the house shortly after eight A.M. He did not go in. His facial features, small and still not fully formed, gave him a childish appearance, which, combined with his slight build, always made him seem younger than he was, no matter how many days he went without shaving.

On this morning, he looked like hell. He hadn't shaved in three days, his spiky brown hair was greasy, his breath foul. He was wearing the same NC State "Wolfpack" sweatshirt he'd had on when he'd collapsed into bed hours earlier. His hands were shaking, his voice was high-pitched, and his eyes were so big and queer-looking that anyone familiar with the effects would have guessed that at some time in the not too distant past he'd consumed a drug stronger than beer.

Angela was sitting on a lawn across the street from her house. A group of her friends, having heard the news, had already begun to gather. They were smoking and talking and looking across Lawson Road at all the policemen running in and out, and at the television trucks starting to arrive.

Chris spoke briefly to his sister, who left her spot at the edge of the lawn long enough to tell him that Lieth was dead and that their mother was in intensive care.

A Washington patrolman gave him a ride to the hospital. He went to his mother's bedside. She looked as close to being dead as anyone he'd ever seen. Tubes seemed to be everywhere, pouring fluid in and sucking fluid out. Her whole head seemed caked with dried blood.

But she opened her eyes as he stepped toward her and made a small sound that let him know that she knew who he was.

As soon as she did, he squeezed her hand and started to

cry. For minutes, he just stood there, bending over her, and crying as if he'd never stop.

Lewis Young, resident agent of the North Carolina State Bureau of Investigation based in the town of Washington, got to the house at nine A.M. A big man, about six two, he was good-looking in the understated way that capable plainclothes investigators often were. He'd been with the State Bureau of Investigation for fourteen years. The SBI was a North Carolina version of the FBI, called in to help local police with major crimes.

Mitchell Norton, the Beaufort County district attorney, had called Young as soon as he'd heard about the murder. This one looked too big to be left solely in the hands of the Washington police.

Of all the SBI's resident agents, Young was one of the very few—in fact, he knew of no other—to have graduated from the University of North Carolina at Chapel Hill. From his superiors, he'd always received the highest possible ratings for thoroughness, intelligence, and ability to get along with both colleagues and the public.

Such was his reputation that even if the murder had occurred hundreds of miles away, Young might have been called to assist with the investigation—he was much in demand for difficult cases—but by geographical fluke, the crime had occurred in his own territory, and thus he was at the scene within hours.

Even before entering the house, Young could tell he'd have problems. In the backyard, blood-soaked sheets hung from a small outboard motorboat. Young winced. This was a crime scene. The scene of a *murder*. At a crime scene, you were supposed to preserve the evidence, not drape it all over a boat.

As he approached the back entrance to the house, Young noticed the slashed screen and the shattered window, the edge of the window being about ten to twelve inches from the edge of the door. He noted also that what looked to be small panes of glass in the door itself, several of which would have given much easier access to the doorknob, had not been broken.

The thought occurred to him that, if one were intending to break into a house, it would have been far easier to crack an eight-by-ten-inch piece of single-pane glass that gave easy access to the lock on the inner knob below than to smash a large Thermopane, double-thick window, in a place from which it would be difficult, if not impossible, to reach the inner knob in order to unlock the door.

From his first look, in other words, Lewis Young, with all his experience and expertise, thought the evidence suggested not an actual forced entry, but rather that someone had tried to *stage* a scene that looked like a break-in.

To Young, it seemed at least a strong possibility that someone had smashed the glass and slashed the screen as an afterthought—on the way out.

As John Taylor had, Young noted that there was little, if any, evidence of theft. And like Taylor, Lewis Young quickly concluded that whoever had come through that door—and however he, or they, had gained entrance—had come with killing, not stealing, in mind.

Young considered the possibility that the killer, or killers, had entered through the front door. But a quick check with the first officers and emergency medical personnel at the scene confirmed that the front door had been locked when they arrived. Thus, it seemed a near-certainty to Young that the back door had been the point of entrance and exit.

John Taylor, before leaving the scene for the day, conducted a small personal experiment to test Young's hypothesis that the shattered window had not provided the killer or killers with access to the inside of the house.

Even discounting the added concern that, in darkness, groping toward the doorknob from the small hole in the double-paned glass meant risking a cut from one of the shards protruding from the edges, Taylor later said that, in order to even *reach* the doorknob, "I had to hold the doorframe and stand on the edge of the steps and reach my hand all the way around and reach around the casing that covers the window, and the casing that covers the door, and it was difficult."

Thus, he, like Lewis Young, from the very first hours,

19

thought that not only had theft not been the motive, but that the shattered glass and slashed screen were meant only to confuse and to distract those who would come to investigate.

As Lewis Young climbed the stairs to the room in which the murder had been committed, he wondered, who were these people?

Like John Taylor, Young had lived in Little Washington for years. As he drove home each day, his route took him through Smallwood, along Lawson Road, right past the Von Stein house. He must have driven past this house hundreds, if not thousands, of times, yet Von Stein was a name he'd never heard.

But unless this murder was simply a random event—a possibility Young considered most unlikely—someone had known the name. Someone had known it well enough to want to kill the man whose name it was.

He called for one of the state's mobile crime labs, but none was available. That morning, all mobile-crime-lab personnel were at a statewide meeting in Raleigh. It would be hours before a van could return to Washington, and the local police didn't feel like waiting. They proceeded to process the scene.

Young did not have authority to make them stop. As an SBI agent, his role was only advisory. He could—and did—advise them to stop. But they could—and did—disregard his advice.

He did, however, have the presence of mind to pay attention to what he saw before the crime scene was forever altered beyond usefulness or recognition.

And one thing he saw was this: next to Bonnie Von Stein's side of the double bed was a typewriter stand, on top of which sat a typewriter, its vinyl dustcover in place. And on top of the typewriter, stacked very neatly, were four pages from a paperback book.

At that point, Lewis Young did not concern himself with the words on the pages, only with the fact that on the top page he saw spatters of blood. Blood-flecked paper next to a bed where a murder and a near-murder had occurred was evidence—and in this case, evidence not compromised by the bungling of the local police.

He placed the pages in a plastic bag and took them with him when he left the house.

Autopsy showed that Lieth Von Stein, Caucasian male, forty-two years of age, five six, 185 pounds, had been hit on the head with a blunt object five times, hard enough to pop open the skin and to cause small, linear cracks in the skull. He had also been stabbed seven times in the back and once in the chest. The stab wound through the chest had penetrated his heart, killing him. A broken wrist, as well as bruise and scrape marks along his forearms, indicated that, for a time at least, he had attempted to ward off the blows.

No alcohol was detected in his blood, though a fatty liver suggested to the pathologist "a rather stiff, consistent use of beverage alcohol." In his stomach, the pathologist found "a rather large amount" of undigested chicken and rice.

3

It has been written of North Carolina that when the essential unpretentiousness of its citizenry is contrasted with the vanity displayed by Richmond aristocracy to the north and the haughtiness manifested by Charleston gentry to the south, the state can be viewed as "a vale of humility between two mountains of conceit."

That being the case, there are few places within it that have more to be humble about than Beaufort County, and that county's seat, Little Washington.

The county lies well to the east of the triangle formed by the relatively thriving and sophisticated cities of Raleigh,

Durham, and Chapel Hill. In size, the eighth largest of North Carolina's one hundred counties, it sprawls all over the state's coastal plain, but fails to reach the sea. There are farms, more farms, then more farms—the biggest crops being soybeans and tobacco—as well as a few lumber mills and an occasional textile plant. And then there is Washington, the county seat.

The town of Little Washington—a name much resented by local residents but widely used by people elsewhere in the state to avoid confusion with Washington, D.C.—sits at the point where the Tar River widens into the Pamlico, thirty miles inland from Pamlico Sound. It has a population of almost ten thousand, a high school, a hospital, a daily newspaper, and a lot of heavy lumber trucks rolling right up its middle, along Route 17. The best motel is the Holiday Inn, where a double room goes for $42 a night. For lunch, even the lawyers eat at Wendy's.

Twenty-six states have towns or cities named Washington. Of these, Washington, North Carolina, its name dating from 1776, is one of three that claim to be the original.

During the Civil War, Little Washington briefly became the "capital" of North Carolina. This was the result of a misadventure that grew out of the erroneous perception, formed by one Edward Stanley, recently returned from California, that North Carolina's allegiance could be transferred to the Union side. President Lincoln, seeing nothing to be lost, named Stanley provisional governor of the new "Union" state, and he set up his headquarters in Little Washington.

The attempt did not prove successful, though Stanley, who survived, was rewarded for his boldness by being appointed, after the war, North Carolina's attorney general. Later, he served five terms in the United States Congress where he earned the dubious distinction of participating in the last duel ever fought between members of Congress. Neither he nor his opponent was injured.

There are some fine, old, well-maintained homes near the center of Little Washington, by the river. In one of these, built about 1830, the great-grandfather of Cecil B. deMille once resided.

The Beaufort County Courthouse, at the corner of Second and Market streets, is a square, two-story brick structure built in about 1800. In the basement is the Beaufort County jail. There, in 1974, a twenty-one-year-old black woman named Joan Little killed a sixty-two-year-old white jailer by stabbing him eleven times with an ice pick. He was naked from the waist down when his body was found. She was charged with murder, accused of enticing him into her cell and then killing him. She claimed self-defense, saying he had tried to rape her. After a nationally publicized trial held in Raleigh, she was acquitted.

Union soldiers burned the town to the ground in 1864, and another fire, in 1900, destroyed it again. In construction since then, grace and charm have not been among the higher priorities. If fresh paint has been applied anywhere in town at any time since the end of World War II, its presence is not readily apparent to the visitor.

Of the residents of Little Washington, much the same can be said as has been written about the natives of Beaufort County as a whole: "The hankering for greener pastures does not infect Beaufort people. Most of them have been here a long time, and it might as well be admitted that they have learned to relax . . . the Beaufort native is not as rich as he'd like to be, but he doesn't see any point in straining himself to earn money so he can buy some leisure for his old age. He already has it."

Neither the county nor the town are the kinds of places you'd be likely to stumble across, and, if you didn't have business there, not places you'd be likely to seek out.

In 1981, Lieth Von Stein was offered the job of director of internal audits for the town's largest employer, a textile company called National Spinning.

Lieth was a native of Winston-Salem, the big industrial city in the central part of the state. His wife, Bonnie, had been born and raised in the farming village of Welcome, a dot on the map about half an hour south of Winston-Salem. For the past two years, they'd been living just outside South Bend, Indiana, where Lieth had been employed in the field of finance. He had just been laid off, however, and he and Bonnie had decided it was time to go back home.

Their first choice would have been something in or at least closer to Winston-Salem. If not there, maybe the Raleigh—Durham—Chapel Hill area, where there was culture and a progressive spirit and economic growth. Or even Charlotte, which, though not big on charm, was the closest thing to a metropolis in the state.

But the first acceptable job offer Lieth received was from National Spinning, located in the backwater town of Little Washington, four hours of hard driving from family and friends.

It was a good job, director of internal audits, paying more than $40,000 a year to start—quite a high salary in Little Washington in 1981—and offering prospects for advancement. Lieth, aware that he had not only Bonnie but her two children from a previous marriage to support, was not inclined to shop for better.

And so they moved, the four of them—Bonnie's two children were Chris, twelve, and Angela, eleven—into a small ranch house on Lawson Road in the new Smallwood subdivision, which, with new homes costing as much as $95,000, came as close to luxury housing as could be found in Little Washington.

But Lieth never grew to like the town. He didn't want to live there, he didn't plan to stay a moment longer than he had to, and it certainly was not the place in which he would have chosen to die.

He was a short, balding man with a trim red beard, a sharp sense of humor, and a quick temper.

Bonnie was a pale, shy, frail-looking woman with thick eyeglasses, and a soft, almost inflectionless voice. She wore no makeup, and acquiring fashionable clothes was not a priority.

They bought a small outboard motorboat and took it to the river on weekends, bringing a picnic lunch and spending whole days on the water. When the children got older, they took the boat over to the little town of Chocowinity, on the south side of the river, where there was a restaurant you could pull right up to in your boat. Bonnie and Lieth had always liked exploring for new restaurants. It was one of their major forms of recreation.

But they were not social people, or even sociable. Outside of work, Lieth had very few acquaintances in town, and the closest that Bonnie came to civic activity was her membership in the county Humane Society. There was no one in Washington whom either Lieth or Bonnie ever came to consider a close friend.

Their families, their friends, their real lives, were four hours away, in Winston-Salem and in the tiny village of Welcome. Little Washington was not a town where you had to do much to be noticed, but Bonnie and Lieth were so private, so withdrawn, that even after seven years— even on the morning of the murder—they remained as unknown to most of the community as they had been the day they arrived.

Bonnie received Darvocet for her chest pain, then Demerol, then Phenergan after a morning episode of vomiting.

She would be awake for a while, then asleep. She felt pressure in her chest. Her head hurt. It was hard to breathe. The worst pain came from where they'd inserted the tube. Lieth was dead. "At least he's not suffering," she mumbled to a nurse. "He tried to save me." Then, "The police said they couldn't do anything for my husband. He's dead."

Chris was there and then he wasn't. But she would never forget the sight of him standing beside her when she'd first opened her eyes. She'd never forget how tightly he'd squeezed her hand, or how hard he had cried.

She slept again. When she awoke, two policemen were there, asking her questions. It was hard to hear them, hard to think, hard to talk. She just wanted to sleep and never wake up. But Angela had not been hurt—the one piece of good news she'd been given.

What happened? they kept asking. How many intruders? Black or white? What did she see? What had she heard? What could she remember?

She'd seen only one, but there could have been ten or

fifteen. She didn't know. She couldn't remember. Her head hurt. Despite seeming "alert" to her physician, Bonnie felt she could not get her mind to focus. They'd already told her she'd lost 40 percent of her blood. How much was that? How long would it take to get it back?

Beneath the bandages that covered her forehead, Bonnie's face was haggard and drawn. She spoke in a voice so soft that listeners had to strain to hear her. Even so, speech exhausted her. Tubes still seemed to be everywhere.

Lieth was dead. Angela had not been hurt. There had been so much blood. So much red, when the police had turned the light on.

She tried to answer their questions. A killer was loose. The man who'd murdered Lieth. The man who'd tried to murder her. These men were trying to catch him. She forced herself to listen, to remember, to speak.

They'd been out to dinner. When they'd come home, Lieth went to bed. That would have been about nine P.M. She'd stayed up to watch television, the first half of a miniseries about Ted Bundy, the serial killer.

Some would later say it was ironic—and others, less charitable, would deem it suspicious, that in the last hours before the murder of her husband, Bonnie, with only her pet rooster for company, had been watching a movie about the crimes of Ted Bundy. But she saw nothing peculiar about it. She simply liked the actor who played Ted Bundy. Harmon was his name. Something Harmon.

By the time she went upstairs, Angela was already in bed. She told the police that Angela had her fan on, and her radio on, and that the door to her bedroom had been closed.

Bonnie had read for half an hour, then fallen asleep just after midnight. What woke her was the sound of Lieth screaming. Never had she heard screams like that. So loud, so sharp. She didn't know how many screams, maybe ten, maybe fifteen. She didn't know what time this was. She, too, had screamed, then she'd been hit by a club, then she'd been stabbed. She'd fallen off the side of the bed.

As she lay on the floor, she was hit again. Then she passed out. It was terribly exhausting to tell all this. And it was all so jumbled in her mind. When she woke up, on the floor, she had reached up and felt Lieth's hand in the darkness. That, she did remember clearly: feeling Lieth's hand. It was sticky, and she knew the stickiness was blood.

She tried to get to the phone, which was on the nightstand next to the bed, but passed out again. When she next regained consciousness, though too weak to sit, she pushed herself backward across the carpet with her heels until she reached her nightstand. Then she pulled the phone down on top of herself by yanking the cord. With the phone on the floor, in the dark, she pushed the buttons, one by one, until she hit the one that brought the operator on the line. Then she'd asked for the police.

No, she couldn't give a description of the attacker. She said she "couldn't see anything but the dark form of a man."

Chris left the hospital that morning in the company of his best friend from high school, Jonathan Wagoner. He asked Jonathan to drive him past his house. There was a big crowd outside. Neighbors, cops, friends, reporters, a TV truck. And Angela still hanging around across the street.

Chris saw the blood-soaked sheets hanging from the boat, garish in the morning light, in plain view of anyone driving by. Chris wanted to stop and find out who'd hung them there and kick their ass, but Jonathan managed to calm him down, driving him away from the house and to the mall a mile away.

He was manic, hyper, on the verge of losing all control. An old friend from high school named Steven Outlaw saw him pacing back and forth outside Frank's Pizza.

"Lieth is dead?"

"That's right."

"How's your mom?"

"Not too good. She's a mess. They stabbed her and they clubbed her in the head."

"Who do you think it was?"

"I don't know," Chris said, lighting one cigarette from

another with shaking hands, "but if I ever find out, I'm going to kill them."

Then Chris turned and walked into Scott's clothing store. He browsed through counters stacked with shirts, and racks of pants. He told Jonathan he'd been working part-time at a clothing store in Raleigh. Then he started chatting with a clerk about prices and styles.

Jonathan Wagoner didn't know much about shock, but he figured whatever it was, Chris was suffering from it.

They went back to the house, where a big crowd was still gathered. Chris spoke to a neighbor who'd just come back from seeing Bonnie at the hospital.

"What did she say?" he asked.

That was strange, the neighbor thought. Not "How is she?" but "What did she say?" And why wasn't he there himself?

"Did she see who it was?" Chris asked.

"No, she just said he had to be young. He seemed strong. She had the sense of a lot of muscles in the chest."

"Young, what do you mean, young?"

"Chris, relax. Calm down. She doesn't know. She couldn't see."

But Chris didn't seem able to calm down. "I'm gonna kill whoever did it," he said. "I can't believe anybody would hurt my mother."

"He was still kind of fucked up," Andrew Arnold said. "Still tore up. He couldn't stand still. Said he'd been par-tyin' all night, taken a few drugs."

Andrew drove Chris and Angela and Donna Brady to Burger King. Nobody ate. They just ordered sodas and coffee. Chris seemed not just nervous now, but angry. He overheard some people in a nearby booth talking about the killing.

"They better stop talking about us!" he said. His voice was loud and shrill, his hands drumming on the table nonstop.

He said he needed to get away, out of town. He hooked up with Jonathan Wagoner again and asked Jonathan to drive him to Greenville, twenty-five miles away. Jonathan went to East Carolina University in Greenville and had an apartment there. Chris said he needed to sleep. He didn't want to talk about what had happened, or hear anyone else talk about it.

They drove to Greenville. When they reached the apartment, Chris turned on the television, found MTV, and then, without another word, lay down on the couch and went to sleep. Shock. This must be shock, Jonathan thought.

Chris slept for two hours, but not peacefully. Jerking and twitching a lot. When he awoke, his face was slick with sweat.

Angela seemed as calm as her brother was hysterical. She seemed beyond calm: casual, even indifferent.

"She's just like her mom," her best friend, Donna Brady, said. "Neither one of them are emotional. They keep everything inside."

To Donna, there was nothing suspicious or even out of character about Angela's apparent lack of reaction. Others, less well acquainted with Angela, formed a different opinion.

She and her friends sat in a neighbor's yard for hours, directly across from her house. Trees provided shade from the hazy July sun. Seated on the grass, legs crossed, they were joking, laughing, smoking cigarettes. Somebody said they should get some beer. Someone else asked about a party that night.

"It looked like a sit-in," one neighbor said. "Or like they were watching a big circus, or a parade. There was no sadness, no sense of danger, no feeling of horror that a ghastly murder had been committed. I finally walked out and said, 'Angela, why aren't you at the hospital with your mother?' And she said, 'Oh, she's fine. Chris has already been to see her.' "

The detectives were gone now. Only a single patrolman stood guard at the front door. In early afternoon, he was approached by a group of five or six neighbors, who said it would be a terrible thing for Bonnie to have to come home to a house that looked like a crime scene. The patrolman agreed and willingly stepped aside as they marched in with their scrub brushes and buckets and liquid detergent and ammonia, and scrubbed all the bloodstains and the fingerprint powder off the walls. There was blood even on the master bedroom ceiling, and they made sure they got that, too. The mattress was saturated with blood, so two of them carried it down the stairs and out the front door. They heaved it into the back of a pickup truck and drove it to the town dump.

By the time the neighbors were finished, you could not have told that Lieth Von Stein had so much as stubbed his toe inside that house.

That afternoon, at police headquarters, Lewis Young read the book pages he'd found, which were the last four pages of a romance novel called *A Rose in Winter* by Kathleen Woodiwiss.

Young was startled by what he read. He didn't know what had transpired over the first 560 pages of the book, but on page 561 alone—the blood-flecked page that had been on top of the stack—Young encountered a young hero named Christopher, who, waving a sword, challenged "the lord of the manor" and said, "You have for too long ravaged this land and escaped your fate. . . . Your time has come. . . . Death, Milord . . . Death!"

Young read descriptions of "a long, blood-darkened blade," a "saber slashing, thrusting, cutting," and a dagger "held ready to test the flesh."

The whole page, and those that followed, described a scene of bloody mayhem. Sabers, swords, and daggers seemed to be everywhere. One character "raised his cane and lowered it over the man's head, crumpling him." The villainous lord of the manor "never felt the thrust that pierced his ribs and heart." The victorious hero, Christopher, gathered the heroine in his arms "as she came to him and softly sobbed out her relief."

Angela went to the home of Donna Brady, whose parents had said that she and Chris could stay with them as long as they needed to. She and Donna and Andrew Arnold and Stephanie Mercer, who lived next door to Angela on Lawson Road, drove around town a little bit. They went to the mall. They went down to the river. Angela did not return to the hospital to see her mother, who had been moved from the emergency room to intensive care. Eventually, they went back to Donna's house.

Angela was very quiet. Donna's father would later describe her as "somber." To others, she seemed detached and blasé. Donna's father said the police had been trying to find her. Apparently, an SBI detective named Lewis Young had a few questions he wanted to ask.

Young interviewed her at four-forty P.M. She was not the least bit impolite, but acted from the start as if she had better things to do. Basically, Angela wouldn't make much of an impression under normal circumstances.

These, however, were not normal circumstances. Her stepfather had just been beaten and stabbed to death and her mother had almost been killed in the same attack, which had taken place some twelve hours earlier, and less than twenty feet from the bed in which Angela had said she'd been asleep.

Something in her nonchalant manner, in her lack of affect, bothered Lewis Young. This whole episode seemed to be something she was watching from a great distance, with very little interest in the outcome.

"She was sometimes in touch, sometimes on Mars," Young would say later. "Kind of spacey. Like, 'Lieth's gone, let's get on with it.' Like she'd just as soon be at the mall, having a milk shake. She just didn't seem to connect."

Angela told Young she knew nothing. She had slept through the whole thing. She'd been horseback riding Sunday afternoon, had come home that night, found nobody there, had gone out again with Donna Brady, and was home again by eleven. Her mother was watching television and working on a design for a Humane Society poster. Lieth was upstairs asleep. This was normal, Angela said. Lieth always went to bed before her mother.

She'd gone to her room, turned on her fan and tape player, and read for a while. Her mother had come in to close her door, saying the music was too loud. Then they'd said good-night and Angela had turned off her light—but not her fan—and gone to sleep. Next thing she knew there was a policeman in her doorway saying, excuse me, someone has broken in and stabbed your parents. It was probably the noise of the fan, she said, that prevented her from hearing the murder. Besides, she added, she was a very sound sleeper.

Angela recited all this in a monotone, as if she found the subject slightly boring. She said they'd been a very happy family with no problems. She knew of no one who might want to hurt either her mother or stepfather, but suggested that the killer could have been someone from National Spinning, maybe someone whom Lieth had fired from his job. That was, she said, "just a possibility." She didn't have anyone specific in mind.

The knapsack? No, she'd never seen the knapsack before. No one in the family had anything like it. She had no idea what it was doing there.

If she didn't actually look at her watch, Lewis Young had the distinct feeling that she wanted to. Like, how long was this going to take? She didn't seem grief stricken, didn't seem curious, didn't seem angry, didn't seem scared. She just seemed as if she had better things to do.

The afternoon paper carried the front-page story "Washington Man Killed, Wife Hurt." Beneath the headline was a picture of the Von Stein house. A police spokesman was quoted as saying the couple had apparently been attacked by burglars, but that details were "sketchy."

An executive of National Spinning described Lieth as "assertive and well-liked," and said he would be missed. "He was respected by one and all for his expertise in the computer area," the executive said.

The story said Mrs. Von Stein was in "guarded" condition in the intensive care unit of Beaufort County Hospital, suffering from a stab wound to the chest and multiple facial cuts and bruises. It said she was sedated and as of press time, had not yet spoken to police.

*   *   *

Angela called a friend, Steve Tripp, who lived in Greenville. She was upset, she told him, because she was being treated like a suspect.

First, a policeman had thought she had blood on her jeans, when it was only saddle soap and oil.

Then, she said, both in the morning and afternoon, she'd had to go to the police station to answer questions. Each time, it seemed to her that the police to whom she spoke had not believed her when she said she'd slept through the whole thing. They'd also seemed to find it odd that she had escaped the assault uninjured, although lying only twenty feet away.

They didn't know, she told Steve, just how sound a sleeper she really was.

She said, "They don't have any idea who might have done it, so I think they're trying to blame me."

By nine-thirty that night, still having been unable to track down Chris Pritchard for an interview, Lewis Young returned to Lawson Road to talk to some of the Von Stein's neighbors about the family. The version of family life he received from them differed rather dramatically from that which Angela had provided him earlier in the day.

Bonnie and Lieth had been extremely reclusive, he was told. While Bonnie herself was intelligent and compassionate, she also was very naive—the sort of person who would say everything was fine, and who might even believe it, when just the opposite was apparent to everyone else.

Lieth had been "very narrow-minded," a Germanic "when I say no, I mean no" type. Also, "a real Jekyll-Hyde personality," especially when he was drinking, which was often.

On weekends, he'd start drinking beer in the morning and go all day. He'd go through a case on a weekend, as well as consuming "a full eight-ounce glass of hard liquor, straight from the bottle." He would go out to a restaurant, have a couple of drinks before dinner, then start cussing out the waiter. At times, it became truly embarrassing. He would have "temper tantrums," throwing food on the floor, or storming out in anger over some imagined lapse in the quality of the service.

"He was an alcoholic and he knew it," one neighbor said. "He wasn't ashamed of it. He'd say, 'It's gonna kill me.' In his mind, he knew he'd die as a young man." There was a pause. "But not like this."

Worst had been his attitude toward Bonnie's children. It wasn't so bad when they were younger, though "as far as love and nurturing went, it wasn't there," and "they never really seemed like a family."

As they'd grown into teenagers, however, Lieth had lost all patience with Chris and Angela, complaining incessantly that they were an "intrusion" and saying over and over that he "lived for the day" when they would be out of his house once and for all.

"Bonnie would put it out of her mind and dwell on the good things, but the way he treated her children, it hurt her in her heart," the neighbor said.

Lieth had been especially hostile and sarcastic toward Chris. A few years earlier, Chris, along with a friend, had gotten into some minor scrape with the law—arrested for possession of alcohol and fireworks, something like that, in the nearby small town of Chocowinity. His name had been printed in the paper.

But the way Lieth had reacted, you would have thought Chris had been charged with . . . well . . . murder. He became "more disgusted than you would believe" and from that moment forward had "never given Chris a moment's peace." He "blew it all out of proportion and he was constantly throwing it in Chris's face."

In turn, "Chris hated Lieth." The stepfather had "turned that boy against him and probably didn't see it." Nor had Bonnie, because she could no more believe that her children were troubled or capable of causing harm, to themselves or to others, than were the helpless pets on which she showered so much affection.

The neighbors advised Young to take a long, hard look at both of Bonnie's children as he investigated the case. Chris was a very strange boy, they said. And as for Angela, "it was like she lived her whole life on some plateau that nobody else could ever get to."

As he left, having been told that Chris was now at the Brady's house and available for an interview, Young was given one last opinion concerning Angela: "There's no way that girl slept through it."

Young had his first talk with Chris Pritchard at ten-thirty P.M. at the Brady home.

He was a scrawny kid, Young thought. He looked more as if he were sixteen years old instead of nineteen. He was wearing a baseball cap, a sweatshirt that looked as if he'd been sleeping in it for a week, and a pair of stained and wrinkled shorts. He was unshaven and bleary-eyed and was chain-smoking cigarettes.

"He was more in line with what you'd expect than his sister was," Young said later. "He came across as more in tune emotionally. You could tell he was upset. In fact, he was shaking. But like his sister, he would flit around a lot in talking.

"Even forgetting what the neighbors had said—neighbors say lots of different things that don't necessarily turn out to be true—what bothered me was that neither one of these kids was doing what they should have been. I mean, Chris had got to town at eight o'clock in the morning and I'd been trying to find him ever since to conduct an urgent interview about a murder committed in his own house, but it's not until ten-thirty P.M. that I get up with him. It just didn't seem right. I didn't like it."

Besides, Young could not erase from his mind the content of the blood-spattered pages he'd read that afternoon.

Chris told Young he was sorry he'd been so hard to contact, but he didn't know anything helpful, anyway. He'd been enrolled at NC State's summer session and hadn't been home much since early June. Hadn't been home much all year, in fact. He'd just finished his freshman year at State. Had a few problems with his grades. You know how that goes. That's why he was in the summer session.

The last time he had seen any member of his family was Saturday night, one of the few occasions when he had been home for dinner. He'd actually cooked the meal himself. With his sister's help, he'd prepared hamburger patties for a barbecue. It had been a nice meal, everyone happy and relaxed. After dinner, he'd driven back to school because he had a term paper to work on.

Sunday night, he'd been up late—*real* late, until about three-thirty A.M.—playing cards and drinking beer with a couple of girls and another friend of his. When Angela had called, he'd been so out of it that it had taken him five minutes to understand what she was talking about. And then he hadn't been able to find his car keys and had wound up calling campus security to get a ride home.

He wasn't aware of any family problems, didn't know of any enemies whom either his stepfather or mother had. He did know that his stepfather had recently come into a large inheritance and spent a lot of time working on stock investments, but Chris himself "did not know about that stuff" and had no idea how much money was involved.

Young was struck by how fidgety and skittish Chris was. Hyper, jittery, all revved up. He couldn't sit still. His head twitched, his hands jumped, his legs quivered. He couldn't seem to focus on the questions.

And neither he nor his sister had seemed to express the slightest bit of sadness at their stepfather's death, or concern about their mother's condition.

At six-thirty the next morning, Lewis Young received a phone call from a woman who identified herself as the wife of Bonnie Von Stein's brother. She said she and her husband were staying at the Holiday Inn, along with other members of Bonnie's family who had rushed to Little Washington as soon as they'd heard the news. She told Young that she and her husband wanted to speak to him as soon as possible. And she said it would have to be kept confidential: she and her husband did not want other family members—and especially not Bonnie herself—to know that they'd contacted the police.

Young told them he'd be waiting at headquarters. They were there within fifteen minutes.

Bonnie's brother, George, stood just less than six feet

tall. He was a thin man, with a mustache and a small beard that covered only his chin, not his jaw. He struck Young immediately as being honest and unassuming. He worked as a chemist for a paint manufacturer in High Point, a city in the middle of the state, not far from Greensboro and Winston-Salem. Young sized him up as a man who would do what he believed to be the right thing, even if it made him uncomfortable.

His wife, Peggy, who had been raised in Washington, D.C., was slim and attractive, with long red fingernails and short brown hair. She, like her husband, spoke plainly and with feeling. They both said, right away, that the decision to seek out Lewis Young had not been an easy one; that, in fact, they'd stayed up most of the night, talking about what they should do.

The problem, they said, was Chris Pritchard, and to a lesser extent, perhaps Angela. From the moment they'd first seen Chris the day before, they had sensed that something was not right.

"It's hard to put into words," George Bates said, "but I don't understand the way he's acting. Yesterday, he didn't act like his mother had just been stabbed in bed and almost died. And like his stepfather had been murdered."

"I never saw a tear in his eye," Peggy Bates said.

"He didn't seem upset," George said. "He didn't seem distraught. He was just his normal, run-here, run-there, can't-sit-still, nervous personality."

Young had thought Chris's nervousness might have been just a reaction to the shocking news he'd been given early that morning. But Chris's uncle said, "He's been that way as long as I can remember."

The big point they wanted to make—and this was a very hard thing for them to say—was that, based on what they'd seen of Chris since their arrival in Washington, they feared he might have some involvement in the crime.

Angela's behavior had bothered them, too.

"I never saw a one of them shed a tear," George Bates said. "It was like *nothing* had happened. It was like if I just went to their house and they've got some friends over and it's, 'Hey, how you doin'?'—same kind of nonchalant way. Like, hey, they're makin' plans to go get pizza and whatnot, up to the mall.''

George Bates looked Lewis Young squarely in the eye. ''I could almost rationalize losing a stepfather and not being in tears, but *their mother is in intensive care. She was almost murdered!* This wasn't a car accident. Someone intentionally tried to *murder* their mother. And they show no concern whatsoever. Why aren't those kids in tears? Why aren't they sitting up at that hospital right now, protecting their mother? If I were them, I'd be there day and night.''

Then Peggy Bates said, ''The first people you need to give your attention to are Chris and Angela.''

And George Bates said, ''Look, I'm not convinced about anything. I'm just bothered. I'm bothered enough to be sitting here talking to you about my own family. I don't like doing it, but I want you to at least be sure you keep someone there at the hospital, looking out for Bonnie. Because, heaven forbid, if the kids did have something to do with it, they might try something else.''

A policeman had been assigned to guard the door of Bonnie's room the day before. Young called to be sure someone was still on duty. Then, at ten A.M., he went to the hospital himself to have his first talk with Bonnie, and to see for himself how badly hurt she really was. Her brother might have feared for her life, and she might have been—as she appeared—an innocent victim, but she was also, Young said later, ''already something of a suspect.''

Lieth had been dead for only a day, but Little Washington was filled with rumors about her possible involvement in the murder.

Had Bonnie been well known in the community, had she had a broad range of friends, acquaintances, or civic activities, the suspicion might have been slower to spread. But who had really known this Bonnie Von Stein? For years, she'd been a stranger beside them. Of such a person, it was easy to believe the worst.

This, as much as anything, might have been what led to the first wave of suspicion, although the existence of a $2 million inheritance—and it was not long before news of this swept the town—was no doubt a contributing factor.

The rumors had begun even before the neighbors had finished scrubbing the blood from the bedroom walls. Even the local paper referred to them, with a spokesman for the Washington police department quoted as saying he had "heard rumors about the incident but discounted most of them as ill-informed or malicious."

Still, even as Bonnie lay in her hospital bed with the chest tube firmly in place, all over Little Washington people she had never met were muttering their doubts about the existence of genuine intruders in the night.

"I must say," Lewis Young recalled later, "she looked pretty incapacitated. Her head looked bad. My head was hurting just looking at her. If there was all that money involved, she obviously had a motive, but I'd never seen a crime where a person inflicted injuries that serious to themselves, or had them inflicted by somebody else, just to take the heat off."

He asked her to tell him about the weekend. She said Chris had been home that Saturday night and had barbecued hamburgers for them all. The next morning, she and Lieth had slept late and then gone to Greenville for breakfast. They'd eaten at The Waffle House.

It was the sort of thing they liked to do on weekends, the sort of thing they considered recreation. Twenty-five miles might seem a long drive just to get to a place called The Waffle House, but if you stayed in Little Washington, your breakfast options were McDonald's or Burger King.

She'd asked Angela if she wanted to join them, but Angela was on her way to the Five Points Equestrian Center to spend the day among horses. Angela loved horses, always had. The chance to ride was about the only thing that could get her up at eight-thirty on a weekend morning. Chris had gone back to school the night before, after the barbecue, saying he had to work on a term paper.

So it had been just the two of them. After breakfast, they'd made a brief stop to look at mobile homes. Having just come into a large inheritance—Bonnie said it was $1.3 million—Lieth had been planning to quit his job at the end of the year and devote full time to managing his investments. With both children finally in college, they'd be free to travel.

That afternoon, they'd spent a couple of hours at the computer, entering and updating stock market data. Then, she said with some embarrassment, they'd enjoyed some "private moments" in their bedroom.

They drove back to Greenville that night, and because their favorite restaurant, The King and Queen, was closed, they'd eaten at Sweet Caroline's. Lieth drank a couple of vodka martinis and Bonnie a Tom Collins before the meal. He ordered the chicken and wild rice special. She had the blackened steak. They'd had wine with the meal, too, though she herself had drunk, at most, a single glass.

He'd gone to bed as soon as they got home. Lieth did that. He went to bed early. As she'd said the day before, she had stayed up to watch the Ted Bundy miniseries. Not because she cared about Ted Bundy: just because she happened to like the actor who played the role. Yes, her rooster had been with her. She'd grown up in farm country, she'd loved animals all her life, and she didn't see anything strange about either having thirteen cats in her house or about bringing her rooster inside while she watched television.

She had turned off the television shortly after the eleven o'clock news had begun. Then she'd gone upstairs and awakened Lieth to ask him if he'd like a glass of tea. He had said no and had immediately fallen back to sleep. Then she'd had her little chat with Angela—Bonnie had been thinking of going to the beach the next day, and they discussed bathing suits, and also a cassette tape of Angela's that Bonnie wanted to bring in her car.

She'd spent a few minutes reading in bed—a paperback Harlequin romance, she couldn't remember the title. But the music from Angela's tape player or radio was distracting, so she'd gone to her daughter's room and closed the door. She'd also closed her own bedroom door. Soon, she had fallen asleep. The next thing she heard was Lieth screaming.

During the attack, she'd heard a "whooshing" and a

"thumping" sound each time that Lieth was hit. She recalled that the attacker, upon leaving her room, had closed the door "softly," he hadn't slammed it. Later, she'd heard the same "whooshing" and "thumping" in the hallway, causing her to fear that Angela was being killed, too.

Young asked if she had any better impression of her assailant than she'd had the day before. Bonnie said she thought he'd been a big man, strong, with broad shoulders that had "blended" into his head, "almost as if he had no neck." She also said she thought he'd been wearing a ski mask.

Young wanted to know more about Lieth. Bonnie said he was a gentle man who would not allow weapons in the house. She was not aware of his having any problems at work. She had no knowledge or suspicions of any extramarital affairs. Their marriage had been filled with happiness.

Lieth had been kind to her children, had wanted them to have good educations. A vocal man, he would let you know right away if something was bothering him, but he didn't carry a grudge. He'd had no problems with Chris or Angela or with any of their friends. They really had been, she said, just one medium-sized happy family. Nothing out of the ordinary in any way, except that maybe, over the past couple of years, faced with the stress of his parents' illnesses and deaths—and the death, too, of an uncle who had been almost like a father to him—and the need, through all this time of sickness and death, to make the four-and-a-half-hour trip to Winston-Salem almost every weekend, Lieth had begun to drink more than she thought was good for him.

He showed her a picture of the green canvas knapsack that had been found on the floor of the hall that led from the back door to the kitchen. She said it did not belong to anyone in her family and that she'd never seen it before.

Next, Young asked about the inheritance. She said Angela and Chris both knew Lieth had inherited a significant sum, but because theirs was not a family in which such matters were openly discussed, she doubted that either child had any idea just how much was involved. One thing the children *did* know was that in the event she and Lieth were both to die, whatever assets they left behind—and when Lieth's life insurance was added to what he had inherited, the total came to almost $2 million—would be held in a trust until Angela, the younger child, turned thirty-five.

When Young asked her if she had any new ideas about who might have committed the crime, she said he might want to consider the trust department of the North Carolina National Bank. Lieth had informed them of his decision to close out their $1.3 million account because he was dissatisfied with their performance and fees. Perhaps, she said, the bank had arranged Lieth's murder to prevent him from taking the money away from them.

This struck Lewis Young as the most ridiculous notion he'd heard yet concerning a motive for the murder. But looking again at Bonnie's battered forehead, he was inclined to think that the combination of physical injury and emotional shock might be responsible for any sort of farfetched idea.

He asked her one more question about the book she'd been reading in bed. She could not remember the title, she said, but she assured him it had not been *A Rose in Winter*.

4

It was shortly after six P.M. on Tuesday, July 26, the day he'd had his first talk with Bonnie in the hospital, that Lewis Young received a call from the Little Washington police informing him that, in the excitement surrounding the murder of Lieth Von Stein, this had been forgotten, but a hog farmer named Noel Lee had called to report that at four-thirty on the morning of the murder he'd seen a fire burning at the edge of State Road 1565, the Grimesland Bridge Road, just across the Pitt County line.

Young called Lee, but he was out. At eleven P.M., Lee returned the call. By eleven-thirty, Lewis Young was standing at his front door.

It was only a quarter mile from Noel Lee's house to the site of the fire. Just beyond a curve and a dip in the road, at the edge of a wooded, swampy area. With a flashlight, Lee pointed out where the fire had been. About eight feet off the shoulder of the road was a burned area, not large, no more than three feet in diameter, and shaped more like an oval than a circle.

Using his own flashlight and crouching at the edge of the oval, Young saw what looked to be ashes. Digging a bit, he detected a faint odor of gasoline. He also found scraps of burnt clothing, a partly burnt shoe, and a burnt hunting knife with a six-inch blade. He placed each of these items into plastic evidence bags.

Then Young played his light out beyond the edge of the burnt area. He spotted a singed and crumpled piece of paper about two feet past the ring of ashes. This, too, he placed in an evidence bag.

It was dark and it was late. He thanked Noel Lee for his help. He said yes, by all means, calling had been the right thing to do. He apologized for the fact that it had taken so long for anyone to respond. Lee said no problem, no need for apology, he wasn't even sure it had been worth bothering anyone about, but then, after seeing on the TV about the murder, he figured, what the heck, might as well call.

Early the next morning, Young received a call from George Bates, who said his fears about Chris's involvement were growing worse. The day before, he told Young, he had driven Chris back to his dormitory at NC State in Raleigh. Chris's roommate had apparently found the missing car keys under a chair cushion, and Chris had wanted to get his car.

All the way up, George Bates said, Chris had continued to act jittery. "Boy, was he nervous. He was shaking." He had not expressed the slightest sorrow about the death of his stepfather or concern about his mother's condition, or even curiosity about what might have happened. Instead, he'd rambled on about how deeply involved he'd gotten in the drug scene on campus, and about how he would have to "get off that junk."

But the really strange thing, George Bates said—and this was what had prompted the call—was that after retrieving his car keys from the dorm room, Chris hadn't seemed to know where the car was.

He had said he thought it was parked in a "fringe lot," about a quarter mile from the dorm. But as George Bates had driven him to the lot, Chris had kept saying he wasn't sure he'd be able to find the car right away.

He'd said, "I was at a party all night and got stoned out of my head."

"But you weren't stoned out of your mind when you parked the car before the party started," his uncle had told him. "What do you mean, you don't know where it is?"

As it turned out, Chris's white Mustang was just about the only car in the whole lot, and so he had been able to spot it right away. But it had struck him as strange, and it troubled him, George Bates said, that Chris had worried that he wouldn't be able to find his own car. It might mean nothing—in fact, all of his talk about Chris might be way off base, George Bates acknowledged—but it was one more thing he thought he should pass along.

Later that morning, at Washington police headquarters, with the young detective John Taylor standing at his side, Young, having already examined the partly burned hunting knife and partly burned shoe and the scraps of burnt clothing, opened the last plastic bag.

He removed the crumpled and singed piece of paper and exercising great care, slowly unfolded it.

He saw lines and squares and drawings of four-legged animals. The word LAWSON was printed above the longest line.

The lines appeared to denote streets, the blocks looked like symbols for houses, and the animals appeared to be dogs. Unlike the lines and blocks, the dogs were not just stick-figure representations, but had been drawn as if to illustrate a medieval fairy tale.

"That's Smallwood!" Young exclaimed.

Although only the word LAWSON indicated a specific street, Young quickly recognized that the other lines, crisscrossing at various angles, represented roads in and adjacent to the neighborhood. There was the Market Street Extension. And behind the line that had the word LAWSON printed above it was another, which would be Marsh Road, and then the one behind that, which was Northwoods.

Of the little square blocks drawn along the line that represented Lawson Road, the fifth from the top was surrounded by more detail than the others. Even with a portion of the map burned away, Young and Taylor could see markings that indicated a fence, a drainage ditch, and a small shed in the backyard.

The drawings of two medieval mastiffs placed them in yards on either side of the fifth house on the block.

The fifth house, Lewis Young knew, from the time he'd already spent at the scene, was the house in which Lieth Von Stein had been murdered.

John Taylor photographed the map. Young sent the hunting knife to the pathologist who'd done the autopsy on Lieth Von Stein. The doctor's findings were what Young had expected: the blade was consistent with the type of instrument used to inflict the stab wounds on Von Stein.

Why the map hadn't been consumed by the flames was something neither Young nor Taylor, nor later, the Beaufort County district attorney, Mitchell Norton, nor anyone else who came to be involved in the Von Stein murder investigation, was ever able to explain.

Had it been just casually tossed at the edge of the pile of bloody clothing, then been blown clear of the flames when the gasoline that was poured on the clothing had ignited?

Or had it been tossed toward the already burning blaze as an afterthought, as the person who'd set the fire hurried back toward a waiting car?

Or was the fact that it had survived the fire nearly intact—survived a blaze hot enough to partly melt a hunting knife—no more, no less than an act of God, as the district attorney would eventually argue to a jury?

For some facts, there are no explanations. But that doesn't mean there are not consequences. It would be many months before the consequences of the map's survival would be felt. But when they were, they would be drastic and everlasting.

5

Welcome, North Carolina, where Bonnie Lou Bates was born, was the sort of small Southern town where the church was the center of all social life; where a mother, over her lifetime, would make dozens of quilts and hundreds, if not thousands, of chicken pies, and where even a shy, plain girl such as Bonnie would grow up knowing everybody for miles around.

Although it was only about ten miles south of Winston-Salem, one of the leading industrial cities in the state, Welcome was not merely in another county: it seemed to be in another world. Driving those ten miles south from the city, one abruptly left behind all traces of urbanization and entered an almost fairy-tale land of Southern farm-country America. If you wanted to go anyplace from Welcome, it would most likely not be Winston-Salem (unless you worked there), but Lexington, a town of fifteen thousand, which was five miles farther down the road.

There may have been about three thousand people in Welcome, or maybe even four thousand. No one was quite sure, since the town was unincorporated. It was the kind of town where the gas stations advertised "Clean Restrooms and Ice Water," and where, if you stopped by Elwood Blackmon's barbershop (Elwood, as a matter of fact, had been in Bonnie's high school class), you could actually hear someone say, "Welcome is so small, it's just a wide place in the road."

Most of the barbershop talk tended to be more specific: whose road just got tarred, how long it took, whose tractor wasn't working, or where the newest patch of dewberries—a cross between raspberries and blackberries—had been found.

There wouldn't be a whole lot of political talk, since almost everyone already felt the same way: Davidson County, of which Welcome was a small part, was more than three-quarters Democratic, and the Republicans, even when in need of a haircut, had the good sense to stick to tractors and dewberries when they spoke.

There were only two ways into town, and either way, you'd pass a sign that said, "Welcome to Welcome." Otherwise, there were no street signs because it was presumed that if you were there, you already knew where you were going. If the Mayberry of television's old "The Andy Griffith Show" wasn't really based on Welcome, it might as well have been.

The townspeople had always been known for three traits: being hardworking, friendly, and religious (as well as for voting Democratic, which was not so much a trait as a reflex).

It was the friendliness that gave the town its name. Back at the turn of the century, the settlement was called Hinklesville, because so many people named Hinkle lived there.

But in 1910, when the Southland Railroad proposed to run its first train through the community and a station was built to receive passengers, the townspeople decided that enough among them were *not* named Hinkle that the town should have a new name. Thinking that the first word a stranger would like to see when disembarking from a train would be "Welcome," they decided to call it that.

Trains still passed through Welcome—one in the daytime, and two at night—but they had long ago stopped carrying passengers, hauled only freight, and no longer stopped. The farmers got up early, raised their corn and wheat for grain, which the flour mill ground for horse feed and glue, and also grew soybeans, tobacco, and fruit. You could also find a lot of livestock in Welcome, mostly cattle, chicken, and pigs.

There was no police department. On the rare occasions when law enforcement was required, the Davidson County Sheriff's Department would do the job. If you were looking for the center of town, the post office would probably be the place to go.

Welcome always had two restaurants—both of them featuring traditional North Carolina barbecue (smoky and vinegary shreds of pork, not to be confused with the gluey, tomatoey concoction consumed in Texas). First, there were Pope's and Dan's; later, Andy's and Kerley's. The Bateses always favored Kerley's.

Only eight hundred feet above sea level, surrounded by low, rolling hills and lots of streams, and a tough, five-and-a-half-hour drive from the beach, Welcome had never fancied itself a tourist attraction. Like Little Washington—though much more of a classic rural, small town—Welcome was not a place in which you'd be likely to find yourself unless you already had relatives living there.

There had been Bateses in Welcome as long as there had been a town, most of them living along Hoover Road, which you got to by turning off Center Church Road (not that there were any signs to point the way).

Bonnie's grandfather Baxter Bates had been a carpenter. The family well remembered the story of how he bought his first car. It was, of course, a Model T Ford. A man drove it into the front yard and Baxter Bates stepped right up and paid cash.

The woman Baxter married, Zealla Sowers, had been born in a log cabin right there on Hoover Road. The family was still living in the cabin when Zealla gave birth to her second child, George, who would become Bonnie's father.

Baxter not only believed, but would state with frequency, "An idle mind is the devil's workshop." He'd go off to do his carpentry in the morning and leave his five children to tend the fields. Zealla died when George was eleven years old, but that only made the Bates children work harder because it meant one less person to keep the home.

The children would sing as they tended the crops of tobacco, sweet potatoes, corn, and even cotton. "When we worked," one of Bonnie's aunts would later say, "the hills echoed with the sound of music."

They might have sung, but they didn't talk. At least not about anything that mattered. For as long as anyone could remember, it had been a Bates family trait not to display emotion. This was something that Baxter Bates taught his children, maybe so he wouldn't have to hear a lot of wailing and keening as their mother slowly sickened and died of stomach cancer.

"You kept your emotions inside," Bonnie's aunt said. "There was no time to talk about how you felt about something, or to cry. There was just too much work to get done."

As a grown man, George Bates, Sr., Bonnie's father, would pass this trait on to his five children. "It is better to be still and be thought a fool," he would tell them, "than to speak and remove all doubt."

In 1941, George had married a tiny eighteen-year-old girl named Annie Erris Moose, from Stony Point, North Carolina. She wasn't even five feet tall, but she was pretty and smart and was made of strong stuff. He had met her at a Methodist church camp. She fell in love with his blue eyes, if not his way with words.

George Bates was a mason. With his own hands, he built the town's Methodist church—the Center United Methodist Church—brick by brick. In Welcome, such an accomplishment brought a man lifelong renown. He sang in the church choir, and Bonnie's mother, who came to be called Polly Bates, was the church organist for many years.

They were good people, the Bateses; solid, reliable, respected, and liked. Bonnie was the second oldest of five children, with one older sister, Sylvia, two younger sisters, Kitty and Ramona, and a younger brother, George Jr.

Welcome was too small to have its own high school, so Bonnie attended one in nearby Lexington, graduating in 1962. The adjective most widely used to describe her by classmates who wrote inscriptions in her yearbook was *nice*. In later years, she came to realize that she must not have made much of an impression.

After high school, she started nurse's training in Winston-Salem. In her first month on the hospital floor she came upon a girl she'd just graduated with, now dying of leukemia. Then there was the dying old man with the high fever whom she had to pack in ice. And the two infants, joined at the tops of their heads. Depressed by it all, she quit in less than six months.

Her next job was as a salesclerk at the Raylass Department Store in Lexington. Here, her mother noticed, she started to bloom. Bonnie was never going to be an extrovert, but at least she developed enough self-assurance to carry on a conversation with a stranger.

Briefly, with a girlfriend who had relatives in the town, she moved to Decatur, Illinois, where she worked as a ward clerk in a hospital. For a member of the Bates family, this was daring: none of the children had ever before lived outside the county, much less the state. Her parents kept urging her to come back. After six months, she did.

She'd saved $500 in Decatur and used it to buy her first car, a Mercury Monterey, the first car that was not a Ford and the first with an automatic transmission ever owned by a member of her family. In her own quiet way, Bonnie was expanding her horizons.

Her big leap, however, was to enroll in an IBM keypunch course at the Lexington Business College. This led to a job with the Integon insurance company in Winston-Salem. Suddenly, Bonnie Lou Bates was a commuter, driving back and forth to a big-city office job every day.

She was an exceptional worker. Reliable, intelligent, and always looking to learn more. Strange, she'd never known she had ambition, but there it was. She stayed at Integon for fifteen years, moving into data processing when the field of data processing came into being. By the time she left, married by then to Lieth Von Stein, she was supervisor of Property and Casualty Systems, the only person in the office at that level of management who didn't have a college degree.

But back in late fall of 1965, another event of great

importance occurred. Driving down Winston-Salem's Main Street, Bonnie looked into a car showroom window and spotted a brand-new teal green '66 Chevy Chevelle SS 396 with four on the floor and a 360-horsepower engine. Much to her surprise, it was love at first sight.

She knew it wasn't appropriate. She knew it was a *boy's* car, not a *girl's* car, but she also knew she had to have it, and right away. Her father was horrified, her mother embarrassed. But Bonnie Lou Bates, twenty-one years old now and gainfully employed, insisted on something for the first time in her life.

The dealer didn't want to sell it to her. He said she was too much of a lady for that car. In fact, the dealer said, he didn't want to sell it to anyone. It was a great attention-getter and he wanted to keep it on the showroom floor.

But Bonnie would not be denied. She worked out a deal with her father whereby he traded his '56 Ford, which, like every other object he'd ever owned, he'd kept in impeccable condition, and she traded him her Mercury Monterey, and he cosigned the car loan and Bonnie zoomed off in her brand-new Chevelle. It was the hottest car that Welcome had seen in years. The car made heads turn when it passed. And then . . . when they saw who was driving it! Was that really . . . ? Could it be . . . ? Bonnie Lou Bates?

The next summer, she and Ramona were cruising along the main street of Lexington in her Chevelle, trying to be noticed. Being noticed in Lexington—population 15,000—was considerably more gratifying than being noticed in Welcome—where everybody already knew you anyway.

The cruising section was generally considered to be that six-block area bordered on each end by a drive-in restaurant. After making several passes up and down this boulevard, you'd pull into the parking lot of one restaurant or the other (in Lexington, in 1966, it was either the Old Hickory or the Bar B Que Center) and park next to the neatest-looking car you could spot and then place your order by speaking into a little microphone attached to a pole that stuck up from the ground.

While waiting for your order to be delivered by the high school girl who was working as a waitress, you'd strike up a conversation with whoever was sitting in the neat-looking car you'd parked next to.

Since Bonnie's teal green Chevelle SS 396 with the 360-horsepower engine was by far the neatest-looking car in the lot of either the Old Hickory or the Bar B Que Center, she found that, even being shy and plain, she had a lot of conversations struck up with her.

On this July night, she saw a car she liked almost as much as her own and pulled in next to it at the Old Hickory.

There were two high school boys in the car. One of them, Steve Pritchard, knew Bonnie's younger sister, Ramona. He was sixteen and about to start his junior year at Lexington West. Bonnie, though twenty-one, had done very little dating in her life. In Winston-Salem, no men paid attention to her. In Welcome, there just were no young men.

Steve Pritchard had already lived a hard life, involving an alcoholic father and foster homes and the sort of turmoil that the emotionally sheltered Bonnie Lou Bates had never known. Even at sixteen, he had developed a smooth-talking veneer to deal with the world at large and with women in particular.

He was no virgin and Bonnie was. He was good-looking and Bonnie wasn't. And he could, in the words of Bonnie's mother, "charm the horns off a billy goat and the skin off a snake."

Everybody Bonnie knew from high school was already married and having children. She had a good job and a hot car, but it looked as if she'd still be living with her parents when she was forty.

Ramona introduced Bonnie to Steve Pritchard, and the two of them began to date. The following summer, a month after Bonnie had turned twenty-three, and when Steve was still seventeen, they got married. Everybody in Bonnie's family told her they thought Steve was no good and she was crazy. She responded that Steve was wonderful and she wasn't crazy, only lonely. Besides, she said, she was in love.

Although they lived only a few miles apart while dating and saw each other almost every day, she would, on occasion, write letters to him, such as this one from January 1967:

Hi Tiger,

Don't expect too much from one of my letters 'cause I'm not quite all right at the moment. You see, I've met this wonderful person whom I love very much. Because of him, I can't quite keep my brain and heart clicking in the same direction. I don't remember his name but they call him Steve Pritchard, or something almost like that.

Hey, do you know him? He has big beautiful brown eyes and lots of cute little freckles on the handsomest nose in the Junior class at West!

I'll go to the next page now and change the tempo a little. Maybe it'll make a little more sense.

I sat by the fire but it was too lonesome without you there to help keep me warm. The fire could only warm me Outside. Steve, you worry me. You work too long and get too little rest. Hope you're strong enough to take it because we'll never make it if you are forced to take a year or two out to recuperate in a psychiatric ward. I love you too much to lose you that way, so please take it easy and don't worry so much.

You and I will probably have to prove ourselves to our parents before they can really accept our attitudes. You know I love you and I know you love me, but it'll be hard to convince them that we can really make it work for a lifetime. I guess it goes back to the same old solution—time. I just get so tired of waiting for everything. I know anything that really means a lot to me is worth waiting for but it's so hard. Much harder than waiting for anything before.

Smile for me now and let's face the future together. . .

Till Friday—

Love always,
Bonnie

In retrospect, what's most surprising is that the marriage lasted almost five years. During the first year, Steve was still in high school. They lived in a rented mobile home. Once he graduated, Steve jumped quickly from job to job, working first for an oil company, then for a dry cleaner, then for a photographer.

As time passed, Bonnie came to suspect that Steve was also jumping from girl to girl, but it was not until the summer of 1972, when Chris was three and a half years old and Angela almost two, that Steve walked out of the new house they'd bought in the Winchester Downs section of Lexington (even though they couldn't nearly afford it), and into the arms of the newest girl he had waiting on the side. The divorce was the first in Bates family history, and as sympathetic as everyone was, there was the whiff of a certain "I told you so" in the air.

At first, Bonnie wouldn't even admit to anyone that it had happened. But her father, whose instinct told him a lot about his children, came over one day and wanted to know if there was anything he could do to help. Bonnie broke down and cried her heart out.

In the years that followed, she proved she wasn't just nice, but tough. She paid every bill Steve left her with and even kept up the mortgage payments on the house. Much later, in her understated way, she would say that the period after Steve abandoned her was "a very lean couple of years."

Steve Pritchard paid neither alimony nor child support. Seldom did he return to see his children. Though surrounded by her family, Bonnie was too proud ever to ask for help. She was a divorced mother of two preschoolers, in rural North Carolina, at a time when women in such circumstances were rarities and viewed with mistrust at best.

She also was not the sort to leave a debt unpaid, even those incurred by her ex-husband. Bonnie worked extra hours and studied at night, trying to master this new field of data processing, all the while telling everybody things were fine. They were eating a lot of beans and potatoes, she said, but they were eating.

Her mother believed her until the night she stopped by—knowing Bonnie was sick with flu—and found little Angela asleep inside the open refrigerator, where apparently she'd gone in a futile search for food.

* * *

When you're a girl from a small town such as Welcome and you take the first big risk of your life by marrying a junior in high school when you yourself are twenty-three and then he leaves you for another woman, in addition to all your other problems you have to deal with the fact that in the eyes of many you've made a damned fool of yourself.

For a while, this made Bonnie bitter. For a while, she felt sorry for herself. She had loved him, in her own way, which was no less real for being not the way of others. She had loved him in the way she'd later love stray cats. People had thought she was strange about Steve. Later, people would think she was strange about cats. But that was Bonnie. If you seemed the least bit helpless or downtrodden, her heart went out. If she could feed you, care for you, give you a warm bed to sleep in, she would. True, her emotions were somewhat inaccessible, not only to others but to herself, but an element of essential kindness was at her core. To many who focused more of their energies on themselves, this made her seem a bit peculiar.

Bonnie had wanted a way to love and still be safe. In Steve Pritchard, she'd thought she'd found it. She hadn't yet had enough experience to recognize that hers was an impossible goal, nor to sense that, at best, Steve was just a restless adolescent with his eye on the main chance, which was always just over the next hill, or in the bar a little farther down the street.

She'd gambled and lost was what it came down to, and it would be some time before she'd gamble again.

For four years, she had almost no life of her own. So much was demanded by her children and her job, and there seemed never enough money or energy. She had refused to sell the house in Lexington because she hadn't wanted Chris and Angela to lose their home just after losing their father—and because she was too proud and too stubborn to give it up.

But that meant leaving at seven every morning for Winston-Salem, dropping the kids off at Salem Baptist, which ran a day-care center and elementary school, then going to Integon and working all day and sometimes far into the night.

Too often, she'd pick up Chris and Angela hours after all the other children had left, then drive home exhausted, feed them whatever cheap starch she could find, and collapse into bed by herself.

Quite a shock, then, to discover that one of Integon's financial executives—the highly regarded and industrious Lieth Von Stein—was expressing an interest in her.

Toward the end of the Depression, Lieth Von Stein's uncle Richard moved to Winston-Salem from New York City. For almost no money at all, he bought a storefront dry-cleaning establishment called Camel City Dry Cleaners & Laundry. The camel was a reference not to any nearby desert, but to the brand of cigarette that had become the mainstay of the Winston-Salem economy.

Through the war and after it, the business grew. Richard added a second location, then a third. He realized he needed someone to run bookkeeping. He convinced Lieth's father—a graduate of Brown University who had lost everything in the stock market crash of '29—to leave New York and join him in Winston-Salem. Together, they built Camel City Dry Cleaners into a regional chain, and Lieth Von Stein, who should have grown up in the borough of Queens, grew up instead in Winston-Salem.

He was an only child and convivial. He played a little football in high school, despite being only five foot six, and got on well with classmates and teachers.

After high school, he enrolled at North Carolina State University in Raleigh, intending to major in engineering. He fared poorly, dropped out, served in the Army (Europe, not Vietnam), and finally earned a degree from a small but well-regarded North Carolina college named Guilford. Then he returned to Winston-Salem and went to work. He was twenty-six, a year younger than Bonnie, but on a considerably faster professional track, when he first became aware of her.

Despite her circumstances, Bonnie had developed into an appealing young woman, with long hair, strong features, a quick mind. She'd come to believe, however, that she would always be just a little country girl who liked hard work: someone of interest only to her parents and her children, and maybe to her brother and sisters. She understood that some men might wish to keep company with her—though she hadn't run into many since Steve had left—but never one as worthy as Lieth Von Stein.

Lieth not only was going places professionally that Bonnie, no matter how hard she worked, could never reach, but he came from much higher social strata. If you grew up in Welcome as a bricklayer's daughter, then the heir to the largest dry-cleaning chain in Winston-Salem seemed like a prince of the realm.

She'd seen him at work but had never considered that she might be of romantic interest to him. She'd just assumed, she said later, that "classy young ladies would interest him." And with her lonely children waiting for her every night at Salem Baptist, and after four years of isolation, exhaustion, and semistarvation, Bonnie Von Stein did not consider herself a classy young lady.

It wasn't until late October of 1976, after Lieth had already decided to take a job with Federated Department Stores in Cincinnati, that they had their first social encounter. Bonnie was thirty-two and Lieth thirty. Angela Pritchard was six and Chris was about to turn eight.

Bonnie needed a pair of boots for a Halloween costume. A friend suggested a good place to find them. Lieth overheard the conversation. The working day was almost over. He said to Bonnie,"I'll ride out with you to find the boots and then you can stop by my apartment for a drink." When they got there, they talked, and then he asked her if she'd like to have dinner. She said she couldn't, she had to pick up her two children at day care.

"Well, pick them up, and then we'll all go out to eat," Lieth suggested. She explained that the children would be tired and shy and not good company at a restaurant. Then, out of politeness—but feeling some spark—she said that if he didn't mind the drive, he could dine with her at her house in Lexington.

And that's what happened. The kids were in bed by eight-thirty and Lieth and Bonnie watched TV.

He was leaving for Cincinnati in two weeks, but he drove

down to Lexington again for Halloween, and then another night the following week, and then once the weekend after that. Then he was gone. He took her address and home phone number, out of politeness, but it was obvious to Bonnie that she'd never see him again.

To her astonishment, he began calling from Cincinnati. He even wrote an occasional letter. His parents were still in Winston-Salem, and every couple of months he'd come to visit. When he did, he'd spend time with Bonnie. They shared an interest in music. Bonnie's grandfather had crafted violins and mandolins out of wood. Lieth's father had earned spending money at Brown by playing saxophone in jazz bands and later (according to family legend) had performed briefly with a Glenn Miller orchestra. But there was getting to be more to the relationship than a mutual appreciation of music.

One Friday, about six months after he'd moved, Lieth said he was coming for a visit and told Bonnie that his parents would like to meet her and her children. He suggested that they have dinner at the Red Lobster on Peter's Creek Parkway, in Winston-Salem. That's when she knew something serious was under way.

Lieth's parents took to Chris and Angela from the start. They told Bonnie they'd always been eager to have grandchildren. They even watched Chris play the role of Pinnochio in a play at the Salem Baptist school.

After that, Lieth visited almost every weekend. He began staying at Bonnie's house. The kids were thrilled. After not hearing from Steve Pritchard for years, they had a father again. They'd spend quiet Saturdays at Finch Park in Lexington, lying by the edge of the pond, watching the swans. Then they'd drive to Kerley's for what its partisans claimed was the best barbecue in North Carolina.

They began to vacation together, traveling to Ocean Isle Beach, on the coast. Bonnie's mother, a staunch member of the old school, did not approve of this intimacy outside of marriage. But she liked Lieth and liked even more seeing her daughter happy again.

Actually, ecstatic would be a better description of Bonnie's state. All week long she'd keep telling herself that this was too good to last, that one Friday Lieth would call and tell her he wasn't coming. Or maybe he'd write her a letter, explaining, as graciously as possible, that he'd met someone else. Someone of his own social class. Someone not saddled with two kids. It was as if he had dropped down from the heavens to rescue her from a life of toil and sorrow, and she couldn't help but fear that one day, without warning, the heavens would consume him again.

How could anybody be as good to her as he was? One day he called from Cincinnati and told her that on her lunch hour she should go shopping at Montaldo's, a department store she'd always considered too expensive. She explained that she couldn't afford to. He told her that for once she was wrong: he'd opened a charge account in her name and had put $500 in it.

One Saturday, they went to Welcome to visit Bonnie's parents. Lieth, of course, was too much the gentleman to comment, even to Bonnie, about certain basics that were lacking at the house. But within two weeks he'd ordered the Bateses a washing machine and an air conditioner.

That could have been a tricky business. Bonnie's parents had as much pride as she did. But Lieth was so gracious and humble and sincere as he explained to Bonnie's mother and father that it would make *him* feel so good to know that they wouldn't have to swelter through the summers, and to know that Bonnie's mother could have more time to tend her orchids if she didn't spend so much doing wash, that they wound up feeling they couldn't disappoint this fine young man by turning away his generosity.

Besides, they saw how much he loved their daughter. They saw how good he was to Chris and Angela. And they saw character beneath the surface. This was no Steve Pritchard, gussied up with a college degree. This was a man they felt privileged to know.

Slowly Bonnie's fears of rejection subsided. In August 1979, Lieth said he was taking a new job with a finance company in South Bend, Indiana. He asked her to marry him. She said yes.

6

The newspaper headline said, "Interview With Wife No Help . . . Woman Is Unable to Give Description." The story quoted a police spokesman as describing an interview with Bonnie as "not fruitful," and said, "She told police nothing that they had not been able to discern from other evidence." The attack was still said to have been "the work of intruders" who had broken into the home, but already burglary was losing credibility as a motive. "Police have said that apparently nothing was taken from the house," the story said.

Bonnie said later that she was never able to untangle her confused impressions of those first days. Lieth was dead. She would live. Angela had not been hurt. Nothing else mattered. She just wanted to be left alone. And she wanted the police to catch whoever did this. Already, she was impatient. Why did they keep asking her questions? Why didn't they just catch him, whoever he was?

And she was tormented by the question of why this had happened at all. The police told her that little, if anything, had been taken from the house. It had not been a robbery gone awry. It appeared to have been premeditated murder. But who would want to kill Lieth—or her?

True, they were not a sociable couple. They'd made few, if any, friends in Little Washington. But neither did they have enemies, unless there was someone at work who hated Lieth, or feared him. Someone he'd never talked about. But she could not imagine even that. Her head still hurt, it was still hard to breathe, and the tube in her chest hurt most of all.

Her mother and father and her brother and sisters and

their respective wife and husbands had come to Washington. It seemed to Bonnie that they should be fearful for their own lives, as well as for hers and for Chris's and Angela's. A madman was out there somewhere. A madman who, for some reason, had singled out Bonnie and Lieth.

A uniformed policeman remained stationed outside Bonnie's door. The killer might not know she couldn't describe him. If he learned she was still alive, what assurance was there that he would not try to silence her?

A representative of the funeral home came. Bonnie told them to cremate the body. Lieth had always said that's what he wanted.

A minister came. He would be conducting the funeral service. He asked questions about Lieth. Neither Bonnie nor Lieth had attended church in Washington, so no minister knew anything about them.

The ex-president of the Humane Society came. Bonnie didn't want to see her. She didn't want to see anyone. But the ex-president of the Humane Society just had to tell Bonnie what she'd heard. Her neighbor had been at the annual summer festival and had seen Angela there with two friends. It seemed strange, she said, that Angela, whom one would have expected to be deep in grief, had been at the summer festival in the first place, but what was even more peculiar, and what the ex-president of the Humane Society just had to rush over to the hospital to tell Bonnie right away, was that a "very, very reliable person" had overheard Angela saying to one of her friends that "Lieth deserved to die." She didn't want Bonnie to get upset about this—Lord knows, Bonnie had been through enough—but it was the sort of thing she felt she had a duty to pass on.

That evening, when Angela visited, in the company of her friend Donna Brady, Bonnie asked what she could possibly have said that would have been so misinterpreted. Donna Brady spoke right up. What Angela had said, Donna explained, was, "Whoever did this to Lieth deserves to die."

Bonnie realized that after any murder in any small town—especially with the murder still unsolved—there would be gossip and rumor. The visit from her Humane

Society colleague made her aware for the first time that after this murder, in this town, some of the rumors could get ugly.

The service was held on the gray, drizzly morning of Thursday, July 28, three days after the murder. By afternoon, the drizzle had become a hard rain.

Bonnie's brother and his wife had brought her a black nightgown and black bathrobe and black slippers to wear. It occurred to her that such items must not have been easy to find in Little Washington in July.

Chris had an even bigger problem. At Scott's, in the mall, he'd picked out a lot of fine new clothing to wear to the service, but when he tried to pay with his credit card, a machine rejected it as being overdrawn. Instead, he had to borrow funeral clothes from his friend Jonathan Wagoner.

A black car from the funeral home picked up Bonnie at the emergency-room door. At the home, shielded by a screen, she sat out of the view of press and public.

Despite his having asked her so many questions about Lieth, the minister got many things wrong, such as describing him as a Vietnam veteran. But what did it matter? Her head hurt, she still couldn't breathe right, the pressure in her chest had not diminished, and Lieth was just a pile of ashes.

She returned to her hospital bed, where she remained for another four days. Her mother and father and sisters and brother continued to visit. Chris and Angela stopped by much less frequently—so seldom, in fact, as to cause comment both from hospital personnel and from other members of Bonnie's family.

Her apparently quick recovery was causing comment, too. Bonnie had never been a complainer. She had a near-fetish about keeping her emotions to herself. To observers, this could easily be mistaken for indifference and could lead to awkward questions about why she wasn't more upset.

The nursing notes for the day of Lieth's service said, "Preparing to leave for husband's memorial service. Patient shows no outward emotion." Upon her return, she was described in the notes as "cheerful and alert, talking with visitors.'' At least to some, this behavior, combined with the fact that nobody in town knew anything about her, and the fact that her husband's death had enriched her by $2 million, caused a great deal of talking behind her back.

To Bonnie, unaware of the reaction, only three things seemed to matter anymore: Who could have done such a thing, why hadn't the police yet made an arrest, and might the killer return?

If the days were long, the nights were longer. No matter who was with her, she felt alone and terrified. She was afraid for herself and for her children. Angela, though seeming tranquil, said she was scared. She told her mother she was afraid the attacker had left her alive only because he hadn't known she'd been there, and that now he might come back to kill her, too.

Bonnie did not know how to respond. She felt incapable of offering reassurance. Above all, Bonnie was a rational person, and reason offered little solace in this instance. Violence had never been part of her world. Since she didn't know where it had come from, she couldn't be sure it was gone.

"Police Say No New Information in Probe,'' the newspaper headline said. The chief said the department was treating the Von Stein murder as "our number-one priority'' and promised that despite a lack of progress, the investigation "will not be put on a back burner.''

No motive had been established, and nothing had been reported missing from the house. Further questioning of Mrs. Von Stein had proven fruitless, as she remained unable to describe the assailants or to tell police how many people had beaten and stabbed her. Questioning of neighbors had proved equally unproductive.

On Friday, four days after the murder and one day after the memorial service for Lieth, Bonnie's ex-husband, Steve Pritchard, paid a visit. He was balding now and had a beard and, as always, was very well-spoken. He could use the phrase *symbiotic relationship* and seem to know what it meant. Also, despite much talk of financial difficulty, he drove a BMW.

For many years, he'd lived out west: South Dakota, Wyoming, someplace like that. He'd been a truck driver. Now he was back in North Carolina, in the western part of the state, working in some other aspect of the trucking business. She didn't know, didn't care.

He'd come to see the kids a couple of times since they'd moved to Washington. Angela treated him as if he were a total stranger, which, to her, he was. Right to his face, she'd tell him she did not consider him her real father. Lieth Von Stein, she would say, was her father.

Chris was more hospitable. Chris apparently still yearned for some sort of relationship with Steve. For Chris's sake, Bonnie had tolerated the visits. As had Lieth. Lieth, in fact, got along surprisingly well with Steve; said he liked the man, said he seemed like a nice guy, the kind of fellow you could sit down and talk to about all sorts of different subjects. Lieth had even insisted that when he visited, Steve sleep right there in the house, in Chris's room. Bonnie herself would just as soon have let him sleep in his car, but she worked hard at not being vindictive.

Now, however, she was not about to act glad to see her ex-husband. In the sphere of existence she presently occupied, there was no room for pretense.

Steve sat on the edge of her bed and told her he was so sorry about the way things had turned out. He said that if he'd never left her, then none of this would have happened.

"Don't apologize," Bonnie said. "You did me the biggest favor of my life."

He looked at her, not comprehending.

"If you hadn't walked out, I never would have had the opportunity to know and love Lieth. I *thank* you for what you did to me."

"Well," Steve Pritchard said, "I guess that's one way to look at it."

Then she asked him please not to sit on her bed. "They don't allow people to sit on hospital beds," she said. And that was the end of his visit.

Bonnie's other visitor that day was Lewis Young. He did not tell her about the fire. He did not tell her about the map. He did not tell her about the suspicions her brother had expressed. He did not tell her about the blood-spattered pages from *A Rose in Winter*.

He was still talking to her for "background," he said later, but he was aware that, despite his own impression of the severity of her injuries—an impression supported by the physicians who were treating her—nine out of ten people in Little Washington already seemed certain that Bonnie had planned the murder of her husband and that her children had helped carry it out.

He'd been hearing a lot about life among the Pritchard children and the Von Steins, very little of it consistent with the picture that Bonnie had painted for him in their first conversation, three days earlier.

He'd been told by high school classmates that Chris was "a tad bit weird," always trying out a strange new hair-style, and driving a noisy car, in an attempt to draw attention to himself. He'd also had "very little luck with the ladies."

Angela had "hung out with a wilder crowd," including, Young was told, boyfriends who had served time in prison.

Regarding Bonnie, he'd already been asked several variations on the same basic question: How could someone kill a man so quick, but couldn't kill a woman?

And this was a woman who had become, literally over-night—with Lieth's $700,000 life insurance added to his original inheritance of $1.3 million—one of the wealthier women in eastern North Carolina.

For someone who'd spent much of her adult life in a state of financial and perhaps emotional deprivation, and whose domestic life on Lawson Road gave rise to so many tales of worsening strain between her husband and her children, it could have seemed an immeasurable fortune—a bonanza for which Lieth's death, and even her own serious injuries, might have seemed a small price to pay.

Lewis Young was gentle and restrained in talking to Bonnie, but he pressed her just a bit about the relationship between her husband and herself, and between her husband and her children.

Again, she assured him that theirs had been a loving, if

private, family, and that if he ever heard anything to the contrary, it could be only from people who did not know them well.

Young could see he'd make no progress in that area, so he asked again about the assailant. Bonnie said she was terribly nearsighted without her glasses, and that all she really had was this *impression* of someone very strong, with broad shoulders, who had acted "methodically," rather than as if in a frenzy.

She added that if she hadn't fallen out of bed, she was sure she would have been killed, too.

She also said that after the assailant had gently closed her bedroom door, she'd heard "three loud whacks," and that she knew, from the sound, that Angela was being murdered, too.

When he asked her again if she had any thoughts as to who might have been responsible for the murder, she suggested, in addition to the Trust Department of the North Carolina National Bank, some disgruntled or frightened employee of National Spinning. As internal auditor, Lieth might have discovered embezzlement, theft, or some other misappropriation of funds. Maybe somebody there had learned that he intended to go public with evidence of wrongdoing and had murdered him before he could.

Young had to concede that the National Spinning theory was not entirely lacking in logic, though early investigation there had turned up nothing to support it.

Indeed, the only disturbing documents his examination of the contents of Lieth's office desk had turned up were letters from a young woman with whom Lieth had apparently become acquainted on a business trip. The letters suggested that at the very least an affectionate friendship had been formed. The letters had been written just one year ago, in the summer of 1987, soon after the woman, a North Carolina native, had moved to California.

In one letter, the woman had mentioned that she'd soon be returning to North Carolina for a visit, and she had seemed to be hinting at the possibility of meeting Lieth, at least for a night, in Wilmington, a coastal town about a hundred miles south of Little Washington.

There was no evidence that any such rendezvous occurred, but several weeks later, the young woman wrote that as midsummer approached she found herself thinking about North Carolina and about Lieth. "These summer days bring back some good memories—that is for sure," she wrote. Then, after asking if he'd been to the beach, she wrote, "I am sure a wild guy like yourself took the weekend once or twice and hit the vacation spots."

She also mentioned she was sorry that Lieth had gone through so much stress concerning his mother, a comment that indicated he had at the very least discussed his personal life with her in some detail. And saying she was anxious to speak with him, she asked him to keep her updated on his travel plans. "I know for a fact that we will see each other in the near future," she wrote.

Only last Christmas she'd sent a card to his office, asking how things were in Washington and whether he was ready to come to Los Angeles. If so, she wrote, "please let me know," adding, "May 1988 be a year of prosperity and travel! (i.e., LA . . . ha ha ha)." She said she'd like very much to see him over the Christmas holidays and gave him dates when she would be visiting family in Raleigh.

Nothing in this correspondence suggested adulterous behavior on Lieth's part, but what did come through clearly was that this isolated, gruff, and taciturn man who had so few friends in his own community, and—according to a number of sources—whose relations with his stepchildren had grown so strained, had succeeded in charming to no small degree a young woman he had met while out of town.

At forty-two, with more than a million dollars he felt confident he could successfully manage by himself, why not a life in L.A. instead of Washington?

As for Bonnie's notion that the trust department of the state's biggest bank might have engineered the killing in order to avoid losing an account, this again struck Young as preposterous.

Indeed, he came away from this second talk with Bonnie feeling that either she was still far more hysterical as a result of the attack than she appeared on the surface, or else that she was desperate to do *anything* to shift his attention away from her family and herself.

On Monday, August 1, eight days after having been admitted, Bonnie was discharged from the hospital.

The doctor who prepared her discharge summary wrote:

This is a 44-year-old white female admitted through the emergency room following an attack in which she was beaten about the head and stabbed in the right chest. The emergency-room physician did the initial resuscitation and work on her, including insertion of a thoracotomy tube in the right chest for hemopneumothorax, and also sutured multiple lacerations of her forehead. She was placed in Intensive Care ... subsequent workup revealed a fracture of the base of the first metacarpal, which required a cast. The patient has done very well. Her chest tube was removed after three days. The lungs have remained clear. The lacerations and contusion of her forehead and her right chest wall are resolving nicely. Chest X ray this morning showed complete resolution of the pneumothorax with some mild reactive pleural changes at the base. She is on a regular diet, ambulatory, and doing very well.

She moved into the double room at the Holiday Inn where her mother and father were staying, and for the next two nights she slept there with them, taking the bed farther from the door and repeatedly asking her father if he was certain the locks had been secured.

On Wednesday, she went to police headquarters to be fingerprinted. It seemed pointless. She was still so weak she could barely walk unassisted and so stunned emotionally that even the slightest conversation required a major effort of the will. Why were they fingerprinting *her?* What good would that do? Why hadn't they yet found the killer?

Lewis Young asked her again about the weekend of the murder. She told him again there had been absolutely nothing unusual about it. Just a typical family summer weekend. One note Young made during this brief talk was of Bonnie's recollection that Chris had spent the early part of Saturday evening "cooking some hamburgers with his sister."

On Thursday, she returned to the police station to pick up a key to her house. Then, in the company of her parents, she returned to 110 Lawson Road.

Some people in Bonnie's situation might have needed to sit for a long time, staring at the house from the security of a parked car, before working up the courage to enter it. Others undoubtedly never would have gone near it. But Bonnie had always believed—with the sort of stoicism that caused some to wonder, on occasion, if she had any feelings at all—that if there's something unpleasant you have to do, then you'd just better go ahead and get it done.

So, with her mother and father at her side, she got out of the car and approached the house. Her clothes were in the bedroom. She needed her clothes. She unlocked the front door. She walked straight to the stairway. She felt nauseated. She felt she might faint.

But leaning on her father's arm, and with her mother close behind her, Bonnie climbed the stairs to the bedroom. She had to pause for breath going up. These were the first stairs she'd climbed since she'd been stabbed.

She did not flinch, she did not turn back. Gulping down air, she moved forward. She walked into the bedroom and went straight to her closet without looking either right or left. With her mother and father helping, she took the clothes she needed. Then she turned and left the room and left the house. Her mother and father loaded the trunk, then drove her back to her childhood home in Welcome.

On the same day, Lewis Young interviewed Chris for the second time. He was "a cocky little college kid," in Young's opinion. Having obviously located his car keys, Pritchard arrived for the interview in his white Mustang with the loud muffler. Like his sister, he acted as if the whole business of answering questions designed to help find the person who'd murdered his stepfather and had almost murdered his mother was just a bit much of an inconvenience on a day when he would really rather have been at the beach. The first time he'd met him, Chris had been so fidgety and so obviously strung out that Young had felt kind of sorry for him. The second time, he just didn't like him.

Chris repeated that as far as he knew, Lieth hadn't had any problems or enemies. He was aware that some stocks had been inherited but had no idea how much they were worth. "I did not know about that stuff," he said as he had earlier.

He described looking for his car keys for "fifteen or twenty minutes" before running out to call the campus police. He said his roommate had eventually found the keys under the cushion of a chair. Again, he described his last visit home as routine. He and his sister had barbecued hamburgers for the family. Then he'd gone back to school, intending to work on his term paper.

In Raleigh, however, he'd run into a friend of his, James Upchurch, at the Fast Fare convenience store, and the two of them had wound up in Upchurch's room, drinking beer. Yes, he'd drunk beer and played cards Sunday night, too. But honest to God, he said, if this hadn't happened, he would have been up at seven A.M. Monday to finish the paper.

Young did not mention the knife and burnt clothing and map that had been found at the scene of the fire.

Nor did he mention the blood-spattered pages found next to the bed—pages in which a young hero named Christopher, and his companions, had slain an evil overlord with knife, club, and sword.

Nor the fact that Chris's own uncle suspected that Chris was involved in the murder.

7

Later, Bonnie would not be able to recall precisely how many days went by with her doing nothing but sitting in the house she grew up in. She slept downstairs, in a room next to her mother and father's.

At least, that was where she tried to sleep. The hours of sleep—as they would be for many nights to come—were far outnumbered by the hours during which she lay awake in the dark, cringing each time a floorboard in the old house creaked.

"She was so petrified," her mother said later, "that she wouldn't even turn over in bed. She kept her lamp burning all night. She was trying to put on a good front, but we knew she was dying inside."

During the days, she'd sit in her father's easy chair with blankets wrapped around her, gazing at the television set and having chills. She'd watch game shows, soap operas, anything that filled the void with motion and sound.

Her mother was constantly trying to make her eat or drink, but Bonnie had neither hunger nor thirst. People stopped by to see her and she received many telephone calls. In Little Washington she may have been a stranger, but in Welcome she was Bonnie Lou Bates and she was suffering, and in Welcome one did not suffer in solitude.

During these first weeks of her recovery Bonnie grew closer to her father than ever before. He may not have been able to articulate the love he felt for his wounded daughter, or the anguish that her suffering caused him, but his daily and nightly presence at her side was enough. "Steady and solid as a rock," was one description offered of George Bates, Sr., and Bonnie felt that from his strength she might be able to replenish hers.

He was a handsome man, tanned from working outdoors, and sturdily built. Even in his sixties, his hair remained dark and full. And to say that he shared and passed on the family trait of not displaying or discussing emotion was not to suggest that he was taciturn or withdrawn. On the contrary, George Bates was known throughout Welcome as a man with a quick sense of humor; a good-spirited and talkative man who loved to tell stories, make up limericks, and sing songs as he walked around the house.

If Bonnie's mother tended to focus on the *business* of life, her father seemed more attracted to its potential for merriment, enjoying its simple pleasures.

For example, George Bates loved sweets. He could not walk past a candy counter without buying something. He even had a candy machine beside his bedroom easy chair. It said, "George's Goody Machine," and his children were always filling it with treats.

Though a bricklayer by trade, his real love was working with wood. It seemed to be in his genes. He was, after all, the son of a carpenter, born in a log cabin hewn from trees that had grown on family land.

During the infrequent chances he'd had for play in his boyhood, George Bates's favorite pastime was to walk the forests of Welcome with penknife in hand, often carving poems into young trees, so that the words and the tree could grow together. He would never speak of the pleasure this form of communing with nature gave him: it was too private. But years later, family members would, in a back section of woods, come upon a tree in which young George Bates had carved a message years before.

At the time he'd met Bonnie's mother, he was working as a bricklayer on an Army barracks at Fort Bragg.

On December 7, 1941, upon hearing the news that the Japanese had attacked Pearl Harbor, he said nothing to anyone, but simply disappeared into the forest behind the house that he shared with his young bride.

There, on a tree that would still stand fifty years later,

he carved the last two lines of the Joyce Kilmer poem "Trees":

> *Poems are made by fools like me,*
> *But only God can make a tree.*

With his wife pregnant with their second child, Bonnie, George Bates was drafted. He got a furlough from boot camp so he could come home when she was born, but then left almost immediately for Europe, where he was an infantryman, trudging and fighting through France and Germany.

In his letters home, he would say nothing of the fighting, but would tell little stories, such as how one night it had been so cold he'd climbed into a barn and had slept among the pigs to stay warm. On another occasion, with his whole unit having been on short rations for days, he'd spotted a field of sweet potatoes and had dug them up and eaten them raw, while his ravenous city-bred comrades had stood by laughing—somewhat enviously—at this country boy able to eat roots.

Home on furlough and awaiting reassignment, he had his first chance to get acquainted with Bonnie, a small and somewhat introverted toddler.

One afternoon in August 1945 they were in the backyard, barbecuing chicken and hot dogs over an open fire, when the news came over the radio that the war was over. George Bates was so overjoyed that he jumped up and tossed the straw hat he was wearing in the air. After retrieving it, still unable to contain himself, he threw the hat in the fire as an act of celebration. It may have been the most uninhibited emotional outburst of his life.

He settled quickly and happily into domestic life. He owned twenty-eight acres of land and set about building a home for himself and his growing family. It was a one-story brick house, with an attic that eventually came to be a bedroom for Bonnie and her three sisters.

Bonnie had grown up listening to her father's stories and hearing his songs. His favorite, which she never forgot, was one he called "The Geography Song":

Maine is an island in Asia,
France is a river in Spain.
Coconuts grow on a mountain of snow,
Deserts are covered with rain.
Crocodiles come from Chicago,
Silver is mixed in a mill,
Grass is quite rare,
The equator is square,
And Kansas is south of Brazil.

He preached and practiced the simple virtues—honesty and fairness and charity—and there wasn't one person in all of Welcome who wouldn't say, "George Bates is as nice as the day is long."

Like almost all other North Carolina families who owned land, the Bateses considered theirs an active resource, not just empty space to gaze across. They grew corn, sweet potatoes, watermelon, cantaloupe, and field peas. To a large extent, in order to supplement George's modest earnings, they lived off their land. At any given time, up to five hundred quarts of canned food would be in their basement.

They raised a few cows, pigs, turkeys, and chickens, which they would then kill and eat. They churned their own butter, made cherry pies from fruit picked from their own trees, and made preserves from their strawberries.

In summers, Bonnie's mother would start making ice cream in late afternoon, so it would be fresh and waiting when George came home, hot and tired from a day of laying bricks. He would sit on the porch and eat that ice cream and tell Polly how it cooled him to the bone. There seemed nothing he wanted that he didn't have. Indeed, his wife would later describe him as the most contented man she'd ever known.

Back in this childhood home, filled with these memories, and sheltered not only by the roof her father had put over her head years before, but by the steadiness and durability of his love, Bonnie struggled to keep her panic under control.

Nothing bad could befall her in Welcome, she told herself. In the aura of her father's goodness, she was safe. All around her were objects he had fashioned from wood: tables, chests, cabinets, bookcases, all made from trees George Bates had cut from his own land.

Most days, and most nights, through early August, it was just the three of them: Bonnie, her mother, and her father. She was grateful for the concern of friends and neighbors, but she wasn't up to seeing many visitors.

The people most conspicuous by their absence—as they'd been from Bonnie's first hours in the hospital—were her children. Day to day, no one seemed quite sure where they were. In Washington, in Greenville, at the beach, down to see Ramona, who lived in South Carolina—everywhere, it seemed, but with their mother.

Her father finally spoke to them about it. He said their apparent lack of concern disturbed him greatly. He told them they were being inconsiderate, unloving, and even cruel.

They said they didn't mean to be, it was just that they were upset and frightened and needed to be with their friends. Besides, there wasn't anything they could do for their mother, now. She was back home in Welcome, getting better. But Welcome wasn't their home, they weren't going to sit wrapped in blankets all day long, staring at the television set. They needed noise and motion and the distraction provided by friends.

And what was the big deal about the hospital? They had stopped by. They'd spent some time there. But it wasn't as if Bonnie had been dying or anything. She'd been well cared for. She'd had lots of other company.

Besides, it upset them to see her with a tube in her chest and with her head all swollen, just lying there asking the same question—who could have done this?—over and over again.

Bonnie seemed less bothered by their absence than was her father. Both children, she could tell, were as grief stricken as she was, but being young and physically unharmed, they were restless, at loose ends, still too shaken to settle in one place for very long.

The fact was, Bonnie did not want *any* company. The

person whose companionship had meant the most to her was gone forever now, and rather than make the effort even to sustain conversation with her children, she preferred to be alone with her memories.

She tried to recall only the good times, of which there had been many, at least until the last eighteen months of Lieth's life.

Things had begun to turn sour in February 1987 when his father had died suddenly of an aortic aneurysm. For the next thirteen months, Bonnie and Lieth had driven back and forth from Washington to Winston-Salem—a four-and-a-half-hour trip—on all but two weekends. After his father's death, his mother had needed constant care. As an only child, it was up to Lieth to provide it. His mother had weakened fast, however, and had died within six months of her husband.

The next to go was Uncle Richard, someone so close to Lieth as to have been almost a second father. He'd become sick with emphysema. Both oxygen and nursing care were required twenty-four hours a day. Eventually, he needed a tracheotomy. Again, Lieth had been responsible for all arrangements. Richard had died in March.

Camel City Dry Cleaners & Laundry had become the biggest enterprise of its kind in Winston-Salem. So successful that when Lieth's father died, having sold the business not long before, he left an estate of more than $1 million. Upon the death of his mother, Lieth inherited the entire estate.

For most people, not having money was a bigger worry than having it, but Lieth—an auditor by trade and a man who'd been raised to respect a dollar sign—found it quite stressful to suddenly control such a sum.

The Trust Department of the North Carolina National Bank in Winston-Salem was managing the estate, but he was not happy with their performance. Since March, often with Bonnie's research assistance, he'd spent nights and weekends formulating a stock-trading program, which, on paper, was achieving far better results than the bank's. Why should he pay them tens of thousands of dollars a year in management fees, he'd asked her repeatedly, to do what he could do better himself? Besides, it was something he enjoyed.

Lieth subscribed to half a dozen sports-betting services and during the football and basketball seasons had a wager on almost every game he was able to watch on television. The stock market, though it required more work, and though the money involved was far more substantial, was, he claimed, just as much fun.

Pressure, to be sure—especially when you were playing with a sum more than twenty-five times your annual salary—but Lieth worked hard at fundamental research and had confidence in his trading instincts. He claimed—perhaps dubiously—that he'd never once lost money even on the riskiest of stock market gambles, the trading of puts and calls. Even so, it took a case of Budweiser per weekend to dull his growing anxiety. And increasingly, the beer had been supplemented by vodka.

By the end of the year, however, he would have been eligible to receive full pension benefits from National Spinning. He could then quit his job—which he'd never liked in the first place—and manage his money full time.

He and Bonnie could live off the income from his inheritance, plus the profits he'd make from investing. He talked about buying a mobile home, which he could use as an office when they were in Little Washington. When the spirit moved them, they could turn the ignition key and take to the road. Or even to the high seas: What about a cruise? With faxes and radiophones and laptop computers there was no reason why Lieth couldn't manage their money just as well while en route to a Caribbean island. Suddenly, horizons seemed limitless. By July, the long months of strain seemed almost over. Soon, he and Bonnie could start to really live.

This had been his mood on the last day of his life, and Bonnie had found herself relieved. Lieth had been so down, so drained, so mentally and emotionally exhausted by the deaths of his parents and his uncle. His nerves had been rubbed raw by the pressure of trying to deal with medical emergencies, then funeral arrangements, then grief, all the while working at a job he didn't like, in a town he despised, and having to cope also with her teenaged children, who, even she had to admit, could be difficult on occasion.

She felt she could drive from Washington to Winston-Salem blindfolded after all the trips they'd made for thirteen months. She'd gone with him on every one, even though it meant leaving the children unattended, because he had told her he needed her. He couldn't face all that misery by himself. She was his wife and her place was by his side, even if that meant nine hours in an automobile every weekend.

Helplessly, she had watched as Lieth's depression deepened, as he grew more irritable and quarrelsome and both physically and emotionally fatigued. He would come home from work, head straight for the beer in the refrigerator, and drink until he went to bed. And he'd taken to going to bed as early as eight P.M. This wasn't healthy, she knew it wasn't, just as it wasn't healthy to go through a whole case of beer on a weekend, plus a fifth of Jack Daniel's or sometimes vodka, or entire bottles of wine.

By the last day of his life, however, she had allowed herself to start hoping that most of the worst might be behind them, and that the new life he envisioned would come to pass. It had been, she'd later say, "a day filled with bliss and togetherness." She reminded herself—and others—that her last meal with Lieth had been one of the happiest and most romantic they'd ever shared.

She said the thought had even occurred to her, as they'd driven back from Greenville after the dinner: *at least there are no more family members left to die.*

A memorial service for Lieth was held in Winston-Salem. Bonnie's mother, who grew orchids in a greenhouse behind their home, made a spray of the flowers and placed it around the urn that held Lieth's ashes. After a service at the funeral home, the urn was taken to a cemetery. How do you bury ashes? Bonnie wondered. It seemed unnatural. But for days now nothing had seemed natural. She no longer knew what natural was and doubted that she ever would again.

She was surprised by how many people stood at the

graveside. People she had worked with at Integon, old high school friends of Lieth's, even her ex-husband, Steve Pritchard. And of course, Angela and Chris.

But that was only one day. There were all the other days to get through, too. The chills did not subside. Nor did the sleeplessness, nor the sorrow.

And as the days passed, despite her father's best efforts, and despite the emotional solace offered by her childhood home, Bonnie could not entirely rid herself of her icy fear.

This was not something she felt she could talk about, because she didn't want to worry others, but as she sat wrapped in blankets in her father's den, she grew more frightened, rather than less, at the prospect that whoever had tried to kill her would come back.

She tried to force the fear into the background by making herself look logically at what had happened. But there had been no logic to it. Who could have killed Lieth? And why? Who could have come so close to killing her?

She knew it might seem farfetched to blame the North Carolina National Bank Trust Department, just as it was farfetched to blame a rival or enemy of Lieth's from National Spinning. But no supposition, no accusation, no crazy guess, could be as wildly unlikely as the fact that it had happened at all.

She grew weary of thinking about it, but there was nothing else to think about.

Why hadn't there been an arrest? How hard could it be to find someone who had done such a terrible thing? This wasn't New York City, Los Angeles or Detroit. This had happened in the Smallwood subdivision in Washington, North Carolina, where nothing like it had ever happened before. Surely, this could not be a hard crime to solve.

In the hospital, Bonnie's only consolation—other than that Angela had not been harmed—was knowing the police would surely make a quick arrest, and the killer would be in jail before she ever set foot on the street. But that hadn't happened. The hours had turned to days and now to weeks. What was wrong with these so-called investigators? What were they doing?

Even in her weakened state, she already was angry at

what she considered police incompetence. She'd read crime books. She'd watched TV. She knew crime scenes were supposed to be preserved so physical evidence could be gathered. Yet her neighbors—*voyeurs* was what she considered them—had been allowed into her home with buckets and mops only hours after the murder, telling police they wanted to clean up the master bedroom so that when she came home from the hospital, she wouldn't have to face the disgusting mess.

And the police had let them—effectively abandoning the crime scene to any do-gooders or sightseers who wandered by. That wasn't right, Bonnie kept saying. It couldn't be. Not only did she feel that her privacy—which she valued strongly—had been violated in an elemental way, but that potentially vital clues might have been lost.

And now, with each call to the Washington police or Lewis Young producing the same unsatisfactory response—there's nothing new, we're working on it, we'll keep you informed—a new and even more desolate feeling spread inside her: *whoever did this might never be caught.*

Even as she sat shivering through the sweltering August afternoons, Bonnie had to consider that she might spend the rest of her life not knowing who had murdered her husband, nor whether they might someday try again to murder her.

8

Unless you are at the beach, or maybe way up in the mountains at the state's western edge, the month of August in North Carolina is hellish. This is nowhere more true than in the steaming flatlands of Beaufort County, which lacks even the temporary diversions that cities of substance can provide. The night is wild with the noise of insects, and by day the sun is a vicious, potentially deadly foe. Even the fish have it bad. In the Pamlico and Tar rivers, fish die by the thousands, literally suffocating in water from which life-sustaining oxygen has been sucked by Carolina summer heat.

One comes to crave air-conditioning more than sex, food, or sleep. Torpor reigns. There seems little, if anything, so urgent that it cannot wait another hour, another day, even a month. In short, it is not the best of times to press forward with a homicide investigation.

Lewis Young tried, but he soon ran into problems beyond the weather. The function of the North Carolina State Bureau of Investigation was to provide assistance to local law enforcement authorities when requested. Young, however resourceful and tenacious he was, had no authority to conduct an independent inquiry. He could not answer a call to action if none was given. If the Washington police didn't ask for help, he couldn't force it upon them.

And in August of 1988, the Washington police were somewhat in disarray. The town manager (who soon would resign for unrelated reasons) was trying to exercise direct operational control over the investigation. The chief of police was preparing to quit. And the detective to whom the Von Stein case had been assigned was not the young

81

and industrious John Taylor, but an older man who often seemed distracted and seldom pursued leads. Interviews were conducted, but at a desultory pace more in keeping with the season than with the gravity of the crime.

Still, reports did drift in. As they did, Lewis Young read them. As he read, he began to sense a pattern. But it was not one that tended to implicate either a frightened or disgruntled employee of the National Spinning Company, or an avaricious vice president of the North Carolina National Bank.

In homicide investigations, Young knew, the old rules were still the best. And the oldest rule of all was that once you've identified your victim, the first place to look for suspects is in the immediate family. This particular family had apparently been unknown to almost everyone in Little Washington, but not so unknown, he continued to learn, as to be immune from unattractive stories:

—An ex-colleague of Lieth's from National Spinning confirmed that Lieth had been upset with his stepson's poor college grades; that he'd said, "If he doesn't make it this semester, that's it; I'm not going to pay for him to flunk out." Another said Lieth would often "fantasize" about how good his life would be once his stepchildren were grown and gone.

—Chris's first-semester roommate at NC State said Chris would frequently get drunk on Canadian Mist and spend hours at his computer. He also said Chris used marijuana, but didn't have the money to buy cocaine. He said Chris spent more time reading Dungeons & Dragons books than studying and barely avoided flunking out.

—Another ex-roommate said Chris had never mentioned his parents, but had a lot of money and just "threw it around" on alcohol and drugs, to the point where he'd have to borrow to pay his bills. He described Chris as "easygoing" but "easily influenced by others." Chris had played Dungeons & Dragons "almost every night" with a tall, skinny guy named Moog, two guys named Daniel and Neal, and some others. Mostly, they'd confine the game to their rooms, but on occasion would act out scenarios in the steam tunnels that ran beneath the university campus. Included in their equipment were darts and knives. Chris "never had much luck with the ladies" and "couldn't get a piece of ass" and didn't do well in class. He had used marijuana and on at least two or three occasions, LSD.

—A high school friend confirmed that Chris had behaved oddly on the day of the murder: chain-smoking, rocking back and forth in a chair, seeming "jittery and nervous but not grief stricken." He'd heard Chris was using marijuana, cocaine, and LSD on a regular basis. He'd heard Angela was a drug user, too. He'd also heard that Lieth had been murdered by drug dealers because Chris owed money for drugs.

—Another high school friend said Chris and Angela were "not in love with" Lieth. There had been many arguments and clashes of personality. Chris would often say, "He lit into me again." He'd been closer to his mother than to Lieth, but even Bonnie, while not "disinterested" in Chris, pretty much let him do what he wanted. Lieth would order a curfew and Bonnie would rescind it. She'd spend a lot of time "trying to keep peace" among the others, but wasn't very "involved" in Chris's life. She was, in fact, such a "bleeding heart," this friend said, that she seemed to give more affection to her animals than to her children. Chris was described as "a smooth talker who gets into messes but thinks in the back of his mind that he can wriggle out of anything."

—Steven Outlaw, the friend with whom Chris had been arrested a couple of years earlier in Chocowinity, said that throughout their teenaged years the two of them had been "serious" Dungeons & Dragons players, largely because "there are not a lot of activities for teenagers in Washington." He said Lieth had been "very upset" by the Chocowinity incident, even going so far as to ban Outlaw from the house. "Lieth was old-fashioned. His views were definitely 'gold' to him. Nothing else mattered. And he was really bossy. He'd yell, 'Bonnie, come upstairs, please,' and then he'd talk to her and she'd have to come down and tell Chris what it was that Lieth didn't want him doing now. Her job was to carry the instructions from Lieth. She tried hard to mediate between them, and between him and Angela, too, but it didn't always work." Then Outlaw described a fight between Chris and Lieth that had erupted in the kitchen or dining room, apparently after Lieth had been drinking and sarcastically berating Chris for poor performance in school. "Lieth stood up and took a swing, but Chris just pushed him away and ran into the little bathroom downstairs. Chris was so mad, though, that he punched a hole right through the door."

—A former boyfriend of Angela's said that Lieth had been strict and hard to get along with; that if Angela had wanted to do something of which Lieth would disapprove—which was almost anything—she and her mother would devise a plot designed to keep Lieth unaware. The boyfriend said his relationship with Angela had ended when she'd caught him with another girl. After that, she had supposedly dated someone who'd served time at a youth correctional facility in Raleigh. Supposedly, she'd used pot and speed. Supposedly, Lieth was worth $3 million after his parents died, but according to Angela, he was so stingy that it probably wouldn't make any difference to their lives. This ex-boyfriend said Angela and Chris seldom referred to Lieth by name, instead calling him simply "the asshole." He added that Chris was "obsessed" with Dungeons & Dragons.

—Donna Brady mentioned that Chris's radio had been stolen from his car, but that he'd been afraid to tell Lieth. She said Angela referred to Lieth as "an asshole" because he was too strict about her hours and the male company she kept, but also that Angela had said the murder could only have been committed by someone from National Spinning. She said Angela was a lot like Bonnie in that she did not easily display emotion, even under circumstances when others might expect it, and that this could be misunderstood as a lack of caring. She said Chris was so immersed in the world of Dungeons & Dragons that even on the way to the funeral service for Lieth in Winston-Salem, he'd read books on how to become a better player. She also said that sometime on the day of the murder Chris had called Angela aside, saying, "I have something to tell you." Angela had never again referred to this incident, and Donna had no idea what Chris might have told her.

—Other acquaintances said that while Chris was "easy to get along with, genuine, and agreeable," it was also true that "he could never understand, after living so poor when he was young, why if his family now had all that money, there wasn't more of it coming his way." These people said they "could not understand" why Chris and Angela had spent so little time at the hospital with their mother. They added that Chris was "in love" with the game Dungeons & Dragons.

—And one of Chris's best friends from high school said there had been "constant tension" between Chris and Lieth. A couple of years earlier, Chris had actually gotten himself baptized by immersion in a river "just because he knew Lieth wouldn't like it." This friend said, "I'd tell him Lieth wasn't that bad, but he'd say I just didn't know how bad he was. Lieth was the kind of guy who would insist that he was always right—you never were. You got the feeling, being around them, that Lieth didn't have much warmth or affection for Chris, and Chris returned the lack of it. Angela, too. And the problem was, Bonnie was always on Lieth's side. She would do almost anything for him. Whatever Lieth said, she'd go along with it." In general, this friend said, Chris "tried too hard to be somebody he wasn't. His major thing was trying to fit in with the crowd. And he always had trouble with girlfriends."

And those were comments made by people personally acquainted with the family. Elsewhere in town, what had begun as simple rumor had, in a matter of days, mutated into a variety of grotesque scenarios. In the oppressive, soggy heat, the murder seemed to be all that anyone in Little Washington could talk about, and the stories ranged from the plausible to the preposterous.

Once word got around about the thirteen cats and the rooster, lurid tales of devil worship and animal sacrifice abounded. But the most common was that Bonnie herself— quite possibly with the help of her children—had arranged, or had even carried out, Lieth's murder. After all, who had more to gain from his death?

Young gave this possibility considerable thought. Maybe Bonnie had been worried about losing access to the money her husband had so recently acquired. Conscious of the letters he'd found in Lieth's desk, he wondered if maybe Lieth *had* a mistress tucked away somewhere in town, or in another part of the state or of the country. Maybe, now that he'd become a millionaire, he'd planned to leave this reclusive wife and her two bothersome children. And maybe she'd had him killed before he could. "Maybe," he said later, "she wanted it done, and Chris set it up for her."

As a theory, that worked fine, except that Bonnie herself had been so badly hurt. Her chest wound was no carefully self-inflicted surgical incision. She'd had a hemopneumothorax—a collapsing lung into which her own blood was pouring, and which could easily have killed her had she not managed to call police when she did, and had not emergency personnel responded so quickly and skillfully. However much she stood to gain financially, that made it difficult—for Young at least—to jump to the conclusion that Bonnie had engineered the crime herself.

"I couldn't totally drop it as a possibility," he said later, "but I don't care how much money there was, or how badly you wanted to get rid of the guy, that would have been a hell of a risk to take."

But what of Steve Pritchard, the truck driving ex-husband? Perhaps, in desperate need of money, and maybe having harbored a decade's worth of jealousy, Pritchard had decided to kill Bonnie and her newly wealthy husband, leaving her children—who were also *his* children—to inherit the estate. Then he could become their loving daddy again.

Young had a problem with that one, too: the map. The map he didn't want anyone to know about. His big secret. His best clue. Bonnie had already told him her ex-husband had visited the Lawson Road home several times. Steve Pritchard, the truck driver, would not have needed a map to find his way.

So what of the map? Lewis Young knew he would have

to try to learn more about it. Who had drawn it? Who had carried it? And who had tried to burn it, and why on that particular lonely stretch of road?

One other document Lewis Young studied carefully was the report of Lieth's autopsy, which had been performed in Greenville by a pathologist named Page Hudson.

The section dealing with Lieth's injuries was straightforward enough. Six different head wounds had caused tearing of the scalp, and in some instances, fractures of the skull. These could have been caused by clubbing with a baseball bat, or something similar.

There had been eight stab wounds: one in the left chest, one high on the right side of the back, and six clustered together lower on the left side of the back. As Young already knew, these could have been caused by the hunting knife found at the fire scene. The stab wound to the chest had penetrated the heart and all by itself, would have caused death "within a very few minutes."

There also were bruises and scrapes on the knuckles and hands, and a fracture of the right wrist, which Dr. Hudson categorized as "defense injuries," meaning that Lieth had sustained them as he tried to fight off his attacker.

Lack of swelling or color change in body tissue indicated that all injuries had been sustained "pretty close to each other in time."

But one aspect of the report troubled Young so much that on Friday, August 12, he drove to Greenville and met with Dr. Hudson in person.

Page Hudson was fifty-nine, and a native of Richmond, Virginia. He'd been educated at Johns Hopkins and Harvard and had become, in 1968, the first chief medical examiner the state of North Carolina had ever had.

He'd held that position for eighteen years before moving into semiretirement as a professor of pathology at East Carolina University and director of autopsy service for Pitt County Memorial Hospital in Greenville, which was where Lieth's body had been taken.

Dr. Hudson was a large man both physically and in reputation. He stood six three, had thick white hair, and spoke in a deep, commanding voice, which, while never overbearing, exuded both knowledge and authority.

He'd served as principal pathologist at more than four thousand autopsies and had assisted in at least that many more. In addition, in his capacity as the state's chief medical examiner, he'd reviewed the records of more than another fifty thousand and had testified in court hundreds of times.

Dr. Hudson did not hesitate to tell Lewis Young he was displeased by the way the crime scene had been handled by Washington police. It was not uncommon, he would later say, that "for political or whatever reasons" local police tended to resist calling the SBI for assistance, preferring instead "to try to do it themselves."

In this case, Dr. Hudson would say, "I question the judgment. Because we're not talking about an ordinary domestic fuss and someone shoving a knife into their spouse in a kitchen brawl." He would have preferred to see experienced SBI lab technicians—in particular a man named Dennis Honeycutt ("the most trained crime-scene investigator this side of Raleigh")—called in. "Not just because the Von Steins were wealthy people," he said, "but because from the beginning it looked like there was a little bit of subtlety involved here."

If Honeycutt had been there, the bloody sheets would never have been draped across the boat; the neighbors would not have been permitted in with scrub brushes and soap buckets; and some crucial procedures that were omitted would have been done.

"In a perfect world," Dr. Hudson said later, "the first officer on the scene, or the first detective, would have gotten a deep body temperature, a rectal temperature. And then, since they're not just going to grab the body and run off with it—they're going to get measurements and photographs and all that stuff—the body is going to stay there a few more hours. So, every half hour, you get another temperature, so you don't just have one point in time. Instead of having a single point, you'd have multiple points on a plot, indicating at what rate the body temperature was falling. That helps you figure back to when it was ninety-eight point six, which can help you determine the time of death."

And the time of death was precisely the point that troubled Lewis Young. The autopsy report suggested that, if almost eight hours had elapsed between the time Lieth had finished his last meal and the time he died, the chicken and rice—especially the rice—found in his stomach at autopsy should have been far more digested than was the case.

Young asked Dr. Hudson about this. "Ordinarily," the pathologist said, "I would have expected the material in his stomach to have pretty well all cleared out and been into the small intestine within an hour or two."

Young asked if the fact that it wasn't suggested the possibility of a much earlier time of death.

"It certainly is consistent with an earlier death," Dr. Hudson said. Another possibility was that Lieth had eaten the meal later than had been indicated. But Lewis Young had already obtained the credit card receipt from Sweet Caroline's, which confirmed that Bonnie's recollection of the meal time had been accurate.

The only remaining explanation, the pathologist said, was that at the time of his last meal, and in the hours that followed, Lieth Von Stein had been under such acute and severe stress that his digestive system had simply shut down.

But that was not at all consistent with Bonnie's account of her last meal with her husband as having been a time of relaxation, warmth, and even romance.

And so Lewis Young left Greenville that Friday afternoon with yet one more puzzle to solve. Besides the blood-spattered pages and their contents, and in addition to the mysterious map found at the edge of the fire, he now had a stomach full of undigested rice to think about.

Much as she dreaded it, Bonnie had to return to Little Washington. Her doctors wanted to take new X rays of her chest. Besides, she felt she needed to talk to Lewis Young in person about the progress—or lack of progress—of the investigation. She was not satisfied with the vague responses she'd been getting when she called.

Bonnie knew the journey would intensify her terror. Her father and mother would drive her because she was still too distressed to travel by herself, but even their presence would not be enough to keep a potential killer at bay.

She called a security agency in Greenville and hired bodyguards to be with her every minute she was in Little Washington. The company arranged motel accommodations for her in Greenville so she would not have to sleep in Washington. They told her they'd put a man in a room adjoining hers and another in the hall outside her door. Even that did not seem sufficient. She could have had the entire U.S. Secret Service protecting her and still she would have been stricken by panic the moment she crossed the Beaufort County line.

She rode to Greenville on Sunday, August 14, and met with Young at ten A.M. the next day. She said she could not understand why they hadn't yet made an arrest. She asked if he had followed up on any of the leads she'd given him—National Spinning, or North Carolina National Bank—and she renewed her complaint about how the Washington police had so quickly abandoned the crime scene to outsiders.

Young, as usual, was polite and sympathetic. But he didn't want to talk about the things she wanted to talk about. He had questions of his own, almost all of which seemed to do with Bonnie and her children, and the life that they had led with Lieth.

This annoyed her because she considered it a waste of time when too much time had already been wasted. She'd made it clear once that their time together had been filled with love and happiness, and now he was making her go over the same ground again, when he should have been out looking for the killer.

Bonnie answered his questions, however, describing again how Lieth had come into her life almost as a medieval knight sent to rescue her from her prison of poverty and loneliness.

She talked in even more detail about their life in Little Washington, saying it was so full and so fulfilling that they really had not had time to form friendships with other people. For a while, Lieth had taught part-time at a nearby community college, and when the data processing instructor there had been hurt in an auto accident, Bonnie had replaced him.

Although her shyness made her uncomfortable in front of a group, she taught both day and night classes for two years. Five days and four nights a week. It had been hectic. She'd have to rush home after the day class, cook dinner, then leave again in fifteen minutes to teach at night. But it had felt good to be back in touch with the field that had been her career.

Eventually, Lieth complained of neglect. He told her he wanted her around the house to fix his meals, and to be there to talk to in the evenings, so he wasn't stuck alone with just her kids. In early 1986, she stopped the teaching.

Not that Lieth didn't love her children. It was just that when they got to be teenagers, he found it harder to relate to them. And their friends running in and out of the house all the time began to aggravate him. Unlike Bonnie and Lieth, both Angela and Chris were very social—if not particularly gifted students—so there was more traffic through the house than Lieth could easily tolerate. "Teenagers," he liked to say, rubbing his balding head. "They'll drive you nuts."

Even so, Bonnie insisted, Lieth was "absolutely wonderful" with both Chris and Angela. "He loved them as if they were his own. He couldn't do enough for them."

While on the subject of Chris, she said—"and if you're going to hear anything bad about my children, I want you to hear it from me"—there had been some "poor judgment" displayed on the so-called Senior Day at the high school, when most of the class that would soon graduate gathered for a preschool party at which drinks were served.

Chris, perhaps, had drunk a bit more than he should have and had then been foolish enough to go straight to school and make a bit of a spectacle of himself, which had resulted in his being given a blank diploma on graduation day, and not formally graduating with his class.

Yes, that had been a disappointment, but it was just teenaged foolishness, and both she and Lieth had let him know that they loved him even when he did make mistakes.

Which was not to say that Lieth and Chris had never had their runins. These, however, were the kinds of things that Bonnie was sure happened in all families.

She told Young how supportive Lieth had been when Chris was arrested. Again, it had been nothing serious—just a typical teenage prank blown out of proportion—but when Chris was sixteen, he and a friend were arrested at a football game in Chocowinity one Friday night and charged with all sorts of ridiculous things, such as "carrying a concealed weapon, assault by pointing a gun, carrying weapons on a public school campus, carrying alcohol on a public school campus, possession of alcohol by a minor, and possession of pyrotechnics."

The incident wasn't nearly as serious as it sounded, Bonnie explained. The day before, Chris and his friend Steven Outlaw had driven through Chocowinity in Chris's Mustang, and Steven, just fooling around, had pointed an air pistol at another teenager they had happened to pass on the street. The other boy had overreacted and had reported to police that he'd been threatened with a handgun. At the football game, Chris's car was identified as having been the one from which the gun had been pointed. When the trunk was searched, a police officer found some throwing-stars and throwing-knives, two air pistols, a hunting knife in a sheath, a hatchet, a nunchaku, some large firecrackers, and several bottles of wine.

Chris had explained to Bonnie and Lieth that he'd just been storing the wine for a friend and that the so-called "weapons" were just toys he occasionally used when acting out a Dungeons & Dragons scenario with friends.

Eventually, she said, he'd paid a small fine—or they had paid it on his behalf—and the charges had been withdrawn. The true importance of the episode, she told Young, was that it demonstrated to Chris that in a pinch Lieth would stick up for him, Lieth could be counted on, in a way his real father could never be.

There had been, however, one "negative incident" that she should probably mention, since Young might hear a distorted version of it from someone else. It had occurred at the dinner table, sometime during Chris's senior year, after Lieth possibly had drunk a bit too much and began to criticize Chris's study habits.

There had been a "disagreement." Suddenly, Lieth had erupted in anger. Bonnie had never seen him so mad. His face got red, he clenched his fists, and Bonnie thought he was about to hit Chris. Shocked and frightened, Chris jumped from the table and stepped away. And that was that. The storm passed as quickly as it had boiled up.

The only aftereffect was that Lieth told her that from that point forward she should act as an intermediary between him and Chris. If there was something he wanted Chris to do, he'd tell Bonnie and she could pass the instruction along. Likewise, if there was anything Chris wanted to share with Lieth, he could tell his mother and she'd communicate it. And while he was at it, he wanted the same policy instituted for Angela, too.

"They're your children," Lieth told her, "and I think it's up to you to discipline them." He said his anger was such that he felt he could no longer deal with them directly.

But that, Bonnie explained, had happened only a few months before Chris had gone away to college, at a time when Lieth was already under terrible stress.

She conceded that it *was* true that Lieth had been disappointed by how poorly Chris did during his freshman year at NC State—getting mostly Ds and Fs and incompletes—but Lieth himself had had trouble making the adjustment to college and understood how hard it could be. As ever, he was encouraging and supportive, as Bonnie, too, had tried to be.

Then, emphasizing that she had *nothing* to hide, *no* family secrets to withhold, Bonnie told Young of two other incidents involving Chris.

Over the July 4 weekend, only three weeks before the murder, while Chris was enrolled in summer session, Angela went to visit him on campus and spend the night. When she got there, she couldn't find him and no one knew where he was. She had to spend the night in her car. The next morning, she'd called Bonnie and Lieth in Winston-

Salem to report that neither her brother nor his Mustang could be found. After making dozens of phone calls to every friend and relative they could think of, Bonnie and Lieth had filed a missing person's report with the Raleigh police.

Returning to campus Saturday night, Chris had been stopped by a school security officer who told him he'd better call his parents right away. They were still at the Von Stein house in Winston-Salem, waiting by the phone for some news. Chris apologized for causing them concern, but explained that he'd gone off with a friend of his named Moog to visit an uncle of Moog's who lived way back in the hills where there weren't any phones. He said they'd drunk goat's milk with dinner and he had become violently ill. A whole day had passed before he was well enough to drive back to school.

Lieth, Bonnie said, had just shaken his head. He didn't even want to speak to Chris, so convinced was he that the whole story was a lie. Bonnie, too, felt that Chris wasn't telling the truth. And this upset her because, as far as she knew, this was the first time he'd ever lied to her.

The second incident had occurred on the weekend of Lieth's death. Chris arrived from school late Friday night and said he wanted to cook dinner on Saturday. He asked Bonnie to buy some ground beef and hamburger rolls. Then, late Saturday morning, he went out to see friends.

When Bonnie came back from the market that afternoon, Lieth told her he'd just received a peculiar phone call from a woman who identified herself as the mother of a fifteen-year-old Raleigh boy.

She'd asked if a Chris Pritchard of that address also had a house in Raleigh where he might have employed her son to do yard work. The boy had presented her with a $35 check signed by Chris and had asked her to cash it. On the bottom, Chris had written the notation "yard work."

Lieth said no, Chris Pritchard did not have a house in Raleigh. He said Chris was out but that he'd ask him about the check as soon as he came home. He took down the woman's number and said he'd call back as soon as he had more information.

As Lieth told Bonnie this story, she began to get a "really bad feeling" that somehow drugs might be involved. But as always with her children, she wanted to give them the benefit of the doubt. And when Chris came back that afternoon he had a ready explanation. He'd been short of cash and he'd been at a grocery store a long way from the nearest cash machine, and this kid who'd been hanging around with him and some of his friends had given him cash for the groceries and Chris had written him a check. When Bonnie asked him why he'd put "yard work" on the check, Chris said he didn't really know.

You hate to accuse your own son of lying was Bonnie's feeling, especially when there's nothing concrete. You want to believe him and to trust him. But she and Lieth talked it over that afternoon and decided they'd better monitor Chris's money more closely. They asked him to start keeping a record of his expenses, because the $50-a-week allowance they were sending him seemed to be running out faster than it should. Quite willingly, he had agreed to do so.

That evening, after Angela and her friend Donna Brady got back from the beach, Chris eagerly cooked dinner for them all, making hamburger patties and grilling them, while Bonnie herself made french fries and baked beans. After the meal, Chris had been "visibly anxious" to get back to school to work on his term paper. That wasn't typical for a Saturday night, Bonnie acknowledged—Chris wasn't exactly a workaholic—but after the phone call about the check and the subsequent conversation, he might just have felt more comfortable away from the house.

When she had walked him out to the car to say goodbye, she'd looked down at the dashboard and had seen a gaping hole where his radio and tape deck had been. Chris explained that the equipment had been stolen while the car was parked on the NC State campus.

"Don't worry about it," she said. "Just go on. I'll tell Lieth sometime next week." She didn't want to burden Lieth with this new piece of bad news after all the strain he'd been under, especially because Lieth was already "apprehensive" about Chris.

Still concerned about the check, however, she'd said to

Chris, "Just be careful. And if there's ever anything you feel the need to talk about, we're here. We love you, and you know you can tell us anything." Chris had said, "I know. Thank you." And he'd kissed her on top of her head.

Then, a few days later, as she lay in the hospital with her head bandaged and a tube in her chest, Chris had tearfully told her he'd been lying. He said he'd actually written the check to try to buy one ounce of marijuana, but the fifteen-year-old had never delivered the drugs. Chris told her a person couldn't walk down a dormitory hall at NC State without encountering drugs. He said "everyone" at State except himself was selling drugs.

He also told her the story he'd made up about the Fourth of July wasn't true. He and his friend Moog had actually gone to Inman, South Carolina, just outside Spartanburg, to visit his aunt Ramona, Bonnie's sister.

This upset Bonnie even more than the confession about the check because Ramona had been one of the people she'd called when she was so frantic with worry about Chris. And Ramona had said she hadn't seen him.

As soon as she felt well enough, Bonnie had confronted Ramona, who was terribly apologetic. She said Chris had been standing right by the phone, begging her not to tell Bonnie he was there because he was supposed to be on campus, studying. Ramona hadn't realized how upset Bonnie was because Bonnie hadn't *sounded* that upset—she never did—and Ramona didn't want to get Chris into more trouble with Lieth, who was already annoyed by Chris's poor grades, so, without thinking, she'd just told Bonnie that she hadn't heard from Chris for weeks.

Bonnie's meeting with Young ended in the early afternoon. She was exhausted by the physical and emotional effort she'd expended and frustrated by the investigators' apparent lack of progress. But at least, she felt, she had succeeded in putting to rest once and for all any questions the authorities might have had about her family.

9

Nine days later, at headquarters, Washington police conducted an interview with Chris. Their questions were somewhat more pointed than Lewis Young's earlier ones.

Drugs? Well, yes, Chris admitted. "A while back" he had done drugs, including LSD. The check? Yes, it had been for marijuana. Drugs were all over the NC State campus, Chris explained.

He described himself as an "arrogant son of a bitch" and "very impulsive," but said he did not remember ever telling anyone he was rich. As a matter of fact, as far as he knew, he wasn't. He did know that Lieth had had some sort of trust fund, but didn't know the purpose of it. That wasn't his business, that was his parents' business.

He said he'd "had a buzz on" but hadn't been drunk when he'd received the call from Angela about the murder. He described again how he hadn't been able to find his car keys, but said his roommate, Vince Hamrick, later found them beneath a chair cushion.

His car had not been parked directly outside the dorm, but in the "fringe lot" about a quarter mile away. He said he'd parked it there Sunday night after returning from supper at a place called Wildflour Pizza. He'd done so in order to irritate the two girls he was with, Karen and Kirsten, by making them walk farther to get to the dorm. He said it had just been a whim, he was a very impulsive guy. The reason he hadn't used the phone in his room to call the campus police was because he'd wanted to let his roommate get back to sleep.

Then they asked him about Dungeons & Dragons. For

the first time, Chris became animated, as if they'd finally hit upon a subject that piqued his interest.

He explained that it was a fantasy or role-playing game that had been his favorite pastime since he'd been eleven years old. You created a character who inhabited a mythical world and embarked upon all sorts of adventures. The game required you to be imaginative and creative and was a lot of fun when played with a good group. At State, Chris had played two or three times a week. Usually, each episode would last several hours, but it could take weeks to play out a whole scenario. Those he played with included someone named Daniel Duyk, and others whom he knew only by their first names, including someone he knew only as Neal. There was also, he said, a fellow whose nickname was Moog.

Yes, he said, on occasion they'd go down into the steam tunnels. For one thing, the tunnels were a good, safe place to "get trashed." For another, he and his game-playing pals had wanted to "map out" the tunnels, so they could incorporate the map into one of their Dungeons & Dragons scenarios.

In the days that followed her return from Little Washington to her parents' house in Welcome, Bonnie found she was feeling worse instead of better. She was still sleeping poorly and often heard noises that alarmed her in the night. By day, she had dizzy spells and was finding it harder to breathe. X rays showed more fluid in her chest cavity. She went to the hospital and they put a catheter in her back and drew out a full liter of bloody liquid.

At unpredictable times, she could feel herself blacking out, or lapsing into a daydream state, almost as if she were having a type of epileptic seizure. She had an EEG and CAT scan done, but nothing abnormal was found.

She saw and heard so little from Chris and Angela that they might as well have been on another planet.

Her scarred forehead began to depress her and she decided to have plastic surgery. "I'm not a vain person," she said later, "but the first thing you see every morning is your face, and it's not mentally healthy to look at that reminder at the start of every day."

Just before the start of the fall semester, Chris and Angela turned up unexpectedly at NC State. Some friends encountered them at Wildflour Pizza, which had always been Chris's favorite drinking spot. He was already drunk by late afternoon, bragging that he now had a gun and he was going to find whoever it was who'd killed Lieth and settle the score. He also said he was tired of hearing people whisper that Angela had been involved. If he heard any more of that kind of talk, he'd settle a few other scores.

Nobody took him too seriously. It was part of Chris's problem in relating to the world that few people ever took him seriously. There was always such a gap between his words and his deeds. Chris talked a great game but seldom played one. After a while, even his better friends tended to discount 90 percent of what he said. More casual acquaintances ignored him entirely.

Drunkenly, he began sobbing that his mother really needed him now and that he was going to clean up his act. Then he talked about Angela, saying how worried he was because she seemed to be in a state of denial about the whole tragedy—trying to act as if nothing had happened. He knew, he said, that couldn't be healthy. As awful as reality might be, you had to deal with it squarely. There was no sense pretending. You couldn't wish your troubles away.

He and Angela stayed on campus that night. There was a party. Chris took acid. He had a very bad trip. He began screaming that he couldn't breathe, that he was dying. People at the party got scared. Some wanted to call an ambulance, call the police. Get Chris some help, fast.

But his friend James Upchurch, whose nickname was Moog, was at the party and took control. Moog said there was no need to call for outside assistance. It was just a bad trip. He'd seen them before and knew how to deal with them. He was Chris's friend and he'd stay right there with him and talk him through it. Everyone else should just leave the two of them alone.

Chris was vomiting and screaming and crying all at once. He was as sick as anyone at the party had ever seen anyone get. But Moog insisted everything would be fine. There was *no need* Moog repeated, to call for help. He knew about bad acid trips. They were scary—both to experience and to witness—but there was nothing life-threatening going on. *Do not,* Moog repeated, *call an ambulance. Do not call the police. That would only get Chris in lots of trouble.*

Eventually, Chris stopped crying and trembling and throwing up. Eventually, he fell asleep. Later, everyone remembered how concerned Moog had been, what a good friend he'd been, sitting there by Chris's side through the worst of it. Later, when Chris was calmer, Moog drifted off, away from the party. He wasn't living on campus anymore—he wasn't enrolled for the fall semester—so no one was quite sure where he'd spent the night. For that matter, no one remembered much about Angela, either.

As the fall semester started, Chris seemed oddly subdued. His roommate, Vince Hamrick, recalled that whenever Chris was asked about what had happened that summer, he'd say only, "I don't want to talk about it." If anyone persisted, he'd walk away. He seemed to be drifting into a world of his own, a world in which he didn't want company.

Angela enrolled at a business college in Greensboro, a city about an hour and a half west of Raleigh, and about half an hour east of Winston-Salem.

In her own way—which was quite different from his— she seemed just as upset as her brother. As she herself put it later, "I shouldn't have even tried to start school. All fall I didn't do anything but waste gas and money trying to be around my friends as much as possible."

She also said, "Gradually, it dawned on me that I was a suspect, but I didn't let that bother me."

In late September, a school psychologist called Bonnie to say that Chris was going through a "very bad emotional period," and that the school's counseling service was not able to provide adequate help.

The psychologist said Chris seemed still so unsettled by the trauma of his stepfather's death and the attack upon Bonnie herself that a medical leave of absence was indicated. Chris lacked the emotional stability necessary to cope with the demands of a new academic year. He needed to be home with his family for a while. He needed more intensive therapy than the school could provide. Quite possibly, anti-depressant and anti-anxiety medication would be required. Apparently, his continuing grief was more than he could tolerate.

With that, Bonnie recognized that she would have to leave Welcome and provide—on her own, once again—some sort of shelter for both herself and her son.

The place she chose was Lieth's parents' house in Winston-Salem. The mechanics of the transfer would be simple because, as Lieth's widow, she already owned the house.

Besides, it had other advantages. It was only ten minutes south of the center of the city, at the very edge of what seemed an endless expanse of shopping plazas, malls, and restaurants. It also was less than a mile from the nearest entrance to Interstate 40, the main east-west road across the state, and less than half an hour north of Welcome.

It was already furnished, which meant she'd neither have to ship anything in from Washington (which she didn't think she could bear to do) or buy anything new (which she didn't feel able to do either). Also, she knew the house well, having stayed there with Lieth during all those weekends when they were tending his sick and dying relatives. And Bonnie's father said he could easily build a shed in the backyard to house her pets.

But beyond that, it was a small house on a busy street—small enough, and with few enough entrances, so that an unbreachable security system could be installed. It had small, dark rooms, the kind in which Bonnie felt more secure, and it was surrounded by many other small houses.

The house, in fact, was so nondescript that it would have been hard to find even if you were looking for it.

Even if you'd been given directions, or had a map.

*   *   *

And so, by the end of the month, Chris left his college campus and moved into the dark little house, locked tight as a bank vault, in which his mother had secluded herself.

They kept the curtains drawn and the alarm system on, night and day. In addition to the outside alarms, there were motion detectors along interior hallways, which they turned on before going to bed.

And each of them, mother and son, slept with a loaded gun under the pillow. Despite her own distaste for firearms—and fear of them—this lover of small, harmless pets, this Humane Society board member, bought handguns for herself and her children.

No action she'd ever taken seemed more out of character, more alien to all that she thought herself to be.

But someone had killed her husband and had tried to kill her, and there was no guarantee he wouldn't try again.

Much later, in writing, she tried to describe her psychological state at the time: "The feelings that come to mind when I try and go back to the time when I armed my children with handguns are these: anger, desolation, agony, fear, uncertainty, aloneness, heartsickness, failure.

"It was one of the most agonizing things I have ever felt the need to do. My frame of mind at that time was beyond comprehension by anyone who has never experienced the fear I felt for my family. I had lost all confidence in the law enforcement officers investigating the case, and knew they were not willing to help protect us. Lieth had lost his life trying to protect himself and me. How could I possibly think I could protect my two children?

"I wasn't sure I would be able to pull the trigger against another person if it came right down to it, but maybe Chris or Angela would in order to protect themselves. There were also times when I was not present in the house, when they might need to defend themselves.

"At that time, I did not know any more about what had happened on July 25 than I did on that night. This act of arming my children was against everything I had ever believed in, but at that time I just didn't know what else to do."

* * *

For Bonnie, that fall, the hardest thing was to go out after dark. But by November, with darkness coming earlier each day, she began to force herself. She knew that otherwise she'd become a total recluse.

It wasn't so bad if Chris was home, but Chris wasn't home much. He'd gotten a job with Triad Tires, at one of their several locations in Winston-Salem. He was working hard, changing and rotating tires all day. He'd come home filthy and exhausted, drop his greasy clothes on the back porch, go up and shower, and then, within the hour, be out again.

He'd made some new friends since moving to Winston-Salem. One was Eric Caldwell, who had been a high school friend of Vince Hamrick's, and who came home most weekends from Appalachian State University in Boone, North Carolina, two hours west of Winston-Salem. Another was a cousin of Eric's named John Hubard, who was training to become a city policeman and working as a security guard at a nearby mall.

Bonnie was pleased that he had made friends so quickly, but concerned that the anxiety and depression that had forced him to drop out of school were growing worse. Her concern caused her to ask the doctor in Winston-Salem whom she was seeing about her chest if he could recommend a psychotherapist for Chris. He gave her a couple of names, but when she called, she was told it would be weeks, if not months, before either of them would have an opening for a new patient. Bonnie did not feel that Chris could go that long without treatment.

Still weak and distracted herself, she took an untypically casual approach: she opened the yellow pages and looked under the heading "Psychotherapy" and called the number of the therapist whose office was closest to her house. He said he had immediate openings and could see Chris that very week.

And so Chris began what Bonnie presumed was a course of therapy. The first consequence was that he was given an anti-anxiety drug called Buspar, which was roughly the equivalent of Valium. When Bonnie herself called the therapist a few weeks later to check on Chris's condition, she was told he seemed to be progressing well, though she herself had noted little, if any, improvement. She and the therapist agreed that the murder of Lieth and the near-fatal attack upon herself must have been a terrible shock to what was apparently already a fragile nervous system.

10

It was true, as Bonnie suspected, that confusion, lack of leadership, and in some quarters, an absence of individual initiative within the Little Washington police department had slowed the investigation's progress.

Lewis Young had been promoted. While still technically the resident agent for Beaufort and Hyde counties, he had also begun to work within an SBI department that handled particularly sensitive investigations, such as those involving judges or law enforcement personnel, all across the state.

His new duties required him to spend more time in Raleigh than in Little Washington. The Von Stein murder, hideous as it was, no longer commanded his full attention. In his absence, little was accomplished.

By late fall, the rumors in Little Washington had convicted Bonnie and her children of virtually every crime of violence committed in the South since the assassination of Martin Luther King. Yet two or three days a week, Bonnie would call to ask about progress, saying she wanted to do more to help, asking if she couldn't look at the files. She would say that perhaps she'd come across some fact or impression that, while appearing irrelevant to detectives, might trigger a helpful memory in her. This, in Young's experience, was not the behavior of someone trying to conceal involvement in a murder.

Yet, there were factors he could not simply dismiss, no matter how badly hurt Bonnie had seemed to be, and no matter how many times she called to inquire about progress.

These were becoming, to Lewis Young, a familiar litany: the large inheritance; the appearance of a staged, rather than a real, break-in; the rice in Lieth's stomach; the blood-spattered pages.

In his mind, he believed her to be innocent, but the nagging doubts wouldn't disappear.

And in the case of her children—especially Chris—Young realized he was dealing not simply with doubt but with outright suspicion.

"From the get-go," he said later, he'd been bothered by both Angela and Chris. Not just by their attitudes, but by facts.

It didn't seem plausible that Angela could have slept through so brutal and noisy an assault. The fan in her room was not *that* loud. She hadn't been drugged. And her bed was less than twenty feet from where Bonnie and Lieth had been attacked. Bonnie's own recollection was that Lieth had uttered a series of sharp, loud screams as he fought for his life. Young had spent time in the house. The walls were wallboard, not plaster. Even with doors closed, sound carried. It defied logic that Angela had slept through it all.

Besides, the first officer to enter her room had reported that when he'd opened her door, she'd sat up immediately, as if already awake. She'd had a phone in her room and, if awake, could easily have called for help. And there was the unanimous opinion of those who'd seen her in the ensuing hours—including Young himself—that she'd seemed neither shocked, grief stricken, nor even particularly surprised by what had happened.

And then there was the question of the unmelted ice. No one had bothered to photograph it, or even to include mention of it in any official report, but it had become one of the most widely told stories in town: there had been *unmelted ice* in the glass observed by the side of Angela's bed when the first officers had entered her room. If she had poured herself a glass of ice water or iced tea before going to bed at midnight, the ice should have melted long before five A.M.

Also, she had not been harmed. As an isolated element in an equation, survival did not imply guilt. But might it be significant that of the three people present in the house, Angela alone had been spared? It was possible, of course, that the killer hadn't known she was there. But it also seemed possible that he had known, had chosen not to hurt her, and had been so confident that she'd never say anything that he'd had no qualms about leaving her undisturbed.

Finally, of course, there was the money. Both Angela and Chris had known at least *something* about the money. Notwithstanding whatever complex trust arrangements Lieth had made, they might have expected that if both Lieth and Bonnie were dead, up to $2 million would be theirs.

Lewis Young had seen many people murdered for less likely reasons than that.

His suspicions of Chris arose from so many reports of quarrels with Lieth, so many reports of heavy drug use, reports of frequent bragging about his parents' wealth, the genuine and serious fears expressed by George Bates, Jr., and his wife, Peggy, and—more than anything—from the map.

All through the fall, even when occupied with other duties, one thought was paramount in Lewis Young's mind: *the killer could not have been a Washington resident or he would not have needed a map.* But whoever had drawn the map was familiar with the town, with the Smallwood neighborhood, with the Von Stein house.

Young had looked often at the report of the late-August interview with Chris Pritchard: while playing Dungeons & Dragons, they'd gone down to the steam tunnels to *make a map.*

He thought he'd like to learn more about the life Chris had been living in college.

And so, in November, while in Raleigh, Young dropped by the NC State campus to interview Vince Hamrick, who had been Chris's roommate at the time of the murder. It seemed to typify the lack of focus and energy that had plagued the investigation from the start that more than three months had passed since the murder and no one had yet talked to Pritchard's roommate, the one person who'd been with him when he'd received the phone call from his sister.

As a graduate of what had traditionally been considered the *real* University of North Carolina—the Chapel Hill campus, twenty-five miles away—Lewis Young could not help feeling a trace of that slight condescension that so many Chapel Hill people felt toward NC State.

The University of North Carolina at Chapel Hill—universally referred to within the state simply as "Carolina"—was recognized as one of the two or three finest state universities in America. Its campus was ivy covered, richly green, bursting with blossoms in spring, and gently shaded by tall, stately trees that added to the sense of tradition. When one went to Chapel Hill, one went to *Carolina*. If you went to NC State, you were simply going to college to get a degree that would help you get a better job.

The attitude was somewhat unfair, given State's excellence in the area of engineering—its student paper was called *The Technician* and it even had its own nuclear reactor on the campus—but it had started as primarily an agricultural school and there were bumper stickers visible in both Raleigh and Chapel Hill that said, "Honk If You Go to Carolina—Moo If You Go to State."

Carolina *was* Chapel Hill, the university being the heart and soul of the small, charming town that had grown up around it. State, on the other hand, even with more than twenty-five thousand students, was just one of six colleges and universities in Raleigh, a rapidly growing city with bigger things on its mind.

In addition to being the state capital, Raleigh was at the eastern point of The Research Triangle—a cluster of high-tech facilities that constituted an East Coast version of California's Silicon Valley. Significant new findings in science and medicine were a regular occurrence at laboratories belonging to such multinational corporations as IBM,

Glaxo, Burroughs Wellcome, Becton Dickinson, and Northern Telecom.

With Chapel Hill at one of the Triangle's western points and Duke University in Durham at the other, it has been said that within twenty-five miles of Raleigh there were probably more library books than anywhere else in the world, as well as more Ph.D.'s per square mile.

Having government and education as its main industries, Raleigh possessed charm and graciousness to a degree almost unique to cities its size (population about 225,000), but it was, undeniably, a *city*. And the NC State campus was only five minutes from the center of downtown.

The first thing noticed by anyone setting foot on campus was the brick. The whole 650 acres seemed to have been constructed of red brick. Dormitories were red brick, classroom buildings were red brick, even the sidewalks were red brick. Officials at State would claim that this was only appropriate for an institution that had sprung from the soil, in an area where the soil was red clay, but the effect was to make State seem strictly functional—a big-city school for small-town farm kids—and a far cry from the pastoral elegance to be found at Chapel Hill.

The university at Chapel Hill accepted only one-third of those who applied; NC State accepted two-thirds. Once enrolled, 75 percent of the freshmen at Chapel Hill eventually graduated, as opposed to little more than 50 percent at NC State. And the attrition rate for freshmen at State was twice that found at Chapel Hill.

There was also, of course, the notoriety attached to the sports programs at State. As opposed to UNC at Chapel Hill, which, especially in basketball, had managed for years to produce nationally competitive teams without compromising academic integrity, athletics at NC State had become a scandal.

Especially after the arrival of Jim Valvano as head basketball coach in the early 1980s, the sports program at State—while enjoying success in the arena—had been embroiled in almost constant controversy. There were allegations of financial impropriety, grade manipulation, and abandonment of any academic standards whatsoever when it came to admitting athletes heavily recruited by the coaching staffs.

In turn, the athletes had been involved in more than their share of on-campus crime: charged with everything from theft of stereo equipment from dorm rooms to rape, sodomy, and other forms of sexual assault.

And it was by no means just the athletes who got into trouble with the law. One statewide survey had shown the per capita crime rate on the campus of North Carolina State University to be the highest of any community in the state.

Drugs, Young knew, were rampant on campus. Anarchy reigned. Kids from small towns all over the state—such as Little Washington—went to State and just got swallowed up by the enormous impersonality of the place, especially during their freshman year. What seemed, at the very least, to have been the emotional, intellectual, and behavioral collapse of Chris Pritchard was a story all too common at NC State.

Chris's summer-session roommate, Vince Hamrick, was a husky young man with dark, curly hair. To Young, he seemed sullen and evasive. He said yes, Chris had dropped out of school; no, he wasn't sure why; something to do with psychological problems. Sure, a group of them had played Dungeons & Dragons a lot during the summer. Daniel Duyk, some guy named Moog. He wasn't sure, he'd heard that Moog had dropped out of school, too. And Daniel, yeah, Daniel had broken up with his girlfriend and had dropped out, too.

Yeah, during one D&D game they'd taken swords—these wooden, Japanese martial-arts weapons—and had gone down into the steam tunnels and acted out their roles. They'd spray-painted their names down there, too.

Chris probably went down in the tunnels five or six times. Vince himself had stopped when he'd gotten too busy with schoolwork. Schoolwork was not something with which Chris had ever seemed busy. Drugs, yes; studies, no. Chris had smoked a lot of pot, then tried to quit, then started again, and had dropped acid a few times, too. Chris lived a day at a time, a spur-of-the-moment type guy, didn't look into the future. He was easily influenced. His bad grades hadn't seemed to bother him. He'd said his father was rich; said he'd once peeked into some sort of stock portfolio he wasn't supposed to know about and had seen that they owned stuff worth millions.

By July, Vince said, Chris had been smoking "a whole lot" of pot. Then he'd disappeared over the July 4 weekend. His mother had called, looking for him, but Vince had had no idea where he'd gone.

The morning of the murder, Chris had been so out of it that Vince had had to answer the phone. He'd handed the receiver to Chris and had gone back to sleep almost immediately. He vaguely remembered Chris saying his parents had been attacked by a burglar, and some kind of fuss about car keys, but it was the middle of the night, Vince was tired, he'd been up late, he didn't really focus, just went back to sleep.

Later, of course, he'd heard all about it. And when Chris came back to school, it had been strange: all he would say was that his stepfather had died, that the police didn't know who did it, and that he didn't want to talk about it. Period.

After his talk with Vince Hamrick, Young was even more persuaded that, despite Bonnie's urgings that he direct his energies elsewhere, he wanted to take a closer look at the surviving members of the family.

Before traveling to Winston-Salem and slapping handcuffs on trust officers of the North Carolina National Bank, or before arresting everyone at National Spinning who'd ever had an item questioned on an expense account, he thought he might lean just a little bit harder on Bonnie and Angela and Chris.

Especially, he thought, on Angela and Chris.

Throughout November and into December, Bonnie made herself leave the house after dark every day. She had nothing to do, nowhere to go, no one to be with, but she would get in her car, drive to a mall, get out, walk around, gaze blankly at the Christmas decorations, then return to her dark house alone.

It was, at first, excruciatingly difficult, but she made herself do it, the same way she'd made herself walk up the stairs and go straight into the bedroom of the house on Lawson Road. Of course, she took her gun with her in the car. Kept it right on the front seat next to her as she drove. Just as she kept it tucked inside the waistband of her sweatpants as she sat in her living room, watching television or reading a book. And just as she kept it at her bedside every night.

For a long time, after dark, she was too scared to go out to the backyard shed in which she kept her thirteen cats and pet rooster. The night she finally did—it was in late November or early December—she felt as if she'd taken a big step on the road back to normalcy.

But how much farther could she go when she did not know who had tried to kill her, or why? She spent a lot of time considering the possibilities. The problem was, when one looked at it logically, the person with the most obvious motive for wanting Lieth dead was herself.

She tried to put herself in Lewis Young's position. If she were him, she would unquestionably consider the surviving widow who had inherited $2 million a prime suspect—injuries or no injuries.

It made less sense to her—in fact, no sense—that anyone could think Chris or Angela had been involved. But here it was, four months later, with the police still dithering and rumors continuing to fly. Every time she called either the Washington police or Lewis Young, they gave the same evasive answers to her questions and did not seem the least bit interested in any theories she'd developed on her own.

One thing she stressed repeatedly was that she didn't see how a lone intruder, armed only with a knife and club, could enter a locked and darkened house in the middle of the night, either not knowing how many people he'd find there, or knowing he'd find at least three.

Every time she raised this point, they came back with the same response: Are you sure you saw only one intruder? And she always gave the same answer: I only saw one, but for all I know there could have been five. And maybe, if you hadn't let so much potential evidence be destroyed, you'd have a better idea of how many there were and who they were and why they came and where they are now and whether or not they're going to try again to kill me or to kill my son or daughter.

Since there was nothing else about which she cared, she found that she spoke of nothing else. Angela would come home from her Greensboro business college—by now, Bonnie realized it had been a mistake for her to go; she was in no shape to be in school; she had scarcely attended a class all fall—and she and Chris and anyone else who happened to be in the house would sit in the cramped living room, alarm systems on, guns close at hand, interior lights burning through the night, and obsessively go over every detail of what they knew and speculate endlessly about what they didn't.

One weekend Angela's friends Steve Tripp and Laura Reynaud drove out from Greenville. On Friday night, they ate at the same Red Lobster restaurant where, years before, Bonnie and her children had been introduced to Lieth's parents. After dinner, they stopped by Action Video to rent a movie. When it was over, they turned out most of the lights, though Bonnie had made it a practice never to let the house be totally dark. Laura quickly fell asleep. Steve, lying next to Angela on a fold-out couch in the living room, began to hear the sound of soft crying.

"What's wrong?" he asked her.

She pointed to a photograph of Lieth on the mantelpiece, barely visible in the dim light.

"I was just thinking that my dad's gone," she said, "and that he's never coming back."

Steve held her until her crying stopped.

The next day, Angela went to the cemetery where Lieth's ashes were buried. Laura went with her. There, Laura said later, Angela cried "for close to half an hour." She said, "Lieth was the best thing that ever happened to me."

On other occasions, Angela would speak of retribution. "If I could catch the person who did this," she'd say, "I'd do the same thing to him." Bonnie would gently suggest that capital punishment could never be justified, and that Lieth's killer should be imprisoned for life, but not executed. Chris, on these occasions, would have little or nothing to say. Often, he'd just leave the house.

To Bonnie, it was obvious that the ceaseless talk about the murder and the investigation upset and depressed Chris, but to her it was all there was left of life. It sometimes seemed that the sole reason she continued to exist was so she could find out who'd tried to put an end to her existence.

As Christmas approached, her spirits sank. She didn't know how she could face the false gaiety of the holiday. What would make it even worse was that everyone—her mother, her father, her sisters, her brother, Chris, and Angela—would tiptoe around her, knowing the pain she was in, and making it worse by trying so hard not to. She'd have to be cordial and congenial for hours on end, at a time when even brushing her teeth in the morning required a formidable act of will.

Also, the little house that had belonged to Lieth's parents, the house that she had hoped would offer solace, had turned out to be drab and cheerless. She felt she was living inside her own tomb. It had been years since the interior had been painted. The walls were a lifeless green that sucked up whatever meager winter light managed to filter through the small-paned windows. She could not make herself put up Christmas decorations. She could not bear the thought of a tree with lights and ornaments.

Nor could she any longer bear the thought that the police were getting nowhere.

On December 7, she reached a point of such desperation that she made the drive to Little Washington to again confront Lewis Young in person.

She insisted that he give her an accounting of everything the SBI and Washington police had done, and an explanation of everything they intended to do from that point forward. She said she was fed up with the continuing gossip, rumor, and innuendo concerning her own possible involvement in the crime, or the possible involvement of either of her children. The time had long since passed for that to have stopped. Not that it should ever have started in the first place.

She told him bluntly that she wanted him and the other investigators to "stop looking at us." She told him she intended to hire private detectives to find Lieth's killer. She would demand that he make available to her and her detectives the entire investigative file.

Bonnie was beginning to wonder if someone in law enforcement *did* know who had killed Lieth, but for some nefarious reason—political pressure, financial payoff, how could she tell?—had decided to cover it up.

Young said he could understand and sympathize with her frustration. But he said a lot of work had been going on behind the scenes. And he said, yes, he'd be happy to share with her all the information they'd developed. But there was one thing she'd have to do first. She—and Chris and Angela—would have to take a polygraph examination administered by the SBI.

He explained that she was under no legal obligation to do so, nor were her children. But he added that until all three of them passed such a test, they could not be eliminated as suspects. And that until the people closest to Lieth had been excluded, investigators could not extend their search beyond this "innermost circle."

The way he presented this request—so tentatively and apologetically, almost as if he were embarrassed to ask— caused Bonnie to feel that he had expected her to refuse. But of course, she wouldn't refuse. If this was what was required to get the investigation moving forward, *of course* she and her children would cooperate. Any one of them would submit to any kind of examination the SBI wanted to give them at any time. *Good Lord, hadn't that been clear from the start?* If this was what Lewis Young wanted, why hadn't he asked her weeks ago?

He said SBI polygraphs were given in Greenville. She and her children would have to come all the way from Winston-Salem to take the test.

Bonnie assured him that this would pose no problem. She said she was "certain" both Chris and Angela would take the test. The only difficulty was with logistics. Because of Chris's job at Triad Tires, the three of them could only come together on a Tuesday, his day off. With the SBI's polygraph operator already heavily scheduled, and with the upcoming holidays adding further delay, it was determined that the test could not be given until Tuesday, January 17, 1989.

Both Bonnie and Lewis Young said they'd prefer to get it done sooner, but that was the date they agreed on. Again, Bonnie said she wished he hadn't let so many weeks go by before he'd asked. Again, Lewis Young was polite and considerate and respectful. And managed to avoid saying much of anything at all.

He knew the polygraph was not infallible. Indeed, results from such tests were still not admissible as evidence in North Carolina, or in most other state and federal jurisdictions across the country. But Young, like many law enforcement officers, had come to value the polygraph as an investigative tool.

If nothing else, it tended to frighten those who had anything to hide. More than once, Lewis Young had seen suspects refuse even to take the test, and run instead toward the protective arms of a criminal attorney.

Christmas was as bad as Bonnie had feared. As always, there was the big Christmas Eve gathering of the Bates family at her parents' house in Welcome, with all her little nieces and nephews running around, oblivious of the aching in her heart. She and Chris and Angela had little to say to one another. This was the first Christmas without Lieth, but as they all knew, it was only the first of many.

In early January, trying to focus on business again, forcing herself, on a daily basis, to do what needed to be done, Bonnie met with an estate lawyer in Winston-Salem.

It was a routine meeting (the lawyer had been a family friend for many years), and toward the end he asked, just in passing, if there had been any new developments in the investigation. Bonnie said no, but added that once she and the children took their polygraph, she was hopeful that things would move forward.

The estate lawyer did not like the sound of that and told

her so. After she left, he made inquiries and was told that the best person to advise Bonnie on whether to take such a test was a man named Wade Smith, a former state legislator who was now chairman of the Raleigh firm of Tharrington, Smith and Hargrove.

Smith promptly told Bonnie's estate lawyer that no one, under any circumstances, no matter how pure of heart or soul they might be, should ever consent to a polygraph examination administered by the North Carolina SBI, or any other law enforcement agency, without prior consultation with an experienced criminal lawyer who would formulate an opinion as to the advisability of such an action only after having made an extensive inquiry into the facts.

In other words, send the woman to Raleigh to see him. Or send her somewhere else to see a different criminal lawyer. But for God's sake, don't let her or her children walk blithely into that SBI polygraph room in Greenville unprepared. Too many stories, Smith said, similar to those involving Christians and lions, came to mind.

And so it was that at one P.M. on January 6, 1989, Bonnie Von Stein found herself standing at the iron gates that marked the entrance to the marble-walled offices of Tharrington, Smith and Hargrove in downtown Raleigh.

Stepping into a lobby replete with atrium, hanging gardens, skylights, and waterfalls, she was, at first, a bit overawed. This looked less like the headquarters of a law firm than it did the lobby of a plush Hawaiian resort hotel.

But she began to feel better the moment she first met Wade Smith. At fifty-one, with short, white, curly hair and a quick, warm smile, he still carried himself with the nimbleness of the Carolina halfback he'd once been.

Eminence rested lightly on his shoulders. He got as much pleasure from flying a kite or painting a watercolor as from making a winning argument to a jury. Both his daughters were grown and gone from home, and his wife was constantly occupied with a variety of worthy causes, but if you could catch Wade in his kitchen with his shoes off and jeans on, he'd still be quick to recite a Bob and Ray skit from memory or to improvise one of his own, or to take out his banjo or guitar and start to sing.

He could easily be drawn into the most serious sort of conversation about metaphysics or epistemology, but he also still played and sang with an acoustic group that performed in the Raleigh–Durham-Chapel Hill area, and he remained one of those rare people in whose company it was impossible to feel anything less than total delight at the happy accident of being alive.

It had been some months since Bonnie had felt anything of the sort.

Still, even as she settled herself into a comfortable armchair in his private office—a far homier and less ostentatious place than the lobby—and Wade came out from behind his desk to sit right with her, face-to-face, she felt a burden lifting from her heart.

As he looked her in the eye with what appeared to be genuine compassion, she sensed that for the first time since the murder of her husband she was in the presence of not only a professional in whose judgment she could place absolute trust, but of a man who—unlike anyone she knew except her father—seemed to care as much about her well-being as he did his own.

And so, looking and sounding, as Wade would say later, "like the saddest, most forlorn person on earth," Bonnie began to tell him the story of her life.

PART TWO

PRESUMED GUILTY

JANUARY–JUNE 1989

11

As he listened to Bonnie, Wade Smith thought: clearly, she was a suspect. He knew nothing of blood-spattered pages or rice in the stomach or reports of family discord. All he knew was that she had gained $2 million from her husband's death, and that she, badly injured or not, had survived. That fact alone would require any competent investigator to put her story to the sternest test.

Invariably, Wade's recommendation to a person in Bonnie's situation would be at least to postpone an SBI polygraph until he could arrange for one to be privately administered. If that result was unfavorable, no one would ever know. She could then simply decline to take the SBI test. If, on the other hand, she passed the private exam, she could take the official polygraph test with little to fear.

There was, however, something so guileless and unstudied about Bonnie Von Stein that Wade felt inclined to waive his normal procedure. She seemed utterly without artifice and to his practiced ear and eye—and Wade Smith had been lied to by the best—thoroughly trustworthy.

He said that while this was not counsel he would normally offer—in fact, he couldn't recall ever having given it before—in this instance, based on his assessment of her, and based on the strength of her desire to do so, he would advise her to take the test.

Without giving it as much thought as he later admitted

he might have, he said he saw no problem with Angela's taking the test, too. After all, she'd been in the house at the time of the attack, and it seemed obvious that she had not participated in it.

In Wade's mind, however, Chris fell into a different category. Because he had not been present when the murder occurred, and therefore could not be considered an intended victim, Wade thought it possible that investigators might look at him through a different lens.

Also, Bonnie had told him that Chris had dropped out of NC State because of psychological problems that had cropped up after the murder and that he was currently seeing a therapist in Winston-Salem. She added that the therapist had suggested that a polygraph test might prove too stressful for Chris at this point and could impede his recovery.

Wade recognized immediately that if Bonnie and her daughter took an SBI polygraph, and her son, for whatever sound medical reason, did not, he would immediately become a suspect, even if he wasn't already. Pressure was going to be put on the boy to take the test. He should have a lawyer of his own.

Not that Wade could foresee any problem, he assured her. It was just that, as a general rule, different interests could lead to different priorities, and he would never want to be in a position where the interests of one of his clients was not fully consistent with the interests of the others, especially when they were members of the same family.

Bonnie was not pleased to hear this. She didn't think she or her children needed one criminal lawyer, much less two. As was her custom, however, she considered Wade's point logically and had to concede it had merit.

Besides, there was something in Wade Smith's manner that inspired belief in what he was saying. His presence was both magnetic and reassuring. He made you believe that what he was telling you must be right—and was certainly in your best interests—even if you wished it weren't so.

* * *

The lawyer whom Wade recommended for Chris was William Osteen, a fifty-eight-year-old former state legislator from Greensboro, who had served for five years as United States Attorney for the Middle District of North Carolina. Osteen, also a graduate of the Law School of UNC in Chapel Hill, was a man as esteemed in Republican political circles as was Wade among Democrats.

As an undergraduate, Osteen had attended Guilford College in Greensboro, as had Lieth Von Stein some years later. He was elected to the state House of Representatives in 1960, the first Republican since 1928 chosen for any public office in Guilford County. He was one of only nine Republicans out of one hundred and twenty members of the House, and, at age thirty, the youngest legislator from either party.

After winning reelection two years later, he did not run again because he'd found politics to be interfering with his first love: the practice of law. In 1968, however, he'd been persuaded to run for Congress. He lost a close, hard fight to Congressman Richard Pryor, but got his picture taken with Richard Nixon in the process. The following year, he was named U.S. Attorney.

In legal circles, Osteen was at least as highly regarded as Wade Smith. Possessing impeccable judgment and an unblemished reputation, Osteen was senior partner of a firm he had founded in Greensboro after leaving his post as chief federal prosecutor in the mid-1970s. (In 1991, he would leave the firm to accept appointment as a federal district judge.)

A hardy and exceptionally handsome man, he was five feet eight inches tall, with solid gray hair. He had a quick sense of humor and unfailingly gracious manners, but when conducting business he functioned in a brisk and direct fashion that left no one guessing about what he thought or where he stood. His voice immediately let one know he was more accustomed to giving orders than receiving them.

Osteen was married, with three sons, the youngest of whom attended The Citadel, the South's foremost military academy. Osteen's oldest son, Bill Jr., who had gone to Chapel Hill for both undergraduate work and his law degree, had joined the Osteen firm in 1987 because he was so eager to practice law with his father.

A traditional family man with traditional family values, Osteen possessed a strong competitive instinct both in the courtroom and on the tennis court. But no one who'd dealt with him in any capacity had ever come away saying that Bill Osteen had been anything less than totally fair and honest.

This would be a simple matter, Wade explained. A young man had been through a terrible family tragedy—stepfather murdered, no arrests made, but the boy had been in his dorm room at NC State and could not have committed the crime. For medical reasons, he would probably not be taking an SBI polygraph test at the same time as his mother and sister. This, no doubt, would cause investigators to start looking at him in a different light. If so, given his age and emotional condition, legal guidance might prove helpful.

Wade was representing the mother, who seemed like a wonderful woman, salt of the earth. He apologized for not sending along a more intricate and challenging case, but said next time he'd try to do better.

Osteen later said he'd been "amazed" upon first meeting his new client. Eventually, he used stronger language. "He was obviously on drugs," Osteen said. "He was surly, insolent, spoiled, brattish—anything in the world you want to say, Chris pretty much resembled that."

Unshaven, with unwashed hair, and wearing a T-shirt that advertised some heavy-metal rock and roll band, Chris had strolled in late for his appointment, with an air of arrogance about him and the smell of alcohol on his breath.

Bill Osteen had grown up on a farm without running water or indoor plumbing, and he well remembered the day in sixth grade when the house first got electricity. His father had been a federal probation officer, his mother a strict Southern Baptist who had made her sons swear never to let a drop of alcohol pass their lips. Bill Osteen had kept the pledge because "that's the way she wanted it."

In law school, Osteen's first ambition had been to join

the FBI. Later, as U.S. Attorney, he directed the activities of federal law-enforcement agents. He had an older brother who had graduated from West Point and had retired from the Army as a major general. In the living room of Osteen's Greensboro home, a large family Bible was always open and on display. His strongest values were family and God, and not necessarily in that order.

"I value some direction in life," Osteen would say later. "I like to see people who are interested in other people. It didn't take long to find out that Chris was not on a road to anything worthwhile, and I didn't like that."

In short, the match between Bill Osteen and Chris Pritchard did not seem to be made in heaven. So strong, in fact, was Osteen's initial distaste that if the referral had come from anyone but Wade Smith, Osteen would have declined to represent Chris. But at least the association promised to be brief.

He explained that, unlike Wade, he *never* made an exception to his rule that no client of his would submit to a state-administered polygraph before passing a private examination.

"Frankly," Osteen said later, "I was a little upset with Wade for allowing Bonnie and Angela to take the polygraph because I didn't think any of them should take it unless we knew what it was going to show. In order to do it properly, I thought we ought to arrange our own examination first."

When he expressed this opinion, Osteen found Chris in full agreement. And that seemed to be the only thing lawyer and client had in common.

On January 16, the day before the polygraph, Bonnie (but not Angela, who said she had other plans for the day and didn't need to talk to any lawyers, anyway) met with Wade to go over the procedure that the operator would likely follow.

Wade said he saw no need to accompany her to Greenville; she'd be just fine on her own. Besides, his presence at her side would send the wrong signal: that she was worried enough about something to have retained the top criminal lawyer in the state. For the present—and quite likely in the future, Wade said—it was best that his involvement not become public knowledge.

Bonnie's recollection of what happened in Greenville the next day was very different from Lewis Young's. She insisted that she had let him know well in advance that only she and Angela would be taking the test; that Chris had been advised not to by his psychologist because it might prove too stressful and set back his recovery.

Young, however, said Chris's failure to appear came as a "complete surprise." After all, the whole point of delaying it until a Tuesday in mid-January had been to accommodate Chris's work schedule.

As recently as the previous Friday, January 13, Young had spoken to Bonnie by telephone, and according to notes he made available later, she had not mentioned that Chris would not be taking the test.

Furthermore, his notes from January 17, the day of the test, stated only that "Christopher Pritchard canceled, due to being emotionally upset and due to strong feelings of guilt about not being present when his parents were attacked and Lieth was killed."

It was Lewis Young's recollection that these notes reflected what Bonnie had told him that morning, and that she'd never mentioned anything, even then, about a psychologist's advising that Chris not take the test.

To further bolster his contention that Bonnie had not informed him in advance, Young offered the notation made by Bill Thompson, the polygraph operator, who had written on Chris Pritchard's file, "This test canceled 8:30 A.M. January 17, 1989."

That, according to Young, substantiated his claim that Bonnie had not called in advance to tell him that Chris would not be present. If she had, a notation would have been made at the time of the call.

In any event, from that day forward, Lewis Young's attitude toward Bonnie changed. Having virtually dismissed her as a suspect, he had begun to feel deep sympathy for her. Now, however, irritation was added to the mix. In his view, she hadn't played straight.

Unlike most of the population of Little Washington, and even other investigators, he still did not believe she had any direct connection to the crime, but as of January 17, 1989, he began to suspect that she might be covering up for her son, trying to shield him from investigators, fearful of what they might learn.

"I don't envy you," he told her that day, in reference to Chris. "You're between a rock and a hard place."

She bristled at this remark. She'd been in a hard place since July, she said, since the night her husband had been murdered, and neither Lewis Young nor the Washington police had done one single thing to help her out of it. So she was in no mood to listen to ugly remarks about her son. Chris's doctor had said the polygraph might prove too stressful. That was the reason—the only reason—why he hadn't come to take the test. He'd been as eager to take it as she was, but they could not ignore a medical recommendation.

Bonnie found taking the test "demeaning." She said later, "It must have upset me a great deal because when it was over, I felt dirty. I didn't feel like a clean person. If I'd had the slightest idea of what it would be like, I'd have never, never agreed to take that test. I'd never do it again under any circumstances and I'd never let any member of my family do it either."

Yet the results, in her case, could not have been better. Of the ten questions she'd been asked, only three were used in the scoring. They were:

—"Did you plan the death of Lieth Von Stein?"
—"Did you help to plan his death?"
—"Do you know who stabbed him?"

To each, she answered no. In the scoring system used by the North Carolina SBI, the highest score possible was plus twelve and that's the score Bonnie got. As Young put it, "She knocked the doors off." John Taylor said, "She blew it out. It looked like she'd never told a lie in her life."

For Angela, the results were somewhat more equivocal. Angela was asked:

—"Did you help someone stab Lieth Von Stein?"
—"Were you involved in stabbing Lieth?"

—"Do you know who stabbed Lieth?"

Angela received a score of plus five. Only weeks earlier, any score between minus six and plus six was considered "inconclusive" by the North Carolina SBI. Then the parameters had been revised, so that any score above plus three was considered passing.

Thus, Angela, too, "passed" her polygraph test, though the difference in score between her and her mother was never far from investigators' minds.

It was, however, as Wade had foreseen, Chris's failure to take the test at all that made by far the strongest impression.

"From that day forward," Lewis Young said, "my suspicions really started kicking in."

Within days of the test, Bonnie's right eye began to swell and she developed blisters on her nose. The ailment was diagnosed as shingles, an extremely painful and debilitating viral condition brought on by an uncommon level of stress. In Bonnie's case, the attack was so severe that except for visits to an eye doctor, she was unable to leave her house for the rest of the month.

12

On February 1, a new chief of police took office in Little Washington. His name was John Crone, and even before his appointment became official he was told that solving the Von Stein case would be his top priority.

He'd been quite candid with the town manager. "Look," he said, "I'm not a crack detective. I never was a homicide investigator."

"You are now, Chief," the town manager said.

Crone was forty-two, and for the previous eight years he'd been a police captain in the resort town of Ocean City, Maryland—one of those places with a winter population of five thousand that swells to three hundred thousand in July. Among his responsibilities had been recruitment and training of the temporary police needed to cope with those crowds. It was not a task he'd found rewarding. In addition, Ocean City had a tradition of always going outside the department to find a chief, so his chances for promotion seemed slim.

Crone's wife was from North Carolina. During a visit to her parents' house, he'd seen a newspaper advertisement stating that the town of Washington, North Carolina, was looking for a chief. On their way back to Ocean City, they'd driven through Little Washington, liked the town well enough, and Crone had applied for the job.

His background alone would have qualified him. The son of a physicist, he had grown up in the suburbs of Washington, D.C, and had worked for seven years as a policeman in the District of Columbia. He'd been promoted to sergeant after four years and earned a bachelor's degree from American University. In 1977, divorced and remarried, he'd moved to a suburb of Denver, but had returned to Maryland after only a year, taking a lieutenant's position in Ocean City.

In addition to his experience, John Crone seemed a congenial fellow. Weighing possibly a pound or two more than he'd like to, Crone had thinning blond hair, a quick smile, and enough self-confidence so he didn't have to swagger into town looking as if he wanted to turn a fire hose on the first person he spotted jaywalking. He gulped a lot of coffee and kept a bottle of Maalox on his desk—and no one who's been married three times and divorced twice can be said to have lived a stress-free life—but Crone's professional manner tended to be more affable than intimidating.

As soon as he assumed command, Crone began to examine the Von Stein file. One thing he noticed quickly was that for a case of such magnitude in the community, the file was notably sparse. In fact—although it had been one of only two murders in the town in the past two years—

there did not seem to be anyone from his department working on it.

"The whole thing was at a standstill," Crone said later. "I come into town, I've got no idea who's even working for me, and here's a six-month-old murder case they want solved tomorrow."

On a nine-man force his options were limited, but one of John Crone's first decisions was to assign a new detective to the case. Hoping that youthful energy and a fresh perspective would make up for lack of experience, he chose John Taylor, the dark-haired, toothpick-chewing twenty-six-year-old investigator who had photographed the crime scene. Taylor was not a man who would need Lewis Young to hold his hand.

The choice turned out to be inspired. Taylor was a slim and graceful man whose speech was a lot slower than his thinking. He had an appealing, self-deprecating wit; in dealing with the public, he was affable, low-key, and direct: the sort of officer who, like Chief Crone, would not tend to frighten suspects into silence. He went out of his way to be generous and considerate even when he had no reason to. People tended to like John Taylor as soon as they met him, and in most cases the feeling endured.

Also, he was thorough and smart. He'd already learned a lot in the months that had passed since he'd taken the Von Stein crime-scene photographs, and he showed an aptitude for learning more, fast.

Taylor had an uncle who'd been chief of the Little Washington department back in the mid-seventies, so he knew the job offered the opportunity for advancement. Especially now that the new chief had put him in charge of the biggest case the town had seen in years.

From the start, as he said later, he saw his new assignment as "the chance of a lifetime, if I didn't fuck it up."

Chief Crone's study of the case file turned up an additional insight.

"Dungeons and Dragons," he said later. "One of the first things that struck me was all these college kids playing this weird game I didn't know anything about."

He also noticed how many suspects there still were, even six months after the crime. "Everybody was a suspect," he said. "We just didn't have any facts."

The three potentially useful objects he did have seemed to be: the knife that had apparently been the murder weapon; the green knapsack, of which all members of the Von Stein household disclaimed knowledge; and the map, which had been found with the knife at the scene of the fire.

To Crone, the bloody—and blood-spattered—climax to *A Rose in Winter,* undigested rice, and an uncle's suspicions were intriguing elements, but they did not constitute physical evidence.

Of the items that might, the map was the one most on Crone's mind. Like Lewis Young, he recognized that whoever had drawn it must have had intimate knowledge of the Smallwood neighborhood, having been able to identify which homes near the Von Stein's had dogs, and having even correctly sketched the way in which the drainage ditch behind the Von Stein home curved.

And like Young, he was struck by the way someone had drawn those strange pictures of dogs—"hounds of the Baskervilles" was how he thought of them—instead of simply having written the word *dog.*

Another element to which he paid close attention was the word LAWSON. He knew, as did Young, that an SBI or FBI lab technician could probably not make a positive handwriting match on the basis of a single printed word, but he still felt it would be useful to obtain handwriting or printing samples from family members and friends.

"What I wanted to do," he said later, "was at least narrow the list of suspects. I wanted to know who might have drawn the map and who might have needed it. For example, Steve Pritchard, the natural father, was in many ways a pretty good suspect, except that he'd already been to the house—he'd actually stayed there two or three times before the murder—so, as Lewis pointed out, he wouldn't have needed a map.

"The same with all of Bonnie's relatives. And with all

the kids' high school friends. None of them would have needed a map to find the house.''

So Crone agreed with Lewis Young that while someone who knew the neighborhood had *drawn* the map, it had probably been *used* by someone who would otherwise not have been able to find his way around.

"We felt pretty sure," Crone said, "that this had been planned. It wasn't just a random, spontaneous event. But the plan didn't work the way it should have. They must not have expected anyone to see that fire, or to find that pile of rubble. Maybe they were careless about burning the map because they never thought we'd find the fire. Take that a step further and maybe whoever drew the map didn't bother to disguise his printing because he never figured we would see it.

"I also thought it was interesting that the road where that fire was burning was a back road that led to Raleigh. It was obvious that the map was the biggest thing we had, but somebody had to get off his ass and do something with it.''

Chief Crone decided the first thing John Taylor should do was take a considerably closer look at Chris Pritchard and his friends from NC State.

In early February, Bill Osteen, troubled by his new client's attitude and demeanor, arranged for a private polygraph test, to be given in Charlotte by a former FBI examiner in whose work Osteen had developed considerable confidence during his years as a federal prosecutor.

Osteen explained that the results would be kept confidential. The police would never be permitted to see them. There was no risk. No matter what the test indicated, it could not do Chris any harm.

Before it, however, Chris consumed such a large dose of Buspar, his anti-anxiety medication, that the results were rendered meaningless. Not negative in any fashion, Bonnie was assured by Bill Osteen. Just meaningless. The polygraph operator would have to repeat the test at a time when Chris was not taking any drugs.

The day after his futile polygraph exam, Chris drove to

Appalachian State University in Boone, two hours west of Winston-Salem, to visit his friend Eric Caldwell. That night, he met a slender and attractive girl with whom he became instantly infatuated.

He called her the next day and the next day and the day after that. He went back to see her again. On Valentine's Day, he arrived laden with roses and gave her a necklace and bracelet on which he'd spent more than $500, once again overdrawing his Visa card.

Chris was this way about everything, but girls especially. He had no control, no restraint. He would call constantly, show up unexpectedly, buy gift after gift. His pursuit had a nervous, even desperate edge: as if he were so starved for love, for affection, for companionship, that a girl who displayed even lukewarm politeness in response to his ardor became for him the sun, moon, and stars all rolled together; the sole reason for his continued existence.

Sooner or later—usually sooner—even girls who had initially been attracted to Chris despite his scrawniness, his jitteriness, his erratic behavior, found the manic quality of his attentions too much to contend with, and they retreated; running faster the harder he pursued.

There was so much he wanted so badly, yet his actions all but assured that his deepest desires would stay unfulfilled. He repelled the very things—and people—he yearned for most.

This was one reason he'd become so obsessed with Dungeons & Dragons: in that game, as a scenario developed, the character you created for yourself could acquire all sorts of powers and charms that you might lack in real life. In the dark realm of the fantasy world, you could—for hours on end—be brilliant and strong and sexually attractive and courageous and rich.

And if you took the right sorts of drugs while playing the game, the illusion became even more convincing.

Slowly, through February, Bonnie recovered. There was no permanent damage to her eye. She continued to receive plastic surgery on both her forehead and chest. She ate lunch with one of her sisters and some old friends from work. She started a class in Lotus 1-2-3 at the Forsyth Technical Institute in Winston-Salem. She had the walls of the house painted in a brighter color and new carpet laid on the floor. She was trying to create a life for herself that would contain at least a few normal elements.

But the alarm system was always on, the guns were always loaded, and the little blue motion-detector lights glowed in the short, narrow hallways all night long.

She took her cats to the vet, she had lunch with an account executive at NCNB (one she did not suspect of having plotted her husband's murder), and she met again with her estate lawyer. On Sundays, she'd make the half-hour drive down to Welcome and teach Sunday school at the Center United Methodist Church, the one her father had built, brick by brick. Often, she'd stay for dinner with her parents. Then she'd drive back to Winston-Salem, her handgun never farther from her than the glove compartment of her car.

In the absence of any news of an arrest, or even of the naming of a suspect, she continued to fear for her own safety and for the safety of her children. The killer or killers had not been caught. No motive for the murder had been established. Anything might happen at any time. Bonnie had few restful nights.

In the weeks that followed her own successful polygraph test, Bonnie's frustration with the Washington police and the SBI had grown into full-blown anger. It seemed obvious that, despite all promises to the contrary, they were still doing nothing to find the person who'd murdered her husband.

She was also becoming even more concerned about Chris's emotional condition. Neither his therapy nor medication, nor his new girlfriend at Appalachian, seemed to be helping. He was moody, jumpy, and seemed under great strain. He drank too much beer, he burst into anger quickly, he would spend hour after hour closed inside his room, playing games on his home computer, and would then spend half the night out with friends, undoubtedly driving too fast and recklessly.

Chris had always had a tendency to be a little wild when he got behind the wheel of a car, but now, given his brittle condition (and alcohol consumption), Bonnie worried that he might be more prone than usual to a serious or even tragic accident.

Chris made a quick trip—a very quick trip—to Little Washington in early March.

He'd spent the night at Eric Caldwell's house, something he was doing with increasing frequency. Both Eric and Chris's other new friend in Winston-Salem, John Hubard, noticed that Chris was spending as much time as possible away from home, away from his mother. Since Bonnie struck them both as an extremely easy person to be around—even, for a mother, fun to talk to—they couldn't understand Chris's apparent avoidance of her.

Maybe, they thought, it was her relentless criticism of the investigators, her repeated complaints that they weren't getting anywhere. That seemed to depress Chris and to upset him.

Or maybe it was just that even on a warm afternoon you couldn't open a window for fear of triggering the alarm system, or that at night, if you had to go to the bathroom, you wanted to be sure to push the right buttons before stepping into the hallway, lest you set off the automatic motion detector and get blown away by a Beretta, a .45 automatic, and a nine-millimeter automatic simultaneously.

On March 8, Chris said he wanted to show Eric the town he'd grown up in. He made the trip in three and a half hours, hitting a top speed of 106 miles per hour along the way. He seemed highly agitated, even frenzied, as he drove.

Once there, they only stayed an hour. Chris drove Eric down Lawson Road and pointed out his old house, but did not stop. Eric started to ask a question about some detail of the crime, but Chris quickly cut him off, saying he did not want to talk about it. Period.

They stopped at NC State on the way back, so Chris could pick up a transcript that he needed to send to Appalachian, where he was applying for fall admission. He took

Eric to Wildflour Pizza, where he drank seven beers in an hour and a half, looking around nervously all the while, as if worried that someone he might not want to see would walk in. Then he jumped in the car—none too sober—and sped all the way back to Winston-Salem.

Three days later, with the first scent of spring already spicing the Carolina air, Chris drove out to Appalachian. He and Eric and John Hubard rented rooms at the Econo-lodge Motel in Boone. Chris's new girlfriend and two other girls came. There was an indoor pool. They thought they'd do a little swimming, have a few drinks, enjoy a Saturday night. But the event turned sour fast. His girlfriend drank too much and Chris drank more. They had sharp and bit-ter—if not terribly coherent—words. She retreated to a bathroom to cry. Enraged, Chris jumped into his car and drove off.

This always seemed his first reaction when confronted with an emotionally stressful situation: to get into his car and drive away as fast as he could, never telling anyone where he was going, probably not knowing himself, and not returning until his anger had subsided. People had been telling him for months that one night he'd get himself killed doing that. Sometimes, it almost seemed that's what he wanted.

During the second week of March, John Taylor compiled a list of all NC State students who had been mentioned in any report as having been friends of Chris Pritchard's. Then—amazed to find that no one had done so before—he ran the names through a statewide computer to see if any had criminal records.

One did. James Upchurch. He was the tall, thin young man, nicknamed Moog, with whom Pritchard had traveled to South Carolina over the July 4 weekend on which his mother had reported him missing.

While in high school, in Caswell County, in the extremely rural north central part of the state—the biggest town in the whole county was Yanceyville, which had a population of only 1,800—Upchurch had twice been arrested for break-ing and entering.

Taylor called Caswell County. A local investigator described Upchurch as "a smart kid" from a broken home, whose father worked for the state department of social services in Raleigh and whose uncle had once been arrested for growing a large crop of marijuana on his farm. He said Upchurch had broken into the local high school and had stolen a computer. Later, he'd broken into a private home and had stolen, among other things, a hunting knife.

Not a bad start, John Taylor told himself. Out of the entire universe of Chris Pritchard's friends, he'd already succeeded in isolating one who had both family drug connections and a record of breaking and entering. And this same friend was the one with whom Pritchard had mysteriously disappeared for two days only three weeks before Lieth had been murdered.

Upchurch had been placed on probation for the breaking and entering offenses, but his Raleigh probation officer told Taylor he had disappeared several weeks earlier and there were three warrants outstanding for his arrest. The offenses included drunk driving with insurance revoked and failure to appear in court for probation revocation. The last time she'd seen him, the officer said, he'd had both sides of his head shaved, leaving only a strip of bleached-blond hair down the middle.

"Well," Taylor said, "at least if he shows up in Washington, he shouldn't be too hard to spot."

On March 13, Crone met with Taylor and established three priorities:
—to obtain a sample of Chris Pritchard's handwriting
—to find James Upchurch
—to learn more about Dungeons & Dragons
From the little he'd heard and read about it, Chief Crone had the sense that the game could inspire unhealthy, even dangerous fantasies: the kind that could lead to violence. He knew it wasn't quite witchcraft or satanism or the occult, but he had the uneasy feeling that Dungeons & Dragons was not the sort of activity with which psychologically well-balanced college students would be obsessed.

What he wanted most, however, was a sample of Pritchard's printing. However unscientifically, he wanted to compare it with the LAWSON on the map.

Officials at NC State said they had a document on which Pritchard had printed LAWSON ROAD. But they said they could not release it without a subpoena.

On March 14, Mitchell Norton, the Beaufort County district attorney, issued the subpoena.

By March 15, Bonnie felt well enough—and desperate enough—to once again drive to Little Washington, this time to confront either Lewis Young or the new chief person to person, in order to ask one simple question: In the two months since she and her daughter had passed the polygraph, what had been done to find her husband's killer?

Young was out of town and the new chief was not immediately available, but she did succeed in speaking to John Taylor, who informed her that Chief Crone had recently placed him in charge of the investigation.

Bonnie was struck by Taylor's youth. How much confidence could she have in someone so inexperienced?

He shook her hand and told her, "I have only one assumption—that you didn't have anything to do with it. I don't have any other assumptions."

She was not comforted by this remark. Of course, *she* didn't have anything to do with it. But who did? Hadn't they made *any* further progress?

"Mrs. Von Stein," Taylor told her, "if we can't clear you and Angela and Chris, we don't feel comfortable going anywhere else." He then reiterated that in his own mind *she* was cleared, but added that he couldn't yet say the same for her children.

Bonnie was openly displeased. This was exactly what she'd heard for months from Lewis Young, and she did not like having it repeated now by some young man who looked more like a *police cadet,* or a prospective boyfriend of Angela's, than a qualified homicide detective.

The next day, John Taylor made the first of what would be his many drives to Raleigh.

He handed his subpoena to the appropriate official at NC

State and was given a small white card on which Chris Pritchard, in applying for on-campus housing, had printed the word LAWSON.

The young detective was tempted to jump into his car and race back to Little Washington as fast as he could, so he and his chief could sit down and compare the printing on the card with that on the map.

But he had other business on the sprawling, crowded campus. He interviewed the two girls, Karen Barbour and Kirsten Hewitt, in whose room Chris had been drinking beer and playing cards the night of the murder. They verified Chris's story, but added other details that Taylor found intriguing. They said Chris and his friends—including James Upchurch, known as Moog—were *heavily* into both drugs and Dungeons & Dragons. Moog, they said, was called the Dungeon Master. He would determine the scenario for a particular game, and the other players would follow his instructions. By rolling dice, he'd determine the outcome of violent confrontations.

At least once, the girls said, Chris and Moog and the others had acted out one of these pretend adventures by wrapping toilet paper around broomsticks and setting the paper on fire. On other occasions, they'd gone down into the steam tunnels.

Kirsten said she had an especially clear recollection of Chris's being in her room the night Lieth was killed because she'd kept asking him to leave. From one A.M. on, at least every half hour, she'd said to him and his friend Daniel Duyk, "I'm really tired. Could you guys please go somewhere else?" The unusual thing was that Chris, who was usually considerate in such matters, had refused, saying he wasn't ready to stop playing cards.

Over the next two and a half hours, with growing impatience, she'd pleaded with him to leave. Finally, he'd asked what time it was. When she said three-thirty, he'd left immediately. It seemed, she said, as if that particular time was what he'd been waiting for all along.

Taylor was back in Little Washington by five P.M. He went directly to the chief's office. He put the housing card on the chief's desk, next to a photograph he had taken of the map.

LAWSON LAWSON

Neither John Crone nor John Taylor was an expert in handwriting analysis. But in this instance, neither felt he had to be.

The words appeared to be a perfect match.

13

After seeing the two words side by side, Lewis Young decided a couple of the SBI's more aggressive investigators should have a talk with Bonnie and her children.

He called her on March 21 to say John Crone felt there had been some fresh developments. Young said he wasn't at liberty to discuss them, but he told her two new SBI agents would be coming to see her the next day. Their names were Newell and Sturgell, and they worked with a special division that handled only the most important cases around the state. He said one of them was tall and thin, the other short and round. Their nicknames were the Thin Man and the Pillsbury Doughboy.

They'd be wanting to talk not only to her, but to Angela and Chris. They wanted to see her at two P.M., Angela at four, and Chris as soon as he finished working at Triad Tires at eight that night.

Bonnie considered this good news. New people might mean new ideas, a new approach. Maybe, finally, some progress would be achieved. It did not occur to her that the meeting was something about which she needed to inform either Wade Smith or Bill Osteen.

With no lawyers present, Newell and Sturgell could play

by any rules they chose. And the rules they chose—while not in any way beyond the bounds of what was permissible under law—were definitely those of what was, psychologically speaking, a contact sport.

Bonnie met them at Winston-Salem police headquarters. They questioned her for two hours. The early stages were not so bad. They asked her the same old questions, and she gave what were, by now, the same old answers. Such as, according to their notes, "Mrs. Von Stein stated that on Saturday night, Chris and Angela cooked hamburgers."

But soon, Bonnie felt, they became rude, confrontational, and accusatory. It was as if she'd never taken and passed the polygraph. She couldn't believe this was happening all over again. They were harassing her, badgering her, as if trying to extort some sort of confession. *Eight months had passed since Lieth had been killed, and she was still being treated as a suspect.*

One of them, the Doughboy or the Thin Man—she never was able to keep them straight—placed some black-and-white photographs on a table and asked her if she could identify them. They were photos of the four pages from *A Rose in Winter.* Bonnie said she remembered it vaguely. The author was one of her favorites. She'd read this particular book a couple of years earlier and had later found it in Angela's room. Thinking, she said, that she might want to reread it, she'd placed it on a typewriter stand next to the bed in her bedroom.

But the book hadn't been found on the typewriter stand, she was told. The book had been found on the floor, with these pages missing. Only these pages, spattered with blood, had been found on the typewriter, next to the bed where Lieth had been stabbed.

So what? Bonnie said. They told her that they considered these pages potentially "significant" evidence. Then they told her to read the text. She did.

If someone hadn't just read those pages—containing a scene where a man is killed with a dagger—and torn them from the book and placed them next to the bed where Lieth was attacked, then why were they spattered with blood?

Bonnie calmly said she didn't know. She hadn't been

reading the book. If she had been, it would have been among a stack of paperbacks on the floor next to her side of the bed, not on the typewriter stand. She had no idea why those particular pages had been torn from it, or when they'd been torn from it, or why they'd been found where they had been, or how they'd come to be spattered with blood.

It seemed perfectly plausible, she said, that the book, which had been lying atop the slippery vinyl cover of her typewriter—*and which had not been the book she'd been reading that night, or at any time in the recent past*—had been knocked off during the struggle, and the last four pages had fallen out as it hit the floor. It was only a paperback, it had been read maybe a dozen times by various members of her family—she and her sisters often exchanged favorite titles—and pages were always falling out of cheaply bound paperbacks, even when there wasn't a life-and-death struggle raging in the immediate vicinity.

It also seemed plausible that one of the first patrolmen or emergency medical technicians to reach the bedroom had spotted the blood on the pages and in order to protect them, had gathered them from the floor and stacked them on top of the typewriter. Or else, maybe her neighbors had done so, while they were destroying what was left of the crime scene that afternoon.

Though she later described her "mode of response" here as "pretty mild and unconcerned," she told the Thin Man and the Doughboy that the fact that even months after the murder they were still trying to develop this sort of absurd scenario—something, she said, that seemed to have been lifted directly from the pages of *Fatal Vision,* where Jeffrey MacDonald had been accused of using *Esquire* magazine stories about witchcraft and the Manson family as inspiration for his fanciful tale of drug-crazed intruders in the night—convinced her that every previous assurance she'd been given had been a lie.

Lewis Young had promised that once she passed the polygraph, the investigation would move beyond her. Well, she'd passed with the highest score possible. Yet now, more than two months later, here were these two new detectives who seemed not only to be back to square one, but even worse: instead of investigating, they were concocting grotesque scenarios that belonged in the kind of escapist fiction they were now attempting to use as *evidence*.

The Doughboy and the Thin Man seemed unmoved. Not only, they said, did those pages suggest that just before her husband had been stabbed to death she'd been reading about a stabbing—in which a young man named *Christopher* had wielded a knife—but before *that* she'd sat up alone, watching a television movie about a serial killer.

They put the photos back in an envelope. Those pages had been removed from the book, they repeated. Those pages had been spattered with blood. Bonnie gazed at them, still in her "unconcerned" mode. They said all right, she could leave now. They were ready to talk to her daughter.

The truth was, neither Newell nor Sturgell considered Bonnie a likely suspect. The location and content of the pages might have been no more than a weird coincidence. But even if the pages had been placed at the bedside for some sort of ritualistic purpose, it seemed improbable that Bonnie would have done it herself, or even known about it.

Like the partly burned map found at the edge of the fire, the pages might have had some sort of mystical significance. But Newell and Sturgell had not been thinking along such tangled lines.

Their tactic had been straightforward. While presuming Bonnie herself to be innocent, they, like Taylor, Crone, and Lewis Young, had grave doubts about her son. They also thought it distinctly possible that Bonnie herself shared their doubts and—by not letting Chris take a polygraph test, for example—was trying to protect him from their scrutiny. The more they shook her, they thought, the quicker she might be to let go of Chris. This assumption, however, was based on a profound misreading of her character.

Bonnie left the office, went straight to a telephone, and called Wade Smith. She was as angry as she'd ever been. At first, she had thought the investigators were merely incompetent. But with each new insult to her and her family, she had begun to suspect them of something worse, and this had been the worst yet.

"I feel like they're trying to build a Jeffrey MacDonald case against me," she told Wade.

He assured her that on the basis of everything she'd told him so far, as well as her impeccable polygraph result, she had nothing to worry about in that regard.

"But they're not following up on any of the things that they should be," she said. And who were these new men, anyway? And why had the old chief of police resigned? What was going on in that little town she'd never liked? It seemed to her, Bonnie said, that *they* were trying to cover something up. She didn't know what, and she didn't know why, but she was not going to stand by and let it happen.

Wade, as usual, counseled patience and caution. He said he was sure that the interview had been a difficult and even degrading experience. He knew how those things could be. But it was over now, she'd answered all their questions, just as Angela was in the process of doing, and just as Chris would be doing that night.

He knew what a strain this was for her, but the hard truth was there really wasn't much she could do. She'd managed to hang on this long, she should just try to last a little longer—at least until they saw what happened next.

Bonnie said she could not wait. She would have to initiate some action of her own. She told Wade that she wanted him to find the best private detective in the state—for that matter, the best private detective in the country—and hire him to solve the case. She didn't care how much it would cost. There could be no better way to spend the money Lieth had left her, she said, than to finance the quest for his killer.

If the police were unable or unwilling to do it, well, then, Bonnie Lou Bates of Welcome, North Carolina, would just have to do it herself.

Angela's interview with Newell and Sturgell lasted only half an hour. Later, she told Bonnie that they'd asked the usual questions and she'd given the usual answers, which were that she'd slept through the whole thing, she knew nothing, and that her best guess was that someone from National Spinning had probably been responsible for the murder.

She said they'd also showed her the pictures. She'd told them she had no idea how the pages had come to be spattered with blood, or how they'd come to be torn from the book. She said she didn't even remember the book. There were a lot of books in the house, a lot of books in her room. Some she'd read, some she hadn't. About this one, she just didn't know.

Chris's interview, that evening, lasted longer. Newell and Sturgell began the way everyone else had, asking Chris to go over in detail his every action on the weekend of the murder.

He'd gone home that Friday night, he told them, and had either stayed in watching television or had gone out with friends, he wasn't sure which. On Saturday night, after cooking supper, he'd gone back to school, leaving his house between seven and eight P.M. He was driving his Mustang fastback.

Sunday, he'd drunk beer and eaten pizza at Wildflour Pizza, a typical activity any day of the week. By ten-thirty P.M. he was in Karen and Kirsten's room, playing cards and drinking more beer. He stayed until three-thirty, when he went back to his own room and to bed.

He described the phone call from Angela, saying that when he couldn't find his car keys in his pants, he'd stopped looking because he didn't want to wake his roommate again. He'd gone to the car, hoping that he'd left the keys in it, but had found it locked. Then he'd returned to his room and continued looking for the keys. When he still couldn't find them, he'd gone to the campus security telephone and called for help, explaining that he had to get home to Little Washington because his father had been murdered and his mother had been stabbed.

Newell and Sturgell began to press him a bit about the car.

When was the last time he'd driven it that night? He said, no later than eleven P.M.

Why had he parked it so far from the dorm? Because that lot was better lit, and a car parked there would be less likely to be vandalized than one parked in the lot closer to the dorm. He explained that his car had been broken into earlier that month while he was visiting his aunt in South Carolina and that his radio and tape deck had been stolen.

Where did he eventually find his keys? He said Vince had found them under a chair cushion sometime after he'd left for home.

Let's go back to that Sunday. Tell us again who you were with. During the day, he said, Hamrick, Upchurch, who was also known as Moog, Karen and Kirsten, and Daniel Duyk.

Where are they now? Where is Upchurch? Where is Duyk? Chris said they'd both dropped out of State. Duyk was working as a bartender. The last time Chris had seen him was about six weeks earlier, when he'd passed through Raleigh. Upchurch, he hadn't seen in months. He said Upchurch's mother lived in Virginia Beach, Virginia, and was either separated or divorced from his father.

Okay, let's talk about drugs. Chris admitted to using marijuana, cocaine, LSD, and Ecstasy. He said his first summer roommate, not Vince, had gotten him started on drugs.

Where'd you get the money to buy these drugs? He explained that he had a job at the Miller and Rhoades men's clothing store in the Crabtree Valley Mall near the campus.

What does that pay? Four dollars an hour, he said.

What kind of drugs can you buy for four bucks an hour, especially if you're only working part-time? Chris said he also got a $50-a-week allowance from home, which he used for drugs, and that he'd charge a lot of regular expenses to his credit cards, which his mother would then pay off. Also, if he got real short of cash, he could always ask her and she'd give him more.

Then they zeroed in on Sunday night. *Tell us again. Take it real slow. Who was where when? Who was with whom? Who did what when?* The answer was that the only ones who'd made it to Karen and Kirsten's room after the beer drinking at Wildflour had been he and Daniel Duyk. He said Moog and Vince had gone to study.

How the hell can you study after drinking beer for four hours? He said he and Daniel had done most of the drinking; Moog and Vince had not drunk that much.

That happen a lot? Five or six of you out drinking for hours and suddenly two guys disappear to start studying late Sunday night? No, Chris admitted, it wasn't common. In fact, he said, that night was one of the first times he could ever remember Moog, in particular, saying he had to go off to study by himself. The truth was, Chris said, none of them had paid much attention to schoolwork that summer.

But you had to rush back that Saturday night so you could work on a term paper? Yes, he said, that term paper had been very important. His grades had been poor and he'd really needed to get it done.

What was the topic? The topic? *Yeah, the topic. You know, what was the paper about?* Oh, Chris said, it was just one of those English things. Kind of vague. With all that had happened since, he didn't really recall the actual topic.

Never got it done, did you? No, he said, not after getting the call from Angela. That had kind of been the end of schoolwork for a while.

But all day Sunday. You're not working, you're drinking beer. And Sunday night. You're not working on any paper. You're playing cards and drinking more beer. You're up until at least three o'clock in the morning. If nobody got killed, when were you going to write the fucking paper?

This was a problem, Chris admitted. He had a lot of good intentions when it came to his studies, but he was just such a jumpy, impulsive, scatterbrained guy that he found it hard to apply himself consistently.

They asked him about Dungeons & Dragons. He said he'd played with Daniel, Vince, and Moog. It was a role-playing game, set in medieval times. Once, they'd gotten high and played in the steam tunnels under the campus. He'd used a wooden sword to act out his role, and a couple of the others had brought along sticks or clubs made of rattan, the sort of thing used in Japanese martial arts. He wasn't sure whom they'd belonged to.

So what do you think? Who killed your stepfather? Chris was ready with an answer. In his opinion, it was someone from the Trust Department at North Carolina National Bank. They'd done it to prevent Lieth from transferring his account.

You think a bank like that—a multibillion-dollar operation—could give such a shit about one lousy little million-dollar trust account that they'd hire somebody to commit murder? You really believe that? Chris just shrugged.

Hey, do me a favor, one of them said. Chris nodded, eager to please.

Here's a pencil and a piece of paper. Draw me a map. Doesn't have to be fancy. Just a little map of your neighborhood. Just so we can orient ourselves.

Chris complied willingly, sketching the lines quickly, as if without thought.

Newell and Sturgell looked at the map.

One more thing. Your street. Lawson. Why don't you print the name of it, just so we know which one it is. Sure, no problem, Chris said. And he printed the word LAWSON on the map. In fact, he printed it twice.

Like the housing card from NC State, these, too, appeared a perfect match with the word found on the original map.

After the interview, Bonnie said, Chris did not seem "nervous or out of sorts." She asked what sorts of questions they had asked him. He said, "Just the usual old crap."

148

14

Two days later, on Friday, March 24, John Crone and his wife drove to Mooresville, near Charlotte, to visit his in-laws for the weekend. He wasn't very good company. He was preoccupied, lost in thought. Chris Pritchard was much on his mind.

And on the way back to Washington Sunday afternoon, as Crone was driving through Raleigh on I-70, he suddenly exited the highway and pulled into the parking lot of a large shopping center called the North Hills Mall.

Crone went directly to a bookstore. He asked if they had any material about a game called Dungeons & Dragons. A clerk showed him a whole section of the store devoted to the game and its many accessories. There was book after book, manual after manual, a dazzling array.

He gazed at the *Player's Manual, Expert Rules, Companion Rules, Master's Set, Dungeon Master's Rulebook, Dungeon Geomorphs, Player Character Record Sheets, Monster & Treasure Assortment*, and game scenario after game scenario, with names like "In Search of the Unknown," "The Keep on the Borderlands," "Palace of the Silver Princess," "The Lost City," "Horror on the Hill," and on and on, all with covers that showed various sorts of warrior types wielding swords and knives and locked in combat with fearsome dragons or other garishly drawn monsters.

The chief bought what appeared to be an introductory set, returned to his car, and resumed the trip to Little Washington. As he drove, he asked his wife to read aloud from the manual.

"It is another place, another time," she read. "The world is much like ours was long ago, with knights and castles and no science or technology. . . . Imagine: dragons are real. Werewolves are real. Monsters of all kinds live in caves and ancient ruins. And magic really works! . . . You are a strong hero, a famous but poor fighter. . . . You explore the unknown, looking for monsters and treasure. The more you find, the more powerful and famous you become. . . .

"A 'dungeon,' " she read, "is a group of rooms and corridors in which monsters and treasures can be found. And *you* will find them, as you play the role of a character in a fantasy world. . . .

"You are carrying a backpack . . . you own a beautiful sword, and have a dagger tucked into one boot, just in case. . . . You will make a map of the dungeon so you don't get lost."

She explained that there were various types of characters, including "thieves" and "fighters" and "magic-users" and that each time a character or group of characters successfully completed an adventure by successfully mapping out a "dungeon" or darkened cave and killing any monster who tried to stop them from finding treasures, they acquired more power, which was measured in something called "experience points."

As his wife read on, John Crone found himself driving faster and faster. He found it hard to keep his eyes focused on the road. As she began to describe the first adventure in detail, he felt his palms grow slick with perspiration.

The players were to enter a castle and kill the overlord in his sleep. The only weapons they were allowed were knives and clubs, which were to be carried in a knapsack. A princess named Aleena was sleeping in the castle near her father, the evil overlord. The players could not tell if she was friend or foe, so they allowed her to continue to sleep. If they were successful in killing the overlord and escaping from the castle undetected, they would inherit all his wealth and develop new and greater powers, which could then be used in subsequent adventures. The more times they stabbed the overlord, the more experience points they would receive. . . .

"Oh, my God!" John Crone said. "Oh, my God . . . oh, my God . . . oh, my God."

Crone paced the floor of his office Monday morning, trying to drink coffee, gesticulate, and read aloud from a Dungeons & Dragons manual all at once. *Listen to this!* he told John Taylor. *And this! . . . And this!*

What had happened seemed obvious. These kids had gotten so deep into their Dungeons & Dragons fantasy world that they'd decided to act out an adventure.

"Look, we know Pritchard drew the map," Crone said. "The question is, who could he get to do the killing? The answer has to be, one of the people he was playing that game with. Which one? I think we can both make a pretty good guess."

"Upchurch," Taylor said.

James Upchurch. Moog. The only one with a criminal record. The one with whom Chris had disappeared on July 4. Also, the only one currently missing in action.

"I can't believe it," Crone said. "I can't believe that for eight months those kids have been sitting up there on that campus and that we haven't been *all over* them."

"I can change that in a hurry," Taylor said.

Crone said yes. Get to Raleigh. Get after those kids. Find out all you can about Upchurch and then find the son of a bitch himself.

"Shouldn't be too hard," Taylor said. "Last thing his probation officer told me was she heard he'd changed his hair color to pink."

Starting the last week of March, John Taylor, as he put it, began to "burn a lot of rubber" between Little Washington and Raleigh. He spent so much time on the NC State campus he felt entitled to an honorary degree. He met many of Upchurch's and Pritchard's acquaintances, and the more he saw of them, the less he liked what he saw.

Daniel Duyk, for instance. He was one of the Dungeons & Dragons players. He was, in fact, the one who'd been up with Pritchard until three-thirty the morning of the murder.

Taylor knocked on his door at noon and Duyk answered it in his underwear. Why the hell weren't these people in classes? What were they doing in their underwear at noon? Taylor wasn't even sure it was *clean* underwear.

Duyk said he didn't know Pritchard well. *He wasn't really a friend of mine.* Or Moog either. None of them. He'd just seen a notice posted on a bulletin board in a dorm lobby at the start of the first summer session, saying anyone interested in getting up a Dungeons & Dragons game ought to come to a meeting in a certain room at a certain time. Daniel had played D&D since seventh grade. He thought it might be fun to play that summer.

Half a dozen people showed. Pritchard, Moog, two black guys, someone named Vince, someone named Neal, and a couple of other guys. It had been Moog, he thought, who'd posted the notice.

Nervously, Duyk explained how the game worked. They were all at a very advanced level, he said, and their "campaigns" lasted fifty or sixty hours, played in segments, four or five hours at a time. They'd played almost every day. They'd gone down to the steam tunnels to write graffiti, but the tunnels, which he called "hell tunnels," hadn't really been part of the game. Once, they'd brought torches down to the tunnels, and on other occasions fake samurai swords belonging to Moog. Drunk or high, they'd wave the swords around and pretend to duel.

Chris Pritchard, Duyk said, had once bragged that he'd found a confidential folder in his parents' home which revealed that they were millionaires. This struck Duyk as ironic because Chris was always over the limit on his credit cards. Of course, Chris—whom he described as "a sweetheart . . . a real nice guy," though "easily led"—*did* spend a lot of money on drugs. Chris had done a lot of acid with Upchurch, who was even more heavily into drugs.

Taylor asked about the weekend of the murder. Duyk said he'd met Chris and Vince Hamrick and Karen and Kirsten at about nine P.M. Sunday and they'd gone to the girls' room to play cards. Vince had been in the room, trying to study, while they played. At some point he'd gotten mad about something and left. Vince was always getting mad about something. Upchurch? No, he didn't remember seeing Upchurch that night.

At seven or eight the next morning, Vince called to say Chris's parents had been attacked, maybe killed, and that Chris had needed a ride home from the campus police because he hadn't been able to find his car keys.

Then Duyk looked right at John Taylor. He said, "That sounds kind of suspicious, doesn't it?" He said he'd been with Chris several times since the murder and Chris had always seemed upset but had never wanted to talk about what had happened.

As the interview ended, Taylor said, "Keep thinking, Daniel. Keep remembering. This isn't the last time I'll be talking to you. I'm leaving now, but I'll be back." Duyk didn't seem happy to hear that.

Next, Taylor visited a friend of both Pritchard and Upchurch's named Matt Schwetz. He'd seen Schwetz's name in several of Lewis Young's reports.

It was raining, but Schwetz would not let Taylor enter his apartment. He stood in the kitchen doorway, keeping Taylor out in the rain.

"Listen," Taylor said, "I'm not here to bust you for dope. I just want to ask a few questions. But I don't want to stand here and get wet."

Schwetz shook his head.

"One step," Taylor said. "I just want to take one step inside your fucking doorway, so I can get out of the rain while we talk."

Schwetz acted as if he'd heard this kind of story before and didn't like it. He was going to put up a goal-line stand. Finally, he relented enough so Taylor could at least shield his notebook from the rain.

Pritchard, yeah, he knew Pritchard. What an asshole. They used to drink together, but he hadn't seen him since fall. Heard he'd dropped out of school for psychological reasons. Wouldn't be surprising. That kid was really fucked up. He'd told a lot of different stories about the murder. One time he said his father surprised a burglar and was killed. Another time, he said the killer had raped his mother first.

Frankly, Schwetz himself wasn't tracking very well. *This*

guy's got a fried mind, Taylor thought. He was jabbering on now about what a swell guy Pritchard was. Always took care of his friends. Always bought the expensive beer, not the cheap stuff. Guy had a real positive attitude, you know? Always talked about his relatives like he loved them. Once, he'd said his family owned 35 percent of RJR Nabisco. His sister had been around when he'd said that. She'd said no, it was only 32 percent.

Dungeons & Dragons? No, not Schwetz. Steam tunnels? No, didn't know anything about them. Yeah, he knew Vince, he knew Daniel, he knew Moog. He'd even seen Moog recently, but only in passing, didn't know where it might have been. You know, you see a lot of guys, don't always pay attention to who was where.

"Listen," Taylor said. "I've been told you supplied Upchurch and Pritchard with acid."

Oh, no. Absolutely not. Acid? Was that the same as LSD? He'd heard of it, but didn't know anything about it. No, no; not acid. Chris, as a matter of fact—now *this* was something he remembered—had never even used acid. Or LSD. Whatever you called it. Whatever it was.

"Stick around town," Taylor said. "I'll be back. And next time I'll bring an umbrella."

Taylor returned to Raleigh on March 29 to talk to Vince Hamrick again. "He gave me one of those 'Y'all leave me alone,' type looks," Taylor said, "which always makes me feel a little more like asking questions."

The night of the murder, Vince said, he'd been studying for a physics test. His best guess was that Chris had come in about midnight. *As best guesses went,* thought Taylor, *that one wasn't very good.* He didn't remember seeing Daniel Duyk or James Upchurch at all on Sunday night. Cards? No, he didn't remember playing cards. No, he didn't remember answering the phone when Angela called. He hadn't woken up until Chris was packing to go home. Car keys? No, he didn't remember anything about Chris not being able to find his car keys. But one thing he did know: Chris loved that car, man, and would *never* let anyone else drive it.

They used to play D&D, he said, but it all kind of petered out after the murder. He hadn't played with Moog or Daniel Duyk since the murder, that was for sure.

"Good luck on the test, Vince," Taylor said. "But don't graduate too soon. I'll be wanting to talk to you again."

Taylor went back to see Karen Barbour and Kirsten Hewitt. Yes, they remembered that Sunday night. They'd been with Chris and Moog and Daniel and Vince at Wildflour Pizza. On the way back to the dorm, they'd bought beer. Karen had bought it because she was the only one of legal age. Yes, they'd thought it unusual that Chris parked the car in the fringe lot, so far from the dorm.

The boys had disappeared for a while, they assumed to play Dungeons & Dragons. The card game hadn't started until late, maybe ten. Daniel got mad because Vince was giving Kirsten advice on how to play. Then Vince got mad at Daniel. By eleven P.M., he'd stormed out of the room, but they kept on seeing him because they'd left the beer up in Chris and Vince's room because Vince had a refrigerator, and every time one of them went up to get a beer they saw Vince studying. They hadn't seen Upchurch at all.

They clearly recalled that from one or one-thirty on, Kirsten had asked the boys to leave. At three-thirty, she'd said, in her most exasperated tone yet, "Can't we *please* stop the game?" Chris asked what time it was. When they told him three-thirty, he left at once. This had always struck them as strange.

John Taylor—being twenty-six and good-looking and comfortable in blue jeans—had established good rapport with these two girls. They felt comfortable talking to him, not intimidated. He wasn't like a cop you had to be afraid of. So they volunteered some additional information.

Kirsten said that Chris had told her once that he'd entered a plan on his computer disc that outlined how he could "come into a lot of money." When she'd asked to see it, he said it was secret. She said he seemed to resent Lieth and Lieth's money, which, he said, Lieth used only to take care of Bonnie, not his sister or him. If they were

155

so rich, Chris complained, how come he and Angela couldn't have more clothes or better cars?

Karen said she'd seen Chris sell marijuana and take acid. But both girls made it clear they liked him. He was good company, fun to be around, even if he was a little obsessed with Dungeons & Dragons.

Leaving campus, Taylor stopped at the security office to show a picture of James Upchurch that he'd obtained from the probation officer. He said Washington police and the SBI were eager to speak to the young man and asked for help in finding him. He said it shouldn't be hard. "Really," Taylor said. "A guy with pink hair. Let's find him."

On March 30, an FBI lab technician phoned Taylor to say that on the basis of the samples submitted, they could deem it "probable" that Chris Pritchard had written the word LAWSON on the map found at the fire site.

15

The next day Bonnie arrived in Little Washington for the annual dinner of the Humane Society, the one social event that could have brought her back to the town she'd learned to fear and loathe.

That afternoon, she went to police headquarters to ask yet again what had become the one question of significance in her life: Was there any news about the investigation?

She was hoping to see John Taylor, who seemed to her to be the only person connected to the case who displayed even a modicum of courtesy.

Taylor was there, but Lewis Young was also present and greeted her coolly. She complained about the rude and insulting manner in which Newell and Sturgell had questioned her. Then she announced her intention of hiring a private investigator and told the two officers that she expected them to cooperate with whomever she brought into the case.

Young flatly told her that it was not SBI policy to cooperate with private investigators.

Bonnie told him she no longer gave a hoot about SBI policy. In eight months, SBI policy had accomplished exactly nothing, except to let a murderer's trail grow cold. She was fed up with SBI policy. And fed up with the incompetence—or worse—of the Little Washington police department. She was taking matters into her own hands, and if they did not cooperate voluntarily, she would take all measures available to her under the law to force them to.

Lewis Young told her she still didn't seem to understand the situation. They were investigating, and they were making progress. Maybe her problem was that it was progress in a direction that made her uncomfortable.

Young might have looked like a banker, and might be an alumnus of Chapel Hill, but he'd grown up in a strict police family. His father had been a North Carolina highway patrolman for thirty-eight years, and Young had lived all over the state as a boy, moving each time his father was transferred. Police work, he would say, "was in my blood."

It had also drawn a bit of his blood. One night, in 1977, while still a bachelor, Young had been standing at his kitchen sink preparing a peanut butter cracker. A shot was fired through the window behind him. The bullet had creased his scalp and skimmed the top of his skull. A quarter inch lower and he would have been dead. His assailant, it turned out, was a former Washington police officer Young had once arrested for theft.

For a while after that, Young ate no peanut butter, but his commitment to his work was intensified by the attempt on his life. And once you've been shot in the head at close range, you are not intimidated by a five two, 110-pound woman, no matter how indignant and determined she may be.

Already, Young told her, "a case could be made," against someone. Already, he said, "there's enough circumstantial evidence to bring someone to trial." No, he said, he was not going to identify the suspect, but rather pointedly he reminded her that Chris had still not taken his polygraph. He said he wanted that done within two weeks. Arrangements could even be made to have the test given in Winston-Salem, so Chris would have no excuse about the inconvenience of traveling to Greenville. He just didn't buy this new story Bonnie was telling him: that some anonymous therapist had said that the test would prove too stressful for the poor boy.

Lewis Young's voice, and his manner, had an edge that Bonnie had not heard or seen before. It both angered and frightened her. What Young seemed to be implying was that in order to get this case taken off the books, in order to wrap it up and move on, they might file baseless and unprovable charges against someone who was, in a very real sense, a victim, too—her own son.

She left the police station and went to her room at the Holiday Inn. She put in a call to Wade Smith, who was not immediately available. Then she sat down and made a few notes to which she could refer when she did speak to Wade. She wrote:

"Current major concern—LEWIS YOUNG—Does not appear genuinely interested in finding guilty party. He feels case can be made—Many cases have been solved on circumstantial evidence. BULL SHIT!!! I will settle for NO LESS THAN a conviction on cold hard evidence. *Facts* must speak, not circumstances."

But when she did meet with Wade, on her way back to Winston-Salem, he counseled patience once again. Because he felt she was already bearing a sufficient burden, he did not share with her, on this occasion, the faint sense of unease he'd begun to develop about the direction the investigation might take once the pace did begin to quicken.

Recent conversations with Bill Osteen had left Wade concerned about Bonnie's son, whom he himself had never met. Couching the opinion very carefully in several layers of lawyerlike euphemism, so as not to risk compromising any degree of attorney-client confidentiality, Osteen had conveyed to Wade the distinct impression that the son of Bonnie Von Stein struck him as an insolent and untrustworthy little thug.

This judgment was so much at odds with the portrait Bonnie had painted of Chris that it caused Wade to have his first twinge of misgiving: If the boy Bonnie described and the boy Osteen had seen were so different, might there someday prove to be a corresponding discrepancy between what Bonnie was so convinced of and what investigators would find?

As April began, the search for Moog intensified. "A really weird fucker," Taylor said. "He didn't seem to live anywhere."

They talked to his father, who, indeed, worked for the department of social services in Raleigh. No, he hadn't heard from James for quite some time. They talked to his mother, who, indeed, lived in Virginia Beach, Virginia. No, she hadn't heard from James for quite some time.

It seemed that Taylor was driving back and forth to Raleigh every day. In the company of Upchurch's probation officer, Christy Newsome, who, in one of life's pleasant small surprises, turned out to be not only competent but extremely good-looking, he staked out virtually every bar in which an NC State student had ever ordered a drink.

Sadlack's, The Watering Hole, the Brewery, the Fallout Shelter, Bourbon Street, I Play Games. Taylor thought The Watering Hole was "the worst damn looking place I'd ever seen. I didn't even want to go in there. Nothing but blacks and motorcycle guys. But Christy had guts. She'd walk right up to the bar and start showing that picture around and didn't even look over her shoulder."

You wouldn't think, Taylor said, that in 1989, as opposed to 1969, some guy with pink hair and a knapsack—and yes, they had learned that Upchurch carried a knapsack with him wherever he went—would be that hard to spot in Raleigh, North Carolina. But even with the help of the Raleigh police, as well as the NC State security officers, Moog could not be found.

* * *

Back in Washington on April 21, Taylor called Bonnie Von Stein. From the start, more than any other investigator, he had treated her with sympathy and respect. It was no act. He liked her. He also felt sorry for her, and he expected that before this was all over she would have to face agonies even worse than she'd already endured.

He said he believed she really did want to help. No matter what anyone else might say or suspect, he thought neither that she'd had anything to do with the murder nor that she was trying to cover for her children. He said he had a couple of questions that might turn out to be important, but added that he couldn't yet tell her his reasons for asking them.

He asked whether she knew where Chris's friend James Upchurch, also known as Moog, might be found. This, he reminded her, was the person with whom Chris had disappeared in early July.

Bonnie said she'd ask Chris as soon as she could. "I knew," she said later, "that I wouldn't get a straight answer from either John Taylor or Lewis Young if I asked them why they were looking for that young man, so I didn't even bother to ask. The only way I was surviving was by taking their questions at face value and doing all I could to answer honestly."

Taylor said his second question concerned a map. He told her—and this was the first time Bonnie had learned this from anyone—that investigators had reason to believe that at some point prior to the murder, Chris had drawn a map of the Smallwood neighborhood, showing the precise location of their house.

She said, in her calm, matter-of-fact tone, "Well, if that were the case, there wouldn't be anything surprising about it. He could easily have done so in order to provide directions for out-of-town friends, or one of his cousins."

But later, when she asked Chris, he said, no, gee, he couldn't remember ever drawing any sort of map of their neighborhood. And when she asked about Upchurch, he said, no, gee, he had no idea what might have happened to James Upchurch. He hadn't heard anyone speak about Upchurch for months.

Angela, however, volunteered that she had met Upchurch once, when she'd gone to NC State to visit Chris. Bonnie asked her what kind of person he was. She responded, Bonnie recalled later, that he was "a nice, quiet young man who might appear a little bit weird."

Taylor's questions might have sounded idle enough to Bonnie, but to the considerably more sophisticated ear of former federal prosecutor Bill Osteen they seemed ominous.

Osteen was already annoyed, to put it mildly, that Chris had drawn a map of his neighborhood and had printed the name of his street for the SBI. He was equally displeased that neither Chris nor Bonnie had even bothered to tell him that the SBI had wanted to question Chris. Had he known, he would never have let such a meeting occur, at least not unless he'd been present himself.

This sort of loose-cannon stupidity got clients into a lot of needless trouble. Why bother hiring a lawyer, he said to Chris, in a distinctly nonavuncular tone, if you weren't even going to tell him you were planning to go off and have little private meetings with investigators who might well consider you a prime suspect in a murder case?

Osteen had no idea why the SBI had wanted the printing or the map, and Chris—who struck him as the kind of kid who you'd think was lying if you asked him on December 25 what day it was and he said, "Christmas"—said he couldn't imagine a map having any possible relevance to anything.

But now that a detective from Little Washington was calling to ask further questions about a map, Osteen could see that Chris was becoming—indeed, had already become—a target, perhaps *the* target of the probe. Another try for a useful polygraph result suddenly seemed a higher priority.

Osteen scheduled the second test for April 25. Chris stopped taking his Buspar well before it. Bonnie drove him to Charlotte. There was little conversation on the way, but, as she recalls it, he didn't seem at all tense. Indeed, she thought that his psychological state had begun to improve.

He seemed much less depressed than he'd been in winter, much less apt to become tearful or to fly into a rage. He seemed, in fact, to be working and living normally. And Angela seemed better, too.

Despite all the harassment from, and lack of progress by, investigators, and despite the fact that the ache in her heart caused by Lieth's death had not subsided, and despite the fact that she and Angela and Chris continued to live in constant fear—their little home a virtual arsenal—Bonnie felt that they were not just surviving, but actually beginning to recover, bit by bit.

Chris's polygraph examination consisted of two questions considered "relevant" by the operator:

First, "Did you set up the murder of your stepfather?"

Second, "Do you know the name of the person who stabbed Lieth?"

To each, Chris answered, "No."

The operator's report said, "Based upon my analysis of the nature and degree of the tracings on the three polygraph charts, it is my opinion that the psychophysiological responses of Mr. Pritchard, when answering the above relevant questions, *are not* indicative of deception."

In other words, he passed. The operator gave Chris and Bonnie the good news immediately. Neither of them seemed to show much emotion. It came, of course, as no surprise to Bonnie. She'd never had a moment's doubt. But Bill Osteen, for one, was greatly relieved.

For the first time since her release from the hospital, Bonnie felt that matters were sufficiently under control so she could take a few days to be by herself, to get somewhere new, to feel something different. And so, at four-thirty on the morning of April 26, 1989, she climbed on a tour bus in Winston-Salem for a four-day trip to Disney World.

16

On Monday, May 1, the decision was made to confront Chris and his mother with the evidence the SBI and Washington police had already gathered.

"It wasn't going to be pretty," Taylor said later, "but we'd decided to have it out with Bonnie and Chris."

Young called Bonnie to say he would be coming to Winston-Salem the next day, bringing with him all the items of evidence she'd been wanting to see since early August. He told her he'd be wanting to speak to Chris and Angela, too. Eight o'clock tomorrow night, he told her, at the Forsyth County Sheriff's Department in Winston-Salem. They were going to lay all their cards on the table.

Without hesitation, Bonnie told him, "We'll be there."

At ten forty-five the next morning, Lewis Young stepped out of SBI headquarters in Greenville and walked toward his car, where a young assistant district attorney named Keith Mason was waiting. On the off chance that, after seeing the case they were building against him, Chris might want to make a statement, the district attorney had wanted someone from his office standing by.

Young was only a few steps from the car when his beeper rang. The message was that an attorney from Greensboro named William Osteen had called his Little Washington office, trying to reach him.

"I'll be right back," Young said to Keith Mason. Knowing he'd be on the road most of the day, Young decided to return the call before setting out on the trip. Having spent most of his career in eastern North Carolina, Young was not familiar with the name William Osteen. He called the Greensboro number.

* * *

The timing of the call was pure coincidence. Bill Osteen had had no idea that, even as he was trying to contact Lewis Young, the SBI agent was preparing to drive to Winston-Salem to try to obtain a confession from his client.

It had just seemed to Osteen—who knew nothing of any comparisons of printing samples—that since Chris had passed a private polygraph exam, the SBI test no longer loomed as a threat. In fact, if Chris passed it—and given the results from Charlotte, Osteen was confident that he would—investigators might finally cross him off their list of suspects.

And so he introduced himself to Young as an attorney who'd been retained "to represent Chris Pritchard concerning the polygraph."

"It's my understanding," Lewis Young said, "that Chris Pritchard doesn't want to take an SBI polygraph."

"That's not necessarily so," Osteen said.

"Well, good," Young replied. "I'll ask him about it when I see him tonight."

There was a brief silence.

"Tonight?" Osteen asked, sounding surprised.

"Yes," Young said, but already with the sinking feeling that he'd said more than he should have. "I'm on my way to Winston-Salem right now. I'm interviewing Chris and his mother and his sister tonight."

"Well, I'm sorry," Osteen said, "but I can't be there tonight."

All the way to Winston-Salem, Lewis Young stewed. *Young, you ran your big mouth off,* he told himself, repeating the thought aloud to Keith Mason. "I blew it," he said. "I've screwed this one right into the ground." Osteen hadn't come right out and said he was going to instruct Chris to cancel his interview, but Young was sure he would. "That lawyer," he said, "is going to call that boy and tell him there's *no way* he's going to talk to us tonight."

Keith Mason had to agree. Lewis Young might not have been familiar with the name, but Mason was. In fact, he'd been in law school at Chapel Hill with Osteen's son. He told Young that Bill Osteen was a former United States Attorney and one of the most respected and renowned lawyers in the state.

At five-ten P.M., as soon as he'd checked into his motel, Lewis Young called Bonnie.

She quickly gave him the answer he'd anticipated.

"I m sorry," she said, "but Chris won't be there tonight. His attorney, Mr. Osteen, does not want him interviewed unless Mr. Osteen can be present himself."

"And how long," Young asked, "has Mr. Osteen been involved in this case?"

"I retained him to represent Chris in January," Bonnie said. "He was recommended by the attorney I retained then, Wade Smith."

Wade Smith! Young was staggered. "As soon as I heard that name," he said later, "it rang all sorts of bells and dollar signs." Young might not have been familiar with Bill Osteen, but every law enforcement officer in the state knew of Wade Smith. He was, quite simply, the biggest name there was in criminal law in North Carolina.

What in the hell, Young asked himself, *are these* victims *doing with lawyers like Osteen and Wade Smith?*

"You mean to tell me," Young demanded of Bonnie, his temper rising fast, "that you've had Wade Smith and this fellow Osteen representing you and your family since *January!*"

"That's right," she said. "One attorney for those of us who were present in the house at the time, and another for Christopher, who was not."

"You never told me a damned thing about having *any* attorneys involved!"

"I didn't think it was any of your business," she said mildly, adding that she'd long ago lost confidence in the ability of the Washington police and the SBI to find her husband's murderer. She said, in fact, that she'd come to fear they might be not only incompetent but dishonest, and that in order to cover up their own mistakes, they might make a serious accusation against an innocent person.

By now, Lewis Young was fuming in a way he seldom did. His charm and courtliness were nowhere in evidence.

Bonnie had never told him about Osteen or Wade Smith. Instead, she'd played so dumb and helpless—jerking him around all year long—as she secretly retained two of the highest-caliber lawyers in the state.

Since January Osteen had been in the case. Ever since Chris had backed out of the polygraph. Goddamn it. *Goddamn it!* She'd promised him that Chris would take that polygraph. Then, at the last minute, she'd changed her mind.

Now, she'd promised him that Chris would appear for an interview. But the very day it was to take place a lawyer whom she'd hired *in January* had intervened to prevent him from talking.

"I guess blood *is* thicker than water," Young said.

"What do you mean by that remark?"

"I mean, you've known all along that Chris was involved and you're doing everything you can to cover for him."

"I assure you," Bonnie said, "that nothing could be further from the truth. Angela and I will see you, as planned, at eight P.M."

Lewis Young slammed down the phone. So much for poor little Bonnie. Tonight, that little lady would see a different and much less pleasant side of Lewis Young's personality.

That night, as Bonnie entered the meeting room, she observed that Lewis Young had not come alone. He was accompanied not only by John Taylor, but by her nemeses of March—the Thin Man and the Doughboy.

Young, still incensed, jumped to his feet before she could even take a seat and picked up a large stack of papers.

"You know," he said, in a much harsher voice than she'd ever heard him use before, "I came to Winston-Salem with every intention of going through this stuff with you, but now I'm not going to do it. As a matter of fact, I'm not ever going to discuss the case with you again."

He threw the papers on a table. Then Newell began to talk. Or maybe Sturgell. Then Lewis Young again. They were coming at Bonnie from all sides. Chris was involved. They had evidence. He hadn't committed the murder himself—he wasn't even in the house at the time—but he was involved. He'd lied to them. They could prove it. No, they wouldn't discuss how they could prove it. They would have been happy to tell her if she hadn't gone out and hired attorneys. The presence of attorneys changed everything. It put her and the investigators on opposite sides of the fence. Since when did victims need attorneys?

Chris's involvement might have been innocent, they said. He might not even have realized he'd provided information that led to her husband's murder. But he realized it now and was lying. They were willing to make a deal with somebody, to plea-bargain, but it would only be with whoever came forward first. And the talk would have to be in the absence of attorneys. If Chris wouldn't talk to them without a lawyer present, they had no further interest in talking to Chris. They'd just go ahead and build their case against him.

Then they told her Chris was in danger. They called him a "weak link" who could lead them directly to the killer and said the killer had strong reason to want Chris quickly and permanently silenced. They said Bonnie and Angela were in danger, too.

"We're stepping up the pressure now," one of them said. "We're starting to push a lot harder. We're closing in. Somebody could come after you at any time. If you don't have any protection, you'd better get some."

This sounded to Bonnie very much like a threat—as if they were trying to scare her into capitulating. They did not succeed—bullying was not a tactic that would ever succeed with Bonnie—but they did make her both angrier and more frightened than she'd been since the previous July.

"I know for a fact," she told them, "that Chris didn't do it. He had nothing at all to do with it. I have my own proof of this."

They sneered at her. One of them said, oh, yeah, she must have arranged a private polygraph. For her poor little darling who was afraid to take a *real* polygraph test.

"You get what you pay for," one of them said. "If you buy the polygraph, you can be sure you'll get the result you want. But it isn't worth a damned thing."

167

Then they got even more personal. "You say you want the truth!" Lewis Young shouted, in a most uncharacteristic manner. "You say you want to find the guilty person! But that's only true as long as he's not your son!"

"That's not true," Bonnie said, her own voice betraying more emotion than usual. "I want the guilty person in jail no matter who it is."

But she couldn't help adding, somewhat desperately, "It's not Chris. I tell you again: Chris is not involved."

And they told her again: the first person to come forward would be the only person with whom they'd deal. This might be Chris's last chance.

She told them again to call Mr. Osteen if they really felt they needed to talk to Chris.

They told her again that they would not deal with any lawyers. Then Lewis Young told her the meeting was over. He said he'd be in town overnight and left a number where she could reach him if Chris was willing to talk—without an attorney.

"It looks to me," she said, her voice quavering, "that since you're not able to find out who really did it, you're going to try to make someone a scapegoat."

She took the number, stuffed it into her purse, and left the office. Angela was waiting outside. Now, it seemed, they didn't even want to talk to Angela. Just Chris. And Chris only without a lawyer.

"Just remember," Young called after her. "There are unknown people still out there. Unknown people who might try to kill you at any time. So take this as a warning: I'm formally advising you that your life is in jeopardy."

"I cried all the way back to the car," Bonnie said later. "I walked a few steps and then I couldn't see through my tears to walk. Angela thought I was going to pass out. She asked me what was wrong and I told her I'd tell her and Chris all about it when I got home.

"I was so upset myself that I don't remember how Chris reacted when I told him. I felt so desolate, lost, run over. I felt as if I'd been raped by the very people I'd been depending on."

One thing she didn't feel was any doubt about Chris's

innocence. She knew that her own son could never have wanted her beaten and stabbed, could never have wanted Lieth murdered.

At nine-forty P.M. she sat down and made notes of her recollection of the meeting, so that when she spoke to Wade Smith in the morning—which was the first thing she intended to do—she would be as organized as possible. The notes themselves, however, reflected not her analytic skills but the raw emotion of what she'd just been through. She wrote:

"I feel like I have just been raped by the law enforcement that I depend on to solve the murder of Lieth. What are my legal rights in obtaining the information these guys have collected? This dangling carrot (blackmail) has gone on for far too long. . . .

"By now I know that all the delays and blackmail used to this point are exactly that—BLACKMAIL! i.e. 'After you take polygraph we will sit down & go over info we have. Then, after Chris takes polygraph—same. Then when Chris will not yet take polygraph they are still prepared to go over info. until Bill Osteen calls and says Chris will not be at meeting.

"My thoughts at this moment: these 4 men are probably feeling pretty good right now about how they must have unsettled me. They are probably sure I will call the number to reach Lewis Young. They're probably 'laughing it up' over the victim they have just emotionally raped!

"Sometime during this Stomp on Bonnie routine, I related to them that my options of a private investigation were destroyed along with all other evidence possibly remaining in my house. . . .

"Lewis accused me of not wanting the investigation to include my family. ('You want to find the persons involved as long as it isn't a member of your family.') I told Lewis I wanted the GUILTY person/persons in jail, no matter who! I also told him again Chris was not involved."

Now, Bonnie was alarmed in a way she had not been before. "They were so adamant," she said, "so certain, that I thought maybe, somehow, without having any idea he was doing it, Chris *had* given someone the idea he wanted his family dead. I also worried that maybe, in a completely innocent way, he *had* drawn a map.

"So I said to him that night, 'Chris, if there is anything . . . if you *ever* drew a map—maybe just playing Dungeons and Dragons . . . if anyone ever questioned you about the house . . . if you remember *anything*, now is the time to let someone know.'

"He went to his bedroom for a while and then came back and said, 'I have given it some thought, Mom, and I just can't think of anything.' "

17

Crone and Taylor returned to the NC State campus and environs, their mood dark in the wake of the futile May 2 meeting, their questions sharp.

They could now see that any further attempts to deal openly with the family—to enlist Bonnie's aid in an effort to get Chris to talk—would be fruitless. At Bonnie's direction, the family had drawn the wagons in a circle. This woman—this *victim*—whom they had been trying so hard to help, seemed willing to let the killer of her husband go unpunished in order to save her son.

So they would just have to do it the hard way.

They interviewed Daniel Duyk again. There was nothing easygoing about Crone now. He said, "I know you were lying in *at least* one of the things you told us. I know Chris Pritchard was involved in *at least* the planning of the murder. Now what I want to know—and you'd goddamned well better tell me the truth—is who Pritchard would go to for advice. Who would he talk to about something like this? Who was he closest to? Who had the most influence over him?"

Duyk's immediate answer was James Upchurch.

Where is Upchurch? they demanded.

Duyk started giving them addresses. Places around the campus where Upchurch had been in the past, might be now. They must have succeeded in scaring Duyk because he suddenly seemed to want to help.

"Daniel never really had a *bad* attitude," Taylor said later. "But after we told him Chris was involved, he got a lot more cooperative. Like, he suddenly remembered an incident a couple of months before the murder when he was in a room with Chris and Upchurch and Vince Hamrick, and Chris was talking about how rich his parents were, and someone—he said it was either Upchurch or Hamrick—said, 'We ought to bump off your parents and get that money.' "

Crone and Taylor met with security officials and received a guided tour of the network of steam tunnels that ran beneath the campus. They saw a lot of graffiti, including the spray-painted initials CWP, which Christopher Wayne Pritchard himself—back when he was still willing to talk to them—had said he'd put there.

For almost three weeks, Taylor spent most of his days and many nights in Raleigh, searching for Upchurch. Every day, he'd hear a new report of where Moog had just been seen or of where he was expected to turn up. It was the most tantalizing sort of hide-and-seek: as if Upchurch, who, presumably, could have fled the city, even the state, were teasing him. As if, to Moog, the whole search were a game—another Dungeons & Dragons scenario.

Taylor leaned on Daniel Duyk a little harder. Duyk said, yeah, he'd heard something: he'd heard that Upchurch was supposed to start a job working for a housepainter. There'd been a flier posted on a campus bulletin board. Taylor checked the board, but the flier was gone. He looked up housepainters in the yellow pages. There were, he said, "about nine thousand" of them. Raleigh was not at all like Little Washington.

Christy Newsome, the probation officer, said she'd heard Upchurch was living in a shelter for the homeless. They checked shelters near the campus. No Upchurch, and nobody recognized his picture.

The rumors and reported sightings continued. There was a witch living in a house on Boylan Street who knew Upchurch, but when Taylor went there, she said she didn't know him, and she didn't appear to be a witch, though Taylor had to admit he might not know a real witch when he saw one.

A Raleigh policeman told him a black guy had been in a fight with Upchurch right out on Hillsborough Street only two days before. Then Taylor was called by a police informant who said he'd actually seen Upchurch that very day, but when he'd approached, Moog had run away.

They were getting closer. Taylor could feel it. On May 19, they staked out a house where Upchurch was supposed to turn up at a party. A big party, but no Upchurch. They went back to Matt Schwetz's house, where they found a note taped to the door. It said: "Matt—Just stopped by for a second. Headed for the cellar for a while." It was signed, "The Killer."

18

On May 22, James Upchurch was arrested near the NC State campus. When first approached, he had run. When eventually caught, he'd given a fake name. Clearly, this was a young man apprehensive about something.

Young and Taylor spoke to him at nine P.M. in an interrogation room on the fifth floor of the Raleigh police department, where he'd been charged with violation of the terms of his probation.

His hair *was* dyed pink, or maybe orange, and it was the longest, scraggliest hair Young and Taylor had seen in quite some time, but aside from his appearance, Upchurch—*after all that hunting*—was a disappointment.

They'd expected him to be hostile and resistant; else why would he have tried so hard to avoid them? Instead, they found a cordial, forthcoming, intelligent young man who talked freely and gave the impression of being sincerely interested in helping them.

Yes, he'd heard that Chris Pritchard's stepfather had been murdered. Terrible thing. Pritchard had never really seemed to recover. After the murder, he'd been "paranoid and upset" and had carried a long-bladed knife with him around the campus. Since he'd dropped out of school, Upchurch hadn't seen him.

He explained that he'd first met Chris in late May or early June, after posting a notice on a campus bulletin board, advertising for Dungeons & Dragons players. Chris had been one of eight or nine people who'd responded and was one of a half dozen or so who'd formed a group to play the game regularly. As he became better acquainted with Chris, he started hanging out in Chris's room, which was two floors below his own, in Lee Dorm. The first time he'd gone there, the room was full of marijuana smoke. Everyone there was smoking pot.

Soon, Chris had grown "bored" with marijuana and moved on to cocaine, but this proved too expensive, even though, as he'd stated often, his family had "more than a million."

From cocaine, Chris had switched to LSD, mostly because it was cheaper. After taking his first acid trip in Upchurch's presence, Chris had become infatuated with the drug and had begged Upchurch to get him more. The morning after the night he'd taken his first hit, he took his second. As summer progressed, Chris began to do acid "constantly." He spent so much on drugs that he wasn't always able to pay in advance and wound up owing money to people Upchurch described as "shady, ex-con types."

The fact was, Upchurch said sadly, Chris had a problem with drugs. Upchurch had found it worrisome. Eventually, he said, he'd felt obliged to warn Chris about the dangers of addiction.

But then again, drugs were a campus-wide problem at NC State. Upchurch explained that he'd come from a small town in Caswell County and hadn't been prepared for the Sodom-and-Gomorrah-like atmosphere he'd found at State. An insecure kid such as Pritchard, he explained, "someone who always worried, 'Do they like me? Am I gonna be accepted?' " could easily get into trouble at a place like State. Fortunately for himself, Upchurch explained, he was unconcerned about social acceptance. He marched to the beat of his own drummer. He was his own man, his own boss; the kind of person, he said—hoping this wouldn't sound immodest—that Chris Pritchard had always wanted to be.

He said that Chris, while likable and outgoing, also was strange and eccentric. He did everything to excess and in a show-offy manner. Like, whenever he got any acid, he'd run around the dorm and tell everyone he had it and ask if anyone wanted any. And he would always blow the limit on his credit cards.

Upchurch said he had a vivid recollection of his July 4 trip to South Carolina with Chris. He said Chris's relatives down there were "real rednecks" and "very rough-type people" and that members of the crowd they hung out with were "always talking about knowing people that would kill other people."

Chris's aunt Ramona had proudly showed Upchurch her .357 magnum the night they arrived. Upchurch found the "rednecks" poor company, so he spent most of his time in a motel with a girl he met. Chris spent most of *his* time with a girl who had brothers who were "criminals." Chris was trying to get into a drug-dealing business with them. Chris was "the type of person who wanted to get into the drug business and wanted to make money dealing drugs." Chris told Upchurch more than once that he'd met people that weekend in South Carolina who could "supply him with anything and in any amount that he wanted."

He said Chris seemed fond of his natural father, Steve Pritchard, and quite obviously loved his mother, who would call school several times a week to check on him. Whenever she called, he'd "hit her up" for more money. He added that Chris and his stepfather "did not seem to get along too well with each other" and seldom spoke.

Still, he had a hard time believing that Chris could possibly have hired anyone to kill his parents. Some of those characters Chris had met in South Carolina, though, were probably capable of murder. He said he was sorry to hear that Chris seemed to be a suspect, but he could understand how it could happen, because Chris was such a weird, flaky kid, and you never knew what he'd do next. Plus, there was always all that talk about how much money his parents had, and how much easier Chris's life would be if he had it himself.

For example, one night he was with Chris and a group of other friends at the Golden Corral restaurant just off campus. The bill had come to over $100 and Chris had insisted on treating everyone. Someone—Upchurch could not remember who—mentioned that if Chris kept spending money at that rate, he'd have to "off" his parents in order to get their money. Chris replied, "Yeah, I have thought about that a few times."

But that wasn't unusual, Upchurch went on. Every two or three days *someone* would suggest to Chris that he "off his parents and inherit the money," but it had always seemed to be said as a joke.

Regarding the weekend of the murder itself, Upchurch's recollection grew hazy. He said he might have been studying for an English exam but wasn't sure. He thought Chris had called him the night before and asked him to come to his room and play a card game called Spades. He thought Kirsten had also called to invite him, but he hadn't gone because he didn't like to play Spades.

But really, he couldn't be sure. The fact was, when it came to that weekend, his memory failed him. He just couldn't remember what he'd done, where he'd been, who he'd been with. All those summer weekends, he said somewhat apologetically, tended to blur.

And, he added—projecting a sense of shame and remorse when he admitted to this—even he, James Upchurch, had been doing a fair amount of drugs that summer. Even he had slipped into bad habits. He was not, therefore, able to remember every last little detail with perfect clarity. But, he repeated brightly, quite possibly he'd spent the weekend studying.

After the murder, he was so concerned about Chris that he contacted several friends on campus and enlisted their support in a campaign to keep Chris away from acid, fearing that after the trauma he'd just undergone, he would be susceptible to a bad trip.

There had been one night, though, when Chris had taken acid and, indeed, had had a very bad trip, screaming that he thought he was dying and begging for help, and Upchurch had to stay with him almost all night, talking him through it. After that, Chris seemed to stop taking drugs, though he continued drinking heavily, and of course he was acting "paranoid" and carrying that long-bladed knife everywhere he went, saying he was afraid someone might try to kill him, the way they'd killed his stepfather.

Chris had told everyone he was dropping out of school because he was under psychological stress and because he "had to go home and take care of his mother." This, however, was "bullshit." The real reason was that Chris was already flunking again and wanted to drop out before he got kicked out.

In September, Upchurch had begun living with Daniel Duyk. They would often discuss the murder and try to figure out what had happened. They were both pretty sure that Chris himself hadn't done the killing because he'd seemed to like his parents—at least his mother—and also because he didn't have the guts. And they had a hard time figuring the motivation because they thought Chris's parents would have been smart enough to put their money in a trust fund or something of that nature, so neither Chris nor his sister would get it all at once if the parents should die.

What they finally came up with was that Steve Pritchard—whom neither of them had ever met—had probably carried out the whole thing, probably still jealous at Bonnie for remarrying and even more jealous at her having all that money, and figuring eventually, as natural father to the children, he'd be able to take control of the trust.

The other thought Upchurch had—and this he seemed to confide almost reluctantly—was maybe Angela and Daniel Duyk had been involved. He had the impression that Duyk was attracted to Angela, but recalled that he'd once described her as "evil." When Upchurch had asked why he'd said that, Duyk replied it was because when he'd spoken to her about the murder, she hadn't shown any emotion.

As for his own difficulties with the law, Upchurch said he'd been a little wild when he was younger, but he'd really matured a lot since. His probation difficulties had begun when he'd overslept one morning and missed a meeting with his probation officer. Fearful that the probation would be revoked, he'd foolishly gone into hiding. Then, when he heard the law from Little Washington was looking for him, wanting to talk about a murder, he'd gotten scared. Not scared because of any involvement, but worried that Washington officials would turn him in to the probation department if they found him.

He apologized for having been so hard to locate. It was just that he'd dropped out of school for a while and was kind of moving around from place to place. But if there was anything else he could ever do to help them, he'd be glad to. He was working now for Triple A Student Painters in Raleigh, a company that hired college students to paint houses in the summer, and was living at the Sylvan Park apartments, 3903 Marcom Street, sharing quarters with his cousin, Kenyatta, from Caswell County, and Kenyatta's boyfriend, who was an old friend of his from high school named Neal Henderson, and another guy.

"It was a major-league letdown," Taylor said. "It was so hard to tell where he was coming from. You couldn't look at him and tell what he was thinking. He was just this cool, detached, real skinny dude with this real funny look on his face."

The interview, in fact, caused Lewis Young to "seriously question whether we were on the right track. We came away a lot less suspicious of him. I guess mostly because of his demeanor. He was so friendly and open, not arrogant. A hundred eighty degrees from Pritchard in terms of the personality we saw. Drugs, yes. He obviously had a problem with drugs and he would have talked to us about drugs for a week. But he did not come across as the kind of person we would normally consider a suspect in a murder case."

Still, Young remained convinced that the answer would eventually be found in Raleigh. He decided to "keep things stirred up at NC State. Make repeated contacts. Keep coming and coming. Make somebody feel, 'They're in our ballpark now. It's time to get on the other team.' We knew all we needed was one. Just from the map, we were convinced there was more than one person involved. And if we could get the first one, we knew he could give us the others."

On June 1, bringing John Taylor with him, Chief Crone traveled to Raleigh to speak to Upchurch for himself. Moog had been released after his probation violation, but was living under a house-arrest system that required him to wear an electronic bracelet around his ankle, so his whereabouts could be monitored at all times.

He was still living in the Sylvan Park apartments—camping out, actually, on the living room floor of the apartment rented by his high school classmate Neal Henderson.

There were games—board games, fantasy games—spread all over the floor. Axis & Allies, Dungeons & Dragons, World War I, The Civil War, The War of 1812, War of the Worlds. You name it, past or future, if it involved battling and bloodshed and fantasy, it was there.

"What it looked like," John Crone said, "was like they took thirty games out of their closet and threw them all over the floor. The apartment was an absolute pigsty." Upchurch and his friend Henderson, a shy, awkward kid who looked and walked a little bit like a turtle, were there when the two officers arrived.

Upchurch seemed surprised—even a bit shaken—to see investigators from Little Washington again. He apparently thought he'd disposed of that little piece of unpleasantness.

"My gut feeling," Crone said later, "was that this guy couldn't be the murderer, but seeing this involvement in all these games—the same kind of obsession Pritchard had—I felt maybe he could tell us who did it. So I decided to take him outside and shake him up a little bit. Not physically, you understand—never physically. Just see how much it would take to make the boy retch. Because maybe if he starting retching, he would talk.''

Crone and Taylor, much less amiable than Young and Taylor had been a week earlier, told Upchurch to step outside. They led him to Chief Crone's car and climbed inside. Taylor sat, unsmiling, behind the wheel, with Upchurch next to him. Crone sat in the backseat.

When they told him they were closing in on Pritchard, Upchurch said, as he had in May, that he didn't think any of the talk about offing Chris's parents had been serious. But, if they thought it was, the person they should talk to was Daniel Duyk, the only truly "unbalanced" member of their game-playing group.

"That's enough," Crone said suddenly. "Stop right there." Upchurch had been pointing them in any and every direction that led away from himself: from thugs in South Carolina to Daniel Duyk, to Chris and Angela, and to their natural father, Steve Pritchard.

Crone wanted to shake the kid up. "Show him the pictures," the chief barked. Upchurch had a smirk on his face.

Taylor leaned across the front seat and stuck a picture of the bloody, beaten body of Lieth Von Stein squarely into Upchurch's range of vision.

"Jesus, this is serious shit," Upchurch said, still smirking but trying to turn his head away.

"Look at the goddamned picture," John Crone said. "This man was brutally beaten and stabbed to death."

Upchurch kept glancing at the picture out of the corner of his eye, but leaned farther from it, toward the car door.

"If you're gonna get sick," John Taylor said, "open that door and puke on the sidewalk. Don't vomit in the chief's car. I got to ride in that seat going home."

Upchurch paled and began to perspire, but the smirk never entirely left his face. Nor did he have anything new to say. It wasn't his thing, man. He didn't know anything about it.

When they walked back inside with him, Crone turned to Henderson, who seemed just a blob in the background, and said, "By the way, what we're trying to do here, in case no one has told you, is find out who committed a murder. It was Chris Prtichard's stepfather who was murdered, and we already know that Pritchard helped to arrange it. What we want now is anybody who knows anything about Dungeons and Dragons. We think the murder might have been just a scenario that got out of hand. Somebody on drugs might have taken it too far without really meaning to. We have no reason to think it was premeditated.

"But the fact is, a man got killed, and we're close to finding out who killed him. If anybody knows anything, pass the word around that we're ready to listen to the first person who talks. But the first person is the only person we'll listen to. Our ship is about to pull out, and we've got room for one person, and one person only, on board."

The same day, Lewis Young was trying a different approach. He was speaking, off the record, to Wade Smith.

Young knew that by having accused her of deliberately covering up for her son, he had forever alienated Bonnie Von Stein. But he still believed that her cooperation could be tremendously helpful.

He remained convinced that Chris *was* the link to the killer, just as he'd said on May 2. But he also knew Chris had not committed the murder himself. That might be a bargaining chip. Maybe his involvement *had* been innocent. Maybe he'd made a map as part of a D&D game and then someone else, acting without Chris's approval or even awareness, had independently decided to drive to Washington and turn fantasy into blood-drenched reality.

If Bonnie could persuade Chris to admit he'd drawn the map and to disclose the identity of the person to whom he'd given it, then they'd know whom to go after at NC State.

Or maybe his involvement was not innocent. Maybe he had confessed to Bonnie and she'd chosen to protect him because he was all she had left. Young could understand that sort of motive, even if he could not condone it. If that was the case, she'd have to be shown—by someone she trusted—that eventually they'd get Chris anyway, and that his ultimate punishment would be far worse than if he stepped forward and told the truth now.

In either case, only someone whom Bonnie trusted— which meant no one from law enforcement—could possibly persuade her that there were valid reasons why Chris was a suspect.

It was Lewis Young's highly unorthodox idea to speak to her lawyer, Wade Smith. With no other attorney in the state would Young even have considered such a gambit. But Wade Smith was said to be different. Not only, in Young's view, "famous," but from all reports, "a gentleman." Young could tell him in good faith that Bonnie was not a target of the investigation. And if he could lay out the details of the case against Chris, maybe Smith could persuade Bonnie that it would be better for her son to admit his role, whatever it might have been.

Young called his supervisor in Raleigh and outlined his plan. The supervisor knew Wade Smith well. He said, "You can trust him with your life. If he tells you something, you can bank on it. He won't shit you. Go talk to him, tell him what you got, and if he agrees up front to try to help you, then he will. I guarantee you he won't tell anybody anything behind your back."

Encouraged, Young approached Mitchell Norton, the Beaufort County district attorney. "It's not standard practice," Young said, "but this is not a standard case." Norton agreed and he himself being aware of the high esteem in which Wade Smith was held, authorized Young to make the contact.

And so, at eleven A.M. on June 1, Lewis Young found himself in Wade Smith's office, as Bonnie had less than five months earlier.

It was an impressive office, no doubt about it. There were books by authors ranging from Chaucer to Thoreau, as well as biographies of subjects as diverse as Winston Churchill and Pete Seeger.

There was a framed newspaper article about Wade, headlined "A Legend in His Prime," in which he was described as "a lawyer who loves life, music and people."

There was a banjo with a plaque on it that read, "This machine surrounds hate and forces it to surrender"—the same inscription found on Pete Seeger's banjo.

And there were photographs: Wade on Annapurna South, Wade with Prince Charles, with Sen. Sam Ervin, with rock musician Bon Jovi. And photographs Wade had taken, such as one of a storm moving across Kenya's Serengeti plain.

But there were also many family pictures: of his parents, of his daughters at various stages of development, of his grandchildren, and one of his wife—dressed as the Great Pumpkin.

It was a warm and somehow comforting office, which seemed to say to a visitor, if life means this much to the man who works here, surely he will care about me.

Lewis Young felt, as had Bonnie, that he had not made a mistake by coming here.

Still, he had a delicate task. He had to explain that he wanted to lay out all his evidence, right there and then, in the hope that Wade would feel it would be in Bonnie's best interests to persuade her son to cooperate. He could do so, however, only if Wade would agree in advance not to share the details with Osteen or Bonnie or Chris.

This request put Wade in a somewhat awkward position. Not only did he represent Bonnie, he'd also brought Osteen into the case. Nonetheless, persuaded that Young was acting in good faith, and with the understanding that there would be no evidence presented that implicated his own client, Wade agreed not to relay any *specifics* to anyone. He did, however, reserve the right to express to Osteen, or to Bonnie, his opinion of the merits of the evidence.

That was just what Young had been hoping for: the chance to show an unbiased, intelligent, and influential third party what they had. So he talked about Lieth's wealth and about Dungeons & Dragons. Then about the fire in the night and the hunting knife. But mostly he talked about the map. He showed Wade the photo of the map. Then he showed him the sample of Chris's printing on the housing card. Then he showed him the map Chris had drawn for the SBI in March.

From all three, the word LAWSON leapt out. Wade did not need an FBI handwriting expert to tell him the printing matched. Nor did anyone have to explain to him just how serious, for Chris, the consequences were.

"What we'd like," Young said, "is for Pritchard to come over to our side. We recognize he didn't do the killing himself. But we believe he's involved and that he knows things he's not telling. You know how it goes, Mr. Smith: whoever comes through the door first. We'd honestly like for that person to be Chris, because, for one thing, we think in the end that would be easier for his mother."

"Nothing about this," Wade said, "has been or is going to be easy for his mother."

For a long time after Lewis Young left, Wade sat alone in his office, not taking any calls. Then he made three of his own.

He called Bill Osteen to say he'd just had a visit from the SBI and without getting into specifics, which he'd promised he wouldn't, all he could say was that from Chris's point of view things were going to get worse fast. Indeed, he said, "Bill, I think you've got to be alert for what you may learn, because I think it is very possible that your client is a prime suspect."

He also apologized. He said, "If I'd had any idea what this was going to turn into, I'd never have called you in the first place."

To Bonnie, he said, in his most reassuring tone, that the SBI had again confirmed that she was not in any way a suspect. That was the good news. The not-so-good news was that they'd done a lot of investigating at NC State because that was where the road seemed to lead.

What road? she kept asking. *What road are they talking about?* They'd always been so vague with her, always hinting, suggesting, implying, but never coming out and talking straight, which was the only kind of talk she understood.

Wade had promised not to tell her about the map, and so he didn't. But he did say that they'd given him the impression that they'd reached a dead end, and that without her help, and without help from Chris, which they were sure he could give, they didn't think they'd ever find the person who'd murdered Lieth.

"If there's anything," Wade said, "anything at all that Chris could tell them that would be helpful, it might be better if he spoke up sooner rather than later."

And then he assured her that whatever happened—whichever way events unfolded—he'd be there for her, as he had been from the start, prepared to offer any help he could.

But what he was already thinking was: *what Bonnie's going to be needing soon is not a lawyer but a psychiatrist. A good one. Someone who can help her prepare for the worst, even without knowing what it is.*

And so his third call was to the best psychiatrist he knew in the area, a woman named Jean Spaulding, who was a member of the faculty at the Duke University medical school and who also had a private practice.

He spoke to her for twenty minutes, not going into any of the specifics of the case against Chris, just saying he had a client who'd been through a terrible physical and emotional ordeal. It seemed likely that the ongoing investigation would produce results that would prove almost unbearably painful for her.

Wade said there was nothing that had to be done yet, but he'd like to have Jean standing by.

19

On June 2, John Taylor headed back to the NC State campus, this time bringing with him the one and only piece of potential evidence found at the crime scene—the green canvas knapsack that Bonnie, Angela, and Chris claimed never to have seen before. He thought it could do no harm to show it around and ask if anyone had ever seen it before, or could remember anyone who'd owned that sort of knapsack.

For the next three days, he trudged around the campus and the off-campus apartments, showing the knapsack to all those to whom he'd already spoken.

"It was disappointing," he said, "There was no reaction from anyone." Daniel Duyk, James Upchurch, Neal Henderson, Vince Hamrick, Karen, Kirsten—no one could identify the knapsack.

But then, on June 6, the day after he'd been shown the green canvas knapsack and had denied ever seeing it before, James Upchurch abruptly cut off the electronic band intended to monitor his whereabouts and disappeared.

Crone and Taylor got back to Raleigh on Friday, June 9. Lewis Young was already there, helping Raleigh and university police search for Upchurch.

Moog could have been a thousand miles away. But as far as they knew, he had very little money. Also, the last time he'd disappeared he hadn't gone far. Hide-and-seek again. Or Dungeons & Dragons. He was a thief or a hero magician, being pursued by agents of the king. Lewis Young half-expected to find him down in the steam tunnels, waving a wooden sword—or pulling a dagger out of his knapsack.

Crone and Taylor hoped to learn more about Upchurch from Neal Henderson, who had not only provided Moog with floor space, but who had known him since they'd gone to high school together back in rural Caswell County.

They met Henderson just off campus, at a Wendy's restaurant where he worked. They arrived at two forty-five P.M., just as the lunch crowd was thinning. The three of them took seats in a plastic booth.

They talked about Dungeons & Dragons for forty-five minutes. Henderson seemed as eager as Chris Pritchard and James Upchurch to talk about Dungeons & Dragons. His face lit up, the pace of his speech quickened, his overall energy level seemed to rise.

Crone suddenly changed the subject. He asked, "If Chris were involved, what would you think?"

"I don't know," Henderson said. "What makes you think Chris was involved?" The question seemed to disturb him.

"Never mind," Crone said pleasantly. Then he asked about Upchurch. Henderson said, "James does know some pretty shady people, and he could find someone to do a murder." He added that Moog had recently seemed worried about "something worse than a probation violation," but that if Upchurch had been involved, it would have been "an uncharacteristic risk."

Chief Crone looked at his wristwatch. It was Friday afternoon. He and his wife were supposed to visit her parents in Mooresville again. He'd told her to meet him at the Apex exit of I-40, just west of Raleigh, at four P.M. If he wasn't there, he'd told her, she should call Lewis Young on his beeper and get further instructions on where and when to meet. The one thing he didn't want was an argument with his wife over his being late, especially if he was just sitting in Wendy's listening to bullshit that would never turn out to be of any use.

It was quarter to four. Even if he left immediately, he realized, he wouldn't get to the Apex exit for at least forty-five minutes. *Oh, shit!* Crone thought. *And I forgot to tell Lewis that my wife would be calling on the beeper.*

"John," he said to Taylor. "Go outside and give the SBI a call and have them get in touch with Lewis to tell him that my wife will be calling him on the beeper. He should tell her to just sit tight. I'm almost done here. I'll be there as fast as I can."

Taylor stepped outside to call from a phone booth in the Wendy's parking lot. He had to wait for ten minutes while Young was located through his pager and called back. Young said there was nothing new to report on the search for Upchurch, but he'd come by and check in with them before they went their separate ways for the weekend.

As Taylor was making the call, John Crone looked back across the booth at this placid, brown-haired, blank-faced young man. *Well, damn,* he thought, *we're not getting anywhere here. I'll try one last hit: give him the old "If you know anything, tell us, because if we find you're withholding anything, it could be trouble."* He'd never been a homicide detective, but Crone had seen enough television and movies to know how it was done.

"So I run that spiel by him," the chief said later. "I say, 'We know *for a fact* that Chris Pritchard is involved!' And I notice again that this scares the crap out of him. So I keep going with it. I say, 'Our attorneys are already talking with his attorneys, and he's just about ready to go down. And when he does go, if anybody knows anything and didn't tell us, they're in trouble.'

"Now Henderson is just sitting there, arms folded, not saying a word. But I'm thinking, just like with a fish, I can feel a nibble. So I yank the rod a little. I say, 'Whoever is found guilty here—of *any* kind of involvement—could get the death penalty. That's the gas chamber here in this state.' "

At that point, Crone paused.

Neal Henderson said, "What if I just gave them advice?"

"I'm thinking," Crone said later, " *'Holy shit! Did I just hear what I thought I heard!'* But outwardly I'm staying calm. You know, chief of police, calm, cool, collected. Got the biggest break of the biggest case of my life unfolding right in the middle of goddamned *Wendy's!* But I've got to sit there like we're talking about the price of bacon cheese-burgers, because I don't want to spook this kid. I'd been hearing so much fantasy bullshit for so long, there's no way I'm sure that this is for real.

"So I said, 'Well, it depends on what kind of advice you gave them. You know, how much you were involved. If it's just a little bit, or if you just know something that could help us, you can clear it up right here and now by telling us.' "

Henderson was still sitting there, arms folded, saying no more.

So Crone continued, "On the other hand, if you're *really* involved, I'd better get the DA up here."

"So he hesitates," Crone said later, "and then he says, in a real calm voice, no inflection, 'I guess you'd better get the DA.' "

"I'm thinking, 'Holy shit! Oh, my God! I don't believe I'm hearing this.' And then I thought, 'Now I *really* don't want to screw this up.' "

"Listen," Crone said to Henderson, "it's a two-hour drive. It's late Friday afternoon. We've got a weekend coming up. Are you really sure it would be worth his while?"

"Let's just say," Henderson replied, still in that eerily unemphatic voice, "I can lay the whole thing out for you. I just want to get it off my mind."

At this point John Taylor stepped back inside Wendy's, having finally made contact with Lewis Young. "I get three steps inside the door," Taylor said, "and here's the chief, coming at me."

"Come back outside a minute," Crone said. Once through the front door, Crone exclaimed, "He says he can lay the whole thing out!"

"Don't fuck with me," Taylor said. "That's bullshit."

"No, it's not. The guy wants the DA! I told him, 'If you know a little bit, tell me. If you know a lot, you'd better tell the DA.' And he says, 'Get the DA.' "

"Shit! Shit!" John Taylor said. "I can't believe it! What did you do, stick your gun into his balls under the table?"

They went back and got Henderson, and the three of them found a seat at one of the outdoor tables, an umbrella shielding them from the late-afternoon sun.

Now that he'd taken the first big step, Henderson wanted to pour out his heart and soul, tell them everything. And this was the news they'd been craving for months. But without a representative from the district attorney's office present, they couldn't let him say a word about it for fear they'd later be accused of violating his right to seek an attorney, remain silent, or whatever other goddamned rights these people had these days.

This time, Crone himself went to the phone and called Young. "We're at Wendy's! He says he can lay it all out! He wants to talk to the DA!" Young called Little Washington and spoke to Keith Mason and said he and his boss, Mitchell Norton, had better get to Raleigh in a hurry because they were sitting with someone who wanted to confess in the Von Stein case.

It took Young only five minutes to get to Wendy's. And then there were four of them, constrained from talking about the one and only subject in which any of them had any interest.

"You've just got to wait, Neal," Lewis Young said. "You've just got to wait until the DA gets here. We want to be sure we do this right." Then Crone's wife called in on the beeper. Crone said, "Better tell her to do some shopping. I'm gonna be a little while."

For the next five hours—Mitchell Norton had been hard to find, and then slow to get moving once he was found, and it got to be nine P.M. before he and Keith Mason arrived in Raleigh—the three investigators sat with Neal Henderson. First, they took him home to change clothes. Then they brought him to the SBI office. Then they all went out to eat.

They went to Captain Stanley's seafood restaurant, choking down french fries and greasy fish and trying desperately not to give in to the temptation to ask Henderson any questions. They also kept declining to answer the one question by which Henderson seemed obsessed: How had they discovered Chris Pritchard's involvement?

As time passed, the three detectives grew more nervous than Henderson. "He was calm," Crone said, "trying to be as cool as he could be. But at any moment he could have just got up and left, and we couldn't have done a thing to stop him. This was strictly voluntary on his part. Not only did we have no evidence on this kid, we hadn't even had any *suspicion*.

"I had no idea what had motivated him to decide to talk in the first place, but I was scared to death the same thing might suddenly unmotivate him. We obviously didn't want him to go anywhere, but he wasn't in custody either. It was really like 'The Odd Couple' for all of us. Every hour that passed I just kept praying harder that that boy wasn't going to change his mind."

Still, it wasn't so bad at the restaurant. At least they were surrounded by other people, and though no one could eat anything, they had the distraction of their food. Only when they got back downtown, to SBI headquarters, and led Henderson into an interrogation room did he look as if he was having second thoughts.

Then, when Mitchell Norton did finally arrive, he announced that he himself would not speak to Henderson for fear of later being called as a witness, which could have prevented him from serving as prosecutor at a trial. He announced that only his assistant, Keith Mason, would speak to Henderson.

"Oh, boy," Crone said later, "I had a hard time coping with *that*. We wait five hours and then the guy won't even talk to him!" Norton remained at the opposite end of a hallway, not even introducing himself, while Crone, Taylor, Young, Mason, and Henderson all filed into an office.

By now it was almost ten P.M. Six hours had passed since Neal Henderson had said he wanted to tell the story of his involvement in the murder of Lieth Von Stein. So far, no one had been willing to let him. Henderson was beginning to look discouraged.

He looked even more discouraged when Keith Mason,

gently and politely, explained that they could not offer any sort of plea bargain, no matter what he might say. They were making no promises. If he wanted to talk, he should talk, but he would have to take it on faith that talking would be in his best interest, because any information given in return for a promise of leniency could be considered less credible by a jury. Of course, a judge might someday take his cooperation into account when imposing a sentence—if matters ever progressed to that point—but there could be no promises made even about that.

Henderson began shaking his head and looking around the room. It didn't happen this way on TV. On TV—which Henderson watched quite a bit of—you came forward and said you wanted to confess and they signed a piece of paper promising to let you off easy, and then you told your story and then the cops were your buddies—or at least they treated you with courtesy—and the whole thing ended, if not happily, at least with no alarming consequences.

It had been one thing talking to John Crone, whom Henderson considered a genuinely nice man, in the comforting din and fluorescent light of Wendy's on a sunny Friday afternoon in late spring.

Now late at night, sitting in some sort of interrogation room that came out of a bad dream somewhere, here was some assistant district attorney they'd suddenly sprung on him—a young lawyer with a manner every bit as pleasant as John Crone's, but a total stranger, nonetheless—telling him that being first to come forward might do him no good at all.

"You could tell," Crone said later, "that he was really getting depressed, upset, in a panic. The very thing I'd been trying to avoid. So I said to the others, 'Why don't you guys go out for a while and let me talk to the boy.' I could see he was getting a little spooked, not just by what Keith had told him, but by the fact we had him outnumbered four to one. And after all, I'd been the one he'd spoken to in the first place."

When the others left, Crone asked Henderson, in the softest tone possible, if he understood why no deals were possible. Glumly, Henderson said yes. Then Crone reminded him that he'd said earlier that he wanted to talk about this to "get it off his mind," and not simply in return for some sort of plea bargain.

"You can still do that, Neal," Crone said. "You can still talk just to make yourself feel better."

Henderson stared at the floor, saying nothing. To Crone, he seemed not simply disappointed or frightened, but despondent.

"I've got a son about your age," Crone said. "And I'll tell you the truth. If you were my own son, I'd tell you to do the right thing. And I think you know what the right thing is."

Henderson, whose own father had left him at an early age—and, like Chris Pritchard's, had kept up only sporadic and unsatisfying contact—looked up at John Crone's concerned and not unkind face.

Later, he would say, "I'd always pictured policemen as guys ten feet tall with blank faces. Chief Crone wasn't like that. He was just a nice man who really seemed to care about me."

Henderson said, "Well, I guess there's still some hope."

"There's always hope," Crone said. "There can't be any promises, but there's always hope."

Henderson nodded.

"Are you going to talk to us?" Crone asked quietly.

Henderson nodded again.

"Well, do me one favor, Neal. No lies. Give us the truth or nothing at all. Will you promise me that?"

"Yes," Henderson said tonelessly, "I'll tell the truth."

Crone paused a moment. There was silence in the room. The two of them could hear muffled voices from the hall.

"Who do you want to tell your story to?" Crone asked.

"You," Henderson said. "You, and I guess John Taylor, too."

Crone stepped into the hallway and informed the others of the situation. Then Crone and Taylor stepped back into the interrogation room and Taylor formally read Henderson his rights and had him sign a form acknowledging that he waived them. Crone then asked, for the record, whether Henderson had been promised any kind of reward or deal, or had been threatened in any way, as an inducement to persuade him to talk. He acknowledged that he hadn't. Crone then asked him to start telling his story. When a question seemed called for, Crone asked it. Taylor took notes.

"The first time through," Crone said, "it was just the bare bones. The whole thing couldn't have taken him five minutes." (John Taylor's notes indicate that this first interview took twenty minutes, but after the day Crone had been through, it was not surprising that his sense of time might have been slightly askew.)

"When he was through, I told him that Lewis Young had been working on this case for almost a year and would undoubtedly need to ask a lot of questions. I asked him if he'd agree to talk to Lewis. He said yes, so I called Lewis in.

"At this point, it was after ten P.M. and all of a sudden it hit me: 'Where the hell is my wife?' I quick called the highway patrol and had them check the Wendy's at the Apex exit, where she had said she'd be waiting, and they went and looked and called back saying there wasn't any Wendy's at the Apex exit of I-40.

"Well, goddamn, I had no idea where she was. I called my in-laws down in Mooresville and asked, 'Have you heard from Cindy? I don't know where she is. Has she called you? Is she there?' First, my father-in-law thought I was joking. Then he goes into a panic. And by then I'm worried as hell, too. The biggest confession of my whole damned career and I can't find my wife.

"Well, it's eleven o'clock before the highway police call back and say, yeah, there is a Wendy's, but it's a mile down the road, not right at the exit. So I say, 'For Christ's sake, go check it, please.' And they called back and said, yeah, she's there, she's been there for hours, and she's pretty upset.

"So I had to have Mitchell Norton, the DA, drive me out there. What the hell, it was the least he could do, he wasn't going to talk to Henderson anyway. We get there and Cindy's on the phone to her parents, crying.

"And Christ, her whole family had been so worried all

night, when we finally get to Mooresville about two o'clock in the morning, she starts crying again and my father-in-law sees this and he's so pissed he doesn't want to talk to me.

"Here, I've just gotten a confession in the biggest case of my life, and it's looking like I'm going to have to sleep in my car."

Young and John Taylor questioned Henderson from ten-twenty until eleven-thirty P.M. Then they broke for half an hour. But Lewis Young was far from finished.

As Crone had said, for almost a year this case had been the primary focus of Young's professional life. Now, here, for the first time, was someone willing and apparently able to tell what had happened.

Young was starved, *famished* for detail. There was no point—no matter how small, no matter how seemingly insignificant—that he was not obsessed with the desire to know more about.

They started up again at midnight. Henderson was tired now, drained both emotionally and physically. But Young was energized, growing stronger as the night wore on, high on the adrenaline rush that comes to good cops when they're finally—for real—breaking open their biggest case.

For most of the hours after midnight, it was just Young and Henderson, one on one. Crone had gone to Mooresville and Taylor was down the hall, conferring with Mitchell Norton and Keith Mason about the next steps to take in light of what Henderson had said.

It was three twenty-five A.M. when Young finally let Henderson go. John Taylor drove him, dazed and weary, to his apartment. They had decided not to arrest Henderson while Upchurch was still at large. "That's all we need," Taylor had said earlier to the district attorney. "Upchurch reads in the paper that we've got Henderson in custody and we'll have to go to Libya to find that boy again."

Henderson had not been a target of the investigation. Upchurch had no reason to fear he would talk.

Exhausted, Henderson had little to say as Taylor drove. But as they pulled up in front of the apartment—with Taylor reminding him not to go anywhere, that they would be back in a few hours to bring him to Little Washington so he could show them just what had happened where—Henderson looked across the front seat and said, as if this could somehow make everything all right:

"You have to understand. I really didn't expect it to happen. When I drove down there, I really didn't expect to see blood."

20

The following Tuesday, June 13, still unaware of even the existence of Neal Henderson, Bonnie drove from Winston-Salem to Washington to work with two friends, making little porcelain dolls that she gave every year to her nieces and nephews at Christmas down in Welcome.

This was so comforting to her: porcelain dolls; decent, quiet, God-fearing people; all the old values with which she'd been brought up. They were like her cats and her rooster. Like poor dumb animals everywhere. They loved and trusted and needed you and would never lie to you or make emotional demands that you could not meet.

If the dark fantasy world of Dungeons & Dragons, or the world of mind-bending drugs or the world of inchoate hatreds or the world of real-life, murderous assaults in the night had an opposite, this was it.

Among the peaceful, Bonnie Von Stein was at peace. If the meek would inherit the earth, she'd own it all—at least judging from surface appearances. The internal toughness, the resilience, the sheer tensile strength of body and mind that had enabled her to survive and move forward—and that would enable her to survive what was to come—were not apparent to the casual observer.

Bonnie was tolerant, not judgmental. What she liked, she did not necessarily expect others to appreciate. What she disapproved of, she recognized others might find of value. She had never sought conflict; indeed, in all her relationships, she had worked to avoid it—even if emotional aridity was the price she sometimes paid.

What she would soon discover was that for such a limitation—if, indeed, that's what it was—few had ever paid a higher price.

On June 14, as Bonnie sat ten miles away, making her porcelain dolls, John Crone, having deduced where to look after listening to Henderson's statement, and disguised as a highway worker so as not to attract undue attention, swung a sickle through high grass and found a baseball bat sunk into the muck of a wooded area fifty yards from the Von Stein house, where Lawson Road met the Market Street Extension.

And on the night of June 15, in the midst of a tumultuous thunderstorm, James Upchurch, carrying a backpack and wearing a Cornell University sweatshirt, and strolling along a street that bordered the NC State campus, was arrested by college police. His hair was bleached a bright blond. By then—on the basis of Henderson's statement—he was wanted not merely for a probation violation but for murder in the first degree.

Chris Pritchard spent that night at his friend Eric Caldwell's house in Winston-Salem. They had, as usual, been out late. The phone rang at eight o'clock the next morning. It was Bonnie. Eric's mother said both boys were still asleep.

Bonnie was calling because she herself had just received a call from Stephanie Mercer, their former next-door neighbor in Little Washington and a close friend of Angela's. Stephanie had said it was on the radio that Chris and someone named James Upchurch had been arrested for the murder of Lieth.

Bonnie had said, "Stephanie, I don't believe Chris has

been arrested. He spent the night at a friend's house. But let me call and be sure he's okay."

So she had called.

Three hours later, she called again. She was a lot more scared than she'd let Stephanie know. This was Bonnie's way. What she really felt, only she had a right to know.

This time she spoke to Eric and told him he'd better wake up Chris, no matter how late they'd been out the night before.

When her son came to the phone, just before noon, she said, "Chris, you need to come home right now because Stephanie called this morning and she heard on the radio that you've just been arrested. We'd better get in touch with Mr. Osteen."

Disheveled, deprived of sleep, and hung over—the same state he'd been in when he'd arrived in Little Washington on the morning of his stepfather's murder—Chris made the twenty-minute drive.

When he arrived, Bonnie fed him a sandwich. The TV was on, minimizing the discomfort that arose from the fact that neither of them was saying anything to the other.

Shortly after noon, Stephanie called back to say it had just been on the twelve o'clock news that arrests had been made and that Chief Crone would be holding a news conference at eight P.M.

At this point, Bonnie called Bill Osteen to report what she'd been told. Osteen said no one from law enforcement had contacted him, and he had long ago learned not to panic as the result of hearing something on the radio or reading it in the paper. He didn't exactly tell Bonnie that there was nothing to worry about, but he himself was unaware of the existence of any evidence that could justify Chris's arrest, so he spoke calmly to her and assured her that he'd be available if anything unexpected was to happen.

Angela was working at Action Video. Returning from a lunch break, she found a message asking her to call her mother. Bonnie explained the situation as well as she could, but being Bonnie, tended to sound a lot less worried than she felt. Angela wanted to know if she should leave work early and come home, but Bonnie said she didn't see any reason to do anything so drastic.

At three-ten P.M. Bonnie looked out the front window and saw four men in suits and ties getting out of two sedans. She recognized Lewis Young, John Taylor, Sturgell, and Newell. She knew this was not a social call.

"Chris," she said, "they're here. I think you need to go to your room and call Mr. Osteen."

When she answered the door, Lewis Young asked, "Can we come in?"

"What do you want?" she said.

"We're here for Chris. Is he at work?"

"No, he's right here at home with me. At this very moment, he's in his bedroom, speaking on the telephone with his attorney. What do you want him for?"

To Lewis Young, Bonnie sounded "stern and irritated," but not out of control.

"Bonnie," Lewis Young said, "we're here to arrest him for murder."

He did not say it unkindly, but there is no kind way that anyone can ever speak such words to a mother about her son. Especially when the charge is the murder of her husband, and the attempted murder of herself.

"Where are you going to take him?"

"First, we're taking him downtown to book him. Then we're going to bring him back to Washington. He'll be spending the night in the Beaufort County jail."

She let the four officers into her living room. "Chris couldn't have done this," she said. "I *know* he couldn't."

"Bonnie," Lewis Young said, "you'd better tell him we're here."

So she went to his bedroom and told him.

As she stepped back into her living room, she asked, "What is your evidence? You still haven't shown me a single shred of evidence."

"We're not going to get into that now," Lewis Young said. "Chris has an attorney. Mr. Osteen can discuss that with the district attorney."

They led Chris from the house without resistance, with

Bonnie following close behind. In the driveway, they put handcuffs on his wrists.

"Can I go back in my room and get my cigarettes?" he said.

"You're not going to smoke in my car," Lewis Young said.

"You be careful with him," Bonnie said. "I don't want to hear about anything happening to him. I've heard too many stories about what happens to people in police custody. I'm holding you personally responsible," she said to Young.

"Bonnie," he said, "nothing will happen to him."

They put Chris in the backseat of one of the cars and started the engine.

"I'll be down there as fast as I can," she called out.

And then, one last time, she told Lewis Young how shameful she thought it was that they could drag an innocent person out of his home in broad daylight and charge him with murder, when they *still* didn't have any evidence and hadn't even considered other suspects.

PART THREE

THE WORST
OF
TRUTHS

JUNE–DECEMBER 1989

21

Under the best of circumstances, the billboard-cluttered drive from Winston-Salem to Little Washington is a four-and-a-half-hour exercise in tedium, relieved, on the interstate west of Raleigh, only by occasional jolts of fright caused by unpredictable, high-speed movements of tractor trailers, and aggravated, from Raleigh east, by the frequent stopping and starting required for passage through such unmemorable towns as Wilson, Farmville, and Greenville.

For Bonnie Von Stein, who left her small house before dawn on Saturday, June 17, bound for the jail in the basement of the Beaufort County Courthouse, where her son was being held on a charge of first-degree murder, the best of circumstances was a condition she doubted she'd ever encounter again.

The day before, determined to maintain her composure, she'd watched the four law-enforcement agents lead Chris away in handcuffs. They'd told her—she was *sure* they'd told her—that they were taking him to the magistrate's office in Winston-Salem.

She'd taken a five-minute shower, thrown on whatever clean clothes were closest at hand, and had rushed downtown.

At the magistrate's office, she was told Chris was not there and had not been there. She was advised to check at the sheriff's office. There, she was told, no, they'd not seen

Chris, either. In a hallway, rattled and anxious, she was approached by a well-dressed, good-looking man in his late fifties.

"Excuse me," he said, "are you Mrs. Von Stein?"

"Yes, I am," she said, "and I'm trying to find my son, who's just been arrested." She thought this might possibly be the sheriff himself.

"Well, I'm Bill Osteen," he said, "and I'm looking for him, too."

And Bonnie realized that, for all the time they'd spent talking on the phone, she'd never before met Bill Osteen in person.

He said he'd just arrived from Greensboro. He quickly located an SBI officer, who told him Chris had already come and gone.

For Bonnie, this news seemed almost as much of a blow as the arrest itself. *It wasn't fair,* she insisted to Osteen. They had *promised* her they wouldn't take him anywhere before she got to the magistrate's office. She was *sure* that was what John Taylor or Lewis Young or both of them had said. This was just another example, she complained, of how they were persecuting her and her family, of how the victims were being treated like criminals.

Osteen was not a man to get sidetracked. He told Bonnie firmly that the details of the arrest were not significant. What did matter was that Chris had now been charged with a crime for which he could face the death penalty. He explained the need for hiring local counsel quickly and asked Bonnie if she had any preference among the attorneys practicing in or near Little Washington. Bonnie said her first choice would be a man named Jim Vosburgh.

The name was vaguely familiar to Osteen. There had been a young lawyer by that name who'd involved himself in a colorful fracas on behalf of the Republican Party during the presidential election of 1960. If this was the same man, at least they'd have someone who didn't back away from a scrap.

Osteen called him. He was the same Vosburgh. He said he'd be pleased to serve as local counsel for Chris Pritchard. Bonnie could meet him at his office the next morning. First, he'd attend the press conference that Chief Crone had scheduled in order to announce the arrests.

Later, Bonnie would remember little of what she'd done or whom she'd talked to for the rest of that day and night.

She had called one friend in Little Washington, a kindergarten teacher named Linda Sloane, who also was active in the Humane Society. She hadn't wanted Linda to learn of the arrest from television or the newspaper. She'd also wanted to assure Linda that Chris had said, "Mom, I didn't do it," and that she was certain he was telling the truth.

She'd also called her father to break the news. He accepted it stoically; not, of course, as if he'd been expecting it in any way, but just as one more of the terrible surprises life could throw at you, and with which you just had to cope. He told her he'd come with her to Little Washington, but Bonnie said no, that first trip to the jail was one she felt she needed to make alone.

That evening, she and Angela had sat together, each attempting to console the other by repeating what an outrage it was, and each assuring the other that it would all be fine in the end because, even if the police can arrest someone without any evidence, they can't keep him in jail forever, and they can't put him on trial, and they certainly couldn't convict him of any crime.

By four A.M., with an optimism she later came to recognize as near-hysterical, Bonnie was packing clothes for herself and for Chris, hoping that somehow, magically—even though he'd been charged with first-degree murder—she'd be able to explain things once and for all to John Crone and Lewis Young, or to some judge who would now have authority in the matter, and they'd apologize for their cruelty and obtuseness and let her have her son back. If that was to happen, she wanted to be sure he'd have clean clothes to wear home.

Bonnie reached Jim Vosburgh's office at ten-thirty Saturday morning. The Washington *Daily News* had already come out, its page-one headline announcing, "Von Stein Stepson Held for Murder." Beneath the headline was a picture of Chris getting out of Lewis Young's car the night before, wearing a baseball cap, an NC State "Wolfpack" T-shirt, shorts, sneakers, and handcuffs.

He looked sixteen years old instead of twenty, and except for the handcuffs, as if he were arriving at summer camp.

Next to his picture was one of Upchurch, wearing a Cornell University sweatshirt. There was, however, nothing else Ivy League about Moog. Staring straight into the camera with an expressionless face, the scraggly hair down almost to his shoulders, he looked more like a member of the Manson cult than he did a North Carolina college student in the post-Reagan era.

All the way from Winston-Salem, panic had mingled with indignation in Bonnie's heart. There was, of course, her fear of the unknown: of the abyss that had suddenly opened beneath her and into which her son had plunged. But there was also resentment at the way Chris had been whisked away from Winston-Salem, and anger that John Crone had been so gloating and boastful and vain as to actually hold a press conference to trumpet news of the arrests, and extreme irritation that someone had tipped off a Washington *Daily News* photographer in time for him to get a picture of Chris arriving handcuffed at the jail. This was just the kind of harassment to which each of them had been subjected from the start.

And *that*, she said to Jim Vosburgh, almost before she sat down, was something she wanted stopped immediately. She'd be calling Wade Smith later in the day, and he, too, would advise her on what to say and do under these new circumstances, but Vosburgh, unlike Wade or Bill Osteen, was right here in Little Washington, around the clock, and he knew personally each of her adversaries in law enforcement. She wanted him to make it unmistakably clear that she would not tolerate one more iota of this sort of emotional and psychological abuse.

Vosburgh looked sympathetically across his desk at her and thought, *Oh, my Lord, this woman has some hard times ahead*.

* * *

Jim Vosburgh ran his one-man law practice out of a long, narrow, storefront office located next to the Mecca Poolroom on Market Street in Little Washington, just around the corner from the courthouse.

He drove to work in a 1986 Ford Ranger pickup truck equipped with CB radio and rifle rack, and conducted the sort of practice in which clients sometimes paid fees not by check but with moonshine liquor, country hams, or dogwood trees ready for planting.

Vosburgh was fifty-six years old, opinionated, voluble, and not infrequently profane. Were you to spend a couple of hours within earshot of him at the bar of the Brentwood Lounge on a Friday or Saturday night—and getting within earshot of Jim Vosburgh was not, generally speaking, hard to do—you'd come away knowing exactly what he thought about almost everyone and everything in Beaufort County. Neither was he a man who had to struggle for words when asked to talk about himself.

He'd grown up in Durham, just a block away from the Duke University campus, where his father had been a professor of chemistry. An adopted child with a very smart older sister, he'd wanted to do something she couldn't do, so for college, he went to The Citadel, the South's premier military academy, and a school that still does not admit women.

After graduation, he'd become an Army paratrooper, meeting his wife at a debutante party while he served as an officer at Fort Bragg. After the Army, he'd gone to law school at the University of North Carolina in Chapel Hill. He had come to Beaufort County, rather than a more invigorating venue, because it was the home of a legendary eastern-shore trial lawyer named John Wilkinson, who had agreed to hire Vosburgh as an associate.

With the passing of the years since he'd last parachuted from a military airplane, Vosburgh's waistline had expanded, his face had reddened, and as a Republican in a Democratic town, his view of local judges, law enforcement personnel, opposing attorneys, and the political establishment had grown, if not exactly jaundiced, at least slightly discolored.

The fact was—even though he sang solo in the choir of

the First United Methodist Church—in some quarters of Little Washington, Jim Vosburgh was viewed with about as much affection as an alligator in a bathtub. He was proud to have earned such animosity, especially from such people as Mitchell Norton, the district attorney: he considered it a mark of his good character and moral worth.

He was also pleased with the location of his office. When working late on a warm spring evening, he could pop into the Mecca for a couple of cold Budweisers and still manage to hear his office phone ring through the wall. Indeed, during his early years in Little Washington, there were months when, if Vosburgh did not actually spend more time in the Mecca than in his office, he certainly won more money shooting pool there than he earned from the practice of law.

Two doors up on the other side of the office was Jimmy's Newsstand and Luncheonette, where a man could not only get a quick sandwich and cup of coffee, but could find out what was *really* going on in the town, and not necessarily by buying the paper.

In the pool hall, the courthouse, and in Jimmy's—the three points that pretty much triangulated Jim Vosburgh's working day—both patrons and staff spent a great deal of time discussing what was *not* in the paper.

Vosburgh, when he was not himself speaking, listened attentively. Thus it was that more than a full day before the warrant was issued, he knew Chris Pritchard would be arrested and charged with first-degree murder in the death of his stepfather.

Vosburgh had been a casual acquaintance of Lieth's. Once, Lieth had come to the office to ask how an individual could incorporate as a business. On a few other occasions, the two had found themselves occupying nearby stools or tables at the Brentwood, the bar and restaurant toward which Washington's professional classes gravitated on their nights out.

His impression had been that Lieth was "quiet and reserved," though Vosburgh's own ebullience would make almost any companion seem so by comparison. Still, Lieth had not been easily approachable. "If you wanted to be his friend," Vosburgh said, "you had to work at it." He, personally, never had; nor, it seemed, had anyone else in Little Washington. Friendship was not something that Lieth had encouraged.

His only other contact with the family arose from a minor automobile accident in which Angela had been involved. She'd been charged with a traffic violation, and Vosburgh had obtained a not-guilty verdict and had later initiated a civil action to recover damages from the driver of the other car.

The younger of his two sons had been in Chris's high school class. The two boys had not been friends, and Jim Vosburgh remembered Chris only as "a very energetic, immature kid, always quick with some smart, facetious remark, but not necessarily insulting."

He had a hard time reconciling the boy he recalled with the charges that were about to be lodged against him.

On the morning of the day Chris was arrested, Vosburgh was called by the district attorney's office and notified that his turn had come in the regular rotation that required all members of the county criminal bar to serve as public defender for someone unable to pay for a private attorney.

Vosburgh was told he was being assigned to represent one James Upchurch of Caswell County, who'd just been charged with the murder of Lieth Von Stein.

A number of thoughts passed quickly through Vosburgh's mind. Being in business for himself, and being also the sole support of his wife and children, one thought was that if he was going to become immersed in something as complex, arduous, and time-consuming as the defense of a client accused of first-degree murder, it would be a far better thing if the client, or the client's family, could pay.

Vosburgh knew that before the day was out Chris Pritchard, too, would be charged with murder. He knew also, from courthouse, newsstand, and poolroom gossip, that Chris's mother, whom he recalled as a bright and pleasant woman, was staunchly maintaining that her son was innocent.

Beyond that, Vosburgh knew that Chris's mother had inherited, by Beaufort County standards, a whopping sum.

And he knew that anyone arrested for the murder of Lieth Von Stein would need a Beaufort County attorney.

He did not know whether he was the first person Bonnie Von Stein would think of in that regard, but he considered it a distinct possibility. He therefore informed the district attorney's office that, due to prior professional involvement with the Von Stein family, it would be a conflict of interest for him to serve as public defender for someone accused of murdering Lieth Von Stein.

Thus, the cup was passed to the next name on the list, while Vosburgh waited for the phone to ring.

The call came at five P.M. The voice on the other end asked, "Is this the Jim Vosburgh of Madison County fame?"

Indeed he was.

On election day of 1960, while still a law student and an active member of the state's Young Republicans' Club, Vosburgh had traveled to the Tennessee border, to *extremely* rural (and Democratic) Madison County, to monitor voting. He'd been told that two years earlier, in the Madison County community of Upper Spring Creek, which had only three hundred registered voters, more than five hundred votes had been cast, none for a Republican. Vosburgh believed that the interests of Richard Nixon would not be well served by having the same feat repeated.

Details had become a little hazy through frequent retelling, but the main point was that Vosburgh had seen some things he hadn't cared for, and his method for trying to deal with them had led the county sheriff, a staunch Democrat, to arrest him on a charge of impersonating an FBI agent.

Eventually, the charges were dropped, but publicity surrounding the incident brought Vosburgh's name to the attention of a number of prominent state Republicans, including a young state legislator from Greensboro named William Osteen.

Now, almost thirty years later, it was Osteen on the phone. He said he'd been representing Chris Pritchard since January, even though no charges had been filed. Vosburgh said he'd be glad to come aboard.

That night, he attended the press conference John Crone held at the Washington police station. He lumbered into the crowded lobby, which was ablaze with television lighting, and saw Crone looking positively military in a freshly pressed uniform and basking in the glow of the attention. Never before in Crone's career had he had occasion to make so dramatic an announcement.

He stated that Christopher Wayne Pritchard, formerly of Washington and currently a resident of Winston-Salem, and James Bartlett Upchurch III, of Blanch, Caswell County, had been arrested and charged with first-degree murder in the killing of Lieth Von Stein.

He said authorities had "testimony from a witness who told us exactly what happened," and he added that a third suspect, who was not a resident of Washington, would soon be taken into custody.

He would not say if the witness and the third suspect were the same person, but stressed that neither Bonnie Von Stein nor her daughter, Angela, were implicated.

The chief added that the first break in the case had come two months earlier and had centered around Pritchard. He said the major break had come just two days ago, but he would answer no questions regarding details of the investigation, nor would he offer any motive.

He did say, however, that Pritchard, who had spoken with investigators on several occasions, had stopped talking about six weeks earlier, at the same time he'd hired a Greensboro lawyer named William Osteen.

At this, Vosburgh, who'd been taking notes as fast as the reporters, began to ask questions.

He hasn't tried to flee, has he? Vosburgh asked. *He's been available for eleven months and he hasn't tried to run away, isn't that right?*

John Crone had been in Washington long enough to know Vosburgh, and he said he wouldn't answer any of Vosburgh's questions, no matter how loudly he asked them, because Vosburgh was a lawyer, not a reporter.

So Vosburgh decided that if Crone wouldn't answer his question, he'd do it himself—forcefully and repeatedly and in the affirmative. Identifying himself as Pritchard's local counsel, hired only that afternoon, Vosburgh told the assembled press that Pritchard had, in fact, been available to investigators for eleven months, had been living in Winston-Salem with his mother, and had never tried to flee, nor had he ever refused to cooperate with investigators.

Vosburgh then left the press conference, climbed into his pickup truck, and drove the few blocks from the police station to the Beaufort County jail, which was in the basement of the courthouse.

Vosburgh saw Chris Pritchard for the first time at ten P.M. and as had Bill Osteen some months earlier, formed an immediate negative impression.

"Most kids of his age and background," Vosburgh said later, "when they see the inside of a jail for the first time, it's culture shock. But Chris was walking around in the orange jumpsuit they'd given him acting like he was in the Syracuse University locker room. I got the feeling he thought he looked kind of cute. He certainly didn't seem very concerned. He didn't even ask me any questions. It was as if he'd been thrown in a drunk tank after being rowdy at a party—not like he was being held without bond for first-degree murder."

For that first night, Vosburgh was willing to assume that Chris's lack of appropriate reaction might be due to the very shock of having been arrested. He figured the next day, after reality had set in—a reality that included the possibility of the death penalty—the orange jumpsuit would not seem quite so cute.

Now, on Saturday morning, Vosburgh spent half an hour with Bonnie in his office, offering the appropriate commiserations, outlining the likely timing and nature of future legal proceedings, and listening to her litany of complaints about the way the Washington police and the SBI had conducted themselves.

As he spoke to her, Vosburgh—like Bill Osteen the day before—was struck by how Bonnie seemed to be focusing on the periphery rather than the core of her son's predicament. He had seen this behavior before. Often, in the first hours or days following an arrest on serious charges, the person arrested, or his family or loved ones, did tend to fixate on the edges of the picture.

What lay at the center was simply too dire to view straight on. That changed with time, Vosburgh had found, as it became apparent where energy needed to be directed. And it seemed to him that Bonnie, being both intelligent and resilient, would soon stop fretting about what investigators had or had not done in the past and would start to worry about what the district attorney might do in the future.

Because it was not during regular visiting hours, Vosburgh, invoking his privileges as attorney, accompanied Bonnie to the jail at noon for her first talk with Chris.

Bonnie seemed most worried about what might have happened to her son overnight. How were they treating him? How frightened was he? What sort of dangerous criminals had he been locked up with? What would happen next? The poor, poor boy, she kept saying.

Chris did not rise to greet them. Instead, he looked up at his mother and asked, "Did you bring me any cigarettes?"

"I don't know about you, Chris," Vosburgh said, "but I think your mom here sure is in need of a hug."

Chris glared at the lawyer and still didn't move. Raising his voice at least one notch, and maybe two, Vosburgh leaned over his new client and said, "Goddamnit, son, she's your mom. For the past twenty-four hours she's been worried so sick about you that she hasn't been able to sleep or eat. Now get the hell up and give her a hug!"

He did stand then and stepped toward Bonnie and gave her a brief embrace. Then he slumped back again in his chair. "What about magazines?" he asked her. "Did you bring me anything to read? And I'm going to need change for the vending machines."

That afternoon, Bonnie went alone to her house on Lawson Road. She carried a camera. She was determined to document everything she could that had to do with the failure of the police and SBI to preserve the crime scene. So great were her shock and anger at what had happened in the past twenty-four hours that for once logic failed her.

She went about the house, eleven months after the murder, taking photographs that she felt could serve as evidence of police incompetence. Then, in desperation, she went to a telephone and called Wade Smith. Though he had often told her to feel free to do so at any time, it was the first time she'd ever called him at his home.

She said she wanted to go public with what she had. She wanted to correct the misinformation that, for months, had been disseminated in the newspapers. She wanted to set the record straight once and for all. The district attorney had already begun to prosecute his case in the media, and she felt the need to fight back.

In his most soothing manner, Wade said, "Bonnie, let's not make a decision on that until we know what the evidence is. We would be flying blind at this point."

"But I've got to say something. I *know* my son is innocent."

Then, aware of how much more he knew than she did, as a result of his June 1 talk with Lewis Young, Wade felt the need to say more. He did not tell her what he knew because he did not think she was yet emotionally prepared to hear it.

So he said, "Bonnie, it's all right. You can believe that as long as you *want* to believe it. But be prepared. There may come a day when you'll have to accept a truth. You are flying over very, very barren territory, Bonnie—pack a lunch. You are flying over territory where there is no food, no shelter, no water. Because you are flying over this horrible landscape, pack a lunch."

If she had asked him, at that moment, what he was talking about, he would have told her. If she had asked, it would have indicated that she was ready to hear. But Bonnie did not ask.

But the data was out there and would not go away. And so, as soon as he finished talking to Bonnie, he called psychiatrist Jean Spaulding and said it would not be long now before she'd be hearing from Mrs. Von Stein.

As Bonnie was speaking to Wade, Jim Vosburgh was back in the county jail, having a further talk with his new client, asking, as he put it later, "some very detailed questions, based on some of the things I'd been hearing. His answers were vague and evasive. That, combined with this goddamned *attitude* of his, really began to bother me. Everything about him seemed wrong."

Vosburgh laid out the evidence as he had come to understand it. While the details of Neal Henderson's statement were being closely guarded by the district attorney's office, Vosburgh knew that some damning allegations had been made. He also knew about the map that had been found at the fire. He told Chris he thought there were serious problems.

"Until then," Vosburgh said later, "he really seemed to think there was no basis for any case against him. It was like he'd really come to believe that the whole thing was a politically motivated frame-up, and that he'd have no trouble beating it.

"But even when I told him, he just shrugged. I couldn't get through that detachment." This boy, Vosburgh kept telling himself, was in a *world* of trouble. Yet he seemed totally uninterested in his plight, or in what it could lead to, which, in his case, was the gas chamber.

22

On Monday morning, June 19, having spent a fretful night at the Holiday Inn, Bonnie went to district court for what she expected to be the hearing that could lead to Chris's release on bond.

While sitting in the courtroom with Angela and Angela's friend Stephanie Mercer, waiting for the proceedings to begin, she experienced an eerie sensation, as if, she later said, "someone was staring holes in the back of my head."

Turning, she saw a man seated a few rows back, gazing straight at her. His hair was tied in a long ponytail and he wore a collarless shirt of the type favored by hospital orderlies. But that wasn't what upset her so. It was that he *was bulky across the shoulders and seemed to have almost no neck*.

This was the first time since the night she'd been attacked that Bonnie had seen a person whose body had the same irregular shape as that of the person who'd tried to kill her. Jim Vosburgh, seated next to her, saw her grow pale and break out in a sweat. He had no idea what was happening, but thought she was about to faint.

The sight of this man so distressed Bonnie that she rose from her seat and left the courtroom, feeling chilled and nauseated. *Those bulky shoulders, the way the head rose straight up from them, almost as if there were no neck:* that was exactly the impression she'd had of her assailant as she'd lain on the floor of her bedroom, looking up.

It turned out that this man was a Little Washington resident who'd come to court on unrelated business and was in no way connected to the murder.

It turned out, also, that there was no bond hearing. Mitchell Norton, the district attorney, succeeded in having the proceeding transferred to Superior Court, which meant there would be a delay of at least a few days.

Vosburgh told Bonnie that the authorities intended to hold Chris without bond as long as possible, in the hope that he would break down and confess.

"He can't *break*," Bonnie replied. "He's innocent."

That night, John Taylor was eating at a Little Washington restaurant called the Stage House, which, while not exactly a haven for gourmets, at least had the advantage of dim lighting.

Several tables away, Angela was seated with Donna Brady and her other friends Laura and Stephanie, and Stephanie's brother, Glen.

Just as Taylor was preparing to leave, Angela walked

over to his table. Grinning, she handed him a red paper place mat on which a note had been written:

> John—Hi! Just wanted you to know everyone (except Glen) over here thinks you are mighty sexy (nice tight ass). It's ashamed [*sic*] that you are a married man, or can you make an exception?———Just may be an experience you will never forget. I realize we are being childish, but—
>
> Desiring you!
> Stephanie, Donna, Angela, Laura.

Taylor folded the place mat and put it in his pocket, smiling at the girls as he left. It was, he reflected, a peculiar message to receive from the sister of someone he'd just arrested on a charge of first-degree murder.

Later, Angela would say she'd only delivered it as a joke, "just fooling around," because she considered John Taylor—whatever his official role—to be almost a friend.

But it was also true that since the day Chris's printing had been found to match the printing on the map, Angela had been relegated to the role of minor curiosity. Since the day of Neal Henderson's statement, investigators had given her no thought whatsoever. And since Chris's arrest, even Bonnie had paid Angela little mind. It may have been that she was just hungry for attention.

On Tuesday, June 20, Bill Osteen and his son arrived from Greensboro, bringing with them a tough and experienced private investigator named Tom Brereton.

Brereton was a heavyset New York City Irish Catholic who had graduated from Fordham University and had spent twenty years in the FBI. In the opinion of both Osteen and Wade Smith, he was as good a private detective as there was in the state. He also had a personality that made Jim Vosburgh's seem positively demure.

The two Osteens, Vosburgh, and Brereton met with Chris that afternoon. Vosburgh, who had seen Chris at least twice a day since his arrest, was now sufficiently uneasy about his new client's demeanor to advise Osteen, "There's something really weird about this guy."

"You don't need to tell me, Vos," Osteen replied. "I haven't liked him from the start."

The meeting with Chris lasted most of the afternoon. Later, Bill Osteen would recall it as one of the most disturbing he'd ever had with a client. "Nothing was right," Osteen said later. "No reaction I saw was proper."

The sheriff had permitted Osteen and his group to meet with Chris in a vacant office adjacent to the jail. He'd come in wearing leg shackles and complaining that they were hard to walk in, but seeming not really bothered by them; indeed, almost *proud* that he was such a dangerous character that this sort of restraint was required.

He also wore thongs on his feet, which he kicked off as soon as he seated himself. Then he assumed what Vosburgh, at least, was beginning to recognize as his characteristic fetal position: knees up to his chin, arms clasped around his legs.

Bonnie was present for the start of the meeting, but Chris's only greeting to her was, as usual, to comment irritably that he needed more cigarettes and that she *still* didn't seem to realize just how many quarters were required for the vending machines.

"He didn't even say, 'Hello, Mom,' " Osteen recalled later. "Just, 'What did you bring me? Where are my cigarettes?' She could have been the canteen manager, or one of the jailers. Finally, I had to say, 'Chris, this is your mother. Say hello.' "

"He wouldn't look at her," Tom Brereton said later. "Even before he opened his mouth, his body language told me something was very wrong. This was his mother, and he'd been accused of trying to have her murdered. You would think, every chance he had, he'd be jumping up to tell her, 'I didn't do it.' Instead, he acted like he wished she'd go away."

Even more troubling to those who witnessed it—Bonnie left early, so Chris could have time alone with his lawyers—was the change in demeanor and energy level triggered by mention of Dungeons & Dragons.

As soon as Tom Brereton asked his first blunt question—
"What the hell is this Dungeons and Dragons bullshit
all about?"—Chris's sullenness and insouciance dropped
away, and an entirely different young man—excited,
engaged, capable of vivid and detailed description—was
revealed.

"It was like flipping a switch," Brereton said later. "You
pressed the D and D button and you got a whole new person. It was like there were two separate sides to his personality. Actually, it was like there were two separate
personalities."

No one present in the room that afternoon—or at any
other time when the subject of Dungeons & Dragons was
raised with Chris—ever lost his sense of amazement at the
totality of the transformation. Bill Osteen termed it "unbelievable." Osteen's son said he was "shocked."

When Chris began talking about Dungeons & Dragons,
the outside world and all its inhabitants seemed simply to
vanish into some black hole deep within his psyche.
Indeed, it was as if the outside world and all its inhabitants
were not real at all, but only a dull and pallid facsimile
of the *true* reality, which was the world of Dungeons &
Dragons.

In this world, the scrawny, drug-abusing, sexually unfulfilled, and academically underachieving Chris Pritchard was
magically metamorphosed into a vibrant and commanding
figure, and his affect when he spoke about it was so completely contrary to that which he displayed under any and
all other circumstances that, to the three lawyers and the
private detective, it was almost as if he'd been possessed
by a spirit or were under some sort of spell.

"It set me reeling," Osteen said. "What in the world
was going on here? To these kids, or to Chris at least, this
wasn't just a game played with invented characters. They
were the characters."

Driving back to Greensboro that night, Bill Osteen took
his thinking about Dungeons & Dragons a step further.

"Are we dealing with a man who knows what he's
doing?" he asked his son and Tom Brereton. "Or is he

219

under some sort of spell? Or, since everything in that game seems to be built around the effort to deceive, could this whole thing be some kind of set-up? Someone else setting him up to get caught?''

Was such a thing possible? Osteen didn't know, and neither his son nor Brereton could help him out. But all three now had to consider the possibility that—quite by accident—they had stumbled into a carefully shrouded world of the occult.

For Bonnie, the weeks following Chris's arrest brought even greater frustration, exhaustion, and stress than the weeks before.

With Angela still to care for in Winston-Salem—''poor little Angela,'' she would say later, ''so horribly neglected through all of this''—Bonnie had taken to commuting between her house there and the Holiday Inn in Little Washington.

She stayed at the Holiday Inn because she could never again stay in the house on Lawson Road, and because, even having lived in the town for seven years, she knew no one in whose home she would feel comfortable as an overnight guest.

There were few nights when she got to bed before midnight, and even fewer mornings when she was not up by four A.M. Day after day, she would settle herself behind the wheel of her Buick Reatta and set off across her own private wasteland. She'd once thought that the days when she'd had to do this with Lieth—drive back and forth between Little Washington and Winston-Salem as his parents had sickened and died—had been among the darkest of her life. But how much she would have given, through late June and July of 1989, to have back even one of those days. How hard life had seemed then, but how easy it really had been. She'd had Lieth then, and she'd had a son who was not charged with murder.

High summer brings to North Carolina a formidable density of heat and humidity: a sticky, cloying, stifling haze that presses down upon the land and its inhabitants, soaking clothes and skin with sweat at the same time it sucks the spirit dry. Bonnie felt utterly and abjectly alone. There was Wade Smith, of course, always ready to offer guidance and comfort; and there was her family, but even in her relations with them, as since her childhood, something firm and unbreachable in her makeup limited intimacy. Only her father, with his quiet wisdom and enduring strength, seemed able to reach out and offer consolation.

By the end of the month, with Chris still in jail, Bonnie recognized she could no longer pass over this barren ground unaided.

And so, at four-thirty on the afternoon of Friday, June 30, she drove the hour and a half from Winston-Salem to the tall, green, needle-topped structure called University Tower that rises from the outskirts of Durham like a lost building from the Emerald City. Bonnie had her first appointment with a psychiatrist.

Jean Gaillard Spaulding was forty-two years old. She was part black, part Caucasian, part Native American. She had long black hair, light brown skin, large round eyes through which she looked both attentively and almost tenderly at those who sat before her, as quick and warm a smile as one was ever likely to find from a psychiatrist, and as fine a sense of clothing fashion as any woman in North Carolina.

Her great-great-grandmother had been a slave in Charleston, bearing four children by the white man who'd acquired her at the age of fourteen. Born in Birmingham, Alabama, Jean Spaulding was, for most of the first five years of her life, separated from her mother, who was confined to a tuberculosis sanitorium in Illinois. Later, Jean was raised in a middle-class section of Detroit.

She graduated cum laude from Barnard College at Columbia University in 1968. She also participated actively in the antiwar riots of that spring, occupying a university building before being driven from it by police. (Her activism had started in ninth grade, when her family had picketed a Woolworth's in Detroit.)

After Columbia, turning down scholarship offers from many other medical schools because she'd just married a man from Durham, she accepted one from Duke, thus becoming the first black woman (and only the third black person) to attend the Duke University School of Medicine.

There were some unpleasant moments, such as the September she returned to school pregnant and a professor said, "You must have been rolling around in a watermelon patch all summer," but she graduated in 1972, despite going into labor during an oral exam. (She gritted her teeth through her contractions and got an A.)

Later, after working in a Veteran's Administration hospital in order to help those who'd actually suffered in the war she'd marched against, Jean Spaulding went back to the Duke University Medical Center for her residency in child psychiatry.

As attractive as she was intelligent, she had married into one of North Carolina's most respected and successful black families. Her husband, Kenneth Spaulding, was a lawyer who had served in the North Carolina state legislature, as had Bill Osteen and Wade Smith.

In addition to her private practice, Dr. Spaulding taught at the Duke University School of Medicine and was a frequent public speaker on the subjects of adolescent depression and teenage suicide. She also cared deeply about her patients and did not stop thinking about them, or feeling for them, even when her workday came to a close. Her warmth and empathy were instinctive, spontaneous, and genuine.

Of all the choices he'd made in his life, selecting Jean Spaulding to try to help Bonnie had been one of those in which Wade Smith had his greatest confidence.

Based on what Wade had told her, Dr. Spaulding viewed her new patient as afflicted by "multiple traumas" or "wearing a number of different hats."

She'd been the victim of a vicious attack, in which she'd been badly hurt. She was the widow of a murdered man and mother to a son charged with the murder. Then there was the unresolved question of Angela, her other child, who, while not accused of a crime, was still viewed with suspicion by some. Lastly, Bonnie herself had been a suspect.

*   *   *

At their first meeting, Dr. Spaulding asked Bonnie to talk about herself and her personal history, deliberately leaving the question open-ended. It soon became apparent that with Bonnie, even more than with many patients, it was not just what was said but what was omitted—not what was emphasized, but what was glossed over—that offered the windows through which insights could be gleaned.

Bonnie started by saying that in 1966 she'd gotten married. (In fact, it had been in 1967.) She did not mention her first husband's name, referring to him only as "a man from Lexington whom I knew for eight or ten months." She said he was much younger than she was, and "very immature."

She mentioned the births of Chris and Angela and then said that in July of 1971 (in fact, it had been 1972) her husband had decided to "move out" and "leave the marriage." She said that after the divorce she kept up payments on both of their cars because she "did not want to hurt her credit rating." She said her ex-husband offered very little in the way of child support, and she stressed that the children had been *her* responsibility.

She talked about meeting Lieth, about how attractive she had found him, about how he had seemed "unattainable." In describing their courtship, she became quite demure, almost to the point of blushing when she talked of how they'd started spending weekends together. She talked in great detail about the progression of the relationship, obviously more comfortable reminiscing about a happier time than confronting any one of her traumas. The marriage, the move to Washington, her job history: it came to seem that Bonnie would get through the entire session without even alluding to the events that had brought it about in the first place.

Eventually, to "nudge" her, Jean Spaulding asked what had happened to Lieth. Bonnie said he'd been "killed." That was it. Not murdered, "killed." "She could have been describing how he'd been killed in an auto accident," Dr. Spaulding said. Rushing right past the event, Bonnie went on to emphasize that on January 1 of the following year, Lieth would have been "fully vested" in his company's pension plan. Then she described Lieth's family history—

his parents, his uncle, the stresses caused by their ill-nesses—but always, in Dr. Spaulding's view, going "around the edges . . . leading up and then going away."

Dr. Spaulding asked Bonnie about her own parents. She said her father had been a bricklayer who'd had to retire when high blood pressure caused nausea and sweats. She described him as a "very strong man." Her mother, on the other hand, had been a "tearful" and "highly opinionated" person when Bonnie was growing up. It seemed obvious to Jean Spaulding that Bonnie felt much closer to her father than to her mother, even describing herself as being more like him in her ability to "get things done." She said neither tobacco nor alcohol had been permitted inside her home, and that she'd led a "secluded and mild" life while growing up.

Then Bonnie described each step of her life after leaving home, going in a big circle that led back to her marriage to Lieth. "There was always a lot of warmth from Bonnie, tremendous affect, whenever she talked about Lieth," Dr. Spaulding later recalled. "She got much closer to tears when talking about him." Dr. Spaulding asked her to say more about her children. She said her son had graduated from high school two years earlier. Quickly, Bonnie moved to the subject of Chris's arrest. What seemed to upset her most was that John Crone had held a press conference. "Agitated" was the word Dr. Spaulding used to describe Bonnie as she talked about the "injustice" of the way the arrest had been handled. Like Osteen and Vosburgh before her, Jean Spaulding was struck by how much more dis-tressed Bonnie seemed about the process of the arrest than by what the arrest itself might imply.

The session ended with Bonnie still not having directly stated that Lieth had been murdered, or that Chris had been charged with the crime.

That same afternoon, Tom Brereton turned up at the small house on the south side of Winston-Salem in which Bonnie and Angela were living.

Walking toward the front door, he was afraid he'd come to the wrong place. This ought to have been the home of

Lieth Von Stein's parents, who had left their son more than a million dollars, money that now belonged to Bonnie. He found it hard to comprehend that, given such wealth, she could choose to live in a house so small and plain. And why had Von Stein's parents, with all their money, lived like this?

The one-story house was so unimposing and the neighborhood so nondescript that Brereton kept looking at the piece of paper on which he'd written the address, concerned that he'd made a mistake. He himself, even with four daughters to raise on an FBI agent's salary, lived in a fine brick colonial on a shady street in a section of Greensboro that, compared to this, looked like the grounds of Buckingham Palace.

He rang the bell and Angela answered. He introduced himself, explaining that he was the investigator who'd been hired by Mr. Osteen to work on Chris's defense. She looked at him as if she didn't know what he was talking about or if she knew, didn't care. She said her mother wasn't home. He said he wasn't looking for her mother. He was there to copy some materials that Chris had stored in his computer.

Specifically, he said, he wanted the description and biography of the Dungeons & Dragons character Chris had been developing through many months of playing the game. Angela looked at him as if he were speaking a foreign language.

It was not Tom Brereton's style, when working a case, to spend time on unnecessary pleasantries, but this girl looked so listless and befuddled that he felt compelled to say *something* that would establish some human connection. So he said it sure was hot out.

In response to this innocuous remark, Angela's blank expression vanished, replaced—quite suddenly and remarkably—by a look of bitterness. She said, yeah, it sure was hot, but it wouldn't be so bad if her mother weren't so cheap that she wouldn't even put air-conditioning in the house. "Even the cats live better than we do," Angela said.

Now it was Brereton's turn to look confused. Angela

gestured toward the backyard. "My mother built a house out there for the cats," Angela said. "She air-conditioned *that,* but we're only people, so we have to sit here and sweat."

Later, when Brereton described the events of the day to Bill Osteen, he said he thought they ought to pay attention to Angela's attitude. First, they'd seen Chris treat his mother as if she were some sort of incompetent servant. Now, even to a complete stranger such as Brereton, Angela had spoken of Bonnie with powerful resentment.

To Tom Brereton's well-worn eye, something was distinctly not right in the chemistry of what remained of this family. The thought he could not escape was that maybe both of Bonnie's children were disappointed by the fact that she was still alive.

Alive, and in control of $2 million, and—except for her willingness to pay for Chris's defense—apparently not eager to spend any of it to upgrade either her own or her children's standard of living.

What these kids were angry about, Brereton suggested, was that neither of them had been given what they might have considered rightfully theirs. Sure, Chris's friends at NC State thought his mother a soft touch when it came to money, but as far as *real* money went, or any significant change in lifestyle arising from the fact that Lieth had become a millionaire—there had been none.

Where were the new cars? Where were the vacations in the Caribbean? Where were the new wardrobes, or for that matter, where was the new house? There was nothing wrong with Smallwood, or with their house on Lawson Road, but nobody would call it luxurious.

Forget right or wrong, forget whether or not, in Lieth's mind or in Bonnie's mind, the children had done anything to earn it. During the first six or seven years of their lives, there were nights when those kids had gone to bed without enough food in their bellies, and even when they did eat, too often it was beans or macaroni. The way they saw it— or might have seen it—once a million dollars came their way, at least some of it should have been *spent,* not squirreled away in some damned trust fund or used to buy a bunch of stocks and bonds that none of your friends would ever know you owned.

Lieth had been so stingy that there might as well not even have been an inheritance. And even now, Brereton said, the kids had gotten less out of the deal than had the cats.

The day's real find, however—or, at least, it would have been a find if Brereton had still been working in law enforcement—had come from Chris Pritchard's computer. It was the biography and description of Chris's own Dungeons & Dragons character, to whom he'd given the name Dimson the Wanderer.

To Brereton—who had come into the case knowing no more about Dungeons & Dragons than had Osteen, and who had to keep reminding himself that he was supposed to be working to *help* Chris Pritchard, not to hang him—what popped up on the computer screen when he hit the keys Chris told him to was not merely bizarre, it was chilling.

There was, first, a section titled "Background Information," which said:

Dimson began her life in the underworld of the Drow. But because of an unfortunate accident involving a cave-in, she was doomed to live the life of an upper-worlder.

She was found by a family of thieves and she was nurtured and taught the ways of the upper-world. She was hidden well by the family so that she would not be ostracized and was taught the ancient art of the disguise. She swore that no other living soul would ever see her as she truly was.

She became a master at disguise to the degree that she could appear to be any kind of elf, male or female. She does not talk much as she does not want anybody to be able to tell if she is female or not. The times that she does allow others to know that she is female gives her the advantage because they will think her weak. She does not like physical combat but she is definitely able to hold her own. She prefers to attack the enemy from behind to optimize her backstabbing ability. She also does not like to be cornered, for when she is she goes into a fighting frenzy and will only stop when her opponents are dead.

Her only disadvantage comes during daylight hours. Unless there is heavy cloud cover, she will not travel freely in daylight. No one living in the upper-world has ever seen her without a disguise on, though she prefers to wear her cloak. If anyone dares to remove her hood when she is not disguised, they are subject to a nasty and painful death. If they escape from her, they should fear her revenge, for she has many names.

She has no friends and she does not care to have them. She prefers solitude and quiet when she is not out looking for a way to destroy all thieves' guilds.

If either Brereton or Osteen had been a psychologist skilled at interpreting the underlying meaning of a fantasy, he might have been intrigued by any number of elements contained in this description of Dimson.

There was the confusion of sexual identity, the "nasty and painful death" that would befall anyone who penetrated her disguise; the "unfortunate accident involving a cave-in" in her early years, which could be seen as a reference to the collapse of young Chris's life when his real father left; of her being "doomed to live the life of an upper-worlder," and her determination that "no other living soul would ever see her as she truly was."

Even the name itself: Dimson. Dim-son. Dim son. Was that not what Lieth had made it clear he considered Chris to be? Or, at least, was that not how Chris had come to perceive himself?

Of course, neither Brereton nor Osteen was a psychologist. Like Bonnie, they tended more toward direct, literal interpretations of data. And on that level, they saw something that they did not like at all.

There was a section in the description of Dimson entitled "Special abilities and spells." A lot of it was jargon that would have meaning only in the context of the game. Such things as, "may fight with two weapons without penalty . . . infravision to 12" . . . detect secret doors . . . can surprise on a 1–4 chance if well ahead of the party and 1–2 if a door must be opened: can only be surprised on a 1 in 8." Weird things, the kind of stuff that, as far as Brereton and Osteen were concerned, a healthy and well-balanced young man would not be engaged by.

But one Dimson trait virtually leaped off the page. Included in the "special ability" category was the capacity to tell an "undetectable lie."

23

Bonnie saw Jean Spaulding again on July 7. The psychiatrist began this session by asking Bonnie how what had happened so far had affected *her*. Bonnie said, very calmly, that, well, the previous November and December had been difficult. She'd been afraid to leave her house after dark. She'd had a "fear of nightfall." But then she had simply made herself go out. She said she'd used her father's philosophy of how to get through things, which was: "You get through by getting through." She had decided to confront her fear, and once she'd done so, things had improved.

It was an incomplete answer to a very small part of a very big question, but Dr. Spaulding didn't press. Already, she had learned that Bonnie would tell you what she wanted to. She would try to be scrupulous about the accuracy of what she said, but she was not inclined to plumb emotional depths.

During the fall, Bonnie continued, "they"—meaning law enforcement authorities—had, for a time, considered her a suspect. Here, Dr. Spaulding got a first glimpse of something that hinted at irritation, but wondered, "Where was the anger?'' Her husband had been killed, she'd nearly died herself, then she'd learned that *she* was a suspect? One might have expected a stronger emotion than irritation.

Next, Bonnie described her own injuries. In talking about them, Bonnie "skipped over *all* emotion." Nonetheless, the description was chilling. To Jean Spaulding, it was also reassuring. This was the first time she had heard the full extent of Bonnie's wounds, and the description laid to rest any concerns that she may have had about Bonnie's possible involvement in the crime.

Bonnie explained how, after she'd gone to her parents' house, she'd had problems with fluid in her chest and the doctor had wanted to put her back in the hospital. Bonnie had adamantly refused. Now, she was quite blunt in stating that her forcefulness had arisen from "fear." She had been terrified that something awful would happen to her if she went back. She said she knew it wasn't rational—and for Bonnie, this was a considerable admission—but she'd had a deep fear that she would *die* if she was readmitted to the hospital.

"Hearing her say this," Dr. Spaulding observed later, "convinced me of the level of trauma she'd been through."

Then Bonnie began talking about how someone named Lewis Young had decided back in August that Chris was guilty, and that there had been a map and she'd asked Chris, but he'd said he didn't remember drawing any map.

It was coming out in a rush now and was quite confusing to Dr. Spaulding, who was not yet familiar with the details of the case. She interrupted with a question about the map. Bonnie explained that, for months, she'd been hearing rumors that a partially burned map, supposedly drawn by Chris, had been found somewhere near the scene, along with bloodstained clothes and a knife. More recently, she'd been told that the boy who confessed had said he'd been only the driver.

Bonnie still wasn't sure whether she'd seen one, or maybe two intruders in her room, but she was sure that the attacker was "not my son."

She emphasized this: "not—my—son."

Angela had been asleep down the hall, and her son had been asleep in his dorm in Raleigh.

She mentioned regaining consciousness in the hospital and seeing Chris—who she again referred to not by name but as "my son"—standing at her bedside, holding her hand and crying.

Then she described her injuries again. She talked of frontal blows, the knife wound in her chest, losing two pints of blood. She said she'd had "memory deficits" and would find herself lapsing into "daydreamlike states."

As the session drew to a close, she started talking about the polygraph. How *demeaning* the experience had been. How, three days later, she'd suffered an attack of shingles around her eye. Even though Bonnie had passed with the highest score possible, Dr. Spaulding noted, "She was *very* upset about the polygraph."

On August 1, six weeks after his arrest, having read many science fiction books and having smoked innumerable cigarettes, Chris Pritchard was released from the Beaufort County jail on bond of $300,000, posted by his mother.

At his hearing, District Attorney Norton, a stocky man with a prominent mustache and a painfully slow way of talking, acknowledged for the first time that the prosecution would not contend that Chris had taken part in the murder, or even that he'd been present at the scene.

Norton reiterated, however, that the state intended to seek the death penalty for Chris, a comment that led to press speculation that Chris would be tried for murder for hire: that the allegation would be that he'd paid Upchurch and Henderson to kill Lieth, and presumably, Bonnie, too.

Bonnie met Chris at the county magistrate's office in mid-afternoon. Outside, the press, such as it was in Beaufort County, had assembled.

"It was a ridiculous scene," Bonnie said later. "Cameramen tripping all over each other, sticking microphones under Chris's face, asking him if he was glad to be out." Neither Bonnie nor Chris made any statement or answered any questions.

Instead, as the Washington *Daily News* reported, "nattily

dressed in charcoal gray slacks, a light gray sportcoat, white shirt and purple print tie, [and] arm in arm with his mother . . . Pritchard crossed Market Street, with lawyer James Vosburgh leading the way.''

That night, Bonnie, Angela, and Chris shared a room at the Holiday Inn. Some might have thought it strange that a young man of Chris's age would sleep in a bed next to his mother and sister, but neither he, Bonnie, nor Angela saw anything unusual about it. Bonnie, in fact, felt the need for physical closeness, even while she and her children were separated by an emotional gulf.

"I was still scared," she said later. "Not only for my own safety, but for theirs. The closer we were, the more comfortable I felt. And even if we weren't having deep conversations, at some level we were still *clinging* to each other."

The next day, Bonnie was back in court to attend the bond hearing for James Upchurch. Bond for Moog was set at $500,000, and unable to raise it, he was returned to the Beaufort County jail.

Bonnie had gone to the hearing not because she was concerned about the outcome—Vosburgh had already assured her that there was no way Upchurch could raise the money needed for his release—but because she wanted, for the first time, to see this person who had been accused of murdering her husband and of trying to kill her. She thought she might experience some shock of recognition.

But there was nothing. If anything, there was a shock of *non*recognition. Upchurch was tall and skinny, with unusually narrow shoulders and a notably long and slender neck.

She did not see Neal Henderson because he'd already been released at an unpublicized hearing held earlier, in a different county.

The following day, August 3, Bonnie and Chris drove back to Winston-Salem. After only one night at home, Bonnie drove to Ocean Isle Beach, at the southern end of the North Carolina shoreline. This was the beach to which she and Lieth had always gone. She'd rented a three-bedroom condominium for a week. Chris and Vince Hamrick drove down together. A day or two later, Angela and Donna Brady arrived.

"We just relaxed and went our separate ways," Bonnie said. "We'd meet occasionally for meals. There was no talk about Chris's situation. After six weeks in jail, the last thing in the world the poor boy needed was to have everybody harping on his problems. This was a restorative time, a time for rest and rehabilitation."

One by one, as the week drew to a close, the others left. Alone, Bonnie walked the beach for miles.

With Chris free on bond, with Bill Osteen firmly in control, and with as capable an investigator as Tom Brereton on the case, Bonnie thought it was not illogical to hope that better days might truly lie ahead.

Bill Osteen's law office was on the third floor of the Gate City Savings and Loan building in downtown Greensboro. It had neither the quaint and rustic charm of Jim Vosburgh's narrow poolroom annex in Little Washington, nor the opulence of Wade Smith's Raleigh headquarters. Plain and serviceable, it was quite obviously a place where business was conducted without frills or fanfare, by a man who knew his business well.

While Bonnie, Chris, and Angela were at the beach, Bill Osteen spent a great deal of time in this office, thinking about what to do next. Chris was no longer a potential suspect, he was now an accused. And not too many months down the road, a trial would come. A trial that could result in Chris's being sentenced to death.

As uneasy as he was about much of what he already knew about Chris, Bill Osteen was even more troubled by how much he still did not know. "There were some gaps," Osteen said later. "I thought we had to press harder to get to the complete truth, because I didn't believe we had been there."

Among defense attorneys—even defense attorneys whose abilities and ethics are beyond question, as in the case of Bill Osteen—there is debate over how hard a lawyer must press his client in an effort to obtain the full truth before trial.

Some argue that while an ethical lawyer cannot let a client take the stand and give sworn testimony that the lawyer knows to be false, in many instances it is in the client's best interest for his lawyer not to be overinformed. In the gray area between certain knowledge and reasonable doubt much strategic maneuvering of the sort necessary to best serve the client can take place. Surely, the one thing a criminal defense lawyer does *not* want to do is come right out and ask a client whether he's guilty, let alone try to make him confess.

Advocates of this approach contend that it is the job of plenty of people on the other side of the aisle—with the full resources of the State at their disposal—to try to demonstrate a client's guilt. And that, no matter what his personal view of the evidence—or his personal feelings about the client—the defense attorney has a clear and compelling obligation not to do the prosecutor's job.

Bill Osteen was not a member of this school. God, family, justice, and truth: these were the cornerstones of Osteen's life. The son of a federal probation officer, younger brother of a West Point graduate who rose to the rank of major general, himself attracted to FBI service, then later, for five years, the chief federal prosecutor for all central North Carolina, Bill Osteen was, by temperament, training, and religious belief, more comfortable with black and white than shades of gray.

Speaking of himself and his colleagues in the firm of Osteen & Adams, he said, "We would never, ever take a case in which we did not try to get at the truth ahead of time. We would never, ever just turn our backs on an area because we didn't want to know the answers. We just don't operate that way. If we're going to represent somebody, we're going to want to know the truth."

Not only did Osteen see this as the moral approach to the practice of law, he'd come to believe, after years of work as both prosecutor and defense attorney, that it also carried with it practical advantages.

Regarding Chris, he said, "We were going to have to make a decision whether to recommend that he go on the stand. In order to make that decision, we had to know what the answers were going to be. And we have a feeling that there is no U.S. attorney we know of, and no state prosecutor, who can ask tougher preparing questions than our office does, in order to get people where they ought to be so they can protect themselves in questionable areas; so that they have answers that are not only truthful, but sound reasonable when they come out. It's often the case that you can give a truthful answer, but the doggone thing sounds so preposterous. We don't want to be caught short, and we don't want our client caught short.

"So we really do grill our clients as if one of us is the prosecutor. All of it is geared toward, 'When you get through answering our questions, you need have no fear that any prosecutor is going to trap you.' We do that every time we have a case. And in Chris's case, there were some glaring weaknesses.

"For that reason, we wanted to make sure Chris had answers. Sometimes, you have to push hard on somebody to get the right thing done. We felt like, if we could break through and get to the truth, it could help Chris."

And also, perhaps, help his mother. For this was the other, less typical, element involved in Bill Osteen's representation of Chris. He was the client, but she was his mother, she was paying the bills, someone had already tried to kill her once, and Osteen felt—as had Bonnie's brother months before—a moral duty in regard to her personal safety.

"There was," he said later, "a side to this that was gnawing at us from the standpoint of, 'Here's Chris, with his mother over there, and we've got to make sure we're not protecting somebody who should not be protected.' So we really did give him a good going over."

To make sure it was good, Osteen brought Tom Brereton in to handle much of the questioning. It was, as Osteen said later that day to Bill Junior, "time to shake the tree and see what falls out of the branches."

The danger, of course, is that if too much falls out, it can make a big mess on the ground.

*   *   *

The session began at nine-thirty Monday morning, August 14, the day after Bonnie got back from the beach.

"We began," Osteen said, "thinking Chris was going to be able to give us truthful answers; answers that really did make sense. But as we got into it, things didn't make quite as much sense. There began to be more questions in my mind. So, then, we sort of zeroed in."

But it was Tom Brereton's recollection that the intent from the start had been not merely to shake the tree, but to uproot it.

"Bill had told me to go at him," Brereton said later. "So I came in that morning fully intending to break him. My intention was to get him to confess. From the first day I saw him in jail, I knew I could take him up or down attitudinally. His character was no stronger than a piece of paper. Once he realized he wasn't floating above it all, in total control, there was nothing to the real Chris Pritchard. Maybe Dimson the Wanderer could tell an undetectable lie, but Chris Pritchard wasn't going to be able to bullshit me."

Osteen began the meeting in his customary smooth and polished fashion.

"Chris," he said, "we have tried our best to look at all the things you've told us and find a way to accept them. But frankly, we're having a hard time. Now, we're going to go through these things in a methodical and orderly fashion, and this time, you're going to tell us the truth."

Then Osteen explained that a previously scheduled court appearance would require his occasional absence from the interview, but that his son and Tom Brereton were well prepared to continue in his absence.

Osteen started by asking about the map. Chris said the only map he'd ever drawn was the one the SBI had asked him to back in March.

"Yeah," Brereton said, "and you printed the word LAWSON on that map."

"So what?" Chris responded.

"I'll tell you so what," Brereton said, leaning forward. "Expert analysis of that printing shows it's *exactly the same* as the printing on the first map you drew. The one you gave to Upchurch and Henderson so they could go down to your house and kill your parents.''

"I never drew them any map.''

"Bullshit!''

"I didn't!''

"Chris,'' Osteen said, speaking softly, "the printing on that map they found at the fire certainly looks like the printing you did in March.''

"I can't help what it looks like. I didn't draw any map for Henderson or Upchurch.''

"Maybe you drew a map for somebody else,'' Osteen suggested.

Chris paused, as if in thought. "Well,'' he said, "you know, I *could* have drawn a map, maybe—I mean, I don't remember this, but I suppose it's possible—for one of our D and D games. You know, mapping out a scenario. Or I could have drawn one for a friend of mine. I had this one friend, I remember, his name was Brian. He wanted to come down to Washington but he didn't know where we lived. You know, maybe I could have drawn a map for him.''

"And did you ever talk, to your friend Brian, or to anyone else, about the possibility of your parents being killed?'' Osteen asked.

"No. No, never.''

"I don't mean seriously,'' Osteen said. "I mean, just maybe as a joke.''

"No, no, I never would even joke about something like that. You know, that would be a really sick joke.''

Except for the fact that he hadn't bothered to shave, Chris was so small and skinny, and was wearing such little kid's clothes, that he looked as if he should have been at day camp, not in Bill Osteen's conference room with Tom Brereton glaring at him, separated from him only by the width of the conference table.

"Well, you know,'' he said, "Upchurch made a couple of jokes about that. Really sick jokes. But I just ignored him. I wouldn't joke about something like that.''

"But you talked about your parents having money,'' Osteen said.

"Well, I don't know. I'm not sure."

"For Christ's sake," Brereton interrupted, "don't deny *that*. Ten people have already told me that you did."

"Oh, no, no. Look, I didn't even know about that. This whole thing about the inheritance. I didn't even know there *was* an inheritance. Nobody ever told me about that."

"Bullshit!" Brereton said. "Your own mother has told me, and she's told Mr. Osteen here the same thing—that she explained very carefully to you that there was quite a large inheritance, and that a trust fund had been established, and that you and your sister would come into the money when the younger of you turned thirty-five."

"No, no," he said. "I didn't know anything about that. I only heard about the inheritance after all this had happened."

"Well, Chris," Osteen said, preparing to leave for the courthouse, "if you stick to that statement, you put me in the position of having to choose between you and your mother in regard to who's telling the truth. And I'll tell you frankly, for me that's not a hard choice."

Once Osteen was out of the room, Brereton moved into a higher gear.

"Henderson says he drove your car. That's in his statement to the police. Why would he say that if it wasn't true?"

"Beats me," Chris said.

"That's not good enough," Brereton said.

"Look, I don't know why Henderson said that, all right?"

"He said it because it happens to be *true*," Brereton said.

Chris sat silently, shaking his head.

"No other answer?" Brereton said.

Chris shook his head.

Brereton showed him pictures of the bat and knife. He denied ever having seen either before.

"You ever take Henderson to your house?" Brereton asked.

"No, never.

"How about Upchurch?"

"Nope. Well, not to my house. There was once, back in June, we were on our way to the beach, just decided to drive down there one night, and on the way back we stopped in Washington. We didn't stay at my house, though. We drove by, I showed him where it was, but we didn't stop."

"So now you're admitting that Upchurch saw your house before?"

"Well, yeah, but I mean, so what? It was the middle of the night."

"It was the middle of the night when Lieth was killed, too."

Chris said nothing.

"And Upchurch, who's been by your house, has a map with your printing on it, showing him just where the house is, and the whole time he's gone your car is gone, too."

"I never said my car was gone."

"You don't have to. You gotta understand, Chris, I've been in this business more than twenty years. I've been bullshitted by a lot better bullshitters than you.

"This isn't bullshit," Chris said. But he was beginning to look a little shakier. "It's just that my memory—look, I was taking a lot of drugs. There's some things I sometimes can't remember."

"Like knowing about the inheritance?" Brereton said.

"Well . . . well, yeah, actually, that *is* a good example. I think I do remember something about that now. I think one time I might have said something to Vince, my roommate, about my grandparents leaving Lieth a lot of money. But I swear to God, he's the only person I ever told."

By late morning, Osteen had returned from the courthouse. He continued the questioning about the money. "Chris," he said, "how could you have told your roommate about the inheritance if your mother didn't tell *you* until after the fact?"

Chris shook his head. "I don't know. I guess that's what I mean about sometimes my memory is bad."

"Your problem," Brereton said, "isn't your own memory. It's other people's memories. And some of them are pretty damned good. I've got some statements here from a few of your friends at NC State. Let's take this Daniel Duyk, for instance. He says he told you that if your parents were dead, you'd have enough money so you could loan him some to start a restaurant.

"And as you may know, Upchurch's lawyer let me interview Upchurch in jail. He didn't say much I believed, but about the money he told me the same goddamned thing. You were planning to have it all."

"Well, maybe they heard it from Vince," Chris said. "I told Vince, I think, about the Camel City Dry Cleaners. And Vince is from Winston. He'd know that would be worth a lot of money."

"I don't give a fuck about Vince," Brereton said. "I'm talking about what *Daniel* says *you* told *him*. Like, if your parents were dead, you'd have a lot of money and you could buy a big house with a long driveway and a fast car, and you could go there and take drugs and play Dungeons and Dragons, and someday you were going to write a book—a fiction book, you told him. One good book that would make you even more money.

Chris's discomfort was becoming increasingly obvious.

"Look, look, I was drinking a lot of beer. I was smoking a lot of pot. I was dropping acid. I might have said some of these things. Like I told you, my memory's bad."

"Chris," Bill Osteen said, "think carefully now. I'm asking you one more time: Did you *ever* leave anyone with the impression—and this is not to say that you wanted to see anything happen—but did you ever give anyone the impression that you would be better off financially if Lieth and Bonnie were dead?"

He didn't answer the question. Instead, he said, "It's *possible* that I printed that word. *Lawson.* It's possible I printed that on the map. I think it may have been James who drew the map. Upchurch. I think he drew it for a new D and D scenario we were just starting, and I could have printed the word on it then."

"So it's 'possible,' " Brereton said. "And, ah, when was it 'possible' you could have done this?"

"Oh, I don't know. About eight or nine days before."

"About eight or nine days before what?"

"You know, before what—before what happened."

"Listen, you silly little son of a bitch!" Brereton shouted. "I'm not swallowing this bullshit! I want to know what the fuck was going on. You might be able to fool a nice guy like Mr. Osteen, but I'm not a nice guy, and you're not fooling me at all."

Chris looked scared.

"Upchurch used that map," Brereton said, "to get to your house to kill your stepfather and try to kill your mother, so you could inherit a million bucks."

"No!" Chris said. "He was only supposed to steal a few things."

The room fell silent.

"All right, look, I'll tell you the truth," Chris said. "I did draw the map. And I gave it to them. And I also loaned them my car. James had said if he could get into the house he could steal a bunch of stuff and take it to a pawnshop and then we'd all have more money for drugs. There was some stuff I told him about. The TV, the VCR, a radar detector, the stereo. And probably some cash in my mother's pocketbook. But it was downstairs! The only things I told him about were downstairs. He was never even supposed to go up the stairs. He wasn't supposed to hurt anybody. Something must have got out of control. I don't know what happened because I've never talked to either one of them since."

Bill Osteen had to make another quick appearance in court. It was almost one P.M. by the time he returned.

"So you drew them a map," he said, "so they could go down to your house and steal some things. You understand, Chris, this is a major difference from any story you've ever told before."

"We just wanted money," Chris said. "So we could do more drugs and keep playing the game."

And it was then—with that reference to Dungeons & Dragons, which Chris habitually referred to simply as "the game"—that Tom Brereton jumped up from his chair. He pounded the conference table with one fist and stuck his other hand about three inches from Chris's nose.

"Look, kid," he shouted, *"this is real life! This ain't no more fuckin' game!"*

And Chris looked up at Brereton and said, to everyone's surprise, "Okay, I did it. I planned it. That's what you want to hear. Now you've heard it."

While Osteen and Brereton and Bill Junior stared at him in utter silence, Chris Pritchard cried for about thirty seconds.

Still in his first year of private law practice, Bill Osteen, Jr., found himself suddenly peering over the edge of a deep abyss, at something very dark and formless far below.

"It was so *foreign*," he said later. "The whole thing was so absolutely foreign to everything in my whole experience of life. I remember feeling so terribly sad, thinking about how much Bonnie loved Chris, and how much faith she had in him, how convinced she'd been that he'd had nothing to do with this at all."

Quickly regaining his composure, Chris lit a cigarette, got to his feet, and in his sandals and T-shirt and short pants, began to pace the length of the conference room.

"I didn't plan on telling you this," he said. "I didn't plan to tell anybody, ever. And I don't know why I'm telling you now."

But then he sat down again and told them the details.

When he was finished, they had him wait in an outer office while they had a private talk.

"Where I come from," Brereton said, "this is when you put the cuffs on him and take him away. But we're working *for* the little bastard, not against him."

"And I'm afraid," Osteen said, "that our real work is just beginning. We still have to defend him at trial."

"How the fuck can we do that?" Brereton said. "What if the son of a bitch is found innocent?"

"I don't know," Osteen said. "He's a mess. But no matter what he's told us, he still stands a chance of being acquitted. In fact, it's our job to get him acquitted. But what happens if he goes free? What happens to him, knowing that he's gotten away with murder, and that we know it? And what happens to Bonnie?"

The thought occurred to Bill Osteen that Chris had just confessed to trying once to kill his mother to get her money. How could they be sure he wouldn't try again?

"Jesus Christ, I don't think I can handle this," Brereton said. "That kid walks, and I've gotta spend the rest of my life down on my knees, prayin' he don't hurt anybody ever again."

"We're going to be down on our knees before that," Osteen said. "Knowing what we know, how do we let him go home to Bonnie tonight? There's no telling what he might do. And she's even given him a gun."

"For his own protection," Brereton said.

"Here's what I think," Osteen said. "For his own protection and for Bonnie's, I don't think we can let him go home. I think we've got to get him straight to a psychiatrist. I don't know if he'll kill Bonnie, but I'm afraid there's a doggone good chance he'll kill himself."

After two hours' worth of frantic phone calls they located a Chapel Hill psychiatrist named Billy Royal, a man experienced in legal matters. By then, an eerie and unnatural calm had come over Chris, as if he'd realized that, for him, the game—whatever it had started as, and whatever it had become—was over now.

Osteen explained to Billy Royal that a young client of his had just confessed to involvement in the murder of his stepfather and the attempted murder of his mother, and that his current condition was something Osteen did not feel qualified to judge, but that it might well be either suicidal or homicidal.

Dr. Royal, much of whose work consisted of evaluating criminal defendants to determine their fitness for trial, agreed to see Chris immediately.

Having sought the truth, and now obtained it, Bill Osteen was faced with the thorniest ethical and moral dilemma of his long and distinguished career.

243

With Chris on his way to Chapel Hill, Osteen had a ninety-minute telephone talk with Jim Vosburgh. Before it was over, the two of them had to confront three unattractive facts:.

First, it remained Chris's right, and might well remain his inclination, to continue with his plea of not guilty. This would put Osteen and Vosburgh in the unenviable position of trying to win acquittal for a client they knew to be guilty not only of murder, but of the attempted murder of his own mother, a woman who continued to believe in his innocence.

Second, Osteen felt he could not permit Chris to testify in his own defense, for such testimony would constitute perjury. An attorney can harbor many suspicions about the veracity of his client's story, but once he *knows* the truth, and *knows* his client intends to lie under oath, he cannot—under Osteen's standard of ethics—allow the client to take the stand. But jurors—especially in a murder trial—no matter how often they're instructed not to infer guilt from a defendant's decision not to testify, can hardly do anything else. Common sense dictates that an innocent man would *demand* the chance to tell his story, especially with his own life at stake. Chris's silence would count heavily against him at trial, yet Osteen could not permit him to speak.

Third—and perhaps worst of all—Osteen and Vosburgh realized *they could not let Bonnie know the truth*.

The State still had the burden of proving the charges against Chris beyond a reasonable doubt. Without question, the State would call Bonnie to testify. She was, after all, the sole surviving victim of the attack. And when Bonnie testified, she'd tell the truth: of that Osteen was certain. He had come to know her well enough to be certain that she would not lie under oath, not even to save her son.

If Bonnie knew the truth, therefore, Chris would lose *all* chance for acquittal.

The only way in which her testimony could help him—and both Osteen and Vosburgh believed it would help mightily—was if she was able to tell a jury honestly that there wasn't a chance in the world that her son had had anything to do with the crime.

But Bonnie had been Chris's intended victim and she might be again. So did they not also have an obligation to her? Could they let her continue in her ignorance, now that they knew her son had tried to have her murdered?

These were questions Osteen and Vosburgh would put to themselves, and to each other, more than once in the months that lay ahead.

But for now, Osteen said, he'd better call the poor woman to tell her not to expect Chris home for supper.

24

Bonnie was at a neighbor's house, having a cup of tea, when the call from Osteen came at shortly after five P.M.

"I'm sorry to have to tell you this," he said, "but Chris is not going to be coming home tonight."

"What do you mean?" For an instant, she thought he was dead.

"We had a very rough session here today," Osteen continued, his voice not quite gruff, but with a certain gravelly, matter-of-fact edge to it. In personal style, he was more the steel fist than Wade Smith's velvet glove.

"Tom Brereton and I found it necessary to put some very hard questions to Chris today. We got quite tough with him, as a matter of fact. By the end of the meeting he was very upset. Frankly, I wouldn't have been comfortable letting him go home in the shape he was in, so I've sent him on to a psychiatrist in Chapel Hill."

Osteen said the psychiatrist's name was Billy Royal, and that he'd been highly recommended by everyone from whom they'd sought a referral. He said Chris was to meet with Dr. Royal at seven P.M., and he was sure that the doctor would be in touch with Bonnie as soon as possible after that and would answer any other questions she might have.

Any *other* questions? She hadn't even started to ask questions. Yet she found herself almost too stunned to begin. It was as if, just as on the night of the murder, she'd been struck a sharp blow in the head.

In an almost trancelike state, she reached out for pencil and paper and wrote the psychiatrist's name. Finally, she managed to ask, "But what happened? What brought this on?"

"As I said, Bonnie, Tom was pretty tough in his questioning. When he got into some of the nuts and bolts, frankly, it seemed a bit too much for Chris to handle. I don't want to go into detail at this point, and I don't want to alarm you any more than necessary, but by the end of the meeting, we all felt—and Bill Junior was here with us, too—that in the state Chris was in there could be a danger that he might harm himself. We agreed that the best thing would be to send him on to Dr. Royal."

After hanging up, Bonnie returned to her own home and sat alone, as the muggy evening turned to dusk and darkness. She knew it made no sense, she knew she was in no greater personal danger now than at any other time since the attack, but she went to her bedroom and got her gun anyway and placed it on the arm of the chair in which she sat, waiting for the phone call from Dr. Royal.

It was ten P.M. before the call came and when it did, the news was not good.

Billy Royal was sixty-two years old, North Carolina born and bred, a soft-spoken man with a gentle manner and a voice that, especially on the telephone, tended to trail off before he reached the end of a sentence. His voice did not possess the crisp authority of Bill Osteen's or the hearty good-fellowship of Jim Vosburgh's or the comforting composure of Wade Smith's. His voice sounded tired, resigned, even maybe a little bit sad about all its owner had been exposed to over the years. It also, quite frequently, was a voice that contained a hint of subtle humor, good cheer, and profound appreciation for those aspects of life that did not involve forensic psychiatry, but those were not qualities that Bonnie would ever have an easy time detecting, and certainly not now.

Billy Royal—and Billy was his given name, not William—told her that he'd had Chris admitted to the psychiatric service of Memorial Hospital in Chapel Hill because, after an extended interview with Chris and a conversation with William Osteen, he thought Chris might be suicidal.

He added, however, that Chris was, for the present, perfectly safe and suggested that Bonnie not visit until the next day.

Early the next morning, Osteen called Wade Smith. As Wade later recalled it, Osteen, speaking "hypothetically," and in the most vague and indirect language he could muster, tried to suggest some of what had occurred the day before, and to describe the dilemma with which he found himself confronted.

In this talk—as can happen when two skilled and experienced attorneys speak to one another about so delicate a matter—information was conveyed so inexplicitly that anyone looking at a transcript of their conversation would have had a hard time determining even what the subject was, much less what conclusions were reached.

"Wade, there are some things I can't tell you," Osteen said.

"Bill, don't tell me anything that you don't want me to tell Bonnie, because I'm going to have to tell her if I know something that I think is relevant to her welfare."

Osteen fell silent.

"So," Wade said after maybe thirty seconds had passed, "I guess there will just have to be a lot of things I don't know."

"That's right, Wade. We're going to have to have this understanding. I'm going to know things that you can't know. But in effect, I want you to understand something, and that is, it is conceivable that Chris did this. I'm not telling you anything more, but I'm telling you it *is* conceivable, and you need to take any action you feel you need to take in that regard. I don't want you to be blindsided."

And so Wade had to engage in his own wrestling match

with his conscience and ethics and sense of professional duty.

"I was walking down a tightwire," he said later. "I had a duty to tell my client things I learned about the case. I can't just keep a secret from my client. But the ethical constraint that is requiring me to tell my client things is not anything like the ethical constraint that is keeping Bill from telling me things his client tells him. Still, I couldn't hold things back very long, and I couldn't hold back things that put Bonnie in danger.

"Was she in great danger? Would Chris try to hurt her in some way? That was a burden. I worried a lot about that. My view was that Chris might do something to himself, but he wouldn't do anything to Bonnie. But it was a risky moment."

Risky, in particular, for Bonnie. Especially given the fact that Wade had never even met Chris.

For the moment, however, he decided that the best thing he could do was to be sure that Jean Spaulding was kept apprised of the direction in which events seemed to be moving.

After speaking to Wade, Osteen called Bonnie. He told her he knew Chris had been hospitalized and that he thought Dr. Royal had made the right decision. But he told her, too, that before she visited Chris, it was imperative that she meet with him.

She reached his office at one-thirty P.M.

Osteen seemed sympathetic and concerned, but his first words struck Bonnie as uncharacteristically vague.

"Some of the things we'd hoped were correct we now have to question," he said. "Certain facts turned out to be not as we had anticipated. Bonnie, there's no way for you not to be concerned at this point, but oftentimes we think things are one way when they're not."

She just nodded, barely listening, not comprehending any meaning behind the words. All she knew was that Chris was suffering a new and more acute kind of pain, and that she wanted to do whatever she could to ease it.

But then Osteen said—with no vagueness whatsoever—

that the real reason he'd asked her to come by was because he had to tell her something extremely important, and he wanted to be sure she fully understood how vital it was in terms of Chris's interests.

Osteen said that beginning immediately, and continuing until he personally told her otherwise, it was imperative that under no circumstances was she ever to ask Chris any questions about *anything* surrounding the events of July 25, 1988.

Before she even had a chance to wonder why this new prohibition was being put into effect, Osteen added that it would not be possible for him to explain. He would not be able to tell her any more than he'd already told her, but it was essential that she follow his instructions to the letter.

She and Chris could talk about anything else, but they were absolutely not to discuss any aspect of the circumstances surrounding the weekend of Lieth's murder.

When she thought about this later, Bonnie said, she'd just assumed that Osteen—recognizing how unscrupulous a prosecutor could be—simply wanted to be sure no ambiguous remark she or Chris might make to one another could ever be twisted into something that sounded sinister.

"He made it very clear that this was important to Chris's defense," she said, "but he in no way indicated that Chris was responsible. And my thoughts, believe me, were elsewhere than on the implications. I was still in a state of shock. My main concern was just to get to Chapel Hill and be with my son."

And so, with that meeting, there commenced a weeks-long sequence of miscommunication and semantic confusion, of vague hints and expressions of partial truths, conveyed in a language thickly encoded so as to maintain at least the appearance of ambiguity. When combined with a loving mother's powerful and continuing desire not to hear the worst of all possible truths about her son, this led to a series of misunderstandings and flawed perceptions which would have been almost comical had the matter not been fraught with such intractable legal and ethical problems, and had it not threatened such potentially tragic consequences.

* * *

Bonnie drove on from Greensboro to Chapel Hill, an hour away. Memorial Hospital was a large, modern, confusing complex, yet the psychiatric wing was reassuring. In many ways, especially given that most of the patients seemed to be about Chris's own age, the setting struck Bonnie as a slightly more orderly version of his dormitory at NC State.

They sat and talked in a small lounge. It was late afternoon by the time Bonnie arrived, and she wound up staying for dinner. She sat with Chris and a few other patients and did not find the conversation to be any less rational or controlled than at any other dinner she'd ever had.

What was not so reassuring was Chris himself. He seemed exceedingly nervous. He could not keep his arms or legs from quivering. He chain-smoked cigarettes, lighting one from the butt of another with trembling hands.

He was, she said, "withdrawn, distraught, and apologetic. Apologetic for having to be in the hospital, for causing me so much concern."

The last thing Bonnie wanted was to put more pressure on him by asking too many questions—or any at all. It was obvious that, for whatever reason, he already was under more pressure than he could handle.

"I just wanted to reassure him," she said later. "I wanted him to see that I was there and that I loved him and that I wanted him to get better and to feel better about himself."

It turned out that although Dr. Royal had arranged Chris's admission to Memorial, he himself was not on staff there and was not present in the hospital that night. On her first visit, in fact, Bonnie was unable to find any doctor to whom she could talk about Chris's condition, or about what treatment he would receive.

That night, however, Dr. Royal called Osteen with a recommendation that complicated matters even further. "We've got to get Chris and his mother together," he said. "Until he sits down and tells her what he did, he can't possibly start to get better."

Dr. Royal explained that, in his view, the cause of Chris's suicidal impulse was guilt about his role in the original crime, and about his having lied to his mother ever since.

What it came down to was this: having broken through such a momentous barrier the day before, by admitting the truth in Osteen's office, Chris was now perched on a suicidal precipice from which he could not even begin to retreat until he made a full confession to his mother and sister.

"I can't let that happen," Osteen said. "I can't let him. I simply cannot let that happen."

"The problem is," Dr. Royal said, "from a psychiatric standpoint, I think we might be talking about a matter of life and death."

"Well," Osteen said, "this may sound melodramatic, but from a legal standpoint, I *know* we're talking about a matter of life and death."

But Billy Royal called again the next day. He said Chris would be "acutely suicidal until he gets this resolved with his mother," then added that the best place for such a confession to take place would be in the supervised setting of the hospital.

Osteen, however, reiterated that he could not allow such a conversation. He also reminded Dr. Royal that he, Osteen, had retained the psychiatrist, and that whatever the doctor's personal feelings might be, he did not have the freedom to do or say anything, or to cause or to allow to happen anything contrary to Osteen's explicit instructions.

"Well, all right," Dr. Royal replied, "but I want to be on record as having given you my professional opinion that this boy is a time bomb waiting to go off."

Chris remained in the hospital for eight days, receiving no treatment, and Billy Royal saw no improvement in his condition. Yet hospital officials determined he was ready for release on August 23.

The night before, Billy Royal called Osteen yet again. He said Chris was still bursting with the need to tell his mother the truth, and that until he did, he would remain not only suicidal but also a danger to others—in particular to Bonnie. If he couldn't relieve his internal pressure by telling his mother he'd tried to have her killed a year ago, there was a risk he would instead kill her now.

Osteen, not normally a man given to spasms of self-doubt, called Vosburgh again. Although the problem of what to do about Bonnie—which was another way of describing this clash between Chris's psychological and legal best interests—had tormented both lawyers since the night of his admission to Memorial, it took on even more urgency now that he was about to be released.

They talked on, late into the night, changing their own minds, then changing each other's, then finding themselves back where they started.

"We've just got to make sure she doesn't learn too much," Osteen said.

"Yeah, but she's gonna be living with this guy again," Vosburgh said. "We already know he's suicidal. We know they didn't do a damned thing to help him in the hospital, so he's just as bad off as when he went in. Even if he doesn't kill her, what do you think it will do to her if he goes home and kills himself?"

"And what do you think it will do to us," Osteen responded, "when we have to tell her the reason he killed himself is because we wouldn't let him talk to her?"

"But goddamnit, Bill, we've got a duty to him, as our client, not to disclose anything that could impair his defense."

Finally, Osteen said, "Vos, if they covered this one in law school, I must have been absent that day."

"Bill, if they'd covered this one, I would have transferred to divinity school the next morning."

25

Chris was released as scheduled on August 23 and did no immediate harm to anyone. Two days later, in fact, he helped Bonnie bring Angela to the small college in southwestern Virginia where she'd enrolled for the fall semester.

To Billy Royal, who saw him almost daily through late August, Chris seemed dejected, said he'd been drinking incessantly since his discharge from the hospital, and displayed "notable mood swings." He said that if he did not have legal problems he could envision a future for himself in which he'd "write a successful novel, have a big house, a fast car." He also said, "You have no idea how hard it is for me to live with my mother and have to keep lying to her."

On August 29, Dr. Royal asked Bonnie to meet with him, thinking that getting to know the mother might give him better insight into the son.

Billy Royal had white hair, a scraggly beard, a shambling walk, and when speaking—as Bonnie had already noticed—a tendency to mutter and on occasion, to drift from what seemed the point. Once one got past this appearance of distraction, however, one found that he possessed a reassuring calmness, and that, even after thirty years in practice, he had a quick and strong sympathy for those who came, or were sent, to seek his help.

"I believe in a goodness in all people," he once said. What he prized most highly in an individual was "a sense of humor in this crazy world. Nobody understands it." He added that most people who were described as being evil "are usually just district attorneys."

Dr. Royal had grown up in the tiny Sampson County village of Salemburg, in the south-central part of the state. Salemburg was so small that the streets didn't even have names. Its center had been dominated by a mighty oak tree, in the shade of which old men sat and played checkers. On May Day, girls and young women did actually dance around a maypole, and the biggest event of the year was the Mother's Day parade. If Norman Rockwell had stumbled upon the town, he would have thought they were putting him on.

Billy Royal's family were merchants. They owned almost every business in the town: the general store, the hardware store, the dry goods store, and the grocery store.

He could empathize with some of the stresses Chris had faced in going from Little Washington to NC State, because when he'd left Salemburg at the age of sixteen, bound for Wake Forest University, he'd lasted only a year before dropping out to join the Navy. He wound up as a hospital corpsman, stationed at Bethesda Naval Hospital, where, on the seventeenth floor, he would occasionally see President Harry Truman dropping in to visit a recuperating senator.

After the Navy, he returned to Wake Forest and earned his degree. Then, unsure of what to do with his life, he went back to Salemburg and ran the general store for four years, selling "everything from bras to pork and beans."

Young men in Salemburg who eyed more distant horizons were generally given three aspirations from which to choose: medicine, the law, or the ministry. Billy Royal knew he didn't want to be a lawyer or a minister, so he drifted into medicine by default.

He did his internship in San Francisco, his psychiatric residency in Chapel Hill, and then, in 1963, with a partner, opened the first private psychiatric practice in the city of Durham.

A first marriage had ended after almost twenty years, and he'd recently married again, to a much younger woman who was also a doctor. From the first marriage, he had four grown children, with whom he stayed in close and affectionate contact, and from the second, a baby daughter.

He was a great fan of the ballet and of the works of

William Faulkner, saying that, in Faulkner, he liked "that Southern craziness and weird behavior."

He was also licensed to fly a single-engine airplane and had spent thousands of hours in the air over his native state, but when traveling to New York City for a psychiatric convention, he would be more likely to take the bus than to fly commercially, even if it meant changing in Pittsburgh, "because people on buses seem to have better stories to tell."

On the evening of August 29, Bonnie found him "a strange bird" and said, "I did not relate well to him at all. He irritated me. He gave me the feeling he was putting *me* under a microscope, asking all sorts of personal questions that I considered irrelevant to what was happening with Chris.

"For example, he dwelled on Steve Pritchard and our divorce. I thought he was looking at me as another potential patient for himself. He even asked me if I thought I needed a psychiatrist, which was a question I considered quite offensive. I can't say I liked him, and that made me wonder if he was really going to be able to help Chris."

The next day, for the first time in weeks, Bonnie saw Jean Spaulding again.

The session began with Bonnie saying she and Chris had been able to go to the beach together and that they "had a very quiet time for a week." Only after that did she mention, with no notable inflection in her voice, that he'd been kept in jail for six weeks and that, since his release, he'd spent eight days in a psychiatric facility, due to "depression."

"Then," Dr. Spaulding said, "she said a boy had confessed. At this point, she didn't use the name. Said a boy had confessed that Chris had said, 'I hate my mom and dad. Let's kill them and we'll be rich.' She did not believe that. That fell into the category of almost extraneous information. There was no way that she could believe that Chris was capable of doing that, or saying that."

* * *

Eric Caldwell, the shy and bespectacled computer whiz who had become Chris's closest friend, spent the Sunday night of Labor Day weekend at Chris's house. "We stayed up talking until five o'clock in the morning," Eric said later. "The crime was definitely on his mind. He made a lot of suggestions and I made a lot of inferences, but nothing was said directly. But he told me without telling me. By the time I fell asleep on Labor Day morning, I knew he had done it."

On Monday night, Chris was explicit. He called Eric at home and told him all he had already admitted in Bill Osteen's office, and all he had told Billy Royal.

He said that, as he spoke, he was sitting on his bed, holding his loaded gun in his hand.

"I'm lying to my mother," he said. "I can't tell her the truth. What reason do I have to go on living? Even if I don't kill myself, I'll get the death penalty. Why wait for them to do it to me if I can do it to myself right now and spare my mother all the extra agony? Not to mention the expense."

Eric had talked people out of suicide before. He'd also contemplated the act himself, on one occasion, and had rejected it, later writing a poem about the experience of coming so close.

He stayed on the phone with Chris for more than two hours. "You've read my poem," he said. "And when you read it, you agreed that nothing was more stupid than suicide. So how can you be thinking of it now?"

"You don't understand," Chris said. "It's my goddamned lawyer. He won't let me tell my mother the truth. And I can't go on dealing with her if I can't tell her. The fucking lawyer isn't giving me any choice."

On Tuesday, Chris had a regular seven P.M. appointment with Dr. Royal. He told his psychiatrist that over the weekend he'd confessed his guilt to his best friend. Then he said he'd also called an ex-girlfriend and had told her.

Dr. Royal asked if finally telling the truth to close friends had made him feel any better.

"No," Chris said. "But it didn't before, either." Then

he explained that during his eight-day stay at Memorial he had confessed his guilt to three other patients.

Well, Billy Royal said to himself, *it's like I kept telling them. The lid was bound to blow off.*

After Chris left, Dr. Royal called Bill Osteen. This, he said, was where the strategy of keeping Bonnie in the dark had gotten them: Chris had confessed to at least five people already, three of whom were mental patients.

For Osteen, this might have been the worst night of them all. In August, he'd obtained an admission of guilt from his client that would severely limit his options at trial. Then, in order to preserve some hope of mounting a successful defense, he'd stuck fast to his insistence that Chris not be permitted to tell Bonnie the truth, even when told that his position might be endangering the lives of both mother and son.

It had not been an easy time for Bill Osteen. At no point had he been sure his course was correct. So far, both suicide and homicide had been averted, but now the crazy little coot had started confessing to boyfriends, girlfriends, and *total strangers from a mental institution!*

Any one of those people could pick up the phone at any moment and call the SBI or the Washington police or the Beaufort County district attorney's office and—just out of a sense of civic duty—report what Chris had told them.

Then where would they all be? Chris would be on death row, Bonnie would probably be in a mental hospital herself—if not a funeral parlor—and Osteen would spend the rest of his life blaming himself for letting the case, the client, the whole mess, spin so far out of control.

He spent a near-sleepless night and arose thinking perhaps he should withdraw from the case before any more damage was done. Let someone else step in and face the hard decisions that still lay ahead. He had given this his best effort, but maybe, for this client, for these circumstances, he was not, in fact, the right man.

He placed a call to Jim Vosburgh. "You sitting down, Vos?" he asked.

These were words that, coming from Osteen, Vosburgh had already learned to dread.

Osteen broke the news about Chris's five confessions. "And these are only the five we know about so far," he said. "There could be more. By the time trial comes, he could be confessing to the jurors while we're up there arguing that the State has failed to prove its case."

"You know, Bill," Vosburgh said, "there are only two things wrong with that boy. He's got a loose screw and a fat lip and both keep running all the time."

Yet, after another long and anguished conversation, they decided they couldn't walk away.

No matter how much they disliked Chris, no matter how much disgust they felt for his crime, no matter how dismayed they were by his current self-destructive behavior, no matter how much fear they had about what each new day might bring, neither lawyer felt comfortable with the prospect of abandoning a young man who was in such obvious, and perhaps terminal, distress.

Nor could they just walk away from Bonnie. It was bad enough that they had kept the truth from her and were still doing so. It would be worse now to leave her all alone.

"The bottom line," Osteen said later, "was that, ethically, I didn't think I could justify leaving a client worse off than he'd be if I continued to represent him. I knew I was no miracle worker and I knew I was making decisions that could prove to be terribly wrong, and that if they were wrong, they could have truly awful consequences. But at least I, and Jim Vosburgh, knew Bonnie and Chris.

"Maybe we didn't really *know* them, but at least we'd had experience dealing with them, and we were familiar— all too familiar—with the case. And this was one that could blow up in our faces at any moment, in any one of a dozen ways.

"So how could we turn everything over to somebody brand new, who didn't know anything? This wasn't a situation where a new lawyer would have the luxury of a few weeks or months to get up to speed. Chris *was* a time bomb, and he had already started to go off.

"If I'd walked away, and then things had blown up completely, I would have wondered for the rest of my life if staying in might have made a difference. In the end, I think

Jim and I both decided that we owed Bonnie—and even Chris—the benefit of our knowledge, at least, if not our wisdom. But there wasn't one day that passed, then or later, when both of us didn't wish we'd taken the other path."

Chris told Billy Royal he'd started confessing because he'd needed to see what would happen if people he cared about knew the truth. Would he be shunned, or would he be accepted despite his crime? As Dr. Royal saw it, these first confessions had been a rehearsal for the moment when he would finally be permitted to tell Bonnie.

More strongly than ever, Dr. Royal felt that that moment could no longer be delayed. The situation had reached such a point of crisis, he told Osteen, that, even contrary to the lawyer's instructions, he might feel bound by his own code of ethics and professional responsibility to ease the psychological pressures that threatened to destroy his patient by orchestrating a scenario in which Chris would admit to Bonnie what he had done.

It is Dr. Royal's recollection that Osteen called back at three-fifteen that afternoon, Wednesday, September 6, to say he agreed that the moment for full disclosure had arrived, legal consequences notwithstanding. He added, however, that he felt it was his responsibility to break the news to Bonnie first, and that he would do so the next morning in his office.

Dr. Royal then arranged to see Bonnie and Chris separately the next afternoon and evening, saying he also wanted to meet with them together at eight P.M. In that joint session, he felt, with the truth finally on the table, he could assess their reactions and perhaps try to help them with the task of going forward under what would be a new and—for Bonnie, at least—appalling set of circumstances.

He would see Bonnie first, so he could gauge her reaction to Osteen's disclosures. He also wanted to tell her how Chris had been stricken, almost fatally, with guilt over what he'd done, and to suggest to her that full and unquestioning forgiveness—if she was capable of it—would be the greatest gift she could ever give her son.

He would next see Chris, in order to report on Bonnie's reaction, and to help prepare the young man for what undoubtedly would be the most acutely upsetting encounter of his life.

September 7 was, for all concerned, if not the worst, perhaps the most confusing, day of the year. Bonnie would later describe it as "the day the bottom dropped out of my heart."

It was Dr. Royal's recollection that Osteen had said the day before that he would tell Bonnie "all that Chris had told him."

Osteen, however, recalled only that he'd said "the time had come to be sure that Bonnie knew, if she didn't already, that things were not as she'd hoped." Osteen said he had no memory of ever stating to Dr. Royal that he would be absolutely explicit.

Indeed, he still felt that Bonnie's knowledge of the details would have to be sufficiently inferential so as to permit her to testify at trial in a way that would be both truthful and not ruinous to Chris's chances for acquittal. So, he would hint, he would imply, he would suggest, and Bonnie—he hoped—would draw the proper conclusion without certain blunt words being spoken.

However he phrased them—and neither Osteen nor Bonnie took notes on this meeting—the words he did utter had great impact.

"There were no specifics," Bonnie said later, "but he did say he had the distinct feeling that Chris was involved. He said, 'I can't tell you certain things that I know.' And he reiterated how important it was to Chris's defense for him not to share with me privileged information. He was very apologetic about it, but he said, 'I don't want you to be placed in the middle here, so it's best that you not discuss anything that had to do with that weekend.'

"He said it put him in an awkward situation, and he realized it put me in an awkward situation, but he knew I was on my way to see Dr. Royal, and he made it very plain that Dr. Royal, too, was not to discuss with me anything about July twenty-fifth, and I was not to ask him anything."

However confusing the day was, and would become, there was one point of clarity: as Bonnie put it later, "This was a bad day. I felt Mr. Osteen's assessment of the situation had changed. Until then, I had believed that he felt Chris was not involved in any way. Now I had the distinct feeling that he had changed his opinion, for reasons I could not be privy to. As much as what was actually said, I could detect a *feeling,* a difference in attitude, and this scared me."

Yet it still did not occur to Bonnie—or she could not yet accept—that any "involvement" Chris might have had could have been anything but inadvertent. She saw Osteen's new "feeling" as reflecting nothing more than an awareness that the strategic problems posed by Chris's defense might be greater than he had at first expected.

So Bonnie left Osteen's office and drove to Chapel Hill for her four P.M. appointment with Billy Royal more fearful than she had been about the upcoming trial, but with her faith in Chris's innocence undiminished.

As soon as she walked into Dr. Royal's office, however, Bonnie sensed that something was not right. "The moment I sat down," she said, "it was obvious that he wanted to tell me what was going on with Chris, what had been causing Chris to be so upset. It seemed plain that he planned to forge ahead with what I assumed was exactly what Mr. Osteen had again just given me instructions not to discuss.

"I interrupted him right away. But when I told him that he couldn't talk about the weekend of the murder with me, he seemed dismayed. He said he would have a difficult time treating Chris unless Chris and I could talk about the things Chris had been holding inside. 'The situation' was the way he described it.

"So I said, 'Mr. Osteen just spent the afternoon telling me there are certain things we can't talk about.' I think he may have gone into a private office and called Mr. Osteen right then. Just how it was expressed I don't remember, but I got the impression that he still wanted to tell me exactly what it was that Mr. Osteen did not want him to tell me. Apparently, he thought he had explained to Mr. Osteen that this was what he was going to do. And Mr.

Osteen thought he had explained to Dr. Royal that this would not be possible.

"It reached the point where I thought it better to stop the meeting. I told him I'd come back to meet with him and Chris together as we had planned, but I left his office in the middle of the appointment and went over to the Chapel Hill shopping center and got something to eat. I was terribly upset and confused. I didn't know what was going on, or what was about to happen next. The one thing I did know was what Mr. Osteen had emphasized so strongly: that it could be dangerous for Chris if certain topics were discussed. And nothing, or no one, could have caused me to do anything that would have endangered Chris."

Billy Royal's recollection and interpretation of the afternoon was rather different. His notes reflect that Bonnie had begun the meeting by saying that she'd had a great deal of experience with computers and thus had learned to put different types of data in different compartments and not get things mixed up. Dr. Royal recalls thinking, as he heard this, *she's been told, and this is how she's dealing with it. She's putting it aside for now, so she can keep functioning and trying to help Chris.*

He did not recall Bonnie terminating the session prematurely, nor his making any call to Osteen, nor any sense of being dismayed by anything Bonnie told him.

His sense was that Bonnie was not comfortable talking about what she'd just learned about Chris before she'd had a chance to talk to Chris directly, and that she didn't want, or need, any sort of planning session to prepare for the joint meeting that night.

She had received the information, she was processing it, and by eight P.M. she'd be prepared to deal with Chris, knowing now the worst about him. Under the circumstances, her calmness and her obviously undiminished concern for Chris's well-being struck Dr. Royal as quite remarkable.

What he didn't realize was that Bonnie *didn't* know the worst, or anything approaching it.

* * *

When Chris arrived at seven P.M., his first question was, "How can I look at my mom?" It would be impossible, he said, for him even to look her in the eye, knowing that she now knew he had plotted the murder of her husband, had tried to have her killed, too, and had been lying about it to her ever since.

But then, it seemed, he wanted to talk about everything *but* telling Bonnie. He said he liked to sit in the woods and play with cats. He said he wanted to have a wife and child. He asked, "What's the point of being alive if I have to be in jail until I'm seventy?" He said Osteen had "jumped my shit" for his having told others about his involvement. He was extremely emotional and tearful, switching subjects even more rapidly, and with less apparent logical connection, than usual.

At one point, he plunged into tearful hysteria, and Dr. Royal said he was prescribing a drug called Serentil, which should help to reduce his anxiety and minimize his symptoms of depression.

"I'm a planner," Chris was saying, talking faster than Dr. Royal had ever heard him talk before. "I plan ahead. I really could be somebody if only I didn't have all these problems." He said he was "very intense" about music, driving, eating, and learning things, that he'd read twenty-nine books while in jail and that he was currently reading a book about the brain.

"He was a weird guy," Billy Royal said later. "He had a lot of feeling about some things; about others, he was totally devoid."

Bonnie returned at eight P.M. Chris seemed terrified. Now, for the first time, his mother would be confronting him, fully aware of the murderous desires he had harbored in his heart, and of the responsibility he bore for the ghastly deeds that had flowed from them.

And knowing, too, that so callously and for so long he had lied to her and had permitted her to trust and to love him when he so clearly had not been deserving of either.

As she entered the office, Chris curled into a fetal position in his chair, hiding his face in his hands, too frightened to look at her. His shoulders heaved with convulsive sobs.

"He was," Dr. Royal said, "regressive and infantile. My impression was that she knew, and she was facing him now for the first time since she knew. This was the point Chris had been trying to get to, but at the same time had been dreading all along. He avoided any visual contact with her. He was like an infant who expected the all-powerful mother to do away with him. He had no defense."

Billy Royal felt that this was perhaps as pivotal a moment as would ever occur in the psychological lives of either Bonnie or Chris, and that his proper role was to remain in the background and let the scene play itself out.

Bonnie took two steps into the office, looked at her son, then stood still, shocked into silence. She'd not been prepared for this. The sight of Chris in such a condition scared her, as much as her presence in the room frightened him.

"I knew he was in pain," she said later, "a lot of pain. But I didn't know what was going on. I'd never seen him like that before or since."

Then, as Billy Royal watched silently, she slowly approached him.

As she drew near, he forced himself to look up at her, and with tears flowing freely down his cheeks, he said, "Mother, I'm sorry. I'm so, so sorry." And then again he sank his face back into the sanctuary of his arms.

At that point, Bonnie said later, "I put my arms around this whole little ball he was curled up in, and I said, 'Chris, I don't know what you're going through, but I'm here and I love you and I want you to know that.'"

To Billy Royal, this was a magnificent act of forgiveness on Bonnie's part—one that might well, he thought, save the life of her son.

To Chris, it was the absolution for which he'd been yearning, but which his legal jeopardy had prevented him from seeking openly. Now, having been granted his own mother's pardon, there was nothing he'd be unable to face.

But to Bonnie herself, her consoling words and actions were no more than a mother's instinctive reaction to seeing her child in pain. When he told her he was sorry, she had no idea what, specifically, he was sorry for.

"There could have been lots of reasons why Chris was in that state," she said later. "And lots for him to be sorry about. His suicidal tendencies, the fact that he'd had to be hospitalized, which he knew was upsetting to me, and maybe even, as Mr. Osteen had suggested that afternoon, the possibility that once, long ago, through some terrible mistake or misunderstanding, he had done something accidental that might have contributed to a situation where the awful events of July twenty-fifth had taken place. And so, I comforted him as best I could, but it was without any idea of why he needed comforting so badly."

Gradually, as Bonnie continued to reassure Chris of her love for him, and of her enduring support, he grew calmer. And then, just as she felt he might be about to say more than she was permitted to hear, under the strictures imposed by Bill Osteen, she told him she'd met with Osteen earlier that afternoon, and he had again stressed how vital it was that she and Chris not discuss any specifics of the weekend of the murder. She quickly added that anything Chris might have said to Dr. Royal in that regard must be held in confidence between the two of them. Under no circumstances should either of them tell her anything that Mr. Osteen did not want her to know.

To Billy Royal, this was a stunning display of the compartmentalization to which Bonnie had referred that afternoon. Here she was, only hours after having been informed of how her only son had tried to have her murdered, yet she not only was able to forgive him, but retained enough presence of mind to remind him, even at such an emotionally overheated moment, that his lawyer had instructed her that they should not discuss the details.

That Bonnie was brave and strong enough to postpone such a discussion until such time as it would no longer pose a danger to Chris at trial so impressed Dr. Royal that he even commented on it to his wife that night.

"Just remarkable," he said, "the way she was able to forgive him, having just been told what she'd been told." In Billy Royal's mind, "there was no doubt about it. Whatever words Osteen had used, it was clear to me that the information had been conveyed."

Bonnie, however, said later that she had in fact been told nothing substantive. She knew only that the attorney in whose judgment she had unquestioning faith was now troubled in a way he'd not been before. But nothing anyone had said had shaken her faith in Chris's innocence. Only facts could do that, and she still hadn't been presented with any facts.

"It got pretty scary," Dr. Royal said later. "The craziness of all of us in this exercise. Nobody could talk to anybody. Nobody could talk about the real issue. It was like a chess game where you weren't allowed to see your opponent's moves. Or the shell game, where the shells are always moving, and you can never guess which one the pea is under.

"I would say, 'This is crazy!' but at the same time there was a prohibition against doing anything differently. Maybe what was hard for all of us to grasp was that you have to noncommunicate at times, or risk destroying the system, even though everybody knows what's being noncommunicated."

Eric Caldwell and John Hubard came by the house on Saturday night, September 9. For five days, Eric had been living in silent terror, aware that he knew a secret that could end the life of his best friend, but one that he also felt driven to share with Bonnie, who had become like a second mother to him.

He'd not had a decent night's sleep since Chris had made his confession. He was burdened by guilt and also by fear. He asked himself continually, *"What the hell do I do if they find me?"* Every day, he expected a call from the SBI or the Washington police, or the Beaufort County district attorney's office. After all, wasn't it logical that, in preparing for trial, they would seek to question Chris's friends? From both Chris and Vince Hamrick, Eric knew how much of an effort they'd made on the NC State campus prior to the arrests, and he feared it would be only a matter of time before the same detectives, or new ones, came to Winston-Salem to interrogate Chris's friends there.

But should he even wait for the police to come to him? Didn't he have some obligation, as a citizen, to contact them? Bill Osteen and Billy Royal could quite justifiably say that their privileged professional relationships with Chris prevented them from sharing the truth with anyone else, but for Eric it was only friendship, and a sense of loyalty, that caused him to stay silent. And the silence caused him severe discomfort.

September 9 was the first time he'd seen Bonnie since Chris had told him the truth. And suddenly, as John Hubard and Chris stepped into the backyard to smoke cigarettes, Eric found himself alone with her.

He felt awkward, guarded, almost furtive. Even Bonnie was quick to notice the change.

"You and Chris's psychiatrist," she said, "seem to think I know a lot more about all this than you're telling me."

Eric did not know what to say. He felt a strong impulse to ease his own burden by sharing his knowledge with her. Once Bonnie knew, *she* could decide what to do, or not to do, after that. But at least she would have the information. And in Eric's opinion, she was certainly entitled to it.

After all, it had been she who'd been beaten and stabbed. And it had been her husband who'd been killed. And now it was she who continued to speak up most forcefully in Chris's defense, and who was spending a small fortune on his legal and medical bills, and who would have to suffer through the trauma of a trial at which Chris's lawyers would argue that he was not guilty of the very offense Eric knew he had committed.

"I get the feeling," Bonnie said, "that you know a lot more than you're telling me."

"Well . . . ," he said. Then he looked away. He could not lie to her, yet neither could he tell her the truth. Or could he? He wanted to. He desperately wanted to. But to do so would be to betray his best friend. But it seemed obvious, just from her comment, that she *knew* Eric had to know something.

"Well . . . ," he said again. But then he stopped.

Bonnie was the one who spoke next. "Chris is dealing with a lot of things," she said. "A lot of guilt."

"Yes, he is," Eric said.

"Eric," she said, "I think the police and the lawyers have convinced Chris that he had something to do with it, when the truth is that he actually didn't. A lot of people have got him feeling like he's guilty, even though he had nothing to do with it."

Eric didn't know how to respond. And before he had a chance to respond in any way, Chris and John came back into the living room and his private conversation with Bonnie was over.

26

A hearing on pretrial motions filed by both the district attorney and by lawyers for both Chris and James Upchurch was held in Little Washington on September 18. Chris, like the other defendants, was required to attend.

The hearing was notable not so much for what was argued or decided as for two other aspects: it gave Mitchell Norton a taste of what it would be like to try a case against Bill Osteen, and it gave Bonnie her first look at Neal Henderson.

For weeks, Jim Vosburgh had been waging a campaign of psychological warfare against Norton. Every time he'd see the Beaufort County district attorney, he'd make it a point to drop some new tidbit of wisdom he'd just acquired from the legendary Osteen, or he'd tell some new (and perhaps, just slightly exaggerated) tale of a courtroom war in which Osteen's skills had reduced an overmatched opponent to ashes.

Vosburgh would say things like, "You know, Mitchell,

Bill is really looking forward to coming down here and trying this case. It's not very often anymore that he gets into the ring against someone with your limited range of experience.''

Mitchell Norton would purse his lips and frown and shake his head. This was the sort of heckling that contributed to Jim Vosburgh's unpopularity in certain quarters, but he could tell it was taking its toll.

Norton, by coincidence, had grown up in the same tiny hamlet as Billy Royal: Salemburg. He'd gone not to Wake Forest or Chapel Hill or even to NC State, however, but to East Carolina University in Greenville, a notable step down the academic ladder. His law degree came not from Chapel Hill or Duke or one of the nationally renowned law schools, but from the Cumberland School of Law at Samford University in Alabama.

He was forty years old, a slow talker but a hard worker, married to a woman he'd known from high school. He had a thick brown mustache and a round and somewhat chinless face. He'd never been in private practice. The year he'd graduated from law school, he'd taken a job as assistant district attorney in Washington. After serving for ten years in that capacity, he'd finally been elected district attorney himself. But his was a sparsely populated, largely rural district, seldom visited by lawyers of Bill Osteen's reputation.

On his office walls, Norton had hung large pictures of Robert E. Lee and Stonewall Jackson. He had meant them to serve as inspiration, but in this instance they were only disturbing reminders of what could happen to even the greatest of men when they found themselves overmatched.

Within a year, Mitchell Norton would have to stand for re-election. If he lost, he'd be off the public payroll for the first time in fifteen years. And he was acutely aware that if he failed in the most notorious murder case he'd ever tried, he'd be an exceedingly vulnerable candidate.

Norton wasn't concerned about Wayland Sermons, the thirty-four-year-old local attorney who'd been appointed Upchurch's public defender, or about Frank Johnston, a more experienced Washington lawyer who would be working with Sermons. Wayland and Frank were perfectly competent, and fine fellows besides, but they were men Norton had known for years, and against whom he had tried many cases. Win or lose, with Wayland and Frank, there was no chance for embarrassment.

The same could not be said about Bill Osteen, whose renown had begun to cast a long shadow over Beaufort County, and particularly over Mitchell Norton's state of mind. To lose the case against Pritchard would be bad enough. But to be made a fool of, in front of his own people—that could spell the end of his career in public life.

In truth, nothing that Osteen said or did in court on September 18 marked him as possessing mythical powers, but that first hearing was really no more than a pregame warm-up: one in which, metaphorically speaking, Osteen didn't even bother to take off his sweat suit.

But even under those circumstances, Mitchell Norton was conscious of a presence that, by its very understatedness, was all the more intimidating. And from that day on, with Vosburgh's continuing encouragement, the county district attorney came to view Chris Pritchard's attorney as someone not only to respect as an adversary, but to fear.

Fear of a much more immediate and acute sort was what Bonnie felt that day. All three defendants, Upchurch, Henderson, and Chris, were required to be present in court as the various motions were argued. Bonnie had seen Upchurch before at his bond hearing and had experienced no reaction whatsoever. But now, upon getting her first glimpse of Neal Henderson, she had an even more severe panic attack than in August when, in district court, she'd noticed the man who'd seemed to have no neck staring at her.

Neal Henderson had exactly the same build. He was bulky across the chest, and his shoulders seemed to flow almost directly from the bottom of his head, as if he, too, were virtually without a neck. *This was what she remembered from the attack. This was the bulky and neckless upper body of the man who'd stood above her, beating her head with a club that made a "whooshing" or "whirring" sound.*

Feeling, once again, as if she were about to faint from fright, Bonnie jumped to her feet and fled the courtroom.

She went directly to Jim Vosburgh's office and stayed there for the remainder of the hearing. *That was the man she'd seen in her bedroom! That was the man who'd tried to kill her!*

Mitchell Norton and the SBI were claiming that all Henderson had done was drive the car, and that James Upchurch, and Upchurch alone, had committed the murder.

But of course that's what they'd claim, Bonnie realized. Henderson, after all, was the one who'd come forward to cooperate, and who would be testifying against both Upchurch and Chris. Of course, Lewis Young and John Crone and John Taylor and the rest of them would want to believe that all Henderson had done was drive the car. That way, he wasn't really a killer. That way, in return for testimony that could send her own son to his death, he'd be rewarded with the lightest sentence possible.

Even as she sat, still trembling, in Vosburgh's office, Bonnie could envision the conspiracy taking place.

She knew one thing, though, and she knew it not logically this time, she *felt* it as strongly as she'd ever before felt anything in her life: *it had been the form of Neal Henderson, not James Upchurch, that she'd seen as she'd looked up, dazed, bruised, and bleeding, from her bedroom floor, and had reached out to touch her dying husband's hand.*

In an attempt to compose herself, Bonnie, the data processor, sat in Vosburgh's office and wrote down her impression of the morning's events. As was so typical of her, even in notes intended only for herself, she did not commit to paper the intensity of emotion that all those near her in the courtroom had witnessed.

She wrote: "All three defendants were present. I looked around for Neal Henderson. My physical reaction was unexpected. It made everything more confused, because his upper-body outline is the same as that of the person in my bedroom on July 25th. Every instinct says I fear this person greatly. The shoulder bulk, the head sitting close to the shoulders, as if there is no neck—it makes the effort to remain unemotional near impossible. . . .

"I went to the rest room to compose myself as much as

possible. Then proceeded to let Mr. Osteen be aware of my concern. I don't know if that was the right thing to do. I really *need* to talk to Wade Smith about what I should do, without involving Chris's attorneys unnecessarily.

"Mr. Osteen felt it could be advisable to not return to the courtroom, so I went back to Mr. Vosburgh's office. I arrived around 12:19 P.M. . . ."

By two P.M., she had regained enough control to return for the afternoon session.

Two days later, on September 20, Osteen and Vosburgh met with Billy Royal in his Chapel Hill office to assess Chris's mental condition and to explore the possibility of an insanity defense.

As was his manner, Billy Royal started slowly and took a good leisurely ramble around the conversational track. For quite some time, he talked about how he had established a very solid professional relationship with Chris, and how—as often was not the case—he'd been given sufficient time and opportunity to formulate an opinion that was supported by extensive contact with the patient.

When he finally reached the first point, he was reassuring: he said Chris's suicidal tendencies seemed to be at least in remission, and that he was "no longer in the danger zone as far as doing immediate harm to himself or to others." Over the longer term, however, Chris would require a "structured environment,' in which to live.

Osteen and Vosburgh recalled that Dr. Royal then said the insanity defense was out of the question. No matter how unstable Chris might seem now, there was no documented history of mental illness prior to the commission of the crime. All Dr. Royal could do would be to testify at the sentencing phase of the proceedings—if and when one occurred—that Chris's emotional problems had undoubtedly predated the planning of the murder, and that his condition should be viewed as a mitigating factor.

"Speaking of that," Vosburgh said, "the question the judge would ask you at that point is whether you think there's any likelihood that he would ever do anything like this again."

"I can't say," the psychiatrist answered. "He might."

"Wait a minute!" Vosburgh shouted. "That's the answer you'd give in court?"

"If court were tomorrow, and I was under oath, that's the only answer I could give."

Later, Vosburgh said, "I felt like I got hit with a baseball bat. I crapped. I didn't know what to do. All the hours we'd invested in this guy analyzing Chris, and the best answer he can come up with is, 'I don't know if he'll ever try to kill his mother again'?

"I'll tell you what. All three of us—Bill Junior was there, too—were devastated after *that* conference. Osteen says, 'Gentlemen, it looks like we go to trial with a client who can't testify, at least five people who could fall out of the sky at any moment, telling the DA that our client has confessed, and now our own psychiatrist, who says he's not insane but it's possible he'll try to kill again.'"

Billy Royal, however, once again had a very different recollection. He said he never thought Osteen seriously considered insanity as a plea. In his opinion, the lawyers did not thoroughly explore all their options. It had been his view, he said later, that if Chris were in treatment he would be no danger to anyone—even himself. Dr. Royal said he expressed this view clearly, but that none of the lawyers seemed to want to hear it.

At seven P.M., Billy Royal met again with Chris. During this session, Chris stressed how scared he'd been by actually having to appear in court. The reality of what was looming in the future seemed to be taking firmer hold.

"Even if I don't get the death penalty," he said, "I'll go away for twenty years. What's life like at forty-one?" He said it had been a very bad day. The sight of Neal Henderson had greatly upset his mother.

He seemed eager to change the subject to girls. "I'll tell them anything to get in their pants." But he said what he really wanted was a child of his own. "Someone to love," he said, "someone to be a part of me."

Two days later, on September 22, he was back. Billy

Royal was concerned about him and wanted to monitor his condition closely.

Chris said he had no childhood memories of his sister, he could not recall ever having been disciplined by his mother, he'd been a lot smaller than anyone else his age, he'd started looking at dirty magazines before he was seven years old, he'd masturbated frequently as a child, he'd had one experience of fellatio with an older male cousin, he and his mother never had philosophic differences.

"What makes you angry?" Billy Royal asked.

"When I don't get my way." He said, "I like to do what nobody I know has done before, so I can brag about it."

"As a child," Dr. Royal asked, "how would you compare yourself to other children?"

"I was smarter. I was a runner, not a fighter. But always a thinker. I'm on a different plane from other people. I can concentrate on two things at once."

By the following Wednesday, September 27, when he next saw Dr. Royal, Chris's condition seemed to be worsening. As soon as he took his seat, he curled himself tightly into a fetal position and said he'd forgotten what he wanted to talk about.

"I feel like standing up and throwing things," he said. He was worried about jail, about getting raped, beaten up, having things stolen. At a weekend party for Angela's nineteenth birthday he'd drunk twelve beers in eight hours. He wanted to scream, he felt as if he were living on borrowed time, he wanted to run away, he knew he would have to go to jail, he'd never be able to have a wife and children.

"I'll be a sixty-one-year-old bum." Then he lapsed again into a recurrent fantasy of living in a big home, of taking care of Bonnie and Angela. It would be a compound, he said, like the Kennedy compound in Massachusetts. He'd have a horse farm for Angela, and for his own children. It would be "one big happy family." He said, "I could be a damned good father." Then he said, "I'd rather take my own life than be raped."

He said, "I used to be a shit, but not anymore. Now I treat girls like they should be treated, I give them roses, I walk and talk with them. I used to just try and get in their pants.''

He said even when he was surrounded by other people, he felt alone. ''I've got to live with the knowledge that I caused my father's death. But there's nothing I can do about that. I can't bring him back.'' The only person with whom he felt secure was his mother. But now, far from feeling compelled to confess, he dreaded the day when she would finally learn the truth.

He said again he couldn't go to jail. What he needed was to be institutionalized. He said he'd always been insecure, ever since his real father had left and his mother had had to work all the time and he'd had to spend so much time with his grandparents. ''I'm not very stable now,'' he said, ''and going to jail isn't going to help.''

On October 2, he told Billy Royal his trial date had been set for January 2, 1990. ''So now I know what time frame I have to cram my life into. I have to live it while I've got it, and that's what I intend to do. But I've totally lost control. My dreams are dashed. I'm good with words, with the English language. I could write a damned good book. And that's what I want to do, write a novel. My first book would be about my life and trial. The second would be more like journalism—about the evils of drugs.''

He added that he had a lot of nervous energy and a constant desire for sex. He also said, once again, that his mother was ''convinced'' that Neal Henderson had been the person in her room.

He seemed to Dr. Royal to be growing more tense, jittery, and depressed as the awareness sunk in that he would indeed be standing trial on January 2, and that even his own lawyer already knew he was guilty.

''All during this time,'' said Eric Caldwell, ''he was drinking a lot, and that would make him depressed. When he was depressed, he'd tell me that he still wanted to tell his mother but he couldn't. But it was strange: he never said he wanted to tell Angela.''

* * *

On October 4, Bonnie saw Jean Spaulding again. It had been almost a month since her last visit.

What clearly was dominating her conscious mind was her vivid recollection of her first look at Neal Henderson. When she began to talk about it, Dr. Spaulding noted a real change in affect.

"This was obviously a traumatic issue. She said he came into the room and she had to leave and could not return until after lunch. For Bonnie, that was just extraordinary. I remember her describing how, when she saw him, it was the neck and the head and the flow between the two that so unnerved her.

"And it was—this is my word—it was more that sense of your hair rising on the back of your neck that she got when she saw him. She had never had that feeling about Upchurch.

"It was hard for her—and this is unusual for Bonnie—even to put into words the impact of having seen Neal Henderson. It was just this kind of in-the-gut sort of reaction that she had. I saw more of an affect bordering on terror. I don't think I'd ever really seen terror from her, but I saw something more in that direction during this description. And she's not the kind to reveal that, if she hadn't had those sorts of emotions. This was really important to her. And this had happened two weeks earlier. She made a point of saying, 'On that Monday two weeks ago . . .' Yet it was very fresh. It gave you the sense that it had just happened like two minutes before.

"I have not been able to dismiss that reaction. I have to give significant weight to it. It is completely unlike Bonnie to have a reaction where she has to leave a room. She is the sort of person who wants to be there for every detail. She wants to hear it all and process it all and see every *i* dotted. For her to have a reaction that strongly, where she has to leave the room, is very atypical. That was a very big thing."

Dr. Spaulding said later, however, that Bonnie "didn't tell me anything" about the trauma of September 7. For her to have made no reference whatsoever to the day that she would eventually describe as one on which the bottom fell out of her heart was an omission that the psychiatrist found "incredible."

Clearly, at their first session together since that day, Bonnie would have been able to recall the events in vivid detail. "But it does not come out. It never comes out. I never hear that. Now we're having real strong evidence of denial. She needed to come and talk about that, and to deal with the emotions about that, and how upsetting it must have been for her to see Chris in that state."

But she hadn't said a word about it.

"She pushed it back," Dr. Spaulding said. "It may have just been so painful for her to even contemplate dealing with it that she would push it back that much more."

Later in the week, Bonnie and two friends went to a doll show in Newport News, Virginia. On her way, she passed through Little Washington, where she briefly visited a former neighbor.

"It doesn't sound good," the neighbor said. "I hear they've got a map that Chris drew."

"Suppose they do have a map?" Bonnie said. "That doesn't prove anything. Here, let me show you what *I* have." Then she took from her pocketbook a copy of the report from the polygraph operator in Charlotte, saying that Chris had passed his test. "You see?" she said. "It's not just me. Here's *proof* that Chris couldn't be guilty."

Bonnie saw Jean Spaulding again on November 6. Almost immediately, she started talking about Henderson. "She went back into the issue of his size. His size was just like the attacker's. That was still fresh. A month later, that was still very, very fresh."

But still—even two months after the fact—she made no reference to the change of heart on Bill Osteen's part that had so shaken her on September 7. At no time, even to her own psychiatrist, did she ever express the slightest doubt about her son's innocence.

Aware that no less an expert than Wade Smith was persuaded that the State's case against Chris rested on a firm foundation, Dr. Spaulding recognized that Bonnie was displaying a classic example of denial mechanism.

"I don't mean that in a negative way," Dr. Spaulding said later. "It's a method for defending against difficult circumstances, defending against conflict, and therefore allowing a person to function. And then when we consider her maternal instincts here, which were quite strong—this is the woman who had had to work those long hours and pay those bills her ex-husband had left her with, and keep that home going for those children—she's going to fight tenaciously.

"But she was not *choosing*. This was an unconscious mechanism. All defense mechanisms like this are unconscious processes—they are things learned so early in life that essentially there is no choice. You kind of automatically kick into whichever one was an operant for you in your family structure. So this was not something she chose.

"She is not a stupid woman. And basic moral values are important to her. If she had known as a fact—if some divine providence, or Mr. Osteen or Wade Smith, came and said to her outright, 'Chris is guilty,' then she's the sort of person who would probably take him right to the judge.

"She would not scheme and plot, but by contrast she's the sort who's going to fight tenaciously for her children, and if that means that she pushes some information back into the far recesses of her mind, consciously or unconsciously, I think she would do that.

"She's also not a cowardly woman. She is very courageous. And when you go back to all these different roles that she's had to play—and not play them out sequentially, but play them out simultaneously—it's almost more than you can imagine a person having to endure."

27

With each passing day, Bill Osteen felt even more keenly the desire not to have to defend Chris Pritchard in court. Trial was only six weeks away, and he not only knew his client was guilty, but that he'd confessed to at least five people, any one of whom, at any time, could notify a law enforcement agency.

Even in the absence of that threat, Osteen didn't want to try the case. The day he'd first met Chris Pritchard and had formed his instant and lasting dislike, it had not even occurred to him that there might ever be a case to try. Now there was, and he knew his client was not only dishonest and insolent, but guilty of murder.

There were lawyers who, even knowing of the guilt, would have let Chris tell any story he wanted on the stand. This question, like that of how hard a lawyer should press his client for the full truth, was one of both ethics and tactics, and honorable practitioners disagreed.

One view was that the adversarial process required the defense attorney to do everything possible—short of making a knowing misrepresentation himself—to win his case. If that meant permitting a client to testify untruthfully, so be it. It was the job of the prosecutor to reveal flaws in the story, and of the jury to make the ultimate determination of truth. The lawyer's job, purely and simply, was to help the client achieve the result the client wanted.

"I know there are people," Osteen would say later, "who perceive defense lawyers as trying to cover up information and even allow their clients to testify untruthfully. But there are a lot of people out here doing good work who do not practice like that, and I believe I was among them."

Having extracted the truth in the privacy of his own office, Osteen was now stuck with it. The result was, he had two reasons for not wanting to defend Chris in court: one, he stood a chance of losing (which meant the strong possibility that Chris would be sentenced to death); and two, he also had a strong chance to win.

"One of the problems," he said later, though not every lawyer would view this as a problem, "was that it looked like we had a pretty good chance."

In July, he'd learned of the content of Neal Henderson's statement to authorities. John Taylor, in an attempt to minimize Bonnie's hostility toward investigators, had taken her to lunch and had spelled it out in detail. In all significant aspects, it comported almost exactly with the story Chris told in August.

Osteen, however, was also aware of the flaws in the State's case: the lack of physical evidence; the mess made of the crime scene; the impossibility of *proving*, on the basis of only three or four printing samples, that Chris had really drawn the map; the flimsiness of the unsupported testimony of one person, Neal Henderson, who appeared to be the only witness who could link Chris to the crime.

"Do we take it to trial and take a chance on winning?" Osteen asked later. "What's going to happen to Chris if we do that?"

The answer was, he would go free, and only then would Bonnie learn that he had, in fact, been responsible for the murder of her husband and for her near-murder, and that he'd lied successfully about it. What would that awareness do to the rest of her life, and to her relationship with him?

Or perhaps she'd never be told. Osteen had noticed that Chris's passion to confess in order to earn his mother's forgiveness seemed to be waning quickly as the date for trial approached. If he was acquitted, would he still feel the need for her forgiveness?

If not, Osteen, his son, Tom Brereton, Jim Vosburgh, and Billy Royal—and even, really, Wade Smith—would live out their days aware that Bonnie's son had gotten away with murder, and that Bonnie herself might never know it.

Unless, as Osteen understood Billy Royal to have said

was possible—knowing that Bonnie was all that stood between him and half of a $2-million fortune—he might decide to try it again.

The fact was, since August, when he'd first learned the truth, or what he supposed was a good part of the truth—with Chris, he felt, one could never be sure one was hearing it all—Osteen had been growing ever more persuaded that the best service he could render his client, and not so incidentally, his client's mother, would be to negotiate a deal that allowed Chris to plead guilty to a lesser charge and receive a sentence of something other than death.

He just didn't know how he could persuade Mitchell Norton that such an arrangement would also be in the best interests of the State.

Bill Osteen and the eight or nine others to whom Chris had confessed by late November *knew* he was guilty. But even within Bonnie's family, some had come to suspect it. Chris's uncle and his wife, of course, had voiced their doubts to Lewis Young at the start, but there was also his grandfather.

Bonnie's younger sister, Ramona, remembered a dinner in Little Washington, while Bonnie was still hospitalized, at which George Bates, Sr., had said to her, sounding truly depressed for the first time in his life, "I'll bet you, when it comes down to it, the young'uns are involved." Whether he meant one or both was not clear, and she did not ask.

Ramona also recalled a later episode. "It was in the summer, but before Chris was even arrested. We'd gone fishing, and suddenly Daddy lay on the ground. At first, I thought he'd had a stroke, but he said, 'No, I'm all right, I just need to rest. I've got a lot on my mind.' " After a long pause, he had added, "I hate it that Chris has done this, but in my heart I know he did."

Peggy Bates, too, could remember a moment, just about at the time of Chris's arrest, when she was sitting under a shade tree in the backyard in Welcome, having just laid wooden steps down to the greenhouse where Bonnie's mother was cultivating orchids.

"We somehow got talking about Chris," she said, "and

his granddad said he knew without a doubt that Chris was guilty. That's the only time I heard him come out and say it, but there were hints in other conversations. He knew it darned good and well.''

And Bonnie's brother, George Jr., remembered feeling, "yes, he thought Chris had something to do with it. Even before the arrest. He just came right out and said, 'Something's rotten in Denmark here. Something's rotten in Denmark.' ''

Knowing how strongly Bonnie believed—and needed to believe—in Chris's innocence, her father had never breathed a word of this to her. It would have broken Bonnie's heart to hear him say it. Instead, he continued doing what he'd done since the day of the murder: being there for her, giving love and support.

At Thanksgiving, he even told her what he'd decided to do for the trial.

Bonnie had cooked a turkey for Thanksgiving. This was something she had not done since she and Lieth had lived in Indiana. In more recent years, they'd spent the holiday in Winston-Salem with Lieth's parents and had dined at a nearby country club.

This year, Bonnie was determined that the holiday would be as homey and traditional and family-oriented as she could make it. The trial was less than six weeks away. She was scared. She knew that, despite the best efforts of Bill Osteen and Jim Vosburgh, by the time the next Thanksgiving rolled around, Chris might not be present at her table.

Her mother and father came up from Welcome. Chris and Angela were there. The turkey was plump and moist and flavorful. There was stuffing, potatoes, creamed vegetables, cranberry sauce, two kinds of pie: the meal was everything Bonnie had hoped it would be.

Chris seemed nervous throughout the day and did not linger for conversation when dinner was done. He was up and out the door as fast as possible.

Sitting in Bonnie's living room after the meal, her father told her he was worried about Chris, and about her, too. Due to extensive and prejudicial pretrial publicity, the trial had been shifted from Washington to Elizabeth City, a fishing and farming town an hour and a half away, near the Virginia border, in the extreme northeast corner of the state.

But even away from the poisonous atmosphere of Little Washington, the trial would be a terrible strain for both Bonnie and Chris. Bonnie had already decided that the best thing for Angela, psychologically, would be for her to continue with her studies at her new college, and to stay as far from Elizabeth City as possible. She'd also asked other members of her family to stay away, insisting that she didn't need "baby-sitters" and could cope perfectly well on her own.

Her father, however, knew better. Regardless of his feelings about Chris's involvement—or maybe even more so because of them—George Bates had no intention of letting his daughter endure the trial alone. He knew how self-reliant she was, and what a point she'd always made of not letting her own troubles affect others, but in this case, he said, she would have to make an exception. He would travel to Elizabeth City with Bonnie and Chris and would stand by the two of them from the first day of trial to the last.

She tried to persuade him that this would not be necessary; that she really could manage on her own; that at his age he ought not to put himself through such stress. But George Bates would have none of it. He said his mind was made up.

And for once, Bonnie did not insist. The truth was, she felt so frightened of what lay ahead that her father's announcement came as a comfort and relief.

On November 30, Bonnie's mother and father drove up from Welcome early in the morning. Her mother climbed into the front seat of Bonnie's car while Bonnie gave her father a hug and said they'd see him the next day. She and her mother were heading for Elizabeth City to find a place for her and her father and Chris to stay during the trial.

The trip took almost six hours. Elizabeth City, even less accessible by modern highway than Little Washington, had a population of 16,500 and was at the lower edge of a vast marshland known as the Great Dismal Swamp. This tangle of cypress and honeysuckle, running almost forty miles from north to south, was inhabited by bear, possum, and an abundance of poisonous snakes.

Elizabeth City itself, a not quite quaint and not quite charming town—though it tilted a bit further in those directions than Little Washington did—was the seat of Pasquotank County, a fringe area of North Carolina that found itself more in the orbit of Norfolk, Virginia, than of any of North Carolina's larger cities.

It also happened to be the home of Superior Court judge Thomas Watts, who would be presiding over the trial.

As in Little Washington, the largest and least offensive accommodation appeared to be the Holiday Inn. But Bonnie did not want to stay there. Judge Watts had already explained in open court that the Holiday Inn was the best place to stay and had offered to make reservations there for all connected with the case.

Mitchell Norton and Lewis Young and John Taylor would be staying at the Holiday Inn. The press would be staying at the Holiday Inn. *Neal Henderson*, still free on bond, would be staying at the Holiday Inn when he came to testify.

There was no way—even with her father by her side—that Bonnie would stay at the Holiday Inn. Instead, she chose a locally owned motel called the Goodnite Inn. It was small. One would be hard-pressed to call it cute. But it was only 1.3 miles from the courthouse, a five- to eight-minute drive, depending on traffic, and in a neighborhood that did not appear disreputable. The management was courteous and the rates were reasonable—$38.95 for a double, compared to $54 at the Holiday Inn.

Bonnie and her mother spent the night there. It was quiet and clean and perfectly tolerable. In the morning, Bonnie made arrangements to book a room beginning Monday, January 1, 1990, with the understanding that she and her father and her son would be occupying it from Sunday night through Thursday night each week for several weeks after that.

On the drive back, Bonnie and her mother stopped in

Burlington to look at fabric and pottery, breaking up what was otherwise an arduous trip. This meant it was well after dark before they drove into Welcome, and down the narrow two-lane road, bordered on both sides by dormant farmland, that led to the house in which Bonnie had been raised.

Even from a distance, she could tell something was wrong.

The driveway outside the house was filled with cars.

That should not be.

There should only have been the one car, which belonged to her mother and her father.

But there was her brother George's car, and her sister Kitty's and Sylvia's and even Ramona's van from South Carolina.

It wasn't right.

She didn't need logic, only gut instinct, to tell her that, as she put it later, "something bad was in the wind."

Chris! Oh, dear Lord, the stress had finally gotten to him and her son had killed himself.

Bonnie parked as quickly as she could, and she and her mother got out of the car in a hurry.

The front door opened and her brother came out to meet them in the driveway.

"What's going on?" Bonnie's mother asked.

"Come on inside and I'll tell you."

"No, tell me outside, right now."

Bonnie didn't wait. She knew the answer as soon as she saw her brother come out the door. For whenever anyone came to his house for any reason, it was always George Bates, Sr., Bonnie's father, who greeted them first. But he wasn't there.

Bonnie ran past her mother and brother and into the house, crying, "Where's my daddy? Where's my daddy!"

He wasn't there. He'd been back in the woods behind the house that afternoon, cutting down a dead tree, an activity he'd engaged in for more than half a century.

But on this day, December 1, 1989, exactly one month before he was to go to Elizabeth City to attend his grandson's murder trial, he'd failed to clear a path for himself and had cut the tree the wrong way and it had fallen on him and killed him.

He'd died right there in the woods—only a quarter mile from where, on Pearl Harbor Day, he'd carved the lines from the Joyce Kilmer poem—with his only living brother cradling his head in his arms.

Later, Bonnie's mother would say, "It was all because of how much he was dreading that trial."

And she would tell her only son, Bonnie's brother, that it wasn't just the trial, but "Chris, and what he had done, that caused his death."

28

What worried people was that Bonnie didn't cry. She didn't cry when she was first told, she didn't cry later that night, she didn't once cry during the two days of the wake, as her father lay in his open casket, and, it seemed, the whole population of Welcome, and half of Lexington as well, came to pay final respects, and she didn't cry at the funeral, which was held Sunday afternoon in the simple brick church that George Bates had built with his own hands.

"What purpose does crying serve?" she asked later. "It doesn't make anything any different."

Instead of crying or praying or grieving in what many would consider the traditional way, Bonnie became even more businesslike than usual. She spent a lot of time on the phone. It was she who called the newspaper to give information about funeral arrangements and all the factual details of her father's life necessary for the obituary. And it was she who called Bill Osteen and Jim Vosburgh, explaining that due to a family emergency she would have to ask that the upcoming motion hearing be rescheduled for later in the week.

The last of the hearings on pretrial motions was held at the Pitt County Courthouse in Greenville on December 14.

As he awaited the start of the proceedings, Bill Osteen heard Mitchell Norton say something to him.

"Excuse me?"

"Your client's a wimp," Norton said.

To Norton's surprise, Osteen did not seem offended by this remark. Instead, he nodded in agreement.

"I think you've put your finger on the heart of the matter," he replied. "Chris *is* a wimp."

While a plea bargain had remained his fondest dream—and while he'd been growing increasingly anxious as trial approached because he still could not view either winning or losing as a satisfactory outcome—Bill Osteen had not yet calculated the best way to raise the question with a district attorney who he thought would reject it out of hand.

He instinctively saw Norton's remark as an opening. He nodded again. "Yes, Mitchell, I think you and I are in complete agreement about Chris. And because he's such a wimp, any part he may have played in this whole thing could only have been inadvertent. He's not like the people who carried it out. They weren't wimps. They were evil."

The district attorney did not interrupt.

"You know," Osteen continued, "maybe when this hearing is over, you and I ought to sit down by ourselves for a few minutes and see if we might not have something to talk about."

Mitchell Norton could hardly believe what he was hearing. Yes, it was oblique, it was tentative, it gave away nothing, it did not in any way compromise Osteen's position, but there was no doubt about it: Chris Pritchard's lawyer was talking about a plea.

To Norton, this seemed almost too good to be true. For, unbeknownst to Osteen, Mitchell Norton was almost equally eager to negotiate a plea bargain.

Like Osteen, Mitchell Norton had certain problems. Foremost among Norton's was Neal Henderson. The district attorney had by now spent many hours in his star witness's company. He believed Henderson's story. But he had also come to feel that the young man from Caswell County, with his 160 IQ and 1500 score on his Scholastic Aptitude Test, and his passion for Dungeons & Dragons and for arcane, bizarre comic books, and such rock groups as Blue Oyster Cult ("That damned old narcotic music," Norton called it)—and with his cold, flinty eyes, his expressionless face, and his detached, inflectionless voice—would make an awful witness.

"He's a plastic man," Norton had complained to his assistant, Keith Mason, and to Lewis Young and John Taylor, who were also helping with pretrial preparation. "He walks like a robot and talks like a robot and nobody's going to believe a damned word he says."

And Henderson was his whole case. He possessed not a whit of physical evidence. To prove the guilt of James Upchurch, he had only Neal Henderson's word. To prove Chris Pritchard's guilt beyond a reasonable doubt, he had only Henderson and the map.

But even if he persuaded a jury that Pritchard had indeed drawn the map (and no expert witness could say so with certainty), Chris could say he'd done so only as a joke, or as part of a Dungeons & Dragons game. Then his mother— who would win the jury's sympathy instantly—would back him up. Bonnie would say there was no way in the world her son could have had anything to do with this tragedy.

And then she'd say the silhouette of the killer she'd seen in her room matched the physique of Neal Henderson and could not possibly have been that of Upchurch.

Unaware, of course, that Osteen would not permit Chris to testify, and also unaware of the various friends to whom Chris had already confessed, Norton had been suffering through his own sleepless nights. The whole case—and with it his career—could so easily go up in smoke, just as the map had not.

Eventually, he'd begun to wonder if he should consider broaching to Osteen the possibility of negotiating a plea bargain with Chris. That way, the district attorney felt, he'd have a much better chance of winning at least one conviction at a trial.

Unfortunately, nothing Norton had gleaned from Osteen's actions or demeanor suggested that the Greensboro lawyer had anything on his mind except fighting like hell, fully confident of the outcome.

It might only make matters worse if Norton raised the question. First, it would be viewed as a sign of weakness. If he were confident of winning, why would he even entertain the notion of making a deal? Second, Osteen might be insulted. His client was claiming innocence, and Osteen was about to step forward and argue that position. He might not take at all kindly to the suggestion that his whole posture had been no more than an elaborate charade; that what he had really been looking for all along was some way to get out from under the worst of the consequences his client might face.

But now . . . but now . . . *Osteen himself had raised the question.*

They met in a small, plain room immediately after the hearing: just Osteen, Norton, and Norton's able and affable young assistant, Keith Mason.

Osteen began by saying, "I haven't raised this before because my client and I are more than ready to go to trial, but I do think that the Code of Ethics requires me to explore any possibility of a settlement of these charges. And so, if either of you have any suggestions, let me know. If not, we'll just proceed."

Keith Mason responded first. "What can you help us with?"

"It's not a question of help," Osteen said. "Our position is that we've got a very good chance of winning at trial because there are some real loopholes in your case that all of us are aware of already. But if you all think there might be any basis for discussions, let me know. If not, so be it.

"And I want you to understand," he continued, "I haven't talked to my client about this. I haven't been authorized in any way to engage in a formal discussion. I am simply inquiring as to what your attitude would be if such a thing ever did become conceivable from our point of view."

Chewing on his mustache, Norton said, well, this wasn't the sort of discussion that he was prepared to really enter into either, but of course, just as Osteen had an obligation to explore all the options available to his client, Norton, too, as a public official, had a duty to his constituents to consider any and all alternatives that might be suggested in good faith.

Then Osteen said, well, maybe they should just leave it right there for a while, not push it any further. Maybe it wasn't an appropriate thing to be discussing, even on an informal basis.

But he added that Mrs. Von Stein had lost her husband at the same time that she'd also almost lost her own life, and then just recently, and so tragically, she'd lost her father, and now she would be testifying that the silhouette she had seen in her bedroom matched that of the State's star witness, Mr. Henderson, and could not have been that of the defendant, Mr. Upchurch.

A jury, Osteen added—a jury that would inevitably have enormous sympathy for Mrs. Von Stein—might well conclude that it was Mr. Henderson rather than Mr. Upchurch who should be sitting at the defendant's table and that, in any event, Mrs. Von Stein had suffered enough. They would not, under any circumstances, want to add to her woes by convicting her son of such a heinous crime.

And then he added that the Christmas season was almost upon them, and that if there was any way, any way at all, that Mitchell Norton could help Osteen bring an end to the agony that that poor woman had been going through, then, "I've just got to know if that's available. What I'm trying to do here is to save people's lives and save people's sanity."

Norton allowed as how that was something that, as good Christian gentlemen, and in the spirit of the season, they all probably ought to spend a bit of time mulling over. "There can't be any harm in talking further," he said, "just so long as nobody thinks anybody is committing to anything."

"Just theoretically," Osteen asked, "what would your position be in regard to sentencing?"

Again, Mitchell Norton was stunned. This was in no way theoretical. This was real.

"Well, I don't know," he said, speaking even more slowly than usual. "I must say, that's something I've never really thought about."

"Here's my position," Osteen said. "I would want you to agree not to argue for any particular sentence. To let me argue for as light a sentence as possible, but to leave it strictly in the hands of Judge Watts."

"I suppose," Norton said, "a lot of what I could agree to would have to do with what it was that Pritchard would say."

"What he would say," Osteen replied, "is that the plan was pretty much what Neal Henderson has said it was."

And with that, Bill Osteen went back to Greensboro, leaving Mitchell Norton almost too flabbergasted to drive himself home.

"I didn't like the thought of dealing with anyone," Norton said later, "but the danger of blowing it all was just too great. The stakes were so high. And I was a public official. I had responsibilities to people in a five-county area. I'll tell you, I stayed up all that night. I looked at those crime-scene photos again. I saw the brutality with which Lieth had been killed. And I asked myself, who was worse morally, the guy who drew the map or the guy who swung the bat?

"I honestly believed that with the map to corroborate Henderson's testimony, we could probably have gotten a conviction against Pritchard. But about Upchurch I wasn't nearly so sure. And he was the man all the evidence, and all my intuition, pointed to as dangerous. He was the type who could do it again, especially after getting away with it once."

Evidence to support Norton's assessment had been provided on November 20 in the form of a letter Upchurch had sent to a friend, a letter that had found its way into the hands of Lewis Young.

Upchurch had mistakenly addressed the letter to a sporting goods store on Hillsborough Street in Raleigh, apparently confusing the store's address with that of his friend. Not long before, the store had been burglarized, but the stolen goods had been recovered. When a sheriff's deputy had arrived at the store on November 20 to return the stolen property, the manager had showed him an envelope containing numerous newspaper clippings concerning the murder of Lieth Von Stein, and a letter obviously intended for someone else, but with the address of the sporting goods store on the envelope.

The deputy had turned the materials over to the SBI. One clipping concerned the value of Lieth's estate. Upchurch noted the estimate of $2 million, but wrote, "He was probably worth ten times this."

He also asked the friend to mail him doses of LSD in jail. He recommended that the friend put the drug tabs under the postage stamps of letters sent through his public defender's office, rather than directly to him, explaining that guards sometimes threw away the envelopes before bringing his mail to his cell.

In the letter, apparently referring to a prior conversation, Upchurch urged his friend not to let any of the specifics he'd mentioned about a bat or knife used in the murder be made public. He said his strategy was to "appear ignorant" to the district attorney. The only story he wanted spread, he said, was that Henderson was lying and he could prove it.

More chillingly, Upchurch had also written that he was enjoying being the center of attention: "It's the ultimate game of me against THEM and winner take all. Win millions of dollars or lose your life. . . . None of this is real, it's just a part of THE GAME OF LIFE and somebody upped the stakes. . . . It looks like I'm going to be a very rich guy a year from now."

Having read that, Mitchell Norton felt even more obligated to do whatever was required to win a conviction against Upchurch—even if it meant making a deal with Chris Pritchard.

* * *

Returning from Greenville to Greensboro, Bill Osteen called Bonnie to tell her he wanted to meet with her and Chris at five-thirty P.M. on Sunday, December 17.

She thought it unusual for Osteen to schedule a meeting for a Sunday evening, and even more unusual for Jim Vosburgh to drive all the way out from Little Washington to attend.

It had been a cold afternoon and was already dark before the meeting began. Because it was a Sunday, downtown Greensboro was deserted, even in the midst of the Christmas season. The heat in Osteen's office building was shut off on Sundays, and he had to use a space heater to warm his conference room. He placed another heater in the reception area outside the room because he knew that for much of the time they were meeting with Chris, Bonnie would have to wait there alone. Inside, they'd be discussing matters about which she still could not be told.

Bonnie and Chris took seats at the same conference table at which, in August, Chris had confessed to a crime Bonnie still did not believe he could commit. Vosburgh was there, as well as Bill Osteen, Jr.

Bill Senior began by saying, "In preparing for a trial of this nature, we have to explore all the options available in the best interests of the client." He went on to say that the time for trial was drawing very near and that Chris would have to make some big decisions. He said that only a few days earlier he'd become aware that the possibility existed for working out an arrangement with Mitchell Norton whereby Chris could change his plea to guilty and promise to testify truthfully, in return for a lesser sentence than he might receive if he was found guilty at trial.

Bonnie wasn't quite sure she had understood Osteen correctly. Had he said Chris could plead *guilty?*

Then they asked her to go out to the reception area because they had matters to discuss with Chris privately.

Once she was outside, Osteen laid it on the line: time was short. Norton would agree to a plea. But Chris would have to decide fast. If they were going to make a deal, they would have to make it soon because, for all they knew, Norton might also be negotiating with Upchurch's attorneys. If the district attorney made a deal with Upchurch, where would that leave Chris? The answer was clear: on death row.

"It is our duty," Osteen said, "to lay out your options, but they're not attractive. In the best possible case, you could go free. In the worst, you'd be put to death." Then he explained the problems that made the best possible case also the least likely: first, he could not permit Chris to testify in his own defense; second, a deal might be made with Upchurch; third, at any moment, any one of the numerous people to whom Chris had already confessed could be discovered by the Washington police or SBI.

"Chris," Osteen said, "you're a very young person and this is a decision that will affect, or might even take away, the rest of your life. Obviously, it's one that we all want you to consider very carefully. But it's just as obvious that you don't have a lot of time."

All three lawyers then gave Chris their best estimates of the percentages of, first, his being found not guilty, and second, of his receiving the death penalty if convicted.

For once, he wasn't snotty, he wasn't arrogant, he wasn't even immature. "I think," Jim Vosburgh said later, "that this was the only time I ever saw him when he wasn't playing a role. I think he finally put the whole thing on the scales intellectually and saw how heavily they were weighted."

The estimates of acquittal ranged from 10 to 25 percent. For avoiding the death penalty if convicted, between 30 and 50 percent. Chris had rolled enough ten-sided dice during Dungeons & Dragons games to find those estimates discomforting.

Just as Chris was starting to ask about the probable length of his sentence, Bonnie was permitted back into the conference room. She heard Osteen say that pleading guilty to accessory to second-degree murder would probably carry a sentence of fifty years to life. A guilty plea to the count of conspiracy to commit murder would add another ten. The most severe sentence that could be imposed for all crimes considered together would be one of life plus twenty years.

What does that mean in "real time"? Chris asked. Estimates varied here because the parole process was notoriously difficult to predict, but Bill Osteen finally said that Chris could expect that even the most favorable plea-bargain agreement would mean he'd be spending at least twenty years in prison.

Bonnie was mystified. What were they talking about? Why were these questions being asked? *"Real time? . . . Life plus twenty?"*

Osteen turned to her and said that while it was still not possible for them to share with her the details that had led them to this point, it would be necessary, within a matter of a very few days, for Chris to decide whether to accept the type of arrangement he'd just described, or to continue forward to trial, aware that the death penalty was a real possibility.

"It was a very precarious time," Vosburgh said later, "because we had tremendous anxiety about Bonnie. That was nothing new, of course—we'd been doing emotional calisthenics over Bonnie every day since August—but now *she* had tremendous anxiety, too, and she couldn't hide it any longer. It was a real dramatic time. Everybody was uncomfortable with the fact that she was the only person in the room who didn't know what the fuck was going on. We all knew we were in the Twilight Zone."

"Chris?" Bonnie was having a hard time getting the words out. "Why is this something you would even consider?"

"I don't know," he said, not looking at her. "There are a lot of things to consider."

"I think, Chris," said Bill Osteen, interceding—for he still did not want Bonnie to start asking direct questions of her son—"that you should go home and think about it very hard. There's no guarantee that I can work out an arrangement no matter what you decide, but I can't even begin to try without being told that that is what you want to do."

"I'm gonna go with your advice," Chris said. Then he did look at Bonnie, adding, "I can't put my mom through a trial."

Immediately, Bonnie objected, saying her only concern

was what was best for Chris. "Mr. Osteen," she said, "this may be the most important decision Chris will ever be forced to make. As his mother, I'd like to help him with it, but I can't if I don't know all the factors involved."

But Osteen just shook his head and repeated that the situation was still so fragile, and its outcome so uncertain, that there were certain details—such as anything that had to do with the weekend of July 25, 1988—that still could not be shared with her.

Then Osteen said he did not want Chris to reach a final decision that night. Go home, sleep on it, call in the morning. Osteen said he'd be there, waiting. If the decision was to go for the plea bargain, he'd immediately begin negotiating with Mitchell Norton. If it was to go forward to trial, well, then, that's what they'd have to do.

But no one had the slightest doubt about which option Bill Osteen preferred.

As Bonnie and Chris walked silently into the cold December night, Osteen said to Jim Vosburgh, "I think we've just ruined their Christmas."

"Forget Christmas," Vosburgh said. "What about the rest of their lives?"

On the drive home, Bonnie asked only, "Chris, is anybody pressuring you? Threatening you?"

He said no. He did not elaborate.

"I can't understand how you could even consider something like this."

He was silent.

"I can't help you if I don't know all the circumstances."

He remained silent.

"I just want to tell you, Chris"—and here, Bonnie's voice trembled just a bit—"that, even if I don't understand it, I will support you in whatever you decide."

Bonnie called Wade Smith in the morning, to describe the meeting and its aftermath. "I don't understand," she kept saying. "I don't understand. Why would Chris be willing to go to prison for a crime he didn't commit? Why is a guilty plea something that Mr. Osteen would even want to consider?''

And Wade, still bound by the constraints he'd been under since the summer, could only say—and there was no way to say this very soothingly—''Bonnie, you've just got to trust Bill Osteen. You've just got to believe that whatever he does will be the right thing to do.''

Chris had an appointment with Billy Royal that morning. He said, among other things, ''I told them to get my sister, too. But to make sure it was painless.''

If everyone was dead, he told Royal, none of them would ever know how very badly he'd really done at school. If they were dead, he said, then nothing he did could ever disappoint them again. And if they were dead, they could never leave him. He'd never again have to fear rejection.

That afternoon, Chris called Osteen and said he had made his decision: he wanted to go for the plea.

That night, he told Bonnie what he'd decided.

Why . . . why . . . why? she kept asking. His only answer was, ''Because it's the right thing to do.''

Later in the week, Osteen called to say he'd arranged to meet with Mitchell Norton the day after Christmas in order to work out the details. He wanted Bonnie, Chris, and Angela to arrive in Washington on the evening of December 26. If all was in order, Chris could sign the agreement, and then, Osteen promised, Bonnie could ask all the questions she liked.

And then it was Christmas again, with Bonnie feeling obliged to put on a happy face.

But for whom? Lieth was gone, her father was gone, and within a few weeks—she now knew—her son would be taken from her, too. But she still felt she couldn't ask why, not only because of Osteen's order, but because she was worried about Chris.

''If we were to get into a discussion, and I were to ask him some pointed questions,'' she said later, ''suppose they caused him to end his life? Then I'd be responsible for that."

So she smiled her way through the day. "I don't like being around people who fall to pieces," she said. "And I certainly wasn't going to fall to pieces myself."

As a Christmas present, she gave Chris a VGA graphics card for his computer, so he'd be able to play his fantasy games in color instead of black and white.

By early evening of December 26, Osteen had reached an agreement with Norton, though it would be the following morning before it would be typed and ready for signature.

The agreement stipulated that Chris would make a complete statement to the SBI as to the extent and nature of his involvement, would answer truthfully and fully all questions put to him, and would later testify truthfully at trial.

In return, the charge of first-degree murder would be withdrawn, and he would be permitted to plead guilty to the crime of aiding and abetting murder in the second degree, and to aiding and abetting an assault with a deadly weapon with intent to kill and inflicting serious injury—the latter charge being the attempted murder of Bonnie.

In addition, Mitchell Norton agreed that he would make no specific recommendation at Chris's eventual sentencing hearing before Judge Watts. It was understood by both sides that the maximum possible sentence would be life imprisonment plus twenty years, which in "real time" probably meant at least twenty years before parole.

That was the good news Osteen was able to share with Bonnie, Chris, and Angela when they arrived in Little Washington that night. As soon as Chris signed the agreement the next morning, he said, they could all meet in Jim Vosburgh's conference room and Chris could tell his mother and sister the truth.

29

Jim Vosburgh's private office was like the man himself: large, comfortable, slightly untidy, and filled with material from which entertaining stories can flow. It looked, in fact, less like a lawyer's office than a shop filled with a life's worth of souvenirs.

The walls were covered with virtually every diploma or letter of recognition he'd ever received, including his diploma from the old Durham High School, and his "Bachelor of Harmony" degree from the Society for the Preservation and Encouragement of Barber Shop Quartet Singing in America, of which he'd been a member for fifteen years.

Over the door hung two gun racks, one holding an 1864 Remington single-shot rifle with shell ejector, and the other an old BB gun, with which he would occasionally shoot a bird.

Five shelves ran the length of the back wall, crammed full of everything from photographs of his parents and autographed baseballs from Little League teams he had coached (plus one from former Brooklyn Dodger pitcher Roger Craig) to his father's old slide rule, a pair of chopsticks brought back from Thailand by a friend, and a plaque with a hand grenade embedded in it that said, "Best Damn Lawyer in Town." That last item being a gift from a grateful client.

Also on the walls were paintings by another grateful client—an arsonist—who'd done them in prison after a conviction that even Vosburgh's best efforts could not prevent. Scattered among these were art projects his children had made in kindergarten years before.

The office was, in short, warm and homey, distinctly not

a place where he wanted the business of this particular morning to be conducted.

Instead, when Bonnie and Chris and Angela arrived at nine-thirty A.M., he showed them to his spartan conference room, where only shelves lined with law books supplemented the utilitarian furniture.

At that early hour, the poolroom next door was quiet. So were Bonnie and her children. Chris and Mitchell Norton had signed the plea bargain. The deal was done. Now, nothing remained but for Chris to tell his story: first here, then in Norton's office, and then at trial. After that, for many years, he would be forced to deal with the consequences of his acts.

Bill Osteen was more grim and drawn than either Bonnie, Chris, or Jim Vosburgh had ever seen him. They took seats at Vosburgh's conference table, Chris at one end, Bonnie at the other. Angela was on one side, Vosburgh and Osteen across from her.

"Chris," Osteen said, "the time has finally come for you to tell your mother and sister what you did."

But now, after all these months—all that yearning to be freed from his prison of deceit and silence—Chris panicked. He froze up. He shook his head. He said softly, "I can't."

Bill Osteen didn't raise his voice. He did not need to raise his voice to make a point. For months, he'd been tormented by the need to keep the truth from Bonnie, and by the pressure of making life-and-death decisions, about the correctness of which it seemed necessary to sound much more certain than he was. Now, almost as if seeking redemption for the weeks of anguish his edicts had caused, he would not permit another moment's delay.

"Chris," he said evenly, "I'm not going to let you leave this room until you tell your mother what really happened."

Chris looked first at Osteen, then at Jim Vosburgh. Then he looked down at the table in front of him. He began to take deep, jerky breaths. Suddenly, he was gasping for air. Vosburgh was afraid he'd hyperventilate and pass out.

"Goddamnit, Chris!" Vosburgh said. "You tell your mother the truth!"

And with that, Chris Pritchard began talking and crying

all at once, precipitating what Vosburgh would later describe as "the most gut-wrenching, emotional day I've ever had in the practice of law."

This was the story he told:

It began during the first summer session, when he responded to a poster on a wall of his dormitory, saying new players were needed for a Dungeons & Dragons game. That was when he first met Upchurch and Henderson, who already knew each other well.

They played the game obsessively. They also did drugs. A lot of drugs. He'd been drinking heavily through the spring semester and early summer and had begun to smoke marijuana. When he met Upchurch, he also started on LSD. He guessed he'd taken about eighteen hits of LSD in the month or so before the murder.

He told Moog and the other Dungeons & Dragons players that his stepfather had inherited millions of dollars. He said his family had seven cars and three houses and two million dollars in cash. He wasn't sure he'd said two million. He might have said, at various times, five million, or even ten. It was that kind of summer. That was what was happening with the drugs, with the booze, with the game. Anyone would say or do anything. Nobody paid attention to real life. Nobody stopped to think.

He told Moog and Henderson and Daniel and Vince—and whoever else happened to be playing the game or drinking with them—that when his parents died, he would inherit the money. Then he'd buy a big house in the woods in north Raleigh, and he and all his friends could live in it together, and they could have Ferraris and expensive stereo equipment and serious computers, which would enable them to play the most advanced and complex of fantasy games.

By the last week of summer session, he stopped going to classes altogether. He only drank and ate and took drugs and played Dungeons & Dragons—and dreamed of the day when all Lieth's money could be his.

Moog became his mentor, his best friend. Moog was, after all, the Dungeon Master. They drove together to Ramona's house on July 4 and did some serious partying. Moog got him deeper and deeper into acid, deeper and deeper into the game.

On the night of Wednesday, July 20, things got serious. He and Moog and Daniel and Vince were eating dinner at the Golden Corral on Western Boulevard, not far from campus. Daniel and Vince went to the salad bar. He was alone with Moog.

He asked a question out of the blue? "What do you think of patricide?" By this, he meant the murder of one's family, although the word actually denoted the killing of one's biological father, and Steve Pritchard was not whom he had in mind.

Moog answered, "Well, you'd better not believe in God."

He didn't know why he'd asked the question. But even through his drug haze, he remembered wondering how many Dungeons & Dragons experience points he might get for killing his stepfather and mother.

Later that night, he went to Moog's dorm room, and they talked more.

"What about if my parents were dead? Real soon. What if I had somebody go kill them?"

"How?"

"I don't know."

"Would a fire do it?"

"Sure. A fire would do it."

The next day, Moog asked, "How would the fire start?"

"Arson."

"That would be suspicious. But if a fuse blew, that would be different."

Chris asked how Moog could make a fuse blow. Simple. Pour gasoline on the fuse box and set a match to it. The fuses blow, sparking an electrical fire that burns down the house.

"We could do it," Chris said, "but suppose they wake up?"

"Sleeping pills. What you got to do is grind up some sleeping pills in their food."

That night, Chris asked, "How about this weekend?" He said he'd give Moog $50,000 from the inheritance money, plus any new car of his choice. Moog said he wanted a Porsche. Fine, Chris said. A Porsche. Moog told Chris to meet him at one P.M. Saturday behind the Sav-A-Center store, just off campus.

Chris drove home Friday night. He stole a back-door key from the rack in the kitchen so he and Moog could enter the house silently the next night. On Saturday, telling Bonnie he was going out to visit friends, he raced back to Raleigh to pick up Moog. They bought a box of fuses in Raleigh, intending to shatter several and sprinkle them near the fuse box, so it would look as if the fuses had exploded, starting the fire. Then the two of them drove back to Little Washington.

They came in by a back road so the car would not be noticed. At three P.M., he dropped off Moog at a small, abandoned tobacco-drying shack behind the small airstrip about a mile from the house. Moog would wait there alone until Chris picked him up after dinner. Once they thought everyone was asleep, they would return to the house to set the fire.

Moog gave him a plastic bag filled with blue powder, which Chris said he thought was ground-up Sominex. He mixed it with the meat as he pressed the hamburger into patties. He grilled the hamburgers and they ate. Donna Brady was there and ate with them. They watched television during the meal. Lieth liked to watch television on weekends. As soon as dinner was over, Chris left, saying he had to get back to school to work on that darned term paper. Instead, he drove to the tobacco-drying shack where Moog was waiting. He and Moog tried to break the fuses, but they couldn't. The two of them were smoking pot. Moog said this wasn't such a good idea. Chris wasn't sleepy, even after having eaten a hamburger. Also, Chris should be at school when the murders occurred. That way, no one would ever suspect him. So they drove back to Raleigh instead of burning down the house.

On the way back, Moog said arson wasn't such a good idea, after all. Too complicated. Too many things could go wrong. Too easy to trace if it worked. Chris suggested staging a break-in, during which Moog could go upstairs and kill Bonnie and Lieth. That way, it would look like just a burglary that had got out of hand.

Moog liked this idea. He said a machete would be the best thing to use. He could just lop off the heads as they slept. One swat was all it would take. Nobody would feel any pain. Chris liked this. He didn't want them to suffer.

But by the time they reached Raleigh, the Army-Navy store that sold machetes was closed for the night. Instead, they went to Wildflour for a pitcher of beer.

Moog said he'd go back the next night and do the killings. Chris should stay on campus and stay up very late, always in the presence of others, so he'd have an airtight alibi. But Moog would have to drive Chris's Mustang because he didn't have a car of his own. Chris said that was no good because Moog's driver's license had been suspended. The whole plan could fail if he was stopped for a traffic violation and he did not have a license.

Chris said he'd better get someone else to drive the car. Moog said, no problem. Neal Henderson could drive the car. Then Chris said chopping off the heads with a machete might be noisy. Angela would probably wake up. If she did, Chris said, it would be all right to kill her, too.

The machete store was also closed on Sundays. They had to go to K Mart instead. The best Chris could do there was to buy Moog a hunting knife. Moog said it sure wasn't any machete, but he'd do the best he could.

Then they went to Henderson's apartment. Moog explained the circumstances and Henderson said he'd be happy to drive. Chris drew a map. He also said they'd better hurry because he really did have a term paper due the next day, and unless his parents were murdered, he wouldn't have a good excuse for not turning it in on time.

At about eleven that night, Chris returned to his dorm from Wildflour Pizza with Vince and Karen and Kirsten, and gave Moog the keys to his car. Then he went upstairs to play cards so he would have an alibi. Moog told him to stay up until at least three or four A.M. He said the car should be back in the parking lot before dawn. The last thing he could remember telling Moog was which side of the bed Lieth slept on, and that he'd better go after Lieth first.

The next thing he knew, Angela was on the phone, telling him he'd better get home fast.

He'd seen Henderson not at all, and Moog only once since the murder. He'd seen Moog in late summer at NC State. Moog had started to tell him about it, saying, "You never told me the back door was Plexiglas," and "I never saw so much blood in all my life." Chris had screamed at him to shut up. That was the night he'd had his bad acid trip, and Moog had stayed with him, so he wouldn't blurt out anything to the police.

Chris stopped talking. He looked at his mother and his sister. Neither Bonnie nor Angela said a word. Osteen broke the silence, asking Bonnie and Angela, "Does either of you have any questions?"

Bonnie said only that now that he'd finally told the truth, she hoped Chris could start to feel better about himself. Angela said nothing at all.

Again, it was Osteen who broke the silence.

"Chris," he said, "I hope you understand just how special a person your mother is. Here, after all the things you've just told her, her first concern is still for you."

30

Bonnie's recollection of what happened during the rest of that day and night would prove very different from notes she took at the time, almost as if, for twelve hours, she'd been plunged into a state of near-amnesia.

She said the meeting in Vosburgh's office hadn't lasted more than thirty or forty-five minutes, that it had to be brief because the prosecutors were waiting for Chris. She recalled leaving the office accompanied only by Angela and returning, dazed and numb, to the Holiday Inn. Angela had asked no questions, but said, "Chris is my brother and I love him, and I know if he hadn't been doing drugs, he never could have done any of this."

Bonnie remembered no other conversation with Angela about what the two of them had just heard. Angela had not stayed long at the motel. Probably, she'd spent the day with friends. Bonnie recalled spending the afternoon alone in the motel room, wondering how she'd ever be able to break this news to her mother, and to the other members of her family.

"I don't remember if Angela and I ate dinner together, or if she ate with some friends," Bonnie said later. She did recall sitting in the motel room with Angela later that night, watching television. If, in all the hours since Chris had made his confession in Vosburgh's office, either Bonnie or Angela had said a single word in reference to it, neither was able to recall it.

Some things, Bonnie said later, were just too painful to talk about. Besides, what good would talking do? It wouldn't change anything. It would not bring back Lieth. To share their pain, even with each other, would have been a sign of weakness. And now, more than ever, Bonnie was determined to be strong.

She did remember Chris arriving at the motel room at ten-thirty P.M., accompanied by Bill Osteen, who said only that it had been a long, grueling day and that he, at least, was ready for bed.

Chris took one step inside and with tears in his eyes said, "I don't see how the two of you can stand to be in the same room with me."

Bonnie's recollection was that she and Angela both told him they realized he was not capable of harming anyone, and that they knew what he'd done must have been caused by drug and mental problems. He cried and said he did not understand how he could have done it, no matter what the circumstances. Then he said to Bonnie, "I love you and Angela and I loved Lieth."

Then he said he was hungry. "He went out to eat," Bonnie said later. "I don't think Angela went with him. When he got back, there was very little talk. We were all so drained, we were beyond talk." They just turned off the lights and went to sleep.

"A sleep," Bonnie said later, "not only of total emotional exhaustion, but of the worst sort of depression I'd ever known."

Bonnie's notes, however, told quite a different story. She and Chris and Angela had actually left Vosburgh's office together and had eaten lunch at the Little Washington outlet of the Golden Corral restaurant chain: an odd choice, since it was in a Raleigh Golden Corral that Chris had first broached the idea of the murder.

Even when her notes were read back to her, Bonnie had no recollection of such a lunch, or even of being in Chris's presence. Nor was Angela able to recall anything she said or did for the rest of the day. Chris had only a vague memory of possibly eating lunch somewhere, but did not remember where or with whom or anything that might have been said.

Bonnie's notes indicated that she returned Chris to Jim Vosburgh's office at one-fifteen P.M., so he could be at the county sheriff's office by one-thirty in order to make his formal statement.

After that, Bonnie did go back to the motel, apparently alone. There, she tried to write about what Chris had just confessed to. "It is so much worse than I had ever feared," she began. But then she stopped.

She called Wade Smith in early afternoon, but was unable to reach him. He returned her call at four P.M., according to her notes, but she felt unable to speak freely to him then because Linda Sloane, her friend from the Humane Society, had arrived in the room.

Bonnie could not remember any of this, but Linda recalled the afternoon and evening clearly. A few days earlier, she and Bonnie had made plans to exchange Christmas gifts in the Holiday Inn, then to have dinner together in the Holiday Inn dining room.

And that's what they did. When Linda arrived at the motel in late afternoon, neither Bonnie nor Angela, who also was there, gave any sign that they'd had an unusually stressful day.

Everything seemed perfectly normal. Indeed, when Linda asked Bonnie how she felt, Bonnie said, "I feel good. I feel positive. Things are going to work out."

They sat in the room and exchanged gifts. Then the three of them went to the dining room and ate. All Bonnie said was that Chris was answering some questions for the police, and she was concerned that if they kept him too long, he might not get a good dinner.

Days later Linda Sloane read in the newspaper that Chris had confessed and was going to plead guilty, and she then realized that Bonnie had known the truth throughout the afternoon and evening they'd spent together.

Even after the story had been printed in the paper, Bonnie never said a word about it. Just as Bonnie never told Linda—perhaps her best friend in Little Washington—that Chris had been hospitalized back in August.

Some things were just not meant to be discussed. Some things were private. Some burdens were not meant to be shared. And maybe, as Linda Sloane suggested later, "to not talk about it can help it to not be real."

* * *

The other discrepancy between Bonnie's memory and her notes involved what happened after Chris had come back to the room. All the restaurants in Little Washington were already closed, and so, according to the notes, she gave Chris and Angela her car keys so the two of them could drive to The Waffle House in Greenville: the place where Bonnie had eaten her last breakfast with Lieth.

Chris and Angela did not return until after midnight. Later, neither could recall anything they had talked about to one another.

The formal interview with Chris had lasted from 1:25 to 10:10 P.M. Present were Lewis Young, John Taylor, Mitchell Norton, Keith Mason, and Bill Osteen. Young later typed a thirty-four-page report of what was said, based on notes he took as Chris spoke. Osteen also took handwritten notes.

Several things Chris said would later give rise to troubling questions. Among them:

—He met Moog for the first time during summer session.

—He did not know whether Moog had ever met Angela.

—When he'd come to Washington on the Friday night before the murder, he'd gone out with his friends Jonathan Wagoner, Steven Outlaw, and Tiffany Heady.

—While home, he'd stolen a key. Young's notes said the key was for "the new back door . . . the outer back door." Osteen's notes confirm this, quoting Chris as saying, "I had gotten a key for the new back door." In the spring, Bonnie and Lieth had enclosed what had been a screen porch behind the kitchen. A new door, with a new lock, had been installed. The original back door, which led from the porch to the kitchen, had become an interior doorway, no longer directly accessible from outside the house.

—Moog was to leave Chris's car keys on a chair in his room upon returning to campus. If they weren't there whenever Chris was first informed of the murder, he would know his car had not yet been returned to the parking lot and he would make up his story about not being able to find his keys.

—Angela was to be a victim. He had no idea why she was not harmed.

—He had never read, or even heard of, the book *A Rose in Winter*.

—Except for the one occasion in August, he'd seen Moog only to say hi to after the murder, had never discussed it with him, and had never again played Dungeons & Dragons with either Moog or Neal Henderson.

At the time, none of these statements provoked much response. In retrospect, however, they could be seen as having disturbing implications.

Bonnie, Chris, and Angela drove back to Winston-Salem the next day. They still did not discuss what Chris had done.

"I'm just not the kind of person who's going to get into a long discussion about an unpleasant subject knowing that we've got a four-hour drive to Winston-Salem ahead of us," Bonnie said later.

Angela said, "I never asked any questions because I didn't want to upset him. That's just the way I was brought up."

And as soon as they reached Winston-Salem, the three of them went their separate ways.

That evening, Eric Caldwell came by the house. He'd already seen Chris, already knew Chris had confessed to Bonnie. Now he wanted to see how she was coping. For months he'd known the moment would someday come when Bonnie would have to learn the truth. Now he wanted to tell her he was sorry for having participated in what everyone had felt was a necessary deception.

"How're you doing?" he asked.

"Very surprised," Bonnie said.

"You had no idea? You really never had any idea?"

"No," she said, "it never once occurred to me that this would be the course events would follow."

Eric told her how hard it had been for him to keep silent. She told him he had done the right thing. He had been loyal to Chris, and she admired him for that. There was nothing for which he should feel sorry; nothing for which she needed to forgive him. Chris was fortunate to have had him for a friend.

Her biggest worry at the moment, she told Eric, was how she would tell her family what had happened.

"They told me about my daddy," she said. "Now I get to tell them about the next death in the family. Because that's what this is. Another death in the family."

Her only consolation, she told Eric, was that, even though it had taken him a long time to work up the courage, to face up to what was right, to what must be done, Chris had, in the end, acted honorably.

"Chris pleaded guilty," Bonnie said, "because he could no longer live with his remorse.

"He didn't plead guilty just to avoid the death penalty. He needed to do it because he couldn't live with it any other way. He wanted us to know. To go through a trial and be acquitted, and then never be able to tell us, that was not something he felt like he could live with. So, at least he acted with honor at the end."

Such were the scraps and tatters to which she clung.

But Eric would say later that he'd reluctantly formed a different opinion of Chris's motive for pleading guilty. "He told me Osteen had said he only had a thirty percent chance of getting off. He said, 'If they told me forty or fifty percent, I would have gone for it.' He said he looked at it like in Dungeons and Dragons, where you roll two ten-sided dice. Bonnie kept insisting that he'd pleaded guilty because of sorrow and remorse, but Chris said it was simply a matter of percentages.

"My biggest fear," Eric said, "was that Chris wasn't really sorry for what he'd done."

Bonnie did tell her mother and her brother and her sisters. Later, she would say, "They were all as shocked as I was."

Then, alone, on New Year's Day, she made the six-hour drive to Elizabeth City, despite the fact that Chris would not be standing trial.

PART FOUR

"THE THREE Ds"

JANUARY 1990

31

For so long, January 2 had been imprinted on Bonnie's mind as the date when the long-obstructed march toward justice would begin. No more of the storm-trooper tactics of the SBI and Washington police. No more intimidation, no more lies, no more being treated like a criminal instead of a victim.

In the courtroom, in Elizabeth City, in front of the stern but fair-minded Judge Thomas Watts, with Bill Osteen and Jim Vosburgh defending him, Chris would finally be given a chance to demonstrate his innocence. And Bonnie would learn for the first time, from hearing *all* the evidence, what had really happened to her and to Lieth.

Now it was not to be. Now, Chris would not be on trial. Now, he would be making only the briefest of appearances to testify against James Upchurch on behalf of the prosecution.

And the prosecution—against which Bonnie had fought for so long and so hard and with such futility—was now *representing* her interests. After so many months of contempt for their tactics and their incompetence, and their stubborn and willful insistence on believing what she knew could not be true, Bonnie was suddenly *on their team*. This was not at all what she had been expecting. But not for a moment did it occur to her to alter her plan to attend every session of the trial. Even if Chris's fate was no longer hanging in the balance, this remained the trial of the man accused of murdering her husband, and of having tried to murder her.

And even though Bonnie was as convinced as ever that it had been Henderson, not Upchurch, whom she'd seen in her bedroom that night, she was now faced with Chris's admission that he had plotted with Upchurch, not Henderson, what he'd hoped would be her death.

Some were surprised that Bonnie was still so committed to attending the whole trial. Yes, of course, she would have to testify; yes, she would want to be there when Chris testified; but why put herself through the agony of being present every day? Why not just wait for a phone call in late January or early February, informing her of the jury's verdict?

Since she now knew for certain that her son would be going to prison for many years, why not take advantage of this last opportunity to spend time with him?

One answer was, she did not want to. And the trial provided the perfect escape. Now that she finally knew the truth, now that her denial mechanism—at least in regard to fact, if not emotion—was inoperable, the only way she could avoid confronting the reality of what he'd done was to avoid Chris himself. Only by spending all week, every week, in Elizabeth City, until the very day Chris was sentenced, could Bonnie spare herself the trauma of such an encounter.

Consciously, of course, she saw her choice not as avoidance but as a last chance to bear witness to the love she'd had for her husband. "There would be other opportunities to be with Angela and Chris," she said. "But this was the last thing I could ever do for Lieth. Elizabeth City was where I felt I needed to be. I had accepted long ago that he was dead and that there was nothing I could do to change that, but I could be there and assist in any way I could to be sure the people who were responsible for his death were punished.

"And whatever the outcome, I needed to feel that when it was over, I would know as much as possible about what had happened on that weekend."

Regarding Chris, she said that during those few hectic and traumatic days between his confession and the start of the trial, "I never had a major talk with him." She seemed surprised, in fact, that anyone might think she'd find it necessary to have a frank discussion—possibly even an *emotional* discussion—about the fact that he had tried to have her murdered.

"The most significant talk we had was me asking him if he wanted me to sell his car. I did ask him once what his concerns were about being in prison, and he said he was worried about sex abuse, but I made a conscious effort not to rehash any of what he'd already told me about the crime because he was facing having to testify, and that would be hard enough for him, without me giving him some sort of grilling in advance. Besides, he'd already told me the basics in Mr. Vosburgh's office."

Judge Thomas Watts was only fifty, but looked at least ten years older. He was balding, bespectacled, and since birth, had suffered from hemophilia. He walked with a cane and wore a hearing aid. His grandfather had been a Baptist minister (a distinction shared, it sometimes seemed, by approximately half the population of the state), and he had grown up in western North Carolina, in the foothills of the Blue Ridge mountains.

"I'm a bleeder," he once said. "One of the few that makes it to this age. When I was born, my parents were told I had a life expectancy of well under a year. So I sort of operate under the philosophy that every time the sun comes up, that's another one on the plus side of the ledger. I had bad knees, I had joint injuries, and there were no treatments in those days except to immobilize the area that was bleeding and put ice on it. I spent probably forty percent of my first ten years in the hospital."

His physical infirmities caused Thomas Watts to become a voracious reader at an early age, and the habit had stayed with him. He grew up a Democrat and still claimed Franklin D. Roosevelt as one of his greatest heroes. He graduated from Davidson College, then Wake Forest Law School, and worked as a district attorney before being appointed to the bench in 1982.

He had Scottish blood in him, even owned a kilt, which he wore to folk festivals in the mountains. He'd been married to the same woman for twenty-seven years and had a twenty-five-year-old daughter who worked in public relations. But the law was perhaps his greatest passion. He read about it, he thought deeply about it, he approached it with a respect bordering on reverence.

His favorite necktie was imprinted with images of the statue of justice from the Old Bailey courthouse in London. "That statue," he once explained when asked, "has three unique things about it. She obviously has the scales, and it's appropriate that justice should have the scales to finely weigh and balance the equities of a case. But she also carries in her right hand an upright sword, because justice should have the power to impose punishment if necessary. That is her strength: the majesty and force to impose the rule of an orderly and civilized society upon the public.

"But the most unique thing about the British figure of justice—which is absolutely different from the statues of justice you see in the United States—is that she is not blindfolded. Her eyes are open, so she can see the truth. And that summarizes my philosophy: justice should have her eyes open and should always be looking for the truth."

It was before Judge Watts that Jim Vosburgh stood at ten A.M. on January 2 and said, "Your Honor, we have entered into a plea agreement with the district attorney. We would like to withdraw our pleas of not guilty and enter pleas in accordance with the plea arrangement and transcript, which will be taken by the court."

Judge Watts, speaking in a deep, scratchy voice heavy with the accent of western North Carolina—more of a flat, slow drawl than the thicker, more purely Southern accent common to the eastern part of the state—told Chris Pritchard to step forward and to place his hand on a Bible that was passed to him, and to swear to tell the truth.

Chris, looking pale and nervous, ill at ease in suit and tie, stood and did so. Then Judge Watts looked down at him with an expression in which no glimmer of sympathy was apparent.

"Just remain standing, if you will, Mr. Pritchard," the judge said, "and answer my questions in a good, loud voice so that the court reporter and all of us can hear what you have to say. First of all, are you able to hear and understand me?

"Yes, sir," Chris said, his voice not loud at all.

"Do you understand that you have the right to remain silent and that any statement you make may be used against you?"

"Yes, sir, I do."

"Are you now under the influence of alcohol, narcotics, medicines, pills, or any other form of intoxicants?"

"No, sir."

"How long has it been since you used or consumed any intoxicating substance of any type?"

"I had a beer last night, sir."

"Is that still in your system?"

"No, sir."

"Do you feel any effects of that?"

"No. I had it with my food."

Judge Watts asked Chris if he'd discussed his case fully with his attorneys (yes), and if he was satisfied with their legal services (yes), and if he understood that he was pleading guilty to two felony charges—aiding and abetting murder in the second degree, and aiding and abetting an assault with a deadly weapon with intent to kill and inflicting serious injury (yes), and if he understood also that on the second-degree murder charge he could be imprisoned for a possible maximum sentence of either life or fifty years (he did), and that the presumed fair sentence for murder in the second degree as set by the state's General Assembly was fifteen years (he did), and that the second charge carried a maximum punishment of twenty years, and that the presumed fair sentence for that one was six years (he did), and if he understood that he had the right to plead not guilty and to have each of those charges decided by a jury, and at such a trial he would have the right to confront and cross-examine any witness who would testify against him (he did), and that by pleading guilty he was giving up those rights and all other important constitutional rights relating to trial by jury (he did).

"Do you now personally plead guilty to the charge of aiding and abetting in the second-degree murder of Lieth Von Stein?" Judge Watts asked.

"Yes, sir."

"Are you in fact guilty of that charge?"

"Yes, sir."

"Do you now personally plead guilty to aiding and abetting an assault with a deadly weapon with intent to kill and inflicting serious bodily injury upon Bonnie Von Stein?"

"Yes, sir."

"And are you in fact guilty of that charge?"

"Yes, sir, I am."

The judge then accepted the change of plea and permitted Chris to remain free under the conditions of his original bond until he was sentenced.

And so Bonnie's new life began. Even as Chris and Angela and Jim Vosburgh left the courthouse and Elizabeth City, Bonnie remained.

Alone in the courtroom, she was approached by John Taylor. He said that now that Chris had pleaded guilty, Mitchell Norton was wondering if perhaps, despite their past differences, Bonnie would sit on the prosecution side of the aisle. It was, after all, Lieth and Bonnie whom the State was representing, and the jury might find it peculiar to have her sitting on the "wrong" side of the courtroom, with the defense.

It was still so hard for her to recognize that the "defense" no longer included her. That these people, whom for so many months she had considered the enemy, were now her friends. Or even if she could never come to consider them friends, that at least they were no longer seeking to do her harm.

She gathered her notepaper and pocketbook and coat and moved in front of the railing that separated the trial's principals from courtroom spectators. There, on the left side, she took a seat alongside Taylor and Lewis Young, directly behind the table at which Mitchell Norton and Keith Mason sat.

The realignment, however, would not prove simple for either side. Grudges long nursed are not easily dissipated, especially when the aggrieved party must, at least implicitly, admit to having been wrong.

The problem worsens when the aggrieved party is a mother whose son has just told her he really did try to have her murdered, and when the district attorney still harbors a faint suspicion that this apparently pitiful victim might be something other than what she seems.

Late in the week, after the jury had been selected and with the trial in recess until the following Monday, Wade asked Bonnie to come to his office. Like Lewis Young before him Norton had turned to Wade for help in solving what he feared could be a serious problem.

Wade explained to Bonnie that Norton would be calling her as one of his first witnesses, but that the district attorney was extremely concerned about what she would say about the shape of the shadowy figure in her bedroom. Her insistence that it could not have been Upchurch would undermine the prosecution from the start.

She arrived at Wade's office, as requested, at nine A.M. Friday, January 5. To her surprise, Mitchell Norton, Lewis Young, and John Taylor were already there. Wade told her he'd been meeting with the three of them since eight-thirty.

Wade said he was almost finished talking with the three members of the prosecution team, and that as soon as he was, they could all talk together. Bonnie sat in the waiting room outside his office and began to make notes. She didn't like this. Even if she was now, in theory, a member—or at least a supporter—of their "team," she didn't like them talking to her lawyer behind her back when she couldn't hear what they were saying.

"9:10 A.M.," she wrote. "He asked for about ten minutes with others.

"9:37—Conference without me still in progress.

"9:50—Same situation. I am still sitting in lobby, waiting.

This is no surprise as far as prosecution group. It *is a surprise* from Mr. Smith.

"9:55—As the minutes pass by, I become increasingly dismayed.

"10:00—All four pass by and enter elevator. Mr. Smith says, 'Bonnie, we'll be ready for you in just a little while. Don't go to sleep!' I made no response other than to nod my head in acquiescence. Actually, I don't quite trust my voice at this point. I really do not want to reveal my total dismay.

"10:05—It's time to release the building tension. I ask Mr. Smith's secretary for a cup of hot tea to help pass the time and calm the rising frustration.

"10:20—Situation has not changed. At 7:45 A.M. Wade Smith said Mr. Norton wanted to meet with him at 9 A.M. and then with me and him at 9:30. I stated this was not desirable to me since I was footing the bill and there was nothing Mr. Norton could not say in my presence. We agreed (Mr. Smith and I) that all would meet at 9:00 *together*.

"10:35—Same situation exists.

"10:40—No change in situation. I still sit here with the clock running. I do not feel there can be any satisfactory explanation for this disregard of our previous agreement that I would be included in the conference I will be expected to pay for.

"10:45—I made a trip to the ladies' room.

"10:50—No change in situation.

"10:55—Finally, Mr. Smith calls me into his office."

By then, Bonnie said, the thought paramount in her mind was, "What's this conspiracy here? They're going to ask me to do something I'm not going to be capable of doing. At that moment, I felt betrayed. On the other hand, I still trusted Wade."

Once again, Wade Smith found himself in the uncomfortable position of balancing what he perceived to be his client's best interests against what she herself might think they were. Wade feared that if the man who stood accused of murdering Lieth went free because of Bonnie's testimony, she would be plagued by doubt and fear for years to come.

She knew now, from Chris, that Upchurch had plotted with him. Upchurch had been with him the night before, waiting in the shack, planning to burn down the house. Upchurch had wanted to buy the machete. Upchurch had the prior criminal record for breaking and entering. Upchurch had tried to flee when the police had come looking for him, in contrast to Henderson, who had stepped forward voluntarily to cooperate.

In fact, even in the absence of physical evidence, the case against Upchurch seemed most persuasive to Wade, especially now that Henderson's testimony could be bolstered by that of Bonnie's own son. The only serious impediment to conviction seemed to be Bonnie's insistence that *it could not have been* Upchurch whom she'd seen.

And so, when Norton asked for a chance to meet with him and his client prior to her testimony, Wade decided that such a conference might serve both her interests and the interests of justice.

During the two hours that Bonnie spent brooding and fretting, Norton and Taylor and Young were explaining to Wade every aspect of their evidence, and lack of evidence.

One new factor was particularly troubling, they said. The story Chris told deviated, in significant ways, from the statement Henderson had given them. They almost felt as if they'd been duped. The murder plot could not have unfolded the way Chris said it had, if Henderson's story—to which they were thoroughly committed—was correct in all details. The basic elements of the two accounts were similar, but especially in the area of timing, glaring contradictions existed.

Norton feared that Chris's confession might have introduced more problems than it solved. This, he said, made it all the more urgent for Bonnie to, at the very least, soften her view that Upchurch could not have been the person she'd seen in her room.

It was bad enough, Norton emphasized, that she would probably insist on telling the jury how back in September she'd jumped up and run from the courtroom in terror upon first laying eyes on Henderson, while the sight of Upchurch had provoked no reaction whatsoever.

Lewis Young argued that Bonnie's increasing certainty about Henderson's being the person in her room had arisen from the fact that she was, and would always be, defensive about her son's involvement. Despite what Chris had confessed to, she would continue to search for ways to minimize and excuse the extent of his guilt. And she'd never forgive Neal Henderson for having been the one who had first pointed the finger at her son. In Young's opinion, her view that Henderson had been the attacker was a function of his cooperation with law enforcement, rather than an honest recollection.

"She couldn't say doodlysquat" about the shape or size of her assailant, Young said, when he had first questioned her in the hospital. This whole "no-neck" business, in his view, had only sprung up after Henderson's statement had led to Chris's arrest. Now, Young said, she didn't care about Upchurch getting convicted. Her own son had been caught, and any other chips could fall where they may.

Bonnie, of course, remained adamant that absolute truth and honesty—as she defined those concepts—were what she owed to herself and to the memory of Lieth. She was not the sort to be bent by pressure. The harder they pushed, the harder she'd resist, as she'd already shown. This was what Wade spent most of the morning explaining to Norton, Taylor, and Young.

Eventually they agreed that Wade and Wade alone would try to find a way to help Bonnie persuade herself that she might not be quite as positive as she thought she was about the identity of the assailant.

And that's what Wade began to do, when, after keeping her waiting for two hours, he led her into his private office and closed the door.

It was, perhaps, the strangest encounter he'd ever had with a client. After apologizing for the long delay, he explained that he wanted to replicate, as closely as possible, the conditions that had existed in her bedroom the night she'd been attacked.

This had already been a very upsetting morning for her, coming after a very upsetting week, which had concluded a very upsetting month, which had come after almost a year and a half of unremitting anguish, which had flowed from as terrifying a moment as anyone could possibly experience. And now the one person left on earth in whom she had absolute faith wanted to reproduce that moment.

He asked Bonnie to lie on his office floor. He then stepped behind his desk and pulled his heavy draperies closed. He turned off the lights. Then he asked Bonnie, who was terribly nearsighted, to take off her glasses.

Then he loomed over her, as had the man who'd tried to kill her.

"What would it take to make *me* look like the person in your bedroom that night?" Wade asked.

She said he would need more bulk in the upper body and less of a neck. Even in the darkened office, even with her glasses off, even Wade—who did have the barrel-chested look of the Carolina halfback he'd once been—did not resemble the figure she'd seen. But if he stepped back a bit, increasing the distortion caused by her nearsightedness, maybe then she would not be quite so sure.

He took two steps backward.

No, she said, he still didn't look like her attacker. He needed more bulk and less neck.

So he went to his office closet and took out his overcoat and put it on, bunching the shoulders up high and squeezing his neck down into the collar of the coat. Then he held his hands clasped high above him, as if preparing to swing down with a bat.

"How about now?"

"Well," Bonnie said doubtfully, "that might be a little closer."

"All right," Wade said, "you see, you can't really be certain of exactly *what* you saw that night. Under the right circumstances, even *I* can wind up looking like the person who attacked you."

"Well," Bonnie said, "I'm not sure."

That, Wade said, was just the point. She couldn't be sure. And not being sure, she could then truthfully testify that it was at least possible that the person she'd seen in her room that night was James Upchurch. And that was all that anyone wanted her to say. Just that, and no more. Just leave open the possibility, so that the case against Upchurch would not totally collapse.

Wade went through the motions again: raising his hands and clasping them over his head, so his neck almost disappeared.

"Yes," Bonnie said, "under these circumstances, and after all your contortions, I would honestly be able to say you've changed your appearance enough so you do bear some resemblance to the person I saw that night."

"That's fine," Wade said. "That's all you'll ever be asked to say. Nothing untruthful, nothing you don't honestly believe. Just that it is a possibility."

Wade told Bonnie to stay right where she was, on the floor. Then he brought Mitchell Norton into his office and duplicated his little demonstration.

Then Bonnie was permitted to get up and to put on her glasses. Wade took off his overcoat with the air of a skilled surgeon who'd just completed a particularly complex and dangerous operation. He opened his draperies. Once again his office was flooded with light.

He asked Bonnie to step outside while he spoke for just a few more minutes with Mitchell Norton. He wanted to stress to the prosecutor—though he did not say this to Bonnie at the time—the importance of wording the question in such a limited and precise way as to allow her to feel that she was being truthful in giving him the answer he needed. Don't push it too far, he cautioned. Honesty is first on the list of Bonnie's virtues. The truth has hurt her dearly in this matter, but it's all she has left to cling to. If you're very careful, he said, and do it just right, you can have her say it's possible. But she's so ready not to, he added, that it wouldn't take but one extra question to have the whole house of cards come tumbling down.

*   *   *

In the waiting room, Bonnie resumed her writing.

"11:55—Still sitting in lobby. Beginning to look like the whole purpose of this meeting is to establish/coerce my testimony to make certain that I do *not* say figure could not possibly have fit size and stature of Upchurch. . . .

"12:05—Still sitting in lobby. My feelings are that there is probably a conspiracy going on here to bend my testimony to fit the prosecution's case. (In speaking to Mr. Smith, I mentioned that I felt the physical evidence the prosecution has should directly place Upchurch in my home on the nite of the 25th. Mr. Smith said he feels there is no physical evidence to that effect. That's what I am afraid of.)

"12:10—Still in lobby. I trust Mr. Smith's judgment, but feel the *evidence alone* should prove/disprove the outcome of this trial. Let me get this in the record: *NO ONE WANTS THE GUILTY PARTY/PARTIES PUNISHED MORE THAN ME!* I CONTINUE TO LOVE LIETH. THE PASSING MONTHS AND YEARS HAVE NOT DIMINISHED THE LOSS I FEEL *IN ANY RESPECT.*"

From twelve-twenty until almost three P.M., in a windowless conference room, Bonnie met with Norton and Young and Taylor to discuss her testimony. From the start, the atmosphere was strained.

"They went over the questions they might be covering when I testified," Bonnie said later. "They wanted to see what kind of answers I would give. We ended up arguing. I would give a full response, but Mr. Norton would want a long, complicated, suggestive question to produce a yes or no answer.

"I said, 'Mr. Norton, if you were to ask me a short, simple question, I could give you a short, simple answer.' But he put his questions in such a form as to tell you what to say. All you had to do was concur, but often what he said was not right. He had hypotheticals that were so long that by the time he got to the end, you forgot what the beginning was. His goal was to create a sense of constant conflict between Lieth and Chris. To make it seem that there was no goodwill. He wanted to create in the jury's mind what he considered a real motive: conflict and greed, not just drugs. And that just wasn't right."

Norton's recollection was that Bonnie grew hostile every time he suggested the existence of any conflict between Chris and Lieth. "She just denied it," he said. "She just kept saying, 'It wasn't that bad.' I sensed a real problem with her, because she'd been on the other side all the way along and just couldn't accept now that we'd been right."

At times, both Young and Taylor would step outside the conference room, leaving Bonnie alone with Mitchell Norton. As soon as they did, it seemed to her that the district attorney, who had never been exactly cordial, grew more antagonistic.

"When I did not answer the questions the way he wanted," Bonnie wrote later in her notes, "he began to say things like, 'You appear to be defending your son. This can only make things harder for Chris at the sentencing. The jury will look at you and think, now, who benefited the most from Lieth's death?' "

Bonnie found it harder than usual to maintain her self-control. *Who benefited the most? How about, who has suffered the most?* This was beginning to remind her of that bad night back in May in Winston-Salem, with Lewis Young shouting at her. But why was Mitchell Norton treating her this way now, when they were no longer on opposite sides?

Then Norton said, "There are a lot of people in Washington who still think you and Angela are involved."

"I couldn't care less what they think."

"But a case could be made," Norton persisted. "There are circumstances."

"Mr. Norton," she said, "your problem from the very beginning has been that all you've had have been circumstances. You've just never had any facts."

"You sound like a mother instead of a victim."

"Unfortunately, I am both."

Bonnie deeply resented Norton's attitude. She had no present, could envision very little future for herself, and now this man was trying to take away her past.

32

On Monday morning, January 8, Mitchell Norton, from whom words came as slowly as unrefined molasses poured from a jug, stood before the jury and delivered his opening remarks.

He said there would be inconsistencies in what the jury would hear. "Inconsistencies insofar as time, place, insofar as when occurrences occurred, and maybe sometimes what actually occurred." But he said not to worry. "That is the normal, the natural state of affairs, not only in trials of criminal cases, but also in our everyday lives. People do not see things the same way, do not hear things the same way, do not remember exactly in the same way." He added that in this case, inconsistencies might have arisen because the first arrest was not made until almost a year after the murder had been committed. He urged the jurors not to focus on the inconsistencies, but to look at the broad picture instead.

"There's going to be evidence of drug usage—acid, marijuana, cocaine. There's going to be elements of repression in this case, people that wanted desperately to forget what had happened." But, he said, the evidence would show "a cold, calculated, brutal killing." He said, "It's going to be unusual in some respects, bizarre in some respects, but when you boil it right down to what it's all about, it's a much more basic motive, a much more basic cause: one of greed. Fast, easy money is what this case is all about."

Norton then launched into his vision of life in the Von Stein–Pritchard household at the time of the murder. "Lieth Von Stein was under a lot of stress. Because of the stress, because of the deaths [of his parents], sometimes

Lieth was on edge. The son, Chris, had gone to North Carolina State University. Lieth Von Stein was paying the bills. The grades weren't good. Chris was spending money. Problems erupted. At times, the relationship was on edge."

There it was: the unhappy home life that would allow a conclusion of premeditation; that would render ineffective any argument that this whole tragedy was the almost accidental result of some kids playing a fantasy game that spun out of control.

Norton then described the murder: Lieth "screaming at the top of his voice," Bonnie's description of the intruder as "a shadowy figure, a person who appeared very methodical, strange, broad-shouldered."

The prosecutor described how Bonnie, "wanting desperately to believe that it was not true [that Chris had planned the murder], supported the son, believed him to be innocent, until two weeks ago." But, he said, "Chris Pritchard himself will talk to you about his use of drugs, the use of alcohol, the fact that he was a student living in a 'me' world, a world surrounded by pizza and beer and alcohol and drugs and a game called Dungeons and Dragons.

"Now," Norton said, "the game has an influence in the case, but it is not a case of a Dungeons and Dragons game gone crazy. It's not a case of Dungeons and Dragons out of control. But Dungeons and Dragons influenced the way that he and Neal Henderson and James Upchurch thought and lived. The game was more of a routine for them than going to class. It's what brought them together: this game that's based on a medieval setting, with clubs and daggers and knives and sticks, in a time before guns were invented. And their minds were accustomed to thinking and living in this world of 'me.' 'What am I going to do?' Fast, easy money."

He said Chris, hoping to "accelerate his inheritance," had "provided the car . . . provided the key so that James Upchurch could come into the house and kill his mother and stepfather."

And, Norton said, it had been Upchurch and Upchurch alone. All poor Neal Henderson had done was drive a car, not really knowing what would happen. Norton said Henderson was "so intelligent that when he was in kindergarten, they put him in second grade. When he got to the fifth grade, they put him in the eighth. The other boys were bigger than he was. They made fun of him because he was smarter than they were. He craved acceptance. Looked for friends, turned to music and fantasy and Dungeons and Dragons."

And so, craving friends, Henderson had agreed to drive the car and "to wait while James Upchurch went into the house and killed Lieth Von Stein."

When Jim Vosburgh had explained that he would not be able to represent Upchurch as a public defender, the next name up had been that of Wayland Sermons, a tall, dark-haired, handsome, well-dressed, soft-spoken thirty-four-year-old graduate of the University of North Carolina at Chapel Hill, and the law school at Wake Forest.

Vosburgh liked to say that he'd known Sermons "since he was a snotty-nosed little kid." A quarter century before, in fact, the day Vosburgh and his wife moved to their home on Honey Pod Road in Little Washington, it was nine-year-old Wayland Sermons who'd come up to their back dock in his small boat and had, in the most neighborly way, taken the new residents on a tour of "his" river. Vosburgh felt he'd entered the pages of *Huckleberry Finn*.

Now Sermons, whose father had served in the state legislature for fifteen years, had the responsibility for a man's life in his hands for the first time in his career. Serving with him as cocounsel was Frank Johnston, an accomplished Washington trial lawyer ten years older than himself.

Though the jury in Elizabeth City would never know it, Little Washington was such a small town that almost everyone involved in this case seemed to have some odd connection to someone else. For Vosburgh, it had been watching Wayland Sermons grow up. For Frank Johnston, it had been having a daughter who'd been in Chris Pritchard's class at Washington High School. They'd never dated, but Chris had been in his home.

Johnston was five eight, on the stocky side, with black hair that was showing its first flecks of gray. He wore wire-framed glasses, had a soft Southern accent, and was blessed with a resonant voice, which provided a contrast to Sermons's smoother, lighter tone. His courtroom style was a distinctive combination of the laid-back (a trait he shared with Sermons) and the no-nonsense. Neither overly folksy nor excessively dramatic, he was noted for his skill at jury argument, and it was he, not Sermons, who made the opening statement on Upchurch's behalf.

Not surprisingly, Johnston suggested that the jury disregard Norton's suggestion and instead look very closely at each and every inconsistency. "Look at it," he said, "examine it, turn it over, twist it around, pull it apart." He said—and with this Bonnie had to agree—that the State "does not have any evidence, any real evidence. They just have a lot of circumstances."

He asked the jurors the same questions about Neal Henderson that Bonnie had been asking herself. "Why is it that it took him eleven months to have this great conscience breakdown and to decide to spill the beans? We submit to you there's a reason for that. We submit to you that he had ample opportunity to develop, to analyze, and to determine what testimony he had to give, and what story he had to give, to put himself in the best position possible."

Johnston said he was confident that by the end of the trial the jurors would find that reasonable doubt existed as to Upchurch's guilt.

33

Bonnie was called to the stand that afternoon. She wore a plain, black linen dress with a big white collar. Though she realized it only much later, she'd bought this dress to wear to the funeral of Lieth's father. She'd only worn it four other times: to the funerals of Lieth's mother, Lieth's uncle, Lieth himself, and less than six weeks earlier, her own father.

"It was not a conscious decision," she said later, "but it must have suggested something about the way I viewed the task of testifying."

Wearing that dress and her thick, rimless glasses, walking slowly and speaking softly, she looked every bit the part of a victim still in the early stages of a recovery that might never be complete. A local paper described her the next day as "a small, dark-haired woman, whose thin, haunted face is framed by strands of gray."

As she gave a brief chronological history of her married life with Lieth—little more than names, places, and dates— Judge Watts had to remind her several times to speak loudly enough so the jurors could hear her. Between the faintness of her voice, and the slow and convoluted manner in which Mitchell Norton was asking his questions—"After Lieth's father died, Ms. Von Stein, was there anything going on in Lieth's life at that time?"—these early moments were awkward.

It was established that by July of 1987, Lieth had inherited more than $1 million from his parents.

Bonnie—determined not to participate in the painting of what she considered a distorted portrait of her family—said that prior to the death of Lieth's parents, he and Chris "got along as good as any loving father and son could get along," and that Lieth and Angela "were good buddies."

After the deaths, Norton asked, was there a change?

"There wasn't any change in the overall relationship."

"But were there problems on a specific basis?" Norton persisted.

"There were specific instances."

Then Norton had her admit that Chris's academic performance at NC State had been "mediocre" in the first semester and that in the second semester "I believe he did not do as well as he had in the first."

"So if he had a mediocre first semester, the second semester was worse?"

"I believe so," Bonnie said. She knew, of course, that it had been; that it had, in fact, been a disaster. But she was determined to make Mitchell Norton work for every inch of this distasteful ground.

She was, however, forced to admit that "a fight almost erupted" between Lieth and Chris during an argument about his grades "sometime during the early summer session of 1988." She said the incident had occurred in the kitchen.

"We were having dinner," she said, "Lieth, Chris, Angela, and myself. I don't remember the specifics of what was being discussed. But Lieth stood up from the dinner table and tried to engage Chris in a fistfight. Chris would not participate in that." She added that afterward she had told Lieth "that Chris had acted in a more adult manner than he had."

But then she added that "Lieth decided at that point that it would be best if I would render discipline to the children instead of him," and she conceded that "occasionally" Chris and Angela would refer to Lieth as an "asshole."

"Was that because he was sometimes?" Norton asked, but an objection to the question was sustained before Bonnie could answer.

As she resumed her testimony the next morning, Bonnie described how, after she'd noticed Chris's sound system missing from his car, she decided that he ought not to mention it to Lieth, and that she would tell Lieth about it later "because Lieth had been under a lot of strain . . . over the loss of both parents and his favorite uncle."

To Mitchell Norton, and to a number of others, this seemed among the least plausible elements of the story Bonnie had told from the start. It had been more than a year since Lieth's parents had died. It seemed simply not credible that those deaths could have been the source of the severe and relentless strain that Bonnie said had brought about such changes in Lieth's personality. If, indeed, there was such strain, its roots must have lain elsewhere. But as to its source, Bonnie provided no clues.

She said Chris had left the house on Saturday "to go and visit some friends" and had then prepared the hamburgers for their dinner Saturday night. She said Angela, too, had been out during the day Saturday, with Donna Brady.

As she spoke, it almost seemed as if—this one last time—she would be able to convince herself that nothing more sinister had been evolving.

On Sunday, Bonnie said, she and Lieth had gone to Greenville for breakfast and then "spent all afternoon working on the computer and with the *Wall Street Journal*," after which they had "shared some private moments in our bedroom."

Then she went through her story of Sunday night: the drive to Greenville for dinner, finding The King and Queen closed, eating instead at Sweet Caroline's, where Lieth had ordered the chicken special with rice.

The dinner had lasted from seven-thirty or seven forty-five to "around nine o'clock," when they'd driven home so Bonnie could watch the Ted Bundy miniseries. Lieth "went straight to bed," which, she said, was customary.

Angela had come home at ten-thirty P.M., an hour before her curfew, which was not customary. She'd gone directly to her room and had gotten in bed.

Bonnie watched the end of the miniseries, then the start of the eleven o'clock news. "Then," she said, "I went to the kitchen, went upstairs, woke Lieth up, asked him if he would like a glass of iced tea. He said no and went back to sleep. I got into bed, and I sat there and read."

This was all routine, Bonnie said. Almost every night, Lieth would go to sleep before her, then would stir when she came into the room. Often, he would want some iced tea to drink; often, he'd even wake up enough to turn on Johnny Carson and watch television for a while as she read. But on this night, he'd simply gone back to sleep.

Angela, she said, "was lying in bed, listening to the radio, reading." Bonnie also said that even though the house was air-conditioned, Angela had a fan on, as had been her habit, "year-round, since she was a small child." She liked the comforting hum, Bonnie said, and the feeling of air blowing on her face.

"After I sat in bed and tried to read for a few minutes," Bonnie testified, "I kept hearing Angela's radio through her bedroom door. So I got up and closed my bedroom door."

"Could you hear anything after that?" Norton asked.

"No. Nothing."

Bonnie said that, as "a guess," she'd gone to sleep "around midnight." Then: "I was awakened to hearing Lieth scream. There was a lot of confusion. Someone was standing at the foot of the bed."

Suddenly, Mitchell Norton was right there, at what he considered the most crucial moment of Bonnie's testimony, and perhaps the whole trial: her description of the intruder.

He established that she wore "thick" eyeglasses, that she was "very nearsighted," that she'd taken her glasses off before going to sleep, that all the lights in the bedroom were off.

But that wasn't enough. He still didn't trust her. So he told her to take her glasses off, right there in the courtroom. Then he asked, standing about twenty feet from her, "Can you see me? Do you recognize me from where you are now?"

"I can tell you have brown hair, have on a gray suit, red tie, and a white shirt."

"Other than that, can you see anything else?"

"I can tell you have eyes and a mouth, but I can't tell what they look like."

"How about my mustache? Can you see my mustache?"

"No."

"Can't see that?"

"No."

"All right. Now you may put your glasses back on." That should be good enough, he thought. No matter how definite she might try to be about the shape of an upper body glimpsed amid that murderous confusion in the dark, he'd already demonstrated that without her glasses the poor woman simply could not see.

"What was it that first awakened you?" he asked.

Until that moment, Bonnie had been in such total control of her emotions that a number of observers wondered if she was feeling anything at all. Now, however, she began to chew on her lip. "The sound of Lieth's scream," she said.

"Can you describe Lieth's scream for us, please?"

"It was short. It sounded piercing right in my ears. Just a series of short screams, very loud to me." She chewed harder on her lip.

But Mitchell Norton wanted more than that. "You say it was very loud. As best you can, can you duplicate for us here in the courtroom the scream that awakened you?"

She tried, but sitting there on the witness stand, in full view of judge, jury, and press, the soft-spoken Bonnie Von Stein was not able to scream loudly. It wasn't good enough for Mitchell Norton.

"No," he said. "I mean with the volume that Lieth used, that you heard that night."

"I don't know if I can or not."

"Can you try? Is there some reason that you feel you can't do it, Ms. Von Stein?"

Now, Bonnie had to fight harder to maintain composure. "Yes," she said. "That's one thing that I've not been able to face."

"Can you explain that?" Norton demanded. "That you can't—I mean, can you explain?"

Finally, Judge Watts stepped in, putting a halt to that line of questioning, allowing Bonnie to say simply that she didn't know how many screams she'd heard, but "when I heard the screams and I was awake enough to know that something was wrong, Lieth was in a sitting position. I believe I reached my hand toward him."

"What happened when you reached over towards Lieth?"

"I was struck with some kind of instrument. I believe, on the hand." This blow, she said, had caused a fractured thumb. Then she said, "The person standing at the—near the end of the bed struck Lieth, hitting my hand in the process. Then I was struck in the head. Then Lieth was struck again. I don't know where. And then I was struck again. And I don't remember after that for a while."

"Was Lieth still screaming?"

"Yes."

"During the time that this individual was striking him?"

"Yes."

Bonnie testified that she'd been struck twice on the right side and once on the left side of her forehead. She said the bedroom was dark, but a light—"it wasn't a bright light"— shone in from the hallway.

Now Norton returned to what was, for him, the crux of the matter.

"Could you tell what type of clothing the individual was wearing?"

"No. Everything looked dark, black, everything looked black to me. It was just dark."

"Could you discern anything at all about the facial features?"

"Nothing. He had his hand raised up over his head, had something in his hand, and was striking us with it. He looked bulky, big through this area"—here, Bonnie gestured to her shoulders and chest. "It looked like he didn't have a neck. It looked like the head just sat right up on top of his shoulders."

At the defense table, James Upchurch sat slender and long-necked. The short-necked and bulky Neal Henderson would not be seen by the jury until he was called to testify.

Mitchell Norton didn't want to talk about shoulders and necks. He wanted to talk about what Bonnie had *not* seen. "Could you discern anything at all," he asked, "about the nose, the mouth, anything at all?"

"No."

"All right, now after you were struck on the hand, struck in the head, you said you didn't remember anything. What was the next thing that you can remember? Lieth is screaming. Your thumb is broken. You are hit in the head."

"I remember being conscious, and I was lying on the floor. There was someone standing at my feet that I assumed was the same person I had seen earlier. Again, with his hands raised and something in his hands. And I was struck again."

"Where were you struck at that time?"

"I don't know."

"Don't know where you were struck?"

"No."

"Where were you?"

"I believe I was lying right next to the bed, on the side that I slept on, with my head near the wall."

"Do you know how you got on the floor, Ms. Von Stein?"

"No."

"Do you recall being struck in the chest?"

"I don't remember that now, no, sir."

"Did you receive some injury to your chest?"

"I was stabbed in the chest. There was internal bleeding and my lung collapsed."

"And were you hospitalized?"

"For seven days, I believe."

"And what about the injury to your head?"

"I had long, open wounds on my head. One on the right side, from my eyebrow up to my hairline."

He made her get down from the witness stand and walk close to the jury and pull her bangs aside and show them— even after all the plastic surgery—the extent of the scarring that remained. And he made her put her fingers on her chest in the exact spot where she'd been stabbed.

She then testified that she'd had "some seizure-type activity," presumably as a result of her head injury. "I would be in the shower," she said, "or driving down the highway, and all of a sudden it was like I was standing on the outside watching somebody else doing something totally different. And it was explained to me as a daydream-type seizure."

No, she said, she'd never had anything like that before being attacked.

"Now," Norton asked her, "how many times did you see—actually see, or look at, the individual there in the room that night?"

"Two times that I recall. When I first awoke and saw the person standing near the end of the bed, and then again when I regained consciousness on the floor, he was standing at my feet."

"And what was the next thing that happened as you were lying on the floor?"

"I heard a whoosh noise and I lost consciousness."

"How many times did you hear the whoosh noise?"

"Directly preceding every time I remember someone being struck."

"How many times do you remember either yourself or Lieth being struck?"

"Four or five times."

"Do you know how long you were unconscious?"

"No."

"What was the next thing you remember?"

"I remember hearing the bedroom door close very softly. And I heard the same type of whoosh sound and some thumps outside of the bedroom behind the closed door. And the thought that came to me was, 'Angela is being attacked now.'"

"What was Lieth doing? Were you aware of where Lieth was at the time?"

"No."

"Do you recall hearing anything from him, any sounds at all coming from Lieth?"

"At that time, no."

"At some time later did you?"

"Yes."

"And when was that, please?"

"I lost consciousness after hearing the whoosh and the thumps outside the bedroom door, as best I recall. And the next thing I remember is becoming awake, being disoriented. I was lying on the floor. I didn't know why I was on the floor. I thought I had had a bad dream and fallen out of the bed. I reached up to get back up on the bed, and I felt Lieth's hand. It was very sticky. It was a very sticky feeling, and his fingers just hung down.''

"Could you hear any sound from Lieth at that time?"

"I believe I heard him breathing.''

"Were you conscious of the fact at that time that you yourself had been struck?''

"At that time, no.''

"What about the chest wound?''

"At the time when I moved my hand, when I reached to try to get up on the bed,'' she said, "I couldn't move. And there was this gushy, yucky, warm feeling that came up on my neck. And I put my hand up on my head. And I felt, like, a big hole in my head. And I realized that something was—was terribly wrong, and I needed to get to the telephone. I remember trying to move towards the telephone, and I couldn't get up. The only thing I could do to make myself move was to push with my heels. So I got turned around in the direction where the telephone was. It was sitting on top of the metal filing cabinet next to the desk.''

Norton asked her how she managed to get to the phone.

"I don't know,'' she said. "I remember moving and trying to reach the phone. And then I remember being right next to the filing cabinet. I couldn't reach the phone. I couldn't sit up far enough to get to the phone. And I reached between the desk and the filing cabinet and caught hold of the cord and pulled the phone, and it fell on top of me.

"I remember becoming conscious again. I had the telephone sitting on top of me. I tried to call, get the operator. I tried to call 911. I couldn't remember where any of the buttons on the telephone were. I kept getting a busy signal, and all kinds of weird noises.

"Finally, I just hung the phone up and thought, 'I have to find the zero.' So I started pushing the buttons one at a time. I would push a button and then hang the phone up until I got to the zero and got the operator.

"Could you describe your emotional state at that time?"

"The only thing I had on my mind,'' Bonnie said calmly,

"was, 'I have to get somebody. I have to get help.' I wasn't conscious of any other emotion at that time."

"At any time during the attack," Norton asked, "did you ever see more than one person?"

"No." That didn't mean she thought there *wasn't* more than one, but the truthful answer to the question he had asked her was no.

"Are you able to identify that person, Ms. Von Stein?"

She paused. Then, very softly, she gave what she knew to be the only truthful answer to the question he had asked. "No."

Norton figured he was through the bad patch now. The rest, from his point of view, was mere detail. But to Bonnie, it involved an anguishing first public description of some of the worst moments of her life.

"I remember somebody knocking on the door," she said. "I assumed it was the police because the lady on the phone said the police were on their way. I remember saying, 'Come in.' But they couldn't hear me. They kept knocking on the door. Finally, somebody opened the door and turned on the light.

"He turned on the light and said something that sounded to me like, 'Oh, my God, I've never seen anything like this.' And kind of fell back out of the room. Everything—everything was red. The whole room looked red to me.

"I remember asking about Lieth. And someone told me that there was nothing they could do to help Lieth. At one point, I asked about Angela. Then I heard her voice. And that was a beautiful sound."

Bonnie paused. She could not go on. There just was no more she could bring herself to say. The moment was, she said later, "unbearable."

But then it got worse. For no apparent reason—Bonnie later surmised, "He was just going out of his way to make me as miserable as possible"—Mitchell Norton handed her one of the worst and goriest of the crime-scene photos John Taylor had taken: one that showed, in full color, Lieth's bloody, battered body on the bed.

"Who is that individual?" Norton asked.

At this point, Bonnie finally began to cry. "That *was* my husband, Lieth," she said.

She held her hand to her eyes and wept softly. It was something she'd promised herself she would not do, but when a person makes as many promises to herself as Bonnie had, it sometimes is not possible to keep them all.

Even when Bonnie was able to continue, Norton didn't let up.

"Did you believe your son could have done such a thing?" he asked.

"No."

"Did you believe your son was innocent?"

"Yes."

"Had you talked with your son?"

"Yes."

"Did he indicate to you initially that he had done nothing?"

"Yes."

"Do you now believe that your son had nothing to do with it?

"No."

"Have you talked with your son about what happened that night?"

"Yes."

"Has he admitted to you that he, in company with others, did in fact plot and carry out not only your death, but the death of Lieth Von Stein?"

"Yes."

"Did he tell you who was involved in the planning of this conspiracy?"

"Yes."

"What did he tell you?"

"James Upchurch and Neal Henderson and himself, Chris Pritchard."

"Did he tell you what the plan was? What each individual was to do?"

"Yes."

"What did he tell you?"

"The plan was for Mr. Henderson to drive Christopher's

car to Washington, and Mr. Upchurch was to go in the house and kill us, and Chris was to stay at North Carolina State."

"When did Chris finally admit to you the things that you've just told us about, Ms. Von Stein?"

"December twenty-seventh, 1989." There was a pause as it sunk into the jury's collective mind that this had been less than two weeks ago.

"And from July of '88 up until December of 1989, had he ever indicated to you, ever admitted to you, that he was involved in this?"

"No."

"And up until that time in December, did you believe or want to believe that your son could not and would not do such a thing?"

"Yes."

Then, after having her testify that the total estate that Angela and Chris would have inherited was approximately $2 million, and that neither she nor Lieth had sat down and explained the trust arrangement to either of them in detail, Mitchell Norton was finished with her.

It was Wayland Sermons, the younger of Upchurch's defenders, who conducted the cross-examination. He began by asking about their family life.

Bonnie said the million dollars Lieth had inherited had caused no changes in their lifestyle.

"You mentioned a fight at the dinner table."

"Yes."

"And that was something prompted not by Chris, but by Lieth's anger, is that not correct?"

"Yes."

"Did that cause any animosity or split feelings between you and Lieth?"

"No."

"For any short period of time?"

"No."

"But I believe you indicated Lieth would have you discipline the children because they were yours, is that correct?"

344

"Not because they are mine, but because I was more diplomatic at handling them than he was."

"Okay. And so that prevented him from becoming involved one-on-one with the children, isn't that true?"

"Yes."

She said "occasionally" both Chris and Angela would call Lieth "asshole" to his face.

In response to further questions she also said. Chris had lied to her in the past; she didn't know why the kitchen telephone cord had been disconnected on the night of the murder; and that Chris alone, with no help from Angela, had prepared the hamburgers the night before.

Returning to the night of the murder, Sermons said, "Now, you talked to Angela in her room and she had a fan on and a radio, and then you closed her door and went to your room. Left your door open, is that correct?"

"Yes."

"And when you began reading you could hear her radio, so you got up and closed your door?"

"Yes."

"Do you know if the door is hollow or not?"

"It is a hollow door."

"It is hollow?"

"Yes."

"And the door to Angela's room would be the same, is that correct?"

"Yes."

He established that she'd indeed had thirteen cats in the house, and then he asked her about the rooster.

"Was this your pet?"

"Yes. I brought him in occasionally. He sat for about an hour each evening and watched TV with me."

Then he asked about keys. "Do you know whether Chris had a key to the back door?"

"To the back door on the porch? No."

"He did not have a key?"

"He did not have a key."

"Have you since heard him state that he did have a key?"

"Yes."

345

This was news. Until this answer, lawyers on both sides had accepted Chris's story of stealing the key to the back door. Now Bonnie was stating he had *not* had a key to the new, outer door. From Sermons's point of view, however, there seemed nothing to gain from pressing the issue.

Instead he began to focus on the murder itself, establishing how much noise there had been, implying that Angela could not have slept through it. He reminded Bonnie that, when first interviewed in the hospital, she'd said Lieth had screamed "at least fifteen times at the top of his lungs."

Then he introduced the subject of Henderson, reminding Bonnie that she had described the assailant as having "very broad shoulders and no neck." He handed her a picture of Henderson. She said she recognized it as being him because she'd seen him in court during pretrial proceedings.

"Can you tell us," Sermons asked, "when the very first time is you saw Mr. Henderson?"

"I saw him in the courtroom in Beaufort County when I was there for some motions to be heard."

"And was that the very first time in broad daylight, in any kind of light, that you had ever seen Mr. Henderson that you know of?"

"Yes."

"Ms. Von Stein, can you describe to us whether or not you had any feelings of recognition of Mr. Henderson at that time?"

Mitchell Norton was on his feet, objecting, but Judge Watts ruled that Bonnie could answer.

"I didn't recognize Mr. Henderson," she said. "I recognized the fact that he had a shape that frightened me. I was upset to the point that when we broke, I left the courtroom and did not return until after the lunch break." Then she described having had the same sensation a few weeks earlier, when she'd seen someone else with the same physique.

Sermons asked whether the sight of James Upchurch provoked an equivalent response.

"No."

"You did not become frightened?"

"No."

346

"You did not feel any scaredness, or any type of emotional uprising in your body?"

"Not with his appearance, no."

"Ms. Von Stein, in your opinion then, do the defendant James Upchurch's physical features match the silhouette you saw in your bedroom?"

"In the conditions I've seen him in, no."

Sermons then attacked Chris's veracity, establishing that during at least four interviews with investigators, he had lied. "It wasn't until December twenty-seventh that Chris began to tell a story different from the four prior times, is that correct?"

"That's correct."

"Did you know then that on the four prior occasions Chris had not been telling the truth?"

"No."

"And I believe you said you did not want to believe that he would have been capable of doing such a thing, is that correct?"

"That's correct."

"And after he made the statement on December twenty-seventh?"

"After he told me, I had to believe him."

On redirect examination, she said she believed him now because "I can't possibly imagine him telling me such a horrible story had he not done what he said he did."

But Norton's main concern was Bonnie's statement that Upchurch's appearance did not frighten her, and that he did not seem to resemble the person she'd seen in her bedroom. All his earlier work was threatening to come undone.

"The conditions in which you have seen Mr. Upchurch," he asked, "have they been in a courtroom atmosphere?"

"Yes."

"In well-lighted areas, just like it is here?"

"Yes."

"Have you had your glasses on?"

"Yes."

"Has he been dressed in a suit, coat and tie?"

"Yes."

347

"White shirt?"

"I don't remember what color shirt, light-colored shirt."

"All right, now, Ms. Von Stein, have you ever seen Mr. Upchurch in a dark room with the drapes drawn and all the lights turned out except some light filtering in from a side door?"

"Not that I know of."

"Have you ever seen him dressed head to toe in dark clothing?"

"Not to my knowledge."

"Do you think that if you dressed him in dark clothing and put him in a dark room, it would be more difficult for you to identify James Upchurch?"

"I believe it would be more difficult."

"Do you think if you took your glasses off in a dark room and he was dressed in dark clothing, it would be even *more* difficult for you to identify him, Ms. Von Stein?"

"I think it would be impossible."

"And if, Ms. Von Stein, you were laying down on the floor, looking up at a subject dressed head to toe in some dark clothing in a dark room, with the lights off, do you feel like that would make it even *more* difficult for you to identify James Upchurch?"

"Yes."

"Furthermore, if you were laying on the floor having been struck in the head, your husband screaming, awakened from a deep sleep, and observed a person in dark clothing head to toe, a dark room, drapes drawn, light filtering through a side door, do you feel like that would make it even *more* difficult to observe or to identify James Upchurch?"

"Yes."

"The times that you saw James Upchurch in the courtroom, Ms. Von Stein, did he ever have a baseball bat, club, or stick or anything raised up over your head?"

"No."

"And if you were laying on the floor, having been struck several times in the head, bleeding from the chest, hearing your husband scream at the top of his voice several times, blood gushing from your chest in a dark room, the defendant dressed head to toe in black or some dark clothing, light filtering through some side door, do you feel like that would make it even *more* difficult for you to identify James Upchurch, or whoever else was in the room?"

"Objection. Same question."

"Overruled."

"Yes."

"Now, you've said that the individual that you saw appeared to be broad-shouldered and appeared to have no neck." He spoke so slowly, so ponderously, that Bonnie seriously questioned if any of the jurors would be able to remember the first part of his question by the time he finally reached the last.

"If you were laying on the floor, looking up, having been struck in the head several times, bleeding from the chest, hearing your husband scream at the top of his voice, and awakened from a deep sleep, saw an individual dressed in dark clothing head to toe, something over his face, drapes drawn, dark light filtering through a side door, a bat or stick somewhere in his hands, with hands raised up over his head"—and here Mitchell Norton clasped his hands above his head, as Wade Smith had done in his office while Bonnie had lain on the floor—"hands raised over the head in this manner with the bat, as you've described it, what happens to the shoulders and to the neck?"

"Objection."

"Overruled."

"Yours," Bonnie said, "just appear to blend together."

Then it was Wayland Sermons's turn again.

"Mr. Henderson caused you to be frightened, is that correct?"

"Yes."

"And Mr Upchurch did not cause you to feel frightened in any way, did he?"

"No."

And then Mitchell Norton: "But again, Ms. Von Stein, the circumstances that he just asked you about, you were not laying on the floor?"

"Objection."

"Sustained. I think we've been over that."

"The truth of the matter is, you can't say who was in there!" Norton said.

"Objection to that."

"Overruled."

"I cannot identify any particular person," Bonnie said softly. "I wish I could."

34

There was testimony from one of the first officers at the scene. He said that from the first moment he saw Lieth, he'd noticed that the dead man's blood had already begun to "jell." This implied a time of death considerably earlier than that suggested by the time of Bonnie's phone call.

Then John Taylor took the stand and remained there for what seemed an interminable day and a half. Mitchell Norton plodded so slowly through his direct examination of Taylor that at one point, out of the district attorney's hearing, Judge Watts called Keith Mason aside and said, "Can't you get Mitchell to go a little faster?"

"Judge," Mason said, "I'm trying to, but he's just a good ol' boy from Sampson County and he's talkin' as fast as he can."

With Page Hudson, the tall, deep-voiced, and extremely authoritative pathologist who had conducted the autopsy, Norton might actually have spoken a bit too quickly—or at least asked one question too many.

He and Lewis Young had spent much time with Dr. Hudson prior to trial. The pathologist was the only truly expert witness Norton had, and the district attorney wanted to use him to maximum advantage.

Most of the testimony was straightforward and not subject to conflicting interpretation. Six different head wounds had caused tearing of the scalp, and in some instances, fractures of the skull. Yes, a baseball bat could have caused them.

There had been eight stab wounds: one in the left chest, one high on the right side of the back, and six clustered together lower on the left side of the back. Yes, these could have been caused by the hunting knife found at the fire scene. The wounds to the back would not have proved fatal, or even brought about "immediate incapacitation." The stab wound to the chest, however, had penetrated the heart and by itself would have caused death within a very few minutes.

The only troublesome question for Mitchell Norton concerned the undigested food in Lieth's stomach, which suggested an earlier time of death than was compatible with the version of events Norton was presenting. But he'd gone over this with Dr. Hudson in advance and had studied the autopsy report, and he thought he could introduce and then dispose of the subject in such a way as not to cause the jury undue concern.

He first asked if tests had been performed that would have indicated the presence of alcohol in the blood.

Dr. Hudson said yes, but that none had been detected.

"Did you also check the contents of the stomach?"

"I did."

"What did you find?"

"I found a rather large quantity of food, rather undigested rice, and a meat which I thought was most likely chicken."

Norton asked the question he knew he had to, because if he didn't, Sermons or Johnston surely would. Had there been anything unusual about the stomach contents?

"Just the fact that it was undigested was remarkable," Dr. Hudson said. "It looked like rice that had been eaten within the previous hour or so."

"Assuming that Mr. Von Stein had eaten around eight

to nine o'clock, and that the attack occurred somewhere around four in the morning, is there anything unusual in that?" He knew the answer, but he also knew what his next question would be, and most importantly, the one after that.

"Yes. In my opinion, very unusual. I would have expected it to be fairly well digested. I would have expected it to have left the stomach in that period of time."

Norton asked if Dr. Hudson had any explanation for why the rice was still in such an undigested state if Lieth had lived until approximately four A.M.

"For the most part," the pathologist replied, "those two facts are incompatible."

But here, on the basis of the autopsy report and his pretrial interview with Dr. Hudson, Mitchell Norton proposed to resolve the apparent contradiction. What about stress? Norton asked. Lieth had been under a lot of stress. Might that have slowed his digestion? In his report, Dr. Hudson had written, "Severe stress can effectively paralyze or 'freeze' the digestion for many hours." They had talked about this ahead of time.

"It is true," Dr. Hudson said, "that under severe stress, particularly severe emotional stress, digestion may simply stop for hours. But it takes a rather considerable stress."

"Concern about family?" Norton asked. "Concern about financial things? Would they create the kind of stress you are referring to?" Norton was confident that Dr. Hudson's affirmative answer would lay the entire issue to rest. The jury already knew about family stress and the pressures caused by newfound wealth. When Dr. Hudson said that these would be enough to freeze the digestive process in its tracks, the question of the rice would be resolved.

"I would not think so," Page Hudson said.

Later, Mitchell Norton would say this answer "dropped like a hammer on my head." In all the talk about stress, he'd just assumed that they'd been talking about the same kind: day-to-day, run-of-the-mill stress caused by work or family problems. But he hadn't gone far enough in pretrial preparation. He hadn't allowed for the possibility that to

Page Hudson stress meant something different and quite a bit more specific.

"In my experience," Dr. Hudson continued, and the jury knew all about Dr. Hudson's experience because Mitchell Norton had made much of it in his introductory questions, "and from what's written in the medical literature, that sort of relatively low-level stress would not slow the digestion to the point that it's scarcely affected in six hours, or whatever the period was."

Norton was too stunned even to try to interrupt. When Dr. Hudson completed his answer, Norton said he had no further questions.

Frank Johnston was on his feet almost immediately. Later, he would say, "This was the first time I'd had a State's witness, in a major criminal case, be on my side. It looked to me like the medical evidence completely overruled what the State was saying happened." He wanted to be sure that even the dullest of the jurors got the point.

"Would you say," he asked, "that it's *very* unlikely for someone to have eaten a dinner of chicken and rice at eight or eight-thirty, and for that meal not to have been completely digested and passed out of the stomach by three or four in the morning?"

"In my opinion, it's very unlikely." The finding was, Dr. Hudson said, "consistent with an earlier death." He added that "ordinarily, I would have expected the material in his stomach to have pretty well all cleared out and been into the small intestine within an hour or two."

An hour or two! Johnston could scarcely believe his good fortune.

And it continued to get better. In the four thousand autopsies he'd personally done, Page Hudson said, he couldn't recall "any at all where stress stopped digestive activity to the point where even some simply digested material like rice doesn't get changed more than this was."

All that Mitchell Norton could salvage on his redirect examination was to establish that Dr. Hudson had never met Lieth Von Stein and had no direct knowledge of his personality or emotional makeup.

It wasn't much. *An hour or two!* If Page Hudson was

right, and there was no one in that Pasquotank County courtroom about to argue the point with the state's first chief medical examiner, then Lieth Von Stein would have been dead by midnight. Now Upchurch's defenders had expert testimony to go with the officer's eyewitness report of the "jelled" blood.

If the jury accepted that finding, there was no way James Upchurch could be convicted. Not only would Lieth have been dead for hours before Bonnie had made her call to police, but according to the testimony that both Chris Pritchard and Neal Henderson would give, Upchurch and Henderson hadn't even left the NC State campus until well after eleven P.M.

As Page Hudson strode confidently from the courtroom, Bill Osteen, who had just arrived in Elizabeth City because his client was scheduled to testify next, introduced himself and asked a question that had not been asked while Dr. Hudson was on the stand.

Osteen wondered if, in Dr. Hudson's expert opinion, the injuries inflicted on Lieth and Bonnie were more suggestive of two assailants than one.

Yes, the pathologist said, they certainly were. And he would have said so had anyone asked.

Chris took the stand the next day. He told the tale of his academic decline and fall, which resulted in a 1.3 grade point average his first semester at NC State, and "nonexistent" grades the second semester. He acknowledged that his poor performance had made Lieth "ill."

He described meeting Henderson and Upchurch for the first time after responding to a flier posted to attract Dungeons & Dragons enthusiasts.

Suddenly, he found himself presented with a chance to talk about his favorite subject, and he was quick to seize it. He said Dungeons & Dragons was a "role-playing game, where a person or group of people get together, create their own little world, so to speak, and have what is known as characters. Now, these characters would be people that you want to be, or people that you would like to be. You could be thirteen years old and be a fire fighter, or you could be a soldier or you could be a knight.''

The game, he said, was "set on the swords and sorcery theme. It would be equivalent to medieval times, but it is actually set on an entirely different planet.'' He was off now, doing his Dungeons & Dragons riff right there in court. He talked of "bards, magic users, thieves, fighters.'' He said, "Those are the general classes. There are subclasses. Subclass of fighters would be—''

But there Judge Watts brought his flight of fantasy to a halt, sustaining an objection on grounds of relevance.

Regarding the murder, Chris said the plot was conceived "about five days prior to July the twenty-fifth,'' when he'd asked Upchurch his "patricide'' question at the Golden Corral. He said he'd told Upchurch that his parents had "about five million dollars between them.''

Even before that, he said, "we were discussing what we were going to do if we got rich, or after we graduated from high school—I mean, from college. Daniel wanted to be a writer, and I wanted to be a writer, and James wanted his own restaurant. I said, 'Well, if something should happen to my parents, then I could set James up in his restaurant. We can all three live in a big house in north Raleigh, a real classy section of Raleigh, and have a real nice stereo; and you know, everybody would have nice cars, something like that.' ''

Yes, he said, during this discussion they'd all been drinking beer and smoking marijuana, and no, he was not serious about it at the time. It was, he said, "just daydreaming.''

But then, he admitted, it got serious. He told the same story he'd told in Vosburgh's office: the further plans, the trip to steal the key, the Sominex powder, Upchurch waiting for him in the shack.

"Had you and James talked about what would happen to your sister, Angela?'' Norton asked.

"We had discussed it. James said something to the effect of, 'Well what about your sister?' And I said, 'Well, if she is there, then I guess her, too. But if she's not, that's fine, too.' ''

"What was your reaction to that talk about going to get a machete?" Norton asked.

"I said, 'Aren't the Army surplus stores closed?' First of all, you know, I wanted it to be painless. But the Army surplus stores were closed."

Then he described buying the hunting knife instead, telling Upchurch he'd have to find a driver with a license, meeting Neal Henderson, and drawing the map.

"What was the purpose of killing your parents?" Norton asked. "What were you going to get out of it?"

"A large inheritance."

"And had you talked with James about that?"

"Yes, sir, I told him I would give him a car and fifty thousand dollars." He added that Henderson was to get $50,000 and a Ferrari. Not a bad deal for Henderson, some thought: getting a payoff equal to that of the killer for doing no more than driving the car. But Norton didn't want the focus to be on Henderson.

"The initial plan," he asked, "whose thought was that?"

"I brought up the idea of killing my parents."

"After that, what part did James Upchurch play?"

"He was an equal in the planning in that he came up with some ideas. I came up with some ideas. You know, it was an equal thing. I mean, neither one of us sat there and talked the other one's ears off."

He said he'd drawn the dogs on the map "so that when James went to the house, he wouldn't accidentally get a dog to barking, because it might have woken up my parents or the neighbors." They had determined that the killing should take place at around two A.M., "because my parents usually went to sleep around eleven or twelve, and at two o'clock they would be pretty deeply in sleep." He said he'd pointed out the best spot for Upchurch to be dropped off, so he could make his way to the back of Chris's house, moving mostly through trees instead of around other houses.

On Sunday night, he'd gone to Wildflour, he said, and had drunk "a lot of beer" and eaten pizza. At eleven P.M., he'd been in his room with his roommate, Vince Hamrick. Upchurch stopped by.

"He said that he was going to go do some homework. I said, 'Well, good luck.' And that was it."

Through all of this, Chris seemed composed, even detached. Later, he said, "I took so much of that medication to calm me down that I almost went to sleep twice on the witness stand."

And neither Bonnie nor Angela—who had chosen to leave school to hear her brother's testimony, though she had not been present for her mother's—displayed any signs of emotion.

"Now, Chris," Norton asked for the second time, "why did you do it?"

"I honestly don't know the answer to that question," Chris said. "There were many reasons that went through my mind, but I honestly do not know why I came up with this idea."

"What reasons were going through your mind?"

"Well, money. I would have inherited a lot of money. I wouldn't have had to do anything else. I wouldn't have had to go back to school or anything. I could sit around, buy a house, and do drugs all the time. I could play D and D all I wanted to. And I had a term paper due that Monday that I hadn't even started on."

He said he'd been taking large quantities of drugs in the weeks leading up to the murder. Alcohol, marijuana, cocaine, Ecstasy, and especially, LSD.

"What effect did LSD have on you?"

"I saw colors. I felt invincible. My mind raced very rapidly. And I had incredible amounts of energy for about six or seven hours straight. Marijuana, it seemed to make music better, it seemed to make TV more interesting, commercials especially. Ecstasy: I felt very mellow. And I just wanted to sit down and contemplate life. Generally, politics. That was what I was contemplating, world politics."

Norton, who was now, in a sense, having the kind of conversation with Chris that Bonnie had not been able to bring herself to have, said, "All right. Now, you also said you had a term paper due. Surely, you don't mean that you killed your father because of a term paper?"

"What I mean is, that was a thought that went through

my mind as one of the reasons, because I was very upset over the fact that I hadn't done it. I was very upset over the fact that my parents would be upset about it. I had already had two talks with my father and mother about my grades. I knew a third would mean that I probably wouldn't go back to school."

After receiving the phone call from Angela, Chris was, he said, "in shock."

"Why were you in shock? This was something you had planned."

"At some level," he said, "I did not really believe this would happen."

"But you had sat down. You had planned. You had provided keys. You had provided an automobile. You had supplied a knife for the killing."

"Yes, sir. But it was just like the game. In the game, you sit down and plan out things. You get your ducks in a row. I knew that this would happen. But at a deeper level, I didn't believe it."

That changed when he saw Bonnie in the hospital. "She didn't look good. She had been injured, beaten, she was on a—she had a tube in her side, in her chest."

"Did you hug her, kiss her?"

"I was just happy she was alive."

"But you'd planned to kill her?"

"Yes, sir."

Now, for the first time, Chris appeared unsettled. He shifted back and forth in his chair, he began to perspire a bit, and he glanced quickly around the courtroom but would not establish eye contact with anyone.

"Did you go to the funeral?" Norton asked.

"Yes, sir."

"Have any feelings about it at that time, about the killing?"

"Yes, sir, I did. Very strong feelings." And now Chris put a hand to his face; now tears began to form in his eyes.

"What kind of feelings?" Norton asked.

"Incredible remorse," he said, quite obviously trying to hold back the tears. "I was thoroughly disgusted."

"Did you think about the police?"

"Yes, sir, I thought about the police. I thought about keeping myself away from them. I didn't want to be arrested, thrown in jail. I didn't want my mama to know what I had done. So I deceived the police as best I could. I lied to my family and my friends."

Bonnie and Angela sat still and expressionless as Chris gave a short, muffled sob. He took a deep breath. He looked around the courtroom again, but not at either his mother or his sister. Then he seemed to regain his composure.

He testified that when he had returned to NC State in August, he'd had no contact at all with Neal Henderson, and had tried to avoid Upchurch as well, because "I was afraid of him, and I was disgusted with him."

There had been, however, one encounter. It was in August. Chris had seen Upchurch at a party and had said he wanted to speak to him "We went to a room," Chris said, "I don't remember where it was. It was in the dorm. And he said, 'You didn't tell me that the window on the back was Plexiglas.' He said he had to cut the screen and break the glass on the side window to get the door. And then, before I could say anything, he said, 'There was blood everywhere.' At that point, I told him to shut his mouth. I didn't want to hear another word. I told him to forget it and to make sure that Neal forgot it, too. And I walked out of the room."

"Why was it, Chris, that you didn't want to hear about what had gone on in the house? Why did you tell him to shut up?"

"Because I was disgusted about the whole thing. I didn't want to hear anything about it. I did not want to hear a word about it. And I was afraid of the boy, you know."

"Why were you afraid of him?"

"Because he was the one that was supposed to have gone in the house and killed my parents."

The next morning, as Chris returned to the stand, Mitchell Norton asked him about Angela.

"You stated that in your initial plan, the fire plan, you did not talk specifically about Angela, is that correct?"

"Yes, sir."

"How about in the burglary plan?"

"Yes, sir, we did."

"What was discussed at that time?"

"She was to be murdered also."

"And was there any particular reason for that?"

"Not any particular reason, no, sir."

"What, if anything, did you stand to gain by Angela's death?"

"The entire insurance," Chris said.

On cross-examination, Wayland Sermons pressed Chris about all the lies he had told, going back to the first time he'd been questioned by Lewis Young, and continuing up to the moment his lawyers negotiated his plea bargain.

"On the twenty-fifth day of July 1988, at ten forty-five P.M., you were not telling the truth, were you Mr. Pritchard?"

"No, sir, I was not."

"On the first of August 1988, at five-fifty P.M. in the Washington police department, you were not telling the truth, were you?"

"No, sir, I was not."

"On the twenty-fourth day of August 1988, at eleven-forty A.M., at the Washington police department, again, you were not telling the truth, were you?"

"No, sir, I was not."

Then Sermons went into the details of the statements Chris had made. Again and again, Chris admitted, tonelessly, "I was lying . . . I was lying . . . I was lying."

Finally, Sermons asked, "Prior to making your statement on December twenty-seventh, isn't it true that you knew Neal Henderson was prepared to testify that you asked him to drive your car down to Washington?"

"Yes, sir."

"And did you not know that Mr. Henderson was contending that Mr. Upchurch actually did the killings?"

"Yes, sir."

"And isn't it true that you knew that if you were convicted of first-degree murder, you stood a chance of being put to death in the gas chamber of North Carolina?"

His face now openly displaying anguish, Chris said, "Yes, sir."

"Isn't it true that by your plea bargain, you no longer face that possibility?"

"Yes, sir."

"And you knew at the time you made the deal that that was saving your life, did you not?"

"Yes, sir."

"You knew that if you had not made that deal, your life was on the line, didn't you, Mr. Pritchard?"

"Yes, sir."

The implication was clear, even to Bonnie. If Chris had lied so many times to so many people in an attempt to save himself, why would he not lie this one more time, falsely implicating Upchurch in the plot, in order to escape the death penalty??

For if Norton hadn't been assured by Bill Osteen that Chris's statement would point to Upchurch's guilt, there would have been no plea bargain.

Outside the courtroom, at the end of the day, Wayland Sermons was even less charitable as he spoke to the press. He said Chris "obviously has a reason to lie. It's not the first time someone has testified to save his own life." He predicted that the jury would "see through" the story Chris had told.

"In four days of testimony," Sermons said, "the only evidence the State has is from someone who did seventeen hits of acid in thirty days."

35
===

On Tuesday, January 16, Neal Henderson was called to the stand. He was well-dressed, composed, and reserved. Even Bonnie noted that he "gave the appearance of being respectful."

She did not experience the same burst of terror as in September when she'd first seen him. Since then, at subsequent motion hearings, she'd grown at least marginally accustomed to the sight of him. Also, she later said, on this occasion, she was fully absorbed by the story he told.

"Speak up as loud as you can, Mr. Henderson," Judge Watts said. "It's obviously important that all these folks hear what you have to say. And it's important that I hear what you have to say. And I have a terrible cold."

Henderson said he was twenty-one years old, lived with his divorced mother and his sister in Danville, Virginia, where he worked as an assistant manager at a Wendy's. Before that, he'd worked at a Wendy's in Raleigh.

As early as fifth grade, he was found so gifted that he'd begun to take eighth-grade classes. Then he'd attended Bartlett Yancey High School in Yanceyville, the seat of Caswell County (and if there was a lesser county than Caswell, with a lesser county seat than Yanceyville, few in the courtroom—even in Pasquotank County—were likely ever to see it).

Two things had happened in high school, he said. He'd met James Upchurch, and he'd become obsessed with Dungeons & Dragons. His junior year had been spent in Durham, at the state's special school for students gifted in mathematics or science.

Next came the same sorry tale told by small-town boys

from all over the state who had gone off to NC State and been overwhelmed by its size and impersonality.

By the end of his freshman year, Neal Henderson, with an IQ of 160 and SAT scores of 1500—760 math, 740 verbal, the highest in the history of Caswell County—had flunked out of college, unnoticed and unmourned.

He had, however, continued to live near the campus, eager to play Dungeons & Dragons, and unwilling to go home and admit failure to his sorrowing mother. At some point in the summer of 1988—he wasn't sure when—his Caswell County buddy James Upchurch had mentioned that the newest player in the game, Chris Pritchard, was heir to a fortune that might be worth $10 million.

And then, he said, "approximately two weeks, maybe three," prior to July 25, Upchurch and Chris paid him a visit.

This was the first of the serious conflicts in terms of time. But there was nothing Mitchell Norton could do about it. Chris had already testified that Henderson had not known about the plot until the day before the murder was committed.

"James and Chris came in," Henderson said. "We chatted for a couple of minutes about Dungeons and Dragons. Then James said he and Chris had a plan for Chris to come into his inheritance early. I remarked to them, 'Oh, you're going to rob the place?' And James shook his head and said, 'No. We are going to murder his parents so that he inherits.'"

"And what did you say?"

"My exact words were, 'Isn't that a little extreme?' Chris laughed. James said, 'No, no. We are serious. Here, let me show you.' And they started outlining a plan."

Henderson—who Mitchell Norton feared would come across to the jury as a "plastic man," and who, to Upchurch's defense attorneys, resembled "a robot"—said mechanically that Upchurch had done "most of the talking," while Chris sat nearby, drawing a map.

The plan was for Upchurch to enter the house, to steal enough small valuables to make it appear that a burglary had occurred, "and then go upstairs and murder Chris's parents. I don't think at that exact time we talked about methods, or anything like that."

That first meeting, Henderson said, had lasted about an hour. They'd gone over the map in great detail, explaining just where he was supposed to drop off Upchurch, how to find the cul-de-sac at the end of the dirt road where he was to park, and the route Upchurch would take on foot from the car to the Von Stein house and back again. But, he said, no date was set.

"They asked me to drive the car down. Just drive it down, drop him off, pick him back up, and drive him back."

They told him they'd give him "either two thousand or twenty thousand dollars, I am not sure exactly which." He said, no problem, he'd be glad to drive the car.

"Two or three days" later, he had dropped by Upchurch's dorm room and had found Chris there. "They were sitting around talking," he said. "If I remember correctly, they were talking about Dungeons and Dragons. When I got there, the conversation turned to the plan. Mostly, about what would happen afterwards. Chris said he was going to become very depressed after the murder, and he was going to listen to a suggestion that someone was going to make, most likely James, to take a beach trip to cheer himself up. He was going to invite all his friends. Everyone was going to the beach—whoever he could find. At that point, he was going to feel much better and then buy everybody a car.

"You see, James was concerned that if only he received a car, people would wonder why he was getting a car. Well, Chris said, that was no problem. He would buy everybody a car.

"Maybe three or four days after that, late evening, I happened to come by James's room. He was there alone, and we started talking about the plan. He pulled a bat out of a closet and laid it on one of the beds in the room. He said he'd been thinking about how he was going to do it, and he had the bat as the primary weapon he was going to use. He also showed me a knife that he had gotten." This, too, contradicted Chris's story. Chris had testified that he'd not bought Upchurch the knife until the day before the murder.

"He said he wanted something that would knock someone out in one hit. He was not at all sure he could use just a knife and quickly do anything. But he said one good hit from the bat should do what he wanted. For as long as I've known him, he's always had a bat like that.

"Then he opened the drawer on his desk and pulled out a pair of gloves. They were the type batters use. And with, I think it was shoe polish, he blackened the gloves. They were black and white batting gloves, and he blackened the portion that was white.

"Then he said we were going to try for a day in the upcoming week. I think this meeting was on a Thursday or a Friday. He said Chris had either already left to go home or was going to go home the next day to find out the family's plans for the upcoming week, and I think, to get a house key. He asked me what my schedule was for the coming week, and I told him I had Sunday night off. He told me to keep it open—that that would probably be the night we would go."

Henderson made no mention of any prior plan to burn down the house, saying only that on the morning of Sunday, July 24, Upchurch came to his apartment to give him the map Chris had drawn two or three weeks earlier.

"He told me he would meet me later that night, at about eleven-thirty, twelve o'clock, and he told me where the car would be parked: in a lot known as the fringe lot, on Sullivan Drive. He told me to just keep the map until that night, look it over."

Henderson said he'd stayed in his apartment for the rest of the day, spending much of it with his girlfriend, Kenyatta, who was James Upchurch's cousin. In order to have an excuse for spending the night away, he'd told Kenyatta that evening that he'd just taken a hit of LSD, knowing that this would infuriate her, and that she'd tell him to get out and stay out until all effects of the drug had worn off.

At about eleven-thirty P.M. he'd met Upchurch by Chris Pritchard's car. Upchurch carried a green canvas knapsack and a baseball bat. The knapsack, Henderson said, "contained some clothing that he was going to change into." He said Upchurch changed as they drove, putting on a black sweater, black running shoes, and a black hood or ski mask.

When they reached Washington—coming in on a back road so Chris's loud and distinctive white Mustang would not be noticed—"James asked me to pull into the Smallwood area on Lawson Road. He wanted to see the area in front of the house. So I pulled in. We went by Chris's house from the front. James kind of counted down five houses and said, 'That's the place.' "

By then, Henderson said, it was about two-thirty A.M.

But by then, in Judge Watts's courtroom, it was five-twenty P.M., and he declared a recess until morning.

That night, Bonnie drove to a waterfront restaurant half an hour out of Elizabeth City. This was not something she'd done before, nor would she do it again. Normally, she would eat a quick, simple, and solitary meal near her motel. Some nights, she would just get a takeout order from a fast-food restaurant and eat alone in her motel room.

But Neal Henderson's quiet recitation of the circumstances that had led to the murder of her husband and very nearly to her own death, had affected Bonnie deeply. She had been stirred by listening to this total stranger describe how casually, how thoughtlessly—almost with indifference—he had involved himself in a scheme that would have seemed preposterous if its consequences had not been so tragic.

For so long, she'd felt it necessary to deny, even to herself, her feelings of sadness and loss. For so long, it seemed, she'd been engaged in combat with law enforcement. For so long, she'd been defending her son as he had lied.

But now it was almost over. Henderson would tell the rest of his sordid tale the next day. And yes, there would be other witnesses. And perhaps some sort of defense from Upchurch's lawyers. And then the verdict, possibly followed by a sentencing: life or death.

Bonnie was not sure it even mattered anymore. Just as, she thought, it did not matter why Lieth had not digested his rice. Her life was broken beyond repair. In only another week or two, her son would be taken from her, less violently but with no less finality than her husband had been.

She felt more weary than ever before, and especially exhausted by the effort of keeping every ounce of emotion locked inside.

Bonnie brought her notebook to the restaurant. After placing her order, she started to write. And for the first and only time during the trial, she wrote something that went beyond fact:

"As I was sitting in the courtroom, listening to Neal Henderson's accounting of what happened, I began to realize the tremendous loss suffered here. It became very difficult to suppress the emotion which began to come forward within me. I had to work very hard to try & prevent any juror from seeing into my feelings. Suppressing one's emotions for as long as I have done is bound to have some effect in the long run.

"As I sit here, I find myself once again dealing with feelings & emotions beyond my control. The realization that Lieth is never, never coming back is overpowering my thoughts at this moment. Maybe it wasn't such a good idea to isolate myself in Elizabeth City. The feeling of complete and total loneliness is like no other I have _ever_ experienced."

There was a pause as the waitress served her meal. Then Bonnie began to write again:

"Thank God for the interruption of my attentive waitress! Enough of this self-sympathy. This is really a nice, quiet, small restaurant. There were only three other tables of guests when I arrived. Two of those have left already. There is soft background music from a local radio station. Just the kind of place Lieth and I could have enjoyed finding together."

And then, for the first and only time, she addressed herself directly to her dead husband:

"Dear Lieth, I need you now as much as I ever have. I miss the time we shared; your compassion; your passion.

Right this moment, I miss our lovemaking together. These things I have desperately avoided thinking about over the past year and a half. Why now? I am alone tonite by choice. Will I always be alone, or will I be brave enough to move forward to new experiences? You always had a lot of faith in my strength. I suppose in many ways I am strong. Why do I feel so weak now?"

The next day, Neal Henderson told the rest of his story.

They parked the car at the end of a dead-end dirt road behind the Von Stein house. "We both got out of the car," Henderson said. "He told me to wait for him for about half an hour, and he would come back to meet me at this point at the end of the road. He put on the sweater. He got a ski mask ready, but he didn't put it on. Went ahead and put his gloves on. He had a flashlight and he turned it on. It didn't work very well. The batteries seemed to be weak."

Mitchell Norton handed Henderson a photograph of a baseball bat.

"This is the bat that James had that night," Henderson said. "I remember him taping the handle. And there's a circle of black triangles around the bat that he drew with Magic Marker. I remember him drawing that."

Then Norton handed Henderson the bat itself. This was, for Norton, one of the trickiest moments of the trial. When Henderson had first told his story to John Crone and Lewis Young, he'd mentioned the bat. He had said he thought Upchurch might have thrown the bat out of the moving car, as they drove back toward Raleigh. Later, he'd revised this, saying he was not sure, but it was possible that when Upchurch returned to the car after having committed the murder, he had already disposed of the bat.

The next day, in a small, wooded area across from Lawson Road, Crone found a baseball bat that had obviously been exposed to the elements for some time. The bat had been sent to a laboratory for analysis, but the report came back negative. There were no traces of blood, no hairs, no fibers—nothing that could link it to the commission of any crime.

Only Neal Henderson could do that. And now he was saying, yes, this was definitely the bat that James Upchurch had brought with him. Those faint and faded traces of Magic Marker were proof enough, even though, he admitted, "there's no tape, and it's a lot darker and it has dirt on it."

He then identified the remnants of clothing found at the fire scene as being similar to what he recalled Upchurch wearing that night.

But that was it. There was no physical evidence that linked either Upchurch or Henderson to the murder scene. There was only Henderson's uncorroborated story, and an old baseball bat that had been lying in a near-swamp for maybe a year. Even the knapsack found in the back hall could not be identified positively as belonging to Upchurch. Henderson said, "He's always had a bag like that. Typically, he put his schoolbooks in it, or Dungeons and Dragons books." But again, there was only Henderson's unsupported word.

Henderson said that after Upchurch had prepared himself for the escapade—donning a disguise that could have been taken directly from a Dungeon Master's manual—"We drove down to a wooded lot behind the house. When I slowed down the car, he jumped out. I never came to a full stop. He disappeared into the lot. I went back down to the other road and parked back where I had parked before."

The road behind the Von Stein house, one block past Lawson, was Marsh Road. It was here, Henderson said, that Upchurch got out of the car. He would have been less than fifty yards from the Von Steins' back door.

The "other road" to which Henderson referred, a dirt road with big bumps and potholes that came to a dead end after only a few hundred feet, was American Legion Road. From the dead end, where Henderson said he parked, the distance to the Von Stein house was about half a mile, across a large, empty field, through woods, across a small street called Northwoods Road, across a backyard or two to Marsh Road, and then through the wooded area that bordered the Von Steins' backyard.

"How long did you stay there?" Norton asked.

"I am not sure. It seemed like forever, but probably, maybe, half an hour. I just couldn't tell. I was supposed to wait until he came back, but I did not."

"Why didn't you, Neal?"

Bonnie felt her stomach tighten as she watched Mitchell Norton, who'd been so emotionally abusive to her, acting positively *fatherly* toward Henderson.

"Up until then," Henderson said, "it didn't seem like anything bad was going to happen, and I wasn't too worried about it. But while I was sitting there, I kept thinking something is going to go wrong, or something is going to go right. Either way, it wouldn't be very good. I was scared to death."

"What did you do?"

"I decided not to wait for him any longer. I pulled out and went looking for him. I couldn't take sitting there by myself anymore. I didn't know what was going on. I had to find out something. So I went down past the Smallwood subdivision, hoping to see some sign of him or something. I kept going past it. Then I turned around and came back. I still didn't see any sign of him."

What he did spot, he said, was a *different* dirt road—not the one where he'd agreed to wait; not where he'd already been with Upchurch; not where Upchurch, fleeing the scene of a murder, would be expecting to find him.

This new road, this little track he saw leading off into high corn, was called the Airport Road and led to a small landing strip. Though a tenth of a mile closer to Lawson than was American Legion Road, it was *on the other side* of the four-lane Market Street Extension, the main road leading past the entrance to the Smallwood subdivision.

Henderson said he'd driven perhaps "a couple hundred yards" down this Airport Road—*a road that, presumably, James Upchurch didn't even know existed*—and turned off the engine and waited.

This didn't make sense. It had never made sense. It never would. Why would the driver of a getaway car move it almost half a mile away from where the killer, fleeing on foot, expected to find it? What was this, a game of hide-

and-seek? Henderson's new location, on the Airport Road, was far from the route he said he'd expected Upchurch to take back to the car.

But this had been his story from the start, and Mitchell Norton was stuck with it, just as he was now stuck with Page Hudson's testimony about the rice in Lieth's stomach.

"Why did you go to the Airport Road," he asked, "instead of returning to the Legion Road?"

"I wanted to be able to see him if he was going towards the Legion Road. I also figured he probably saw me. I figured that he saw me as I was driving back and forth on the main road. And if he did see me, he would see where I turned into."

To Bonnie, this was the least plausible testimony she'd yet heard. The driver of a getaway car used in a murder decides all on his own to switch locations, *assuming* that the killer would be able to figure out where to find him in the dead of night, fleeing the scene of what might well be a multiple homicide, in a neighborhood that neither one of them had ever seen before?

Asked how long he sat there, Henderson said, "It wasn't too long. Ten minutes, maybe more, maybe less. I just wasn't sure."

"And what were you thinking?"

"Well, I was hoping we wouldn't get caught. But I was hoping that he wouldn't do anything to get caught for. I didn't know what to think. It seemed like whichever way I was thinking, it wouldn't turn out right."

"And while you were sitting there thinking, did you see James Upchurch?"

"Yes. First, I heard him running towards the car. I heard *someone* running and I immediately looked around to see if it was him. And I saw him coming up the road from the main road.

"He got to the car, and he opened the door. He jumped in and said, 'I did it! I can't believe I did it! I never want to see that much blood again the rest of my life. Let's get out of here!' "

This, too, seemed somewhat improbable. Why would Upchurch's first words not have been, "What the hell are you doing *here,* when you were supposed to be parked at the end of the Legion Road?''

And since the whole assault had been carried out in near-darkness, how could he have even seen the blood?

Henderson described driving off at high speed, looking for the road back to Raleigh, but missing what he thought to be the proper turn, and instead turning down a dark road he'd never seen before.

"Once we got off that main road, James told me to find a dark place, to pull over so he could change clothes. He said he had blood on him. And somewhere along that road, there was a farmer's path off to the right or the left. I just don't remember. I pulled over. There were no lights around, no houses. He walked up ahead of the car, about twenty, thirty feet where some bushes were. And he changed clothes and threw his old clothes in the trunk. He threw everything he had in the trunk."

"What did he say, if anything, about what had happened inside the house?"

"He told me someone made a loud noise while he was in there. And he thought the whole neighborhood would wake up because of it."

Instead, however, not even Angela, twenty feet away, had woken up.

"When he got back to the car," Norton asked, "do you recall anything that he brought back with him?"

"He had what he was wearing and he had the knife."

"Do you recall the bat?"

"No, sir."

The bat continued to pose a problem for Mitchell Norton. But he decided to tackle Henderson's inconsistent statements about it head-on. Why, he asked, had Neal said two contradictory things about the bat?

"At that point," Henderson said, "I was just trying to give them ideas of where to look. I told them I wasn't sure. James might have had the bat. He might not have. I just couldn't remember."

Henderson said he and Upchurch had eventually spotted

a road sign that said, "To 264," which was the road that would take them back to Raleigh.

"I was still very scared," Henderson said. "I didn't hear any police sirens, so I figured they weren't coming after us right away. But someone had still been killed."

Had they talked? Norton asked.

"I don't think either of us was in any mood for talking. I was thinking what I was thinking. And he wasn't saying anything. Once we got out of Beaufort County, though, James told me to find another place and turn off."

"How did you know you had gotten out of Beaufort County?"

"There was a sign saying, 'Entering Pitt County,' I believe. And then at every intersection we came to, I would slow down and we would look to both sides, looking for a place that was dark, that didn't have any houses in it. Eventually, we came to one. It was very empty. We could see a house off in the distance, but nothing close to the road. I drove forward until we were in a dark area, right at the beginning of a curve. I stopped the car, and I got out and went to the bushes to use the bathroom. James asked for the keys to open the trunk up. I came over and opened the trunk for him. He took out the knife. He took out the sweater, the jeans, some shoes, and a can of gasoline. He threw the stuff on the ground and poured the gasoline on top of it. He lit it somehow. I don't know if he had a lighter or a match. I wasn't paying close attention to him. My back was to him, but I heard a whoosh of the gasoline igniting. He went to the front of the car and took out the map, and he threw the map on top of the fire."

Then they got back in the car and headed home. But they were only as far as Greenville when they decided to stop for gas.

"It was a place that also had a drive-through car wash, and when I got out to go pay for the gas and get something to eat, I noticed the car was very dirty. It had mud all over it. And James came into the place, and I said, 'Let's get the car washed.'

"Neither one of us said much, if anything, after that. I kept thinking about what James had said when he got back in the car. I didn't know what to do, so I just listened to whatever James said to do and drove the car back to Raleigh. I glanced behind me and listened for any police sirens, but I didn't hear anything. And the closer we got to Raleigh, the more it seemed like everything was behind us. Maybe I could just put the car away and forget it ever happened.''

Henderson said the sun was already coming up by the time they reached Raleigh. Again, from their point of view, not an advantageous situation. A college campus on a Monday morning, with summer session still in full swing, was a busy place. A lot of people up, taking showers, getting ready for class. A lot of people who might have noticed a white Mustang pulling into a campus parking lot.

"James told me he was going straight to his room and for me to go up to Chris's suite and put the keys in the bathroom closet. I did, and then went back to my apartment. I couldn't get in the front door because it had been locked, so I knocked on the window and Kenyatta let me in. I came inside, I lay down, and I told her I had spent the night in the steam tunnels.''

"Why was it that you told her you'd been in the steam tunnels?''

"Well, I didn't want her to know where I had been all night. And to spend the night in the steam tunnels seemed like a plausible excuse.

Maybe not everywhere, but apparently at NC State.

"Kenyatta left to go shopping, and I lay there for a while, and eventually I got to sleep. Later that afternoon, when Kenyatta was at the apartment, James came in. And he told us that he'd heard that Chris's parents had been assaulted the night before. He said Chris's father had been killed and his mother was in the hospital in serious condition. And he suggested that I stop by his room later to talk about D and D.''

"Dungeons and Dragons?''

"Yes, sir. And I went over to his room and I asked him if he had heard anything else. He said, 'Don't worry. As far as I know, the police don't suspect anything.' He said he thought he'd made it look like a burglary. I asked him to keep me posted if anything happened, or if he found out anything. Then I went back home and went to work."

Henderson said he'd never again spoken to Chris Pritchard. And as time passed, he saw less of James Upchurch. But also, as time passed, he said he began to feel troubled.

"It wasn't so bad when I was busy, when I was working or doing something. But whenever I had quiet time by myself, I could remember what he had said that night and what I had done. And I couldn't tell anybody about it. I couldn't talk to anybody about it. And that went on for months."

Then, toward the end of April, he ran into Upchurch on the street, and Upchurch said he needed a place to live for a couple of weeks. So Upchurch moved in with him. And then one day John Taylor and John Crone came looking for Upchurch. That was bothersome, but what was worse—much worse—was that day in early June when Taylor had returned, carrying Upchurch's green knapsack.

"He admitted to me," Henderson said, "that he had forgotten the bag. Then he said he would be leaving very soon. He said the police were closing in and he was heading out of town. He told me that I didn't have anything to worry about. His exact words were, 'Look, you just drove the car. If worst comes to worst and Chris confesses, it's your word against his, and no one's going to believe Chris over you, so don't worry about it. But I am getting out of town.' "

"Did Bonnie Von Stein have any participation in the planning or the murder of her husband, Lieth Von Stein?" Norton asked.

"No, sir."

"Did Angela Pritchard have any participation in the planning or the murder of Lieth Von Stein?"

"No, sir. It was just James Upchurch, Christopher Pritchard, and myself."

And that was his story, however rich in improbability and inconsistency it may have been, and however much it contradicted so many aspects of the story Chris had told.

He'd returned the keys to a bathroom closet? Chris had

said on innumerable occasions that they'd been found beneath the cushion of a chair.

They'd not left campus until midnight and had not returned until after the sun was already up? Chris had said he'd wanted the murders done by two A.M., when both Lieth and Bonnie would be most deeply asleep. He'd also wanted his distinctive white Mustang safely back on campus before dawn.

They'd stopped for gas—*and to wash the car*—in Greenville? Chris had said earlier that he'd not only filled the tank on Sunday night, just before giving Upchurch his keys, but had told Moog that although the gas gauge was broken, it was possible to make it down and back without having to refuel. Just in case, however, he'd given Moog twenty dollars for gas. Presumably a driver with Henderson's IQ and gaming ability would have thought to stop for gasoline, if he thought any might be needed, *before* a crime was committed, not after.

Beyond these details, there was the extraordinary discrepancy regarding the duration of Henderson's involvement. Had it spanned weeks, or only the final twenty-four hours?

Given this embarrassment of riches from which to choose on cross-examination, Frank Johnston, in a manner that Bonnie described in her notes as "offensive and harsh," probed hardest at Henderson's story about moving the car.

"You say you drove down that road a couple of hundred yards?"

"No more than that."

"And you parked there?"

"Yes, sir."

"Did you have your lights on or off?"

"They were off, sir."

"Isn't it true that there is a cornfield located immediately to the south of where you were parked, between Airport Road and the Smallwood subdivision?"

"I think so, yes."

"And isn't it true that corn was growing there at the time?"

"I think so."

376

"And you say you pulled down this road hoping to *see* James, or that *he* would see *you?*"

"I pulled down the road hoping to see James. I was hoping James would see me when I drove back and forth."

"Well, you only drove back and forth once."

"If he was on the road, that would have been enough." Henderson seemed a little less forlorn and pathetic now; a little more surly.

"And you are telling us that you expected him to walk down this highway, with all his goodies, about a quarter of a mile back to the Airport Road, rather than walking through a field that would provide camouflage for him?"

"I expected to park the car where I was told to park the car and wait where I was told."

"But you didn't do that?"

"No. I got scared and I left."

In Bonnie's mind, that still did not answer the question of how Upchurch, fleeing her house after a murder—and by a longer and more exposed route than he needed to take—had managed to see a car parked in an unexpected location, maybe two hundred yards down a road that was little more than a driveway through a field of corn that in North Carolina, in late July, was already almost six feet high. And even if he had seen it, why would he have assumed it was Chris Pritchard's car, with Neal Henderson behind the wheel, instead of, for example, the police?

She was also bothered by two of his other answers. Henderson admitted that when he'd first spoken to Lewis Young, he'd described Chris's car as black. Not only was it white, but he'd even paused on his way home to get it washed. So how could he have thought it was black?

And in his original statement to John Taylor and John Crone, as he described the trip back to Raleigh, he'd said he and Upchurch had not talked much—instead, they had listened to the radio. But weeks earlier, the radio had been stolen from Chris's car.

As he neared the end of his cross-examination, Frank Johnston seemed to become more openly sarcastic with each question.

"Isn't it true, Mr. Henderson, that you were termed by many as a 'genius'?"

"Some might say that," Henderson answered. "Some might not. It depends who you ask."

"And isn't it true that you had, from the time this incident occurred, eleven months before you ever came forward and made any statement to any officers?"

"Eleven months sounds about right."

"And isn't it true that there have been an additional six or seven months since you first came forward?"

"Yes, sir."

"And during all this period, you have certainly had ample opportunity to think about your situation and what would be in your best interest, have you not?"

"Yes, sir."

"In recognition of your plea, is it not true that the State reduced charges against you and has agreed not to prosecute other charges?"

"That was the plea bargain, yes, sir."

"And isn't it true that by your plea, you are not facing the death penalty?"

"Yes, sir."

"And isn't it true that it was explained to you that the sentence you would receive would be based upon His Honor's discretion?"

"Yes, sir."

"And depending on how you did in court and what you said, that might have a significant impact on what type of sentence you might receive, isn't that true?"

"I was told it would be entirely up to Judge Watts."

"Weren't you told, Mr. Henderson, that if you got on that stand and verified the facts that the State wanted you to verify, that it may help you in your sentencing?"

"No, sir. I was told to give truthful testimony. And that's all I am doing."

Now it was Johnston's turn to carry forward the appalling crime-scene photograph of Lieth Von Stein.

"I ask you to look at this again. Isn't it true that the last time you saw Mr. Von Stein you saw him in that condition, or *put* him in that condition on July twenty-fifth, 1988?"

"No, sir. That is not true. I did not do that and I could not do that."

"And isn't it true that on none of these occasions you've testified to, James Upchurch was even with you?"

"No, sir. That is not true. He was with me and he did do what I said he did."

36

Bonnie went home for the weekend. She met with Billy Royal on Saturday. "This time," she said, "*he* talked to *me*."

Now that he was free to speak openly to her, Dr. Royal wanted to try to explain how her son had turned out the way he did, and what might have driven him to the desperate point he'd reached by July 1988.

Bonnie wanted to know, yet she didn't. She needed to know, but not too much. The defenses that had enabled her to survive not only the previous eighteen months, but the grim years that had followed Steve Pritchard's departure, were not about to crumble all at once.

Besides, she still did not have the rapport with Dr. Royal that she enjoyed with Jean Spaulding. Indeed, Bonnie's notes of the meeting suggest a certain defensiveness. "Once, during our conversation," she wrote, "I called Chris 'Christopher.' Dr. Royal seemed to want to make a big deal out of that. There is no hidden reason for this. Usually, when saying the possessive form, it is easier to say 'Christopher's' than 'Chris's.' "

She also wrote, "I asked Dr. Royal what his assessment of Chris is. He beat around the bush with a lot of 'ahems' and double-talk. I asked him to tell me what he would say if asked a direct question about the reasons for Christopher's involvement & his seeming detachment. He went through another long, meaningless dialogue about how each of us possesses the ability to do most anything under given circumstances.

"Finally, he reached the core of the question. He feels Chris was deeply affected by his abandonment by his father at a very young and impressionable age. Since that time, he has had a fear of losing me. He has constantly sought assurance from me and has always feared rejection.

"Lieth came into his life and filled the father-figure void. He and Lieth did have a few problems, but certainly not more & maybe less than most fathers & sons. Chris has always felt like he needed a lot of friends.

"Dr. Royal also said Chris has had several fantasies concerning becoming a great writer, providing a home for me & Angela (having us dependent on him). Another fantasy is that he is married and we all live together in a giant home. Me, Lieth, Chris, his wife, Angela. His need for family seems to be overpowering at times. Almost to the point of desperation.

"In 1987, when Lieth's father died and we began spending so much time in W-S on the weekends, Chris felt a loss. The loss of Lieth's mother only made Chris feel more insecure. He saw Lieth's parents leave him. He also knew there was what seemed to be a large amount of money involved. His move to NC State was a further separation from the family. Being removed from the close relationship & dependence on me, he began to feel not so good about himself. His grades were slipping.

"Chris became more involved in the game D&D. This allowed him to remove himself from his real feelings and situations. He could set himself aside and become the character he was playing. Then came the increased use of alcohol, then the drugs. This combination became a deadly force: Chris's loss of confidence & self-esteem, D&D, alcohol & drugs.

"Chris also idolized 'Moog' to a degree. He often talked about how smart he was & how he could keep all the characters in his head. 'Moog' was the Dungeon Master. Dr.

Royal feels when Chris mentioned patricide to 'Moog' that 'Moog' jumped on the idea & didn't lose sight of it. Although there were several occasions when the plans were talked about, they were never in a 'real life' aspect or setting. Chris was detached, like it was 'all a big game.'

"Another observation Dr. Royal had was that he felt Chris was trying to prove by killing his entire family that he could show he was not dependent on anyone. He could survive without any of us."

Absent from the notes was any expression of feeling about what Chris had done. This was her son. He'd tried to have her murdered and had taken from her forever the man she'd loved. Yet she herself could survive only by reducing Dr. Royal's insights to a form of data she could process.

Billy Royal later made several other observations. Among these were that Bonnie's anger at Steve Pritchard for leaving her had communicated itself to both Chris and Angela; that the need for Bonnie to work such long hours, and sometimes to be gone for as much as a week at a time for training programs, made Chris extraordinarily insecure. Night after night, he and Angela would be the last two children to be picked up at the Salem Baptist day-care center. Chris, in particular, developed a chronic fear that his mother was never coming back.

Billy Royal also said, regarding Dungeons & Dragons, that the game put Chris in a place where he was in control, instead of dependent, and in a universe where he could "do" things that deviated dramatically from the value system he'd been brought up to believe in.

"He decided to take his fate into his own hands," Dr. Royal said, "and just get rid of everybody he was close to before they had a chance to abandon him."

But on that Saturday in January, as Bonnie's meeting was drawing to a close, Chris arrived for his regular appointment. This would be one of his final sessions with Billy Royal. In little more than a week, he would be sentenced and locked up for many years in a place where neither Billy

Royal nor anyone like him would be able to help Chris get better.

Chris walked in, Bonnie looked at him, then suddenly started to cry. Almost immediately, so did Chris.

It was as if she could now see him, maybe for the first time, as the hurt, frightened, and angry little boy he'd always been.

37

James Upchurch's lawyers chose not to have him testify in his defense.

This may have been simply because they feared the jury would neither like him nor believe him. Though he'd gotten his hair cut and wore neat and subdued clothing each day, Moog, even on trial for his life, could not rid himself of the smirk that had attracted the attention of every investigator who'd ever spoken to him.

Lewis Young called it "a weird smile" and saw it accompanied by "that crazy stare." Frank Johnston termed it more euphemistically "a facial mannerism that was not positive for his position." In either case, a silently smirking murder defendant was bad enough. One who seemed to be grinning at the jury while denying his guilt from the stand would be worse.

Wayland Sermons later said there was another reason for the decision not to have Moog testify. "We felt that even though he would have had some good points, they would have been overshadowed by the open-door rule on cross-examination in North Carolina. That rule says that if a defendant, or any witness, takes the stand and swears to tell the truth, the prosecutor can ask *any* question—it doesn't have to have been raised on direct examination—

relevant to either the facts of the case or the credibility of the witness.

"The State took three weeks to put on its case. Three weeks' worth of information that the DA laboriously put in front of the jury. And we felt he would laboriously spend three more weeks asking the defendant, 'Isn't it true that this happened?' And we felt the damage from that—from hearing that again, with the defendant sitting up there saying, 'No, that is not true, I did not do this'—we felt like there wasn't any advantage to that.

"In the eyes of the jury, whether he says yes, no, or 'I was in Hawaii,' it just reiterates those points."

The risk, of course—as would have been the case with Chris—was that no matter how often a jury was instructed that a defendant's decision not to testify should not count against him, it almost always did. Presumption of innocence was a splendid concept in the abstract, but what was found far more frequently in the real world of the courtroom was a presumption of guilt. After hearing two former friends spend days describing how he had plotted and carried out a murder, why wouldn't James Upchurch—or any innocent defendant—have *demanded* the right to personally tell the jurors it was not true?

In any event, with Upchurch having chosen to stay silent, closing arguments were made on Monday, January 22. In the absence of any direct denial of guilt from the defendant, it was up to his two public defenders to argue that the case against him had not been proved beyond a reasonable doubt.

Frank Johnston spoke first. He had not written out his presentation in advance, nor even outlined it. He never did. His approach was to "think through" the weak areas in the State's case and focus on them. Here, he felt, he had an abundance from which to choose.

"I don't think this case falls into the realm of good, old, everyday common sense," he said. "I think it's in the realm of the supernatural. I think it's in the realm of imagination, science fiction, the movies. This is not a case where you simply go out and say, well, it must have happened because Neal Henderson and Chris Pritchard said it did."

Then he began to chip away, piece by piece, at the evidence the State had presented. The inconsistencies, the unanswered questions, the elements that defied rational explanation.

He began with Angela, suggesting, without saying so outright, that perhaps she should have been a defendant, too. "Angela's bedroom," he said, "was ten to twelve feet from Mr. and Mrs. Von Stein's bedroom."

He reminded the jury that the doors of both Angela's bedroom and the master bedroom were "hollow-core doors—not as good a sound protector as a solid door would be." And that Bonnie had awakened to screams. Yet somehow Angela had managed not to hear the screams. Somehow, she'd managed to sleep through it all.

"And what did the officer say who spoke to her?" he asked. " 'Angela showed no emotion, nor any interest in the situation.' "

Bonnie, when awakened by the screams, saw someone standing above her. "And how did she identify this person? Very broad-shouldered; no neck. Very broad-shouldered; no neck. Now, this is interesting. Remember how she describes this. She says there was light filtering through the door. She had testified there were no lights on in the bedroom. It was completely dark. So this intruder had evidently turned a light on somewhere. She is telling us now that there is a light on somewhere in the hall—or is it coming from Angela's bedroom?"

Whatever its source, Johnston emphasized, "even though she may not be able to see his face, that light would silhouette his form. And it did. And that is why she is able to give that kind of description. Broad-shouldered, and no neck. But not just broad-shouldered. *Very* broad-shouldered. It made a distinct impression on her. And the specific question was asked of her, 'Mrs. Von Stein, does the defendant look like, or does his size appear to you to be the same as, the person you saw in the room on that morning?' 'No, it does not.'

"The State tries to say, oh, well, now, if you were in a completely dark room with the lights out, with somebody standing up holding a bat, could you tell who that person was? Well, no. But if that's the case, why does she see Neal Henderson and James Upchurch in the courtroom in Washington, North Carolina, under the same circumstances, at approximately the same time, and it's the figure, the physical appearance of *Neal Henderson*, that bothers her so badly that she gets scared and has to leave the courtroom and go to an attorney's office across the street.

"The State would contend to you that doesn't make any difference. But Neal Henderson fits the picture. You've seen a picture of Neal Henderson. You've recognized and identified him. Seen him on the stand. You can see that there's a marked difference in his physical stature and that of James Upchurch. But the State would contend to you that, well, you ought not to pay any attention to that. That's not important.

"Well, you are trying this man for some awfully serious crimes. And it is important. And it needs to be considered, seriously considered, by each one of you when you get in that jury room."

Next, he spoke about the bat. "Who is the only person," he asked, "who has indicated that this bat was in the Von Stein residence? Neal Henderson. What does Bonnie Von Stein say? She said she heard a whooshing sound, even after someone left the room and shut the door. Now, you swing that bat as hard as you want to, you are not going to hear a whooshing sound. 'Oh, but we found a bat in the woods eleven months later.' The scientists, the SBI, the FBI, nobody can say anything about that bat except it's a bat and it was found in the woods—except Neal Henderson.

"Who knows what his thought processes were, his defense tactics? There's no way to tell that. But I think it's awfully strange that a bat was found in the woods near Smallwood that can only be identified by Neal Henderson. A bat that was not identified by Bonnie Von Stein. A bat that could have been put there anytime after July twenty-fifth. No blood on it, no fibers, nothing to connect it with this case except for old Neal saying, 'Yes, I saw James take it out of his closet two or three days before this happened. I saw him draw something on it.'

"But isn't it conceivable, doesn't it make sense, that that bat could have been planted there, or could just have been there, period?"

Then he voiced doubt about Bonnie. "You've got to weigh Bonnie Von Stein's testimony in the totality of this situation. What's happening here? What's going on? Have you seen any good Alfred Hitchcock programs lately? Her husband goes to bed. She watches TV. Ted Bundy story. Any of you familiar with that? Remember what it was like? Took her rooster in to watch it with her. Daughter came home. Went upstairs to get ready for bed."

But what happened next? Johnston asked. "She says, well, I was unconscious for part of the time. When did it happen? Did Lieth get assaulted and killed sometime earlier in the evening, and then Bonnie get assaulted three, four, five hours later?

"What do we know? We know she called the police at four twenty-seven A.M. We know that the gentleman saw the fire about ten miles away in Pitt County at about quarter to five. Those times certainly check out. But what do we know about old Lieth?

"The blood had jelled. Blood had jelled. He's lying across the bed. Are we going to believe that she was passed out for hours and that the attacker waited around for her to regain consciousness before he attacked her again? Is that what the State wants us to believe?

"It's like a game of Clue is what the State wants you to believe. Have you ever played Clue? You draw little cards. It says the knife is in the kitchen, so you move your man over to the kitchen. Try to figure out who did something. The State wants you to draw all these cards, and the ones you can't fit in the puzzle, just throw them away and don't worry about it.

"And where is Angela all this time? Safely tucked away in her bed, sleeping through all the screams, through all the noise, through all the batterings. What did Bonnie say she told Detective Taylor? 'Yes, I could have told him that Lieth screamed as many as fifteen times. I heard piercing screams, and I screamed.' The insulation was so poor that she had to keep her door shut to keep from hearing her daughter's radio.

"They rush her off to the hospital. And obviously, she is injured. Got some cuts and bruises on her forehead where she says she was struck. Had a collapsed lung from a knife wound." He paused there, apparently hoping that the jury would, on its own, contrast the relative insignificance of these injuries to the massive and murderous wounds inflicted on Lieth.

"Then Detective Taylor and the rest of Washington's finest come in and do the crime scene," he said. "And what do they find? Nothing. Nothing. And what does the SBI find? Nothing. What does the FBI find? Nothing. There is not one thread of physical evidence that ties anything that happened in this case to the defendant, James Upchurch. Not one.

"The State has introduced approximately one hundred and seventeen exhibits, and there is nothing in any of them that ties the defendant to being in that house, or to being with Neal Henderson on that evening, or to having anything to do with this. There's only the statements of Neal Henderson and Chris Pritchard."

Neither of those two, he argued, was worthy of belief. "Why aren't they telling you the truth?" he asked. "Who are they protecting?" It was not a question he attempted to answer directly, hoping instead that the jurors might come up with a few tentative answers of their own—enough, at least, to have reasonable doubt about the guilt of James Upchurch.

Johnston said it was awfully important to keep in mind that Neal Henderson was a genius. "I don't know about y'all, but most of us don't run into contact with geniuses every day. And I don't know how to weigh and to approach a genius mind. I fall much inferior to that. We've got a person here who has immense capabilities, not only of developing and focusing and directing and imagining, but we don't even know what we are dealing with. We do not know the ramifications. Perhaps some of you are geniuses and you understand, but I don't think good common sense can even help us to understand the magnitude and thought processes that geniuses have.''

But he wasn't just a genius, he was an unfeeling, mechanical man. "Look at Neal Henderson's demeanor on the stand," Johnston said. "Have you ever seen anybody testify that looked more like a robot? . . . 'James told me to do it. James told me to stick my hand in the fire, so I did it. I do everything James tells me to do. I don't make any independent decisions of my own. Look, I wouldn't even have got involved in this if I didn't need some friends.'

"He played Dungeons and Dragons with two groups of people, lived with his girlfriend, but he needed friends? Does that sound to you like somebody that's a recluse, that doesn't have friends?"

And he wasn't just a genius and a robot, he was a liar. Take, for instance, his mention of the radio. They hadn't talked on the way back to Raleigh, they'd just listened to the radio. *Except there hadn't been a radio in the car.*

"If you're going to tell the truth," Johnston said, "you tell the truth fifteen times, you tell it the same way. But if you're going to tell a lie, you get mixed up. You get confused. You tell it different ways. 'Well, I think the car was black.' If he can remember every road he came out of Raleigh on, if he can remember every little detail on that map, you mean to tell me he can't even remember what color the car is?"

Of all Henderson's lies, he said, the most preposterous was the account of moving the car from the American Legion Road to the Airport Road while Upchurch was presumably inside the Von Stein house, committing murder.

"He wants you to believe that after this defendant killed Mr. Von Stein, he strolls on out to Market Street with the big streetlights out there, with blood all over him, and goes on down the road.

"Now, is somebody going to go on a straight line back through some woods where they are going to be protected, where they won't be seen—go in a straight line back to the car—or come out on the highway, walk down the road that's well lit, one of the major roads in Washington? And from what Neal tells you, this defendant didn't even know the car was there! He didn't know Neal had moved his location. Does that make sense to you?"

Then Johnston closed with a summary of what he considered to be the most glaring inconsistency.

"Dr. Page Hudson," he said. "As good an expert, as informed, educated, experienced, an expert as you could have in any case. Highly renowned, tremendous background and experience, dedicated, responsible.

"With Dr. Hudson, we come to a situation that is totally and irrevocably unexplainable. With Dr. Hudson, ladies and gentlemen, the bottom falls out of this case.

"Because what does he tell you about the medical evidence? 'It's undisputed that Von Stein ate supper eight-thirty, or seven-thirty at Sweet Caroline's. Had a chicken and rice dinner. I would expect a dinner of chicken and rice to be completely digested and out of the stomach within one to two hours after consumption. If he finished supper at eight o'clock and the death occurred at between three and four, we are talking about seven hours. At best, we are talking seven hours. Highly unlikely. Very unusual.'

"Now, the State is saying, wait a minute, can't his bodily processes be slowed down or stopped because of all this emotional trauma that he's experiencing? 'Yes, that could happen,' Dr. Hudson says, 'but it's an absolutely unusual scientific thing to happen, for somebody's bodily processes to stop functioning because of stress. It just is not likely. And not because of a financial situation, or a family-death situation from some time back.'

"And I say to you again," Johnston went on, "where is all this stress, other than Bonnie saying the parents died and that he was upset about it. Which was a year before this, for his parents—a year or more—and four or five or six months for his uncle. But he wasn't so stressed out that he couldn't get on his computer and figure out how to invest his stocks and his bonds and how to improve his station in life.

"Which is okay. I am not criticizing him. But there's no medical evidence that he'd been to see doctors, that he was having digestive problems, that he was having a nervous condition. Nothing.

"There's a big hole in this case. Common sense? This doesn't make *any* sense. What's the answer? I don't know. But I think it tells us something about this case. We ain't getting the truth. When you get through listening to all this evidence and hearing this case in its entirety, you still are not going to know what's happened. I don't believe *any-body* knows.

"Well," he said in conclusion, *"somebody* knows. But we don't even know who that is. I don't know what the truth is. But I do know that we haven't heard it in this courtroom."

Johnston had spoken for almost two hours. After a short break, Wayland Sermons gave a shorter, lower-keyed pre-sentation. He said, "The State spent almost two weeks establishing that Lieth Von Stein suffered a horrible death. There is no question about that. There's no one here to tell you he did not. There's no one arguing he did not. You've been shown horrible pictures. No doubt Mr. Norton will strut those in front of you again.

"But is that evidence of the defendant's guilt? Absolutely not. Absolutely not. Don't let that tactic shock you into thinking that there must be some evidence of guilt. Because just as horrible as that death was, equally horri-ble is the thought that an innocent man may be found guilty upon the uncorroborated testimony of two confessed mur-derers. There's absolutely *nothing* to link the defendant to the crime which the State says he committed. Absolutely nothing.

"You have the power over this young man's life. There's no question about that. Mr. Norton doesn't decide it. Judge Watts doesn't decide it. We don't decide it. Y'all decide it."

Then, as had Johnston, he suggested that Neal Hender-son had committed the murder, pointing out that one of Lieth's worst head wounds had been sustained on the left side of his face, as it would be if a right-handed person were swinging a club at someone facing him. Henderson, he reminded the jurors, was right-handed. Upchurch was not.

390

He also suggested that Henderson had suffered from a failure of imagination in being unable to describe more dialogue between himself and Upchurch after the crime. "He said they didn't really say anything. They didn't feel like talking. They listened to the radio. Now, I contend to you that he told us that for this reason: he made that journey and came back and that car was utterly silent and he was with his own thoughts." And then there turned out to be no radio.

The couple of remarks Henderson had attributed to Upchurch—"I can't believe I did it. . . . Blood was everywhere"—indicated nothing. By the time Henderson first told his story, "anybody connected with the case" knew there had been a lot of blood.

Next, he focused on the return of Chris's car keys. He had the jury picture the scene: "driving into Raleigh as the sun is up, seven o'clock Monday morning, summer school at North Carolina State." They parked the car in the same place they'd found it seven hours earlier, and then, despite the fact that "Mr. Henderson lives a mile away in an apartment and James Upchurch lives two floors up above Chris Pritchard's room," it is Henderson, not Upchurch, who returns the keys, "because James told him to."

But what was the real reason? It was, Sermons said, "because Henderson realized that he had to say he went up and put the keys up there in case somebody saw him that morning. He had no reason to be up there unless he actually took the keys up there by himself when he returned from Washington by himself."

Then Sermons trained his sights on Chris. "Y'all remember him. I think you can see that Chris Pritchard was ready to say and do about anything to save his life. He admitted that to me on the stand. Chris Pritchard is lying.

"Why did he feel compelled to lie in every instance about forming this conspiracy with Upchurch? I contend that it was because he never formed a conspiracy with Upchurch—he formed a conspiracy with Neal Henderson."

Just look, Sermons told the jury, at the story Henderson told about Kenyatta demanding that he leave their apartment. "How did he know she would kick him out?" Sermons asked. "Was that a regular type thing? I mean, that's just too pat. I would argue that what actually happened was—you remember Chris Pritchard's description of LSD. You see colors. It makes you feel invincible. It gives you incredible energy.

"I contend to you that Mr. Henderson was telling the truth when he said, 'I took LSD,' and that he was telling Kenyatta the truth when he said, 'I took LSD.' And that after taking LSD, he went and did this murder."

Then, Sermons, too, hit hard at the implausibility of Henderson's story about moving the car. He had been parked in what was, from his point of view, a perfectly good location: at the end of a dead-end dirt road that anyone fleeing the Von Stein house could reach by passing through a vacant lot and a wooded area, running only a small risk of being seen.

"But Neal Henderson says he got scared. Didn't know what was going on. Couldn't stand to wait." So he drove back out to the well-lit and well-traveled Market Street Extension, drove past Lawson Road, turned around, came back up the Market Street Extension, and then pulled down a long, narrow pathway called Airport Road that was shielded from view by both woods and high corn. And pulled in there, Sermons emphasized, "in hopes that the defendant would *see* him!"

That Upchurch, "in the dark of night, never having been there," would somehow stumble across Henderson parked a hundred yards or more down the Airport Road?

That instead of fleeing out the backyard and across the vacant lot and through the woods to where Henderson was supposed to be, Moog had ambled out the front, loped down the middle of Lawson Road, hit the well-lit Market Street Extension, decided to toss his bat in the woods right there, and then run along the highway in search of his getaway car, having somehow *intuited* that his Dungeons & Dragons buddy would have chosen, all by himself, to switch locations?

"I think you should question that finding," Sermons said. "You should look at that very carefully."

He then asked the jury of three men and nine women to

consider one final point: "woman's intuition, the feeling of déjà vu."

He said, "You all know what that is, the feeling that you've seen something before or been in a situation before. Mrs. Von Stein testified that the silhouette was bulky, broad-shouldered, and no necked. Look at Neal Henderson. You saw him on the stand. He's bulky, broad-shouldered, and no-necked.

"I contend that the evidence shows that Mrs. Von Stein's woman's intuition was correct that day in court when she became so frightened of Neal Henderson that she had to leave the courtroom and go to her attorney's office. She also told you that on a separate occasion, seeing the defendant Upchurch, she had no such fright. That should weigh heavy in your mind."

He closed by discussing reasonable doubt, defining it as "a sane, a sensible doubt, an honest substantial misgiving," and citing a North Carolina Supreme Court ruling that said a reasonable doubt could exist if jurors "after considering, comparing, and weighing all the evidence . . . are left in such a condition that they can't say they have an abiding faith in the defendant's guilt."

Had the State, he asked, presented evidence that caused the jurors to have an "abiding faith" in the guilt of James Upchurch? *"Abiding,"* he said, "means not only that you will feel the State has proven its case when you are back in the jury room, but that you will abide by that, that it will carry with you, that you will feel good about it . . . into this week, next week, next month, next year.

"If not," he concluded, "then you should return a verdict of not guilty."

After the jurors had left for their lunch, Judge Watts spoke from the bench. "All right," he said. "I am going to say it on the record. Mr. Johnston, I was most impressed by your remarks to the jury. Mr. Sermons, I was most impressed by *your* remarks to the jury. I think both you gentlemen did a fine job in this case, and I think you ought to be commended for it publicly."

38

Mitchell Norton was aware that, quite apart from the quality, or lack thereof, of his evidence, his presentation of it had been less than dynamic. He knew Judge Watts thought he'd moved far too slowly. More importantly, he'd been told by such people as Keith Mason and Lewis Young that the jurors seemed less than enraptured by his style. And so, somewhat unconventionally, he began his closing argument with an apology:

"I didn't come here the last couple of weeks to irritate you. I didn't come here to irritate the judge. We didn't come here to drag this case out. We came here to present the evidence. So if I have said anything, if I have done anything which would irritate you—you don't like the slow manner in which I speak, you don't like my bushy mustache—hold that against me personally, not against Lieth Von Stein. He can't speak for himself. I must speak for him. That's why I am here."

Then Norton tackled the question of reasonable doubt: "Lawyers, when they talk about it, sometimes want to make it such a heavy burden that you feel like you want to put it in a wheelbarrow and push it around." But really, he said, it was just a matter of common sense—"good old, plain old, everyday common sense."

Then he said, "Let me give you an example. This is a hunting area up here, Pasquotank County—deer hunters, duck hunters. Suppose I were to go out in the field during the deer season, and I were to spy this buck deer standing out in the field. And I were to take my rifle and I would take aim and I would fire and the deer would fall over. And I would look at Mr. Sermons and Mr. Johnston and say,

'Oh, look, what a fine buck there I have killed.' And they would shake their heads and say, 'Oh, no, you didn't kill that deer. That deer died of a heart attack.' Well, I suppose that's possible. But is it reasonable? Does it make good common sense?"

Physical evidence, Bonnie thought. You could tell whether you shot the deer or whether the deer died of a heart attack by just walking up and looking to see whether there was a bullet hole in the deer. Just as, in this case, the mysteries might have been solved by physical evidence, if only the Washington police had not so badly bungled their handling of the crime scene.

But now Norton was trying to deal with that: "I told you when we started that there were no fingerprints that will link anybody to it. I told you there were going to be inconsistencies. I told you right from the start. I also told you that in some respects, the evidence in this case was unusual, strange. Mr. Johnston tells you that we don't rely on common sense. That this is a case of the supernatural. He talks about Ted Bundy murders, about roosters, about Alfred Hitchcock.

"But no. The motive in this case is not strange. It's not supernatural. It's not Dungeons and Dragons gone crazy, although Dungeons and Dragons played a part in this case. It's what brought them together. It's what got them thinking about medieval times, with daggers and knives and swords, in the days before guns were invented. That's what got it started.

"But the motive, the reason for this, is age-old. Nothing different about this case. Fast money. Chris Pritchard didn't want to work for it, didn't want to go to school and study. Fast money, fast cars, easy living. When? After you've put in the work and the effort and the time? No— now. Now. The motive in this case is greed. The motive is fast, easy money."

Then Norton spoke about the inconsistencies: "These cases do not come tied in nice little neat packages. They come turned and twisted sometimes by time and faulty memories. People see and hear things differently. They remember things differently. Perhaps some of you, when you were children, remember a little game. It was called Gossip. We might could try it right here just with you right now. You know how it works. You take a series of facts and phrases and you lean over and whisper in your neighbor's ear, and the neighbor whispers to the neighbor and tells her what he heard, and so on, and on and on down the line.

"You will be surprised, when you get back up here to Mr. Foreman, how it's changed. It don't say that you are lying about it, that you're trying to cover up and not tell the truth, but it is the normal, natural, human, everyday experience of life.

"The only way, ladies and gentlemen, the only way that you can get everybody to say exactly the same thing every time is to walk in and give them a script. But we didn't do that in this case. There hasn't been any scripts."

But then he began to speak from what might have been his own script. He had his own version of "Life With Lieth and Bonnie," and the fact that Bonnie had been fighting him about it every step of the way was not going to prevent him from presenting it now, at the close of his case.

"Bonnie Von Stein," he said, "is in a unique position. She is a wife—a widow now—a mother. She is also a victim in this case. She was married to Lieth Von Stein for approximately nine years prior to his death. Chris Pritchard was ten years old when Lieth married her, took in her family, provided for her.

"But you heard Bonnie say there were problems. There were problems about school. There were problems about the trip to South Carolina when the missing person report was filed. And who was he in South Carolina with? James 'Moog' Upchurch. And when he got back, Lieth and Bonnie changed the way in which Chris was allowed to handle money. He would have to account for the money.

"And she relates to you that one time they almost came to blows, and that after that Lieth began letting her discipline the children. Chris had the car stereo stolen. He didn't want to let Lieth know about it. He was going to let Bonnie take care of it, because they didn't want to upset him.

"His parents, his entire family, wiped out from February of 1987. The father died, his mother died, the uncle died, and they were going back and forth to Winston-Salem, getting the estate settled. He had inherited a million dollars. Now, you say, well, give me some of that stress. I would like to try that sometime.

"But think about it. Stress is a change in your life. Bonnie said he was under a great deal of stress. Chris flunking out of school, no grades at all. Caught in a world of pizza and beer and drugs and Dungeons and Dragons, with no responsibility whatsoever. A world centered around 'me' and self-gratification. Instant gratification. House in north Raleigh, all the drugs I want, play Dungeons and Dragons anytime I want.

"Remember what Chris said? 'They had talked to me twice about my grades. I knew that when the third time rolled around, that I won't be going to school, won't get the money. I was going to have to go to work.' But it wasn't weighing heavy on his mind because he had already resolved how to handle it. He was going to kill him. Kill him and get the money. Yes, it's cold. Yes, it's heartless. Yes, it's cruel."

Then, abruptly, Norton shifted his focus to Bonnie. He talked about her wounds, about how serious they had been, about how she still bore the scars. "This is important," he said, "because the defense lawyers insinuate to you that that woman right there"—and here he pointed directly at Bonnie—"had something to do with the murder of her husband, or with concealing it."

This, Norton suggested, was the most outrageous suggestion he'd ever heard.

He *didn't* tell the jurors that Bonnie still "just didn't feel right" to him. That there remained a little part of him that kept on doubting her story. That was an opinion he would not express until well after the trial.

For now, to deal with the problem of Bonnie's testimony that the intruder had been broad-shouldered and no-necked, Norton suggested she *wanted* to believe Henderson had been her attacker because of the deep resentment she bore toward him for his having gotten Chris in so much trouble.

"At the time she saw Henderson she knew he had made a statement and had implicated her son and her son's friend." Thus, he suggested, Bonnie *needed* to believe the worst about him.

Besides, he said again, in the dark, with glasses off, lying on the floor, how much could she really tell? And he referred to Bonnie's own testimony, to the answer she had so much not wanted to give: "Yes, it could have been him."

Besides, Norton said, "why frame James Upchurch? Why say something about James Upchurch that isn't so? Have they presented any evidence, any intimation, any innuendo, as to why they would have selected James Upchurch to frame? Not one mite.

"Chris and Upchurch were friends. They went to the beach together. They went to South Carolina together. They played Dungeons and Dragons together. They went to Wildflour together, to eat pizza.

"Now, Neal Henderson played Dungeons and Dragons with Chris, but there is not one other indication that they had anything at all socially to do with each other."

As he progressed with his argument, Norton seemed more like a defense attorney than a prosecutor: defending, in this instance, his own case. There were so many problems, so many holes—the inconsistencies, the lack of physical evidence, the improbable story about moving the car, Bonnie's impression of her assailant, and not least, the puzzle posed by the chicken and rice.

"What about the food? Dr. Hudson said this was unusual, that he normally would have expected the rice to have been gone from the stomach in about two hours. He said finding the rice was consistent with an earlier death than, say, four o'clock. But he couldn't or didn't give you an exact time of death. Could not say. And there is not one bit of evidence that Lieth Von Stein died prior to the time Neal Henderson and Bonnie Von Stein say, except for the chicken and rice.

"But what else did Dr. Hudson say about that? That under severe emotional stress, digestion may simply stop for hours. Now, Dr. Hudson had never met Lieth Von

Stein. He didn't know anything about his personality or his emotions. All of you know that different things affect different people. Things that affect me may roll off your back. Something that may be minor to you may be devastating to me.

"The doctor said he had done four thousand autopsies and assisted in four thousand more. But how many did he do with a man that had lost his entire family within a thirteen-month period? How many of those four thousand autopsies had just inherited a million dollars? How many of them had the combination that the child was flunking out of school and he'd had to file a missing person report? How many had put in a stock quotation? How many of them, as Bonnie Von Stein said, were under a lot of stress? How many of them had had rice suppers? And how many had been stabbed eight times and bludgeoned in the head with a bat?

"Page Hudson is a very fine physician. One of the top men in his field. But how many autopsies did he perform on Lieth Von Stein? Only one. Only one. And he didn't know anything about his personality or his emotions.

"And look at it from another standpoint, because you've got to face this, too. If, as they contend, the rice had to be gone in two hours, then Lieth Von Stein was dead at eleven o'clock. And if Lieth Von Stein was dead at eleven o'clock, then Bonnie Von Stein had to know about it. She had to be part of it.

"Neal Henderson and Chris Pritchard have admitted their part in this. But after an investigation of over a year and a half, there is not one bit of evidence, not one piece, not one statement anywhere, that it didn't happen just like she said it did.

"And if he was dead at eleven o'clock—think about this—if he was dead at eleven o'clock, what in the world was Neal Henderson doing coming down here from Raleigh for five and a half hours with the body lying in the bed and him sitting around and waiting until four-thirty or so to go out and dispose of the clothes?

"Does that make any sense? And after having five and a half hours to think about it, and destroying everything else, leaves the only piece of evidence that will connect him or anybody else to the crime: and that's the map. The map that went directly back to Chris Pritchard. The map that he has identified as having written. If he had all that time to think about it and plan it, you know that the map would have been taken care of better than it was.

"And if Bonnie Von Stein was in it, if she planned it, does it make any sense that she would involve her own son, subject him to the death penalty, or life imprisonment plus twenty years? Why not go out and hire a hit man? It would be a whole lot cheaper than legal fees with all this going on in court.

"And what about the vanity of women? They would have you believe that she either did it to herself or allowed someone to put permanent scars in her head, leaving her very near death, seven days in the hospital with a collapsed lung.

"And then they throw out another little innuendo. They say, well, Angela slept through it all, safe and snug in her bed. But there is not one bit of evidence either that Angela knew anything about it other than being awakened from her sleep and being told by the officers to go downstairs. You've heard the tape from the mother herself: 'Don't let her come in here and see this.'

"They said, oh, well, she was calm, unemotional. That's one way to describe it. What about shock? What about shock? Wouldn't that apply just as well?"

The contradictions in the stories told by Chris and by Henderson could easily be explained, Norton said. Chris was confused. "And why is it that Chris is confused? Well, for a year and a half he has denied it to his lawyers, to everybody else, even his own mother right up until December of 1989.

"The only thing these boys differ on, basically, is the time in which the conspiracy came about. Chris, after a year and a half, with the drugs he was taking, the denial to his mother, tries to think back. Try to think about if you had to go to your mother or your father and tell them, 'Yes, Mama, for money—for thirty pieces of silver—I planned your death.'

"If you had any conscience at all, think how difficult that would be. And think why it was that even after his arrest— that it was December of 1989 before he ever told his mother. He denied it right up until then.

"He got what he wanted. Half of what he wanted. That was the death of Lieth Von Stein. But once he got what he thought he wanted, he found that he didn't want it at all. When he went up and hugged his mother and kissed her and saw the tears running out of her body, as he says, 'On another level, I was disgusted with what I had done.'

"So, there's denial, and there's the drugs. He was smoking marijuana three times a day; every week he takes cocaine; he's taking acid, some seventeen hits of acid. Chris Pritchard, because of drugs or whatever other problems that he has, just got the times and the places disjointed. It's a wonder he remembers as much about it as he does."

And the lack of physical evidence? Norton tried to put a reverse spin on that, too. "There was no evidence to connect Neal Henderson to it, either," he said. "And yet Neal Henderson, on the ninth day of June, without any promise, threat, or reward, gave a statement which put his own head in a noose. That sure is a funny way to put it off on somebody else, when you are not even a suspect: to confess your own part in a murder."

Besides, he added, there was one piece of physical evidence: the green canvas knapsack that belonged to no one in the Von Stein family. No, it could not be proven beyond a shadow of a doubt that Upchurch had brought that knapsack to the house, but there had been testimony that he'd owned one just like it, testimony that he'd used it to carry around his Dungeons & Dragons books, and further testimony that the day John Taylor showed up in Raleigh with it was the day Upchurch said he was getting out of town.

But then, having derided opposing counsel for suggesting that the case contained "supernatural" elements, Mitchell Norton concluded his argumenr by getting positively mystical.

"What was it," he asked, "that caused Noel Lee to be leaving the hog farm that day? What was it that caused the map to be saved from the fire? Was it luck? Was it fate? Was it some other power that saved that map out of all the things in the fire? The one thing that kept the investigation going, which put them on the trail of Pritchard and Henderson and Upchurch, was the map.

"Now, like I said, I don't know what saved this map. I don't know if it was luck or fate or whatever you want to call it. This map survived fire. And out of all the burns there was on it, the Von Stein house was saved, and the other major portions. Now something did that. Something or somebody wanted this case solved.

"That map kept the case going. I don't know what to say. I don't know what saved it from the fire. Was it luck? Was it fate? Or, was it some other power?

"They want to talk to you about supernatural things? Look at the map closely. Look at the burn marks on the map. Are you looking at the face of death? Or, when you reverse it, are you looking at something more sinister?"

Here Mitchell Norton turned the map upside down and held it to his face like a mask. He looked at the jury through two holes that had been burned through the map.

And as he held the map in that position, pressed close to his face, two diagonal edges jutted above his head, as if they were the horns of Satan.

From studying the jurors' faces, Bonnie could not tell what they thought. But she did believe that were she a juror, she would have had no choice but to find James Upchurch not guilty.

To Bonnie, it all came down to proof. And proof, to her, meant physical evidence. Not the uncorroborated statements of two coconspirators who had made deals in order to save their lives—even if one of them was her son.

In the absence of a single piece of physical evidence that linked James Upchurch to her house, Bonnie felt she would have had no choice but to acquit the man accused of murdering her husband and of trying to kill her.

The jurors began deliberations at nine fifty-five A.M. on Tuesday, January 23. After two and a half hours, they went to lunch. At one-fifty P.M., they resumed deliberations. Shortly after five P.M., Judge Watts sent them home for the night, with no verdict reached.

As Bonnie was leaving the courtroom, she was approached by Wayland Sermons. He had an unusual request. It was, of course, uncertain what the jury's finding would be. But if—if—the verdict turned out to be guilty, then both prosecution and defense would be permitted to offer testimony in a further proceeding relating to punishment. The jury would then engage in a new deliberation about whether or not James Upchurch should be put to death.

The natural thing, the obvious thing, the thing that happened in almost every death-penalty case heard in any court anywhere across the land, was for grieving relatives of victims to want to take the stand and plead, implore, or demand that the jury sentence the convicted murderer to death.

Sermons asked Bonnie if she would do the opposite. Would she, if it came to that, take the stand and ask the jury to spare the life of the man convicted of killing her husband, convicted of trying to kill her?

Without a moment's hesitation, she said yes.

Bonnie believed the death penalty to be wrong. It was wrong in all cases. And if it was wrong in all cases, then no exception could be made here.

Still, she could have replied that while she personally believed the death penalty to be wrong, she could not find it within herself to plead for the life of the man who had so brutally taken the life of her husband, and who had tried to take her own.

But it never occurred to her to say no. If Upchurch was convicted, he should be punished. That would be fair. But no one, under any circumstances, should be put to death by the state.

Bonnie knew a lot of people—Wade Smith among them—who held this belief as strongly as she did.

But who had ever been put in her position? Asked to intercede with a jury on behalf of the man convicted of entering her home in the middle of the night, walking up the stairs and into her bedroom, and beating and stabbing to death the man she loved?

Under such circumstances, many people, regardless of their personal feelings about the death penalty, undoubtedly would have declined such a request.

In this way, however, as in so many others, Bonnie was unlike many people. If she believed in something, if she thought it was the fair, the just, the proper thing, she'd fight for it as hard as she could—whether it was the innocence of her son or the life of a stranger found guilty of having tried to murder her.

It was just after four P.M. on Wednesday, after ten and a half hours of deliberation, that the jury returned its verdict.

James Upchurch was guilty on all counts, including murder in the first degree.

39

Two days later, after a high school teacher had said he was smart, after a court-appointed psychologist had said he did not seem psychotic or prone to violence, and after his weeping mother had said he was a loving and church-going young man, Moog's lawyers approached the bench and said the next witness they wanted to call, in an attempt to persuade the jury not to sentence their client to death, was Bonnie Von Stein.

Judge Watts temporarily excused the jurors from the courtroom. Once again, Bonnie took the stand. It was during this brief appearance that she was most openly emotional.

Tears filled her eyes and her voice was unsteady as she said she did not want Upchurch put to death because "I just simply don't believe that taking another life could make amends for the loss of Lieth."

Mitchell Norton, her adversary once again, quickly established that Bonnie's opposition to the death penalty was total and absolute and was a feeling she'd had for many years.

After hearing legal argument about the admissibility of Bonnie's testimony, Judge Watts made his ruling.

"First of all," he said, "I respect Mrs. Von Stein's opinion and her beliefs. It took considerable courage for her, in this case, to go on the witness stand and say those things." Then he turned to speak directly to Bonnie.

"I commend you for speaking," he said. "For backing up your beliefs with the force of your words. And I certainly appreciate and sympathize with the difficult circumstances in which you have found yourself throughout this entire thing."

Then he turned back to the lawyers and said, "But it strikes me, gentlemen, that to permit this evidence to come in would invite this jury to render its decision upon the basis of passion, upon the basis of emotionalism, upon the basis of bias or prejudice."

Therefore, he said, he would not allow Bonnie to testify. Ample case law supported Judge Watts's ruling: ironically, it arose from instances in which a victim's family wanted to speak in support of, not in opposition to, the sentence of death.

On the morning of Monday, January 29, unaware of Bonnie's feelings, the jury heard arguments for and against sentencing Upchurch to death in the gas chamber.

Mitchell Norton delivered a ninety-minute talk that was interrupted thirty-four times by objections from Frank Johnston. Nine of the objections were sustained.

Norton stressed that the murder was premeditated, committed in the hope of monetary gain, that Upchurch "was not somebody who came from a slum neighborhood, somebody who was mentally defective, somebody who never had a chance in life." Thus, he said, the murder was not the act of a "deprived" person. "Depraved, maybe, but not deprived."

He mocked Upchurch's well-groomed appearance at the trial, urging the jurors not to be misled by it. "Trying to put his best foot forward. He's got his hair cut. Looks like a little choirboy." But this man, Norton said, "sliced through the rib cage like you would cut up a chicken."

And, he said, as he had in his earlier summation, that no one should look upon the murder as being "a case of Dungeons and Dragons out of control." He said, "Dungeons and Dragons didn't cause this. The game helped develop the mind-set of killing dragons and other people in this imaginary fairy-tale land, got them accustomed to thinking of killing, brought them together, but that's the only connection Dungeons and Dragons has with this case, no matter how people want to look at it."

Toward the end, Norton said, "Sometimes lawyers like to tell the story about the old wise man, the oracle up on the mountain, the one who knew the answer to every question. These two men decided they would trick the oracle. They wanted to prove him wrong, so they captured a small bird, put the bird in their hand, and went up to the old man and said, 'Master, I have within my hand a bird. Can you tell me, is the bird dead or alive?'

"You see, they had planned that if the old man said the bird was dead, they would open their hands and the bird would fly away. But if the wise man said the bird was alive, they would then crush the bird to prove him wrong.

"And a lot of times, lawyers like to stand here and say to you that the life of the defendant is in your hands, like the bird. James Upchurch, however, is not like the bird, because the bird in that case was truly innocent. The bird in that case was like Lieth Von Stein, asleep in his own house.

"And James Upchurch is like the two men that went to the oracle. He had premeditated. He had deliberated. And he was the one who had the option to determine whether the bird lived or died. And instead of crushing the bird, he took a baseball bat and crushed Lieth Von Stein's head.

"And he took a knife, like you would cut up a chicken."

"Objection."

"Overruled. Well, sustained."

"And the only way you can be assured that he won't do it again is to impose the sentence of death."

Then, Norton offered some of his own more general philosophy of life. "Part of what's wrong with society today," he said, "is nobody wants to take responsibility. Over the last twenty years or so, our society has become one of excuses, quick fixes on drugs and alcohol, and instant gratification in a me-centered world. Society is pervaded by a lack of responsibility, people who seek to avoid responsibility. But I say to you that you ought to hold him responsible for what he did."

And what had he done? Once more, Norton reminded the jurors of just how awful a crime it was. "Covered in dark clothing, head to foot, he entered the Von Stein residence while Lieth was asleep in his bed. Asleep in his bed, away from the world and tribulations. Safe in his own home, just like you or I, when you leave this courtroom and go home to wherever you live, whether it's an apartment, a mobile home, or a tent—the most important place on the face of this earth, where you ought to be able to feel safe and secure. And to be awakened in the nighttime by the swish of a bat and the slap of it, crushing the skull. And the knife, as it came down through the rib cage."

He granted that "yes, yes, Christopher Pritchard is more morally responsible, guiltier, perhaps, than the others, because he planned the execution not only of his stepfather, but his own mother." However, Norton added, "when Chris Pritchard was in Raleigh, James Upchurch—that man right there—had the bat in his hand, knife in his bag."

And because he was speaking to a jury in Pasquotank County, in fundamentalist-Christian eastern North Carolina, he closed with a quote from the Bible:

"If you look at the Old Testament, and even some parts of the New, you will see that not only is the penalty of death enacted by the state, but in biblical terms, and in our spiritual existence, it's commanded!"

* * *

In response, Wayland Sermons spoke first, and spoke softly. "You have decided the case. I am not here to quarrel with you over that. But is it fair for James Upchurch to die?

"Chris Pritchard said he wanted to buy a house in north Raleigh so he could lay up and play Dungeons and Dragons all he wanted to. They were playing Dungeons and Dragons every day. Doesn't that tell you something? Doesn't it tell you about the blur of reality and fantasy? And I think it should tell you that money wasn't exactly what it was done for—that this game of Dungeons and Dragons led them into the swords, and led them into the clubs, and led them into thinking it was all a fantasy. I would contend that it goes a long way toward explaining how such a horrendous act could be done.

"Neal Henderson said, 'It was just like in the game.' Just like in the game. I contend to you that you can reasonably infer that this powerful fantasy role-playing game goes a long way towards explaining how these three intelligent young men would find themselves in such a sinister affair."

Then he asked the jurors to consider James Upchurch's youth as a mitigating factor. "Mr. Norton would have you believe that at age nineteen you are equipped for everything the world throws at you. I think all of us were nineteen at one time. And probably, while we were not doing drugs and playing Dungeons and Dragons and living in a fantasy world, we certainly had misgivings. We certainly had immaturity.

"You're just out of high school. Where you've been living on a farm. Where you've just gotten through walking the halls and signing the yearbooks, and your lives are all of a sudden changed. You are no longer in the high school cafeteria. You are thrust out into a community the size of Raleigh. North Carolina State University. Twenty-some thousand students. And all of a sudden, rather than being a big fish in a little pond, you're a tiny fish in an ocean. And at nineteen, you are not developed mentally. You are not mature. You are impressionable."

Then Sermons said if anyone *did* deserve the death penalty in this case, it was Chris. "Is it just and appropriate that Chris Pritchard only face life plus twenty, and now Mr. Norton is asking you to return the penalty of death against Mr. Upchurch. Is that fair?

"Chris Pritchard is the most culpable here. He is the Ayatollah. Mr. Upchurch is only the guard over the hostages. Chris Pritchard is the Manuel Noriega. Mr. Upchurch is just the soldier with a rifle in his hand. I contend to you that were it not for Chris Pritchard, we would not be here today. James Upchurch would never have done what you have convicted him of.

"So, is it fair that Chris Pritchard entered into this agreement only five days before trial, when he was the one who started this whole mess, and is not facing the death penalty? Is that fair?"

Frank Johnston spoke last and went right to what Bonnie believed to be the heart of the question. How could this have happened? How could this be?

"You look at these young men," Johnston said, "and you say, *how,* how could this happen? I don't know. Mr. Norton has presented a picture to you that it's a cold, calculated murder. Certainly, it's a bad situation. There's no question about that. We have never contended it was not. But how do you explain it? There has got to be an answer. There has *got* to be an explanation. But I don't know what it is.

"If it's a case of greed, where is all the discussion and the bickering and the fighting afterwards about 'Where is my money? I want at least a portion of it, because I did the act. I want part of the money.' But there's never any mention of money again.

"If you can go into that jury room and say, 'I am convinced beyond a reasonable doubt that this act was committed for pecuniary gain and for no other reason,' then, yes, vote for the death penalty. But I don't believe you can do that in clear conscience.

"What does the culmination of using drugs, using alcohol, playing Dungeons and Dragons, have upon a young person's mental stability? I don't know. But is there any other answer?

"You know, it's strange that Mr. Norton says to you that this is not a case of Dungeons and Dragons going wild. Because he also says it's a case where Dungeons and Dragons teaches people how to kill and use swords and talk about ancient times of swords and sorcerers. So, obviously, even Mr. Norton thinks that Dungeons and Dragons had some effect upon these young men. And I think it did.

"I think it's also strange for us to talk about how that game could affect and influence a young person, since none of us have ever played it. We don't know the full ramifications it may have upon someone. Along with the influence of alcohol and drugs. There's just no other explanation for it."

And then Johnston closed with his own appeal based on religion. "I was thinking yesterday, when I was sitting in church, about the mask Mr. Norton—the map Mr. Norton presented to you in his final argument. He put it up to his face to imply a mask, or some type of a cult symbol, and suggested to you that it was for some supernatural or divine reason that the map was not burnt up in the fire. And that the only way this investigation continued was because they were able to find the map and link Pritchard to it, because of the word *Lawson*.

"And as I thought of that during the minister's sermon yesterday on mercy, I could only think that I hope that God's mercy will be with you in your decision."

As the jury left the courtroom to deliberate whether James Upchurch should live or die, Judge Watts began the sentencing hearings for the two accused who had pleaded guilty.

Henderson's was first. As with Upchurch, witnesses testified in his behalf. The first was the same high school teacher from Caswell County who'd testified for Upchurch. He said Henderson's IQ scores were "the highest of any student we've ever had in the twenty years that I've been there."

He said, "Even in fifth and sixth grade, he so far outstripped his teachers that he basically would be sent to the library every day—the public library down the street, where he would simply read a great deal and play."

On his Scholastic Aptitude Test, taken while a senior in high school, Henderson scored 1500, the highest score ever recorded in Caswell County. "He did not always work as hard as he could have," the teacher said, "but he was certainly the most gifted student I've ever dealt with."

Socially, however, the teacher said, Henderson was looked upon as "an oddity. Socially and emotionally he was always out of place. He often was laughed at." Even outside of school hours, he lived an isolated life. To get to his house, where he lived with his mother and grandmother and sister—the father having left long before and moved out of state—"you had to drive down a tiny little dirt road, through trees, off the highway a good bit."

The teacher also said that Henderson was "intimidated" by physical violence. "I've never known him to get into any kind of physical confrontation, even in play."

Then John Taylor testified that from the moment Henderson had first come forward, he'd cooperated fully with investigators and had been helpful. "He wasn't sure of a lot of things," Taylor said, "but he did the best he could. He cleared things up for us on the course of events."

Judge Watts asked Taylor why he thought Henderson had decided to talk.

"He never come right out and stated he had done this for such and such a reason," Taylor said, "but I got the impression it was a conscience-clearing effort on his part. Because there was no other reason for him to be doing it."

Bonnie, however, could think of an obvious one: to get the best deal for himself, at the expense of the others who'd played the game. You would not have had to score 1500 on your SATs in order to figure out that.

Lewis Young then testified that Henderson had been "totally cooperative" throughout the investigation. "Anything we've asked him to do, he has done."

To Young, Judge Watts said, "I've known you, what, fifteen, twenty years now? I don't mind saying that I have the highest regard for your instincts as an officer and as an investigator. But it struck me in reviewing your notes of your conversations with Mr. Henderson that, in many instances, he was at least vague. Did you get that sense—that there were just some areas he was extremely vague on?"

"Yes, sir," Lewis Young said. "I found him to be very vague in areas concerning certain details that night. One was what happened to the bat. Another was the car. I immediately recognized I was talking to someone of superior intelligence, but I felt like maybe the mundane, the ordinary, the everyday, did not seem to register with him."

"It was not your impression," the judge asked, "that he was at all deceiving, or being intentionally vague?"

"No, sir. I think he was trying to be helpful. I didn't think he was trying to throw us a curve, if you will."

And that seemed to satisfy Judge Watts, who again noted the "tremendous respect" he had for Lewis Young's integrity and ability.

Then the judge revoked Henderson's bond and ordered him taken into custody, pending a decision on sentencing, which would not be made until after the jury had returned with its verdict on Upchurch's punishment.

"If ever he was going to try to flee," the judge said, "this would be the time to do it, because it's all been prologue until now. We are near the final curtain of this drama, tragic tale that it is."

The next day, Tuesday, January 30, as the jury continued its deliberation of Upchurch's fate, Chris's sentencing hearing began. Billy Royal was the first witness called, and it was Bill Osteen, speaking for the first time in the Elizabeth City courtroom, who put the questions to him.

One thing he wanted to get into the record was at least a bare outline of the miasma of doubt and confusion through which lawyer and psychiatrist had groped between mid-August and the end of December.

"Dr. Royal," he asked, "as part of the work you were doing with Chris, did you note a concern on his part as to how his mother was going to accept this situation, or what her reaction would be?"

"That was probably the foremost concern."

412

"Now, at that time, I told you that Chris could not discuss what actually had happened with his mother, didn't I?"

"Yes."

"Were you having some problem dealing with the mother and the son on the basis of that catch-22 situation?"

"Absolutely."

"Describe what kind of dilemma that created for you."

"My initial response," Dr. Royal said, speaking so softly that the judge had to ask him to raise his voice, "was that the suicide and depression could not be resolved without resolution of the issue between him and his mother. A resolution that allowed him to tell her what he had done, which was something he wanted to do. And I thought that should occur during his hospitalization, so that the issue could be dealt with in a therapeutic setting."

"And you even explained to his lawyers that you thought that ought to be done at that time?"

"That's correct."

For Osteen, but even more for Billy Royal, this was the strangest sensation: to have all those desperate, searching, frantic phone calls reduced to this formalistic question-and-answer exchange.

"And what response did you get from his lawyers?"

"His lawyers did not feel that should be done if there was any way to cut around it."

"Did his lawyer explain to you why?"

"Yes," Royal replied.

"Why was that?"

"Because if he had told his mother and it came to trial, she would have to relate that. And as I understood the contract you had with his mother, she had told you to do what you could to protect Chris. And in that sense, as I saw it, you were in a difficult situation about how to do that. But that seemed to be the direction that you had received from her. And in my discussions with her from time to time about her relationship with you, that seemed to be what she was stating."

This exchange would not produce testimony that could lessen Chris's sentence. It almost seemed as if lawyer and doctor were engaging in mutual catharsis. To establish that, however uncertain each may have been about the likely outcome of the chosen course, he was doing what he thought Bonnie wanted done.

Dr. Royal then delivered his professional opinion of Chris in the simplest terms possible: "Chronic anxiety has been a problem since his youth. Just never being able to relax. Always, in a sense, as Satchel Paige aptly put it, looking behind to see if something were gaining on him."

The abandonment by his father, Dr. Royal said, "affected Chris very much in terms of anxieties. In my view, it's been an insult to his psyche that he has never compensated for, because you can't go back and compensate for something like that at that age. So, he has therefore been insecure, anxious, depressed throughout his life, and his psyche has always been engaged in an attempt to deal with that, to deny that, to cover that over."

Chris had also found it impossible to communicate with his mother about his inner turmoil and dread. In the fall, Billy Royal had noted that Bonnie's understanding of Chris was "superficial." He'd written that she was "not reading Chris, what's going on internally."

This condition extended back many years. Chris and his mother had never talked deeply and openly about feelings; they'd never dealt with what was going on inside his mind, with how he really felt about himself. Bonnie had never opened that avenue. How could she, when it did not exist within herself?

The result was that Chris had been locked inside himself, just as Bonnie was cut off from aspects of herself. By example, she had taught her children that emotional turmoil was a weakness best overcome by refusing to recognize its existence. Feelings were messy and threatening: do not express them. Do not acknowledge them. Do not discuss them with others, do not admit their existence to yourself.

Even in this psychological environment, Dr. Royal said, Chris had been able to cope until he'd gone away to school. Then, for the first time, he'd had to face the consequences not only of his lifelong difficulties, but of the more acute phase—the thirteen-month period that covered the deaths of Lieth's parents and uncle.

In this period, Dr. Royal explained, both Lieth and Bonnie had had less contact with Chris, had given less support, had almost—although Billy Royal did not actually use the word—*abandoned* Chris emotionally. As Bonnie had grown increasingly concerned about the stresses that were plaguing her husband, she had inevitably become less aware of whatever anxieties and pressures had been building in the lives of her children.

The NC State environment had not been a healthy one for Chris—nor was it for most other students, in Billy Royal's opinion. "Chris did not do well academically," he said. "He got involved gradually in drugs, alcohol, and Dungeons and Dragons."

Osteen asked more about the game.

"It has, I guess, received notoriety in the last few years," Dr. Royal said. "There has been a great deal in the press about different aspects of it. It most often attracts young people who are bored or need something to do. It's a game that involves skill, daring, a lot of intellectual adventure. But there have been a number of tragedies. Meaning, not infrequently, that some people get hurt or killed through playing the game."

Dr. Royal stressed the impact that the game had had on Chris. "In his case, this and a combination of drugs and alcohol became a kind of modus operandi for him and the group he was involved with. To some degree, this group became a family. This game, with the alcohol and drugs, created for Chris a situation where there was a separation from life, from his ordinary functioning, from what's going on in reality. He moved into this fantasy world. And in my view, the plans that were carried out regarding his stepfather and mother were a direct result.

"Chris was trying to find a solution where he was not going to be abandoned; where he was going to live a life in which he didn't have to depend on other people; in which he was not going to be hurt."

"But, Dr. Royal," Osteen said, asking this question almost as if he himself were seeking the information, because he himself was still trying to answer the question of how all this could have happened, "there are a lot of young people unfortunate enough to grow up in the poor circumstances that Chris did, and a lot of young people who get caught up in drugs, and apparently at least some people that get caught up in playing Dungeons and Dragons. Is there anything else that might relate to why that combination affected this young man as it did? Why him, in other words?"

To Bonnie, listening attentively, this was the most important question asked all year. Even more than whether or not Neal Henderson had been her attacker, this was the question to which she most wanted an answer. But this was also the one question she'd not been able to bring herself to ask, either of Chris or of anyone else: *Why him? Why my son?*

"You get to the bottom line," Dr. Royal said, "and I think it's because there have been tremendous stresses, primarily internal, which have never been talked about, never been dealt with. Chris, throughout his life, has developed a lifestyle of denial, of compartmentalizing things and not dealing with them."

There were consequences, in other words, to a lifestyle of denial.

Consequences, Bonnie realized, such as the possibility that one day your poor, lost, befuddled, forlorn son will discover that he wants you dead.

40

Just as she had been for his testimony, Angela was present in court for Chris's sentencing hearing. Throughout all proceedings, she'd made a strong impression on those who observed her by seeming thoroughly uninterested.

Bill Osteen had noticed this same disturbing lack of reaction on December 27, when Chris had first confessed that he'd planned to have her killed in her sleep.

"You could just as easily have been reading her the *Wall Street Journal*," Osteen would say of that day. "*No* reaction. None. It was as if nothing in the world had been said to her that was of any consequence whatsoever. She could easily have said, 'I think I'll just go to Hardee's and get a hamburger while y'all talk about this.' "

During her brief appearances in Elizabeth City, it had been the same. At night, she would spend time not with her mother or brother, but at the Holiday Inn, socializing with John Taylor and others.

In court, she showed no signs of caring about what was said. Wayland Sermons would say later that he'd thought— perhaps erroneously—that Bonnie had seemed "cold" throughout the trial. Regarding Angela, he said, "My impression of that kind of coldness was probably tripled. Angela would look around, play with her fingernails, adjust her clothing. She acted very bored, uninterested in what was going on."

Shortly after four P.M., however, one event prompted a dramatic change in her demeanor. Chris's sentencing hearing was interrupted by word that the jury had decided the fate of James Upchurch.

The verdict: "We the jury unanimously recommend that

417

the defendant, James Bartlett Upchurch III, be sentenced to death.''

And Angela, to the amazement of all who saw her, began to cry.

Though she shed no tears, the sentence came as a shock to Bonnie, to the extent that she was still capable of feeling shock. It had seemed to her that, just as in closing arguments during the trial, Upchurch's two lawyers had argued more forcefully and more persuasively than Mitchell Norton. She realized, however, that her view of Norton's performance might be colored by her view of Norton, and that the members of the jury, having been spared the sort of personal contact with him to which Bonnie had been subjected, might have been less unimpressed.

But beyond that, she didn't see how a jury could say that a nineteen-year-old boy deserved to die when there still wasn't one single piece of physical evidence that proved he had even committed a crime.

After the verdict was delivered, Judge Watts offered Upchurch the chance to speak. When he stood, Bonnie was again struck by how skinny he seemed, how prominent his long, thin neck was. Considering that he hadn't found it desirable to utter a single word throughout the entire trial, he made quite a little speech on this occasion.

"First off," he said, "I want to thank my attorneys. They have done a remarkable job. And that's got my utmost respect. And I want to thank you, Your Honor. You obviously have gone a long way to keep this trial from becoming any more of a circus than it already is. And, you know, I respect the trouble the jury has gone through to deliver their verdict."

He was sounding more like someone who'd just been given an Academy Award than a death sentence.

But then he said he was "appalled and shocked" by the verdict. "I find it utterly amazing that the testimony of two confessed murderers would be enough to convict anybody to death. I am forced to believe that I am merely being convicted by the assumption of guilt by association. I am an innocent man.''

Or a guilty man who had incorrectly calculated the odds. A man who had thought, as had Bonnie, that in the absence of any physical evidence, no one—least of all, a white college student—would be convicted of first-degree murder. Especially by a jury which, under the law, was not allowed to learn of his prior criminal record.

The Dungeon Master had spent so long devising his own scenarios, then watching others act them out, that he might not have realized that this had been a game whose outcome he could not control.

The next morning, when Angela was called to testify for the first and only time, her display of emotion over Upchurch's sentence was well behind her. She managed to seem both nervous and indifferent. She gave the impression of being there because she had to be, even if she provided all the right answers to Osteen's questions.

"Angela, for a long time after this tragic event, you and your mother believed that Chris had nothing to do with it?"

"Yes, sir."

"And there did come a time when Chris sat down and talked to you about it?"

"Yes, sir."

"And did he tell you everything that he testified to here in court?"

"Yes, sir."

"Since that time," Osteen said, "you obviously have had time to think about your relationship with Chris. And you know he's going to prison. Just tell the court what you expect your relationship to be with your brother from this day forward."

"I expect us to stay as close as we ever were. Keep in contact with letters, or however. And I expect to be there to pick him up when he gets out."

"Angela, as a result of what has happened, do you have any fear of Chris to this day?"

"No fear at all."

Next, with both Bill Osteen and Jim Vosburgh present, Bonnie spoke to Judge Watts on Chris's behalf:

419

"Dr. Royal basically has the overall picture pretty well covered. We struggled very hard—or I struggled very hard—to maintain the home that we were living in when my husband and I separated, so the children wouldn't have to be uprooted. And we suffered in lots of ways. By not having balanced meals, I guess, on occasion."

This was not easy for her. This was like asking for pity. But in the realm of the law, it was the last chance she'd ever have to help Chris.

"I just tried to maintain Chris's and Angela's environment as well as I could under the circumstances and continue with my job so we could move forward at some point in our lives. My sisters kept the children on many occasions. My mother and father kept Chris and Angela a lot. At the time, I was traveling for my company, and on many occasions I would be out of town for as much as a week at a time."

Once more, she tried to counter the impression of perpetual discord that Mitchell Norton had attempted to create:

"We had a very close-knit family relationship. Lieth was very proud of Chris. On many occasions he would tell me—and he would tell Chris also—that even though Chris wasn't doing as well at North Carolina State, gradewise, as he would like to see him do, he was doing much better than Lieth did when he went to State.

"And you know, occasionally Lieth and Chris would have a disagreement. But it was always a very short disagreement. And when it was finished, or they finished the argument or discussion or whatever they were in, everything was back to normal, and there was no problem."

It seemed that might be how it would always be in Bonnie's mind, no matter what anyone else might feel or say: there was no problem.

In talking about the period in August when Chris had been hospitalized, she sounded almost upbeat. "He made a lot of friends in the hospital. And I think he acted a little bit happier than he had in previous months, acted like he was a little bit more relieved, or there was some pressure taken off him."

"Do you know," Osteen asked her, "whether Chris

wanted to talk to you after he entered the hospital about the facts of this case?''

"Oh, yes. Dr. Royal said Chris wanted to talk with me. And you specifically asked me not to talk about July twenty-fifth. And Chris said you asked him not to talk to me about it. So we just avoided discussing anything about July twenty-fifth.''

"Throughout this time, Chris was, in effect, wanting to tell you?''

"Oh, absolutely. And it really bothered him, from what I saw.''

"And did you notice any change in Chris after he was able to tell you what the facts were?''

"Oh, yes. Complete relief. He just had a totally different attitude—like he didn't have anything to hide anymore.''

"Mrs. Von Stein, you have heard what Chris has had to say about this, and of course you were a victim. You are a mother and a victim. Would you please relate to the court what your feeling is about Chris presently, as he is getting ready to serve his time for what he's done?''

Bonnie took a deep breath, then another. She had very much wanted not to cry in public at this moment, but she did.

"My feeling with Chris now,'' she said, wiping her eyes, "is that he indicates to me in every way and every action and everything he says that he is basically looking forward to serving his time to pay for the things he was involved in, things he really can't explain to me.

"I feel like Chris, without the effects of the drugs, could never have even considered doing the things and saying the things that he did. It's totally foreign to everything he was brought up to believe in. It's totally foreign to his personality.

"Chris has always been the kind of person—he's kind of like me in the respect that instead of stepping on a cricket in the house, he'll pick it up and carry it outside and turn it loose. He's always been like that. That's one of the reasons I was absolutely sure Chris had no involvement in this, when the investigation started going in that direction.

"Now I am going to stand by him and be there for him.

I will love him as I've always loved him. I don't approve of the things that happened, but that can't be undone. I know in my heart that without the drug situation it never could have happened.

"And if he gets out of prison in my lifetime, I will do everything I can to help him get on his feet and start a new life for himself. He has my support."

She paused, then said, "I will also make arrangements that if he's not out during my lifetime, those things will still be possible for him."

When Bonnie returned to her seat in the front row, Lewis Young walked over to sit beside her.

"I just wanted to apologize," he said, "if I ever caused you any unwarranted hurt during the investigation. Sometimes, I have to take steps that others just may not understand at the time."

She thanked him and said she fully understood that he had just been doing his job.

And as Bonnie finished, Judge Watts said, "Incidentally, Mr. Osteen, let me observe that I certainly recognize the difficult situation that this placed you and Mr. Vosburgh in, and placed Mr. Pritchard and Mrs. Von Stein in. And I must say that you handled it in a very responsible manner, in accordance with the code of professional responsibility."

But then Mitchell Norton stood to say that of the three people involved in the killing "Chris Pritchard, from a moral standpoint, is more guilty than the other two." He again called the killing "savage and brutal" and despite his earlier agreement not to ask for any particular sentence, noted that the maximum was life plus twenty years and said, "I would ask the court to look at that whole, entire maximum."

This brought Jim Vosburgh to his feet almost immediately. *Goddamnit,* he thought, *if Chris was the most morally guilty of the three, then Norton should have had the balls to try him—Bill Osteen or no Osteen.*

Vosburgh said, with some indignation, "Any one of these three people could have ducked out of this at any time. Nobody forced Mr. Henderson to drive. Nobody forced

Mr. Henderson to go to a place and pick Upchurch up. Nobody forced him to do anything. He could have bailed out at any time.

"And nobody forced Mr. Upchurch to do the things that were done. Just like nobody forced Mr. Pritchard to draw a map. The district attorney thinks he's *more* guilty—we don't have comparative negligence in this state. We don't have comparative guilt. They are either innocent or guilty. That argument about greater guilt is a specious one. It just doesn't hold water when you take into consideration the roles of all three people."

Rather than saying that Chris had "induced" the other two to commit the crime, Vosburgh suggested that the real inducement had been Dungeons & Dragons.

Or, he said, "Dungeons and Dragons and drugs. The three Ds. Those were the inducements. The idea may have originated as a joke, but the more they played and the more drugs that were induced into their systems, the plan became reality as opposed to fantasy."

Then, for the first and only time, Bill Osteen spoke on behalf of this client whom he'd so disliked from the start, who'd caused him such stress and anxiety for so many months, who'd presented him with the least rewarding, most distasteful case of his career.

Personally, Osteen was inclined to agree with Norton. He did not express this opinion in court but would say later, "By far the worst of the lot is the son who participates in something like this. The people who came in and helped, even doing the act, are no more at fault than the son. From the prosecutor's standpoint I would have had a hard time seeing Upchurch where he was and Chris where he was."

This, however, was not the time to share that view. Until sentencing, he was obligated to act as Chris's advocate.

At first, as he spoke, it almost seemed a form of therapy. As if, after going for so long saying so little to so few, he now felt a compulsion to put in the record some observance of the difficulties that had beset him. As if, by reciting them to a judge in a public forum, he might be able to put to rest his own inner doubts about the way he had handled the case.

"This was," he said, "a most difficult situation. Leaving out what happened on July twenty-fifth, but just dealing with the mother, who was concerned and offering her help, and a son who was concerned and wanting that help, and lawyers who were trying to help but were caught in the middle, with the psychiatrist saying we needed to come to a resolution of this between the people immediately.

"If there is a responsibility that Chris Pritchard did not carry out in regard to telling his family earlier, then I assure Your Honor, it was at the direction of his lawyers, who were caught in the position of saying, 'We can't do it because she may be required to testify. They just have to accept our word for it that there's more involved here than anybody thinks there is, and at the proper time we can make it all known.'

"And if Your Honor please, when it came time to make a decision on what to do, there is nobody in this courtroom who knows, or will ever know, whether proper decisions were made or not. We live with our decisions. They become history. They are subject to second-guessing. They are subject to many things.

"But in keeping with the responsibility that Mr. Vosburgh and I and my son had, we evaluated this case from the standpoint of its being a one-witness case. And we evaluated it from the standpoint that we thought there were serious discrepancies, or areas that could not be confirmed by the prosecution, as a one-witness case. That witness being Mr. Henderson.

"And we had an obligation to tell Mr. Pritchard how we evaluated his case if he went to trial. And we did that. And after hearing us tell him that this was not by any means, in our opinion—and I am not asking anyone else's opinion at this time, I am just trying to set the tone of what Mr. Pritchard heard from us—rightly or wrongly, his attorneys thought there was at least anywhere from a small chance to a good chance that if these matters were put before a jury, Mr. Pritchard had a good chance—as would Mr. Upchurch, based on the evidence at that time.

"We told him our opinion. We also told Chris that we did not know what could be worked out in the way of an agreement to plead guilty, but that we would explore it if he wanted us to. And we said we doubted that Chris Pritchard could walk out of our office that day, or after a trial in which he might be found not guilty, and ever feel good about himself again. And his lawyers would not have felt good about it.

"And Chris sat there and said to us, 'I participated, and I understand I am responsible for it, and I don't want to walk out.' And so we did work something out with the State."

Osteen paused. He had needed to get that off his chest. He had needed to leave in some appropriate forum some objective record of the agonies he'd been through along the road to where he now stood. To those who knew him well, this public display of personal feeling about a professional matter was entirely uncharacteristic. But this case had affected him as had no other during his thirty-year career. And since this would be the only time he'd talk about it publicly, he wanted to say a few more things—perhaps hoping that by trying to explain to Judge Watts how this had happened, he might succeed, at least in part, in explaining it to himself.

"There are a few things, Your Honor, that I want to call to your attention that I thought were bizarre in this case, and that have never, perhaps, occurred before.

"Chris Pritchard had a record in his community of being an honorable person as he grew up. And it's just almost *inconceivable* that things could have gone as wrong as they did. But it's not a unique situation when coupled, as Dr. Royal said yesterday, with whatever there was in his genetic or environmental makeup, and with his early years and the difficulties that he encountered then.

"It seems to me that it is reasonable to say that when he got to a school—and it could have been State or any other school. I certainly don't say it's because he went to State. I say that wherever he went at that time, whatever group he became part of at that time, was likely to have a great influence on him.

425

"And it did. There was just an ineffable pattern of things going from good to not so good, bad to worse. But greatly to my surprise, I find that this is not an unusual situation. This week I was reading a book called *Understanding the New Age*. I don't know where it came from. My wife got it somewhere. And I picked it up and started reading it.

"There is, in this country, if Your Honor please, a 'new age,' which has moved away from some of the things that many people were taught in their youth and clung to, still cling to, as being the things that perhaps make people act in a better manner.

"This new age—and I guess one of the people that comes to mind is a lady named Shirley MacLaine, an actress who has been involved deeply in this new-age theory—this seems to be a theory that says, 'I am a being, and I am capable of transferring my own powers to a greater power, and therefore I am God.' That's the thinking.

"And there was a writer in the *L.A. Times*, Russell Chandler, who set out to look into and explore this new age. I would like to refer to him for just a moment if I may. Because he said something that hits this case. At least, it did for me. He said, 'We are all aware that a warning label must be attached to psychedelic drugs, for in the "new age" this is the entry level for altered states. For tens of thousands of people, psychedelic drugs bring back not a past Xanadu, but lead to a mental hospital for a fried brain. By the late 1980s there was growing experimentation and research with high-tech "Designer Drugs" including Ecstasy'—which has been mentioned in this court.

" 'Warnings about opening up the mind to hallucination and sinister entities are regularly sounded by critics of the "new age." The alarms include the dangers of fantasy, role playing, and imagination games like Dungeons and Dragons, which swept the youth culture several years ago. Dungeons and Dragons is a doorway to the occult.'

"It goes on," Osteen said, "to discuss Dungeons and Dragons, saying it's laced with references to magic, occult wisdom, violence, and power. And what this man, Russell Chandler, is saying in his summary is that the hallucinogenic drugs, the Dungeons and Dragons game, the other mind-altering games, are an attempt to harness a segment of society that's never had much religion—to create an alternate religious worldview.''

This was Bill Osteen, the old Republican representative and federal prosecutor speaking now, but speaking to a judge who, except for political affiliation, clearly shared almost all the same values.

"In my view," Osteen said, "it's the kind of pathology where the more fascinated a person gets with it, the more likely it is that he can become mentally unbalanced by the process itself.''

He again quoted from the book. " 'Auto-hypnosis is a powerful tool, not totally understood. It is manipulation.' If Your Honor pleases, I submit that is essentially what we see in Chris Pritchard's case. I am sure there are people who can play Dungeons and Dragons and never have any lasting results. There are people who, unfortunately, can use drugs and not have any lasting results. And there are people who can grow up in deprived homes and do wonderfully well. But once in a while, those categories come together and create what has been created here.

"And I submit that Chris Pritchard, at the time this dastardly act happened, was changed to such an extent—not only his personality, but his pathology, as Dr. Royal has said—that he had moved himself into a position of imagined power and control over his own destiny, which he now understands is not his to determine.

"And through it all, there is a mother who sat on this stand, and who has sat for months and gone through *pure hell* not knowing what was out there, but knowing something was.

"Who has gone from the belief that 'My son was not involved' to the understanding that 'Some way, something is not as I understand it' to the full understanding.

"And a mother who sits there and says, 'I am going to help him. I am going to give him my love and I am going to work with him.'

"I hope Your Honor will take those things into consideration."

*   *   *

Then Judge Watts gave Chris a chance to speak.

Chris stood. In jacket and tie that would soon be exchanged for prison jumpsuit, he looked anguished, frightened, and still only about sixteen years old. Whatever combination of arrogance and surliness he had used to mask his guilts and fears over the preceding year and a half, they were now gone. More than ever—and not just to Bonnie—he seemed a victim himself.

"I just want to say, first of all, that I believe Mr. Norton was extremely fair in allowing me to take this plea bargain agreement. I know that I am guilty and I do deserve to spend time in prison. And I think it was fair of him to allow me to have that opportunity.

"I want to speak with my family." Chris looked unsteady on his feet. Also, he was starting to cry. "As Dr. Royal has mentioned, I seem to deny my feelings. I don't know why, but I do. And they build up like pressure in a cook pot."

He was crying now, and finding it hard to go on. "They build up like pressure in a cook pot," he said, "and they overflow, as right now."

He turned away from Judge Watts to look back at the closely packed rows where his mother, his sister, his grandmother, his uncle, his aunts, and so many of the friends he'd had in high school—and even the parents of many of those friends—sat watching him. A number of them were crying, too.

"I just want you to know that I love all of you," Chris said to them, crying so hard he had to pause. "And I thank you all for being here and supporting me. I honestly feel I do not deserve this support. But the Lord has given me strength to stand here today and do what I know is right. And I ask that he give you all the strength and support in the coming years, for I will not be here to do that myself."

Then, trying to compose himself, he turned back to face the judge.

"I can't hold anything against James Upchurch or Neal Henderson for what they did. The Lord asked me to forgive them, and I have. Just as He has asked me to forgive myself, which I have not quite been able to do just yet.

"That's all that I have to say. Thank you."

Judge Watts called for a ten-minute recess.

When court resumed, the judge spoke. As with everyone else involved, elements of this case had touched him in ways he'd not forget. Having spent more than twenty years in the criminal justice system, Thomas Watts was no stranger to horror, sadness, and waste. Yet, he, too, seemed shaken by exposure here to something more—to something mysterious and malignant.

He began, however, by talking about Bonnie. "It was indeed a difficult situation counsel found themselves in, in this case. But if there's anybody in this courtroom that I personally have the deepest of sympathy for, it is Bonnie Von Stein, a lady who has lost her husband. It was just very obvious from her testimony, from all that she has ever said, that he was the light of her life. And she's a lady who is now about to lose her son, at least in a physical sense of separation."

Then he spoke directly to her. "I hope, Mrs. Von Stein, based upon what Dr. Royal has done, that you may in fact regain a son who had been lost previously. The difficulties and conflicts that Mr. Osteen and Mr. Vosburgh encountered pale in comparison with the things that you've been through. And my heart goes out to you, ma'am. I think this matter shouldn't conclude without me saying that."

Judge Watts turned his attention back to Chris. "Now, having dealt with some heinous crimes, some terribly, terribly tragic things, I honestly and sincerely would still have to say that this case is, as you put it, Mr. Osteen, bizarre and just atrocious in its consequences for all concerned.

"But particularly for Lieth Von Stein, who, without benefit of jury, without benefit of judge, without benefit of due process of law, had the ultimate punishment imposed upon him savagely and brutally, as the consummation of a plan that originated in the mind of his stepson, whom he loved and cared for.

"You gentlemen," he said to Osteen and Vosburgh,

"appeared before me with a motion in Greenville, back in December. And while you were getting organized and putting your things out on the table, there was a Bible lying open on that judge's bench in Pitt County. I had not placed it there. I don't know who did.

"But as you gentlemen were getting ready to speak, I glanced down and the book was open to Proverbs 28:24. I made a note of it at that time and I've carried it with me ever since.

" 'Who so robbeth his father or his mother and sayeth, it is not transgression, the same is the company of a destroyer.' That's old law, but that's still good law.

"And when Upchurch was apprehended, he had a backpack that had many things in it that I did not admit into evidence. But among those books he was carrying with him was the collected works of William Shakespeare. *King Lear,* act one, scene four: 'How sharper than a serpent's tooth it is to have a thankless child.' How sharper than a serpent's tooth."

Now he looked directly at Chris.

"I believe you are now remorseful, Mr. Pritchard. I don't doubt your remorse in the slightest. I believe, if you had it to do over again, if you could go back and undo those whom you have wronged, you would do so. But you can't. And you must pay the consequences of those events which you put into motion.

"And the genesis, the genesis was Christopher Pritchard. The midwife may have been Dungeons and Dragons and drugs—I would not argue with that—but the genesis was Christopher Pritchard.

" 'How sharper than a serpent's tooth.' "

Then Thomas Watts imposed the maximum sentence: life plus twenty years. It would be, probably, more than twenty years before Chris even became eligible for parole.

Chris was permitted to walk to the front of the spectator area and give farewell hugs to family and friends. Then Osteen asked the judge if Chris could have just a moment alone with his mother and sister before being taken away.

Chris, Bonnie, and Bill Osteen were led to a small room

adjacent to the judge's chambers for a private farewell. Angela did not accompany them. "I don't understand why," Osteen said later, "because the purpose was to give them a chance to at least say good-bye."

But even Bonnie stayed only briefly. She said she'd be in touch once she was told where he'd been sent. A time might come for a deeper and more personal exchange between mother and son, but in Bonnie's mind, it was not now.

She knew that Neal Henderson was about to be sentenced, and after having attended every minute of the legal proceedings thus far, she did not want to risk missing that moment.

And so, as she put it some months later, "I exited the room," leaving Chris in the company of only the lawyer who had so disliked him from the start.

As the door closed behind her, Bill Osteen found himself, for the first time, feeling something approaching sympathy and even affection for Chris.

"We knew this was coming," he said. "We knew, essentially, what the judge was going to do. But the best thing that happened here today was that I perceived something genuine coming from you. You appeared to me to be saying, 'I love my family and I know what I've done is wrong.' I think that's a big first step for you, Chris. And if you stay on that road, I think you're going to make it."

Chris looked Osteen straight in the eye. He said, "Yes, sir. It was too long in coming. I really have hurt them. But I'm going to try to make it up any way I can."

Back in court, Judge Watts termed Henderson a "bright star," praised his SAT scores, and complimented him for his honesty and cooperation, without which the crime might never have been solved. He then sentenced Henderson to a term that, with recommendation for "study release," might mean he'd be out of prison in less than five years.

To Bonnie—who still firmly believed that Henderson was the man who'd tried to kill her—this sentence seemed unconscionably lenient. It so rattled her that the moment court recessed she headed straight for the prosecutors' table and had sharp words with the first person she found, who happened to be the young assistant district attorney Keith Mason.

A tall, kind, thoughtful man, he came from a Beaufort County farm family of which it could be noted, and often was, that "there are no better people than the Masons." He spoke with a country accent much thicker than Bonnie's, despite his having graduated from both college and law school at Chapel Hill, and he shared the same small-town values that she had grown up with in Welcome.

"This means I'll have to sleep with a gun in my hand for the rest of my life," Bonnie said.

When Mason did not respond, she added, "I hope one day you'll tell me what *really* happened."

"Excuse me?"

"I hope one day you'll tell me what really happened."

Keith Mason was slow to anger, especially toward a woman who'd been through as much as Bonnie, but it had been a long day, a long week, a long month, a long year.

"Bonnie," he said, "why don't you just say what's on your mind."

"Are you aware of Dr. Hudson's opinion about two assailants? One person could not have used a bat *and* a knife at the same time."

"Yes, I am aware of Dr. Hudson's opinion."

"Well, what do you think of it?"

"Opinions are funny things. Everybody's got one, especially when it doesn't have to be part of their testimony. I assure you, we are not covering up for Neal, or anybody else."

Then, his temper rising, he added, "Bonnie, I don't know who was in your bedroom other than Upchurch. I don't know because I wasn't there. But whether you know it or not, there are an awful lot of people who have the opinion that you were the one who killed your husband. I'm not one of them, because there's no good, hard evidence. You may have killed him, but there's not any evidence. And I can assure you that we have gone where the evidence has taken us, and not where we thought we ought to be."

And so it ended for Bonnie as it had begun: with her as

victim, as suspect, and as a mother whose trust in her son had been sadly misplaced.

She walked out of the courthouse and into a small park across the street where, seated on a bench, in bright sunlight, the air calm and surprisingly warm for January, she made her first and only public comment on the case.

Reading from a statement she and Wade Smith had prepared in advance, she said:

"The events of the past eighteen months have been tragic for me and my family. We have endured sorrows beyond any I have known before. I loved my husband, Lieth, and loved our quiet life together. On the night he died, I almost died from wounds I suffered during the assault. I do not understand why I survived.

"Now my son, Chris, and two of his companions have been sentenced for participating in this tragedy. I love Chris, as I am sure Neal's and James's parents love them. I hope and pray that these three young men can someday find peace within themselves.

"We now have the difficult task of picking up our lives and trying to move forward. With the continuing support of our family and friends, we will succeed."

And then, after checking out of the Goodnite Inn, she drove home alone to the small, empty house in Winston-Salem.

When she got there, she walked straight through the house and out the back door to the shed where her cats were waiting. She opened the door and stepped inside and sat on the floor of the shed, leaning against a wall, her eyes closed.

"And I sat there for an hour petting them," she said. "Just letting those poor, sweet, innocent, trusting creatures climb and purr and rub all over me."

PART FIVE

FOREVER
A STRANGER

FEBRUARY 1990–JULY 1991

Which of us has known his brother? Which of us has
looked into his father's heart? Which of us has not
remained forever prison-pent? Which of us is not forever a stranger and alone?

—Thomas Wolfe
Look Homeward, Angel!

41

It was only three weeks later that I met Bonnie, in the same small, windowless conference room at Tharrington, Smith and Hargrove where, in early January, Mitchell Norton had said he still could make a case against her for the murder of her husband.

The next day, she drove me to Little Washington and we walked together through the Lawson Road house.

She said there would be no secrets, no closed doors. She would ask everyone with whom she'd ever had contact in relation to this case to answer any questions I might have.

"Very firmly and very forcefully," Jean Spaulding recalls, "she said, 'This book is not for me. The truth is to be told in this book. I want you to tell him the truth, and however it turns out is how it turns out.' "

Through the late winter and into the spring and summer of 1990, I spent many hours in the dimly lit living room of Bonnie's small house in Winston-Salem, talking to her about dark and cheerless things.

Staying at a nearby motel, I'd arrive, usually, at nine A.M., and we'd talk all day. She made me iced tea, fed me sandwiches for lunch, answered every question I asked, and volunteered information on subjects I would not have known to ask about if she had not introduced them.

Usually, after such sessions, we'd go out for dinner at one of the many nearby restaurants and make an effort to find other things to talk about. But there wasn't much. Bonnie was trapped, alone, inside a very dark and private cave from which there was little hope for escape, and there was no use pretending she wasn't.

We were in close physical proximity, but emotionally she was always distant. She talked about Chris and Angela and about the frightful things that had happened to her with a flatness and detachment that was bothersome at first, until I realized that in order for her to speak, or to function at all, she had to keep the part of herself that dealt with the outside world (including me) isolated from her deeper feelings.

On rare occasions, usually late into our long afternoons—and only when the subject would be her father or Lieth—there would be a sudden catch in her voice, a halting, what might have been a misting of her eyes, a quick breath, a look away.

She acknowledged that she might be, herself, "at the extreme other end of the spectrum, perhaps too much so," but said, "I take a dim view of people who get overly emotional. I don't ignore difficult situations, but they're not what I dwell on. Why should I burden others with my feelings?"

Over the next year, I would learn that the refusal to display emotion was not merely a protective mechanism Bonnie had adopted to survive in the aftermath of her trage-dies; it was, perhaps, the Bates family's dominant trait. From childhood, it had been especially strong in Bonnie.

She had been born with her tear ducts sealed. "We might as well not even have bothered to get them opened," her mother once told me, "because Bonnie was a child who just didn't cry. And if she was sick, just leave her alone, don't bother her. She didn't want to be comforted." Bon-nie's younger sister, Ramona, recalled, "Even when she was a little girl, you never knew what she was thinking."

Bonnie feared only one thing: going upstairs by herself, to the bedroom she shared with her sisters. Not that she ever spoke of this—even as a child, Bonnie did not admit to weakness. However, when her mother would give her clean, folded clothes and tell her to take them to her room, they'd be found hidden in the kitchen or den instead. Only years later did Bonnie confess that she'd hidden them, changing into them when no one was watching, because of her fear.

It seemed a peculiar phobia. Forty years later, however, it was in her upstairs bedroom that Bonnie experienced the most terrible moment of her life.

Whatever emotional openness she had had vanished when Steve Pritchard abandoned her. "He shut down forever a part of Bonnie that I miss," Ramona said.

"We didn't want her to marry Steve," her mother told me. "George and I talked to her until we were blue in the face. But the more we talked, the more determined she became."

Even before he walked out on her, he caused her pain. While she was pregnant with Chris—just how pregnant no one seems sure—she had an epileptic seizure. Bonnie herself first told me this. She'd been rushed to a hospital. She'd had to undergo a spinal tap. She'd stayed in the hospital for a week, receiving then and for the rest of her pregnancy large doses of the antiseizure drug Dilantin. She wondered if this might have done some prenatal damage to Chris's brain that could have made him less responsible for his actions twenty years later.

What she didn't tell me was what seemed to have caused the seizure. "She had that seizure because of Steve," her mother said. "She found out he was running around. I can even tell you who it was with. Right down there at the corner of Center Church Road and Route 150, there was a store, and the girl lived upstairs over the store. Steve was seeing her. One night, she even came down to the car to talk to him while she was wearing nothing more than her nightgown. Bonnie found out, and that's when she had that seizure—right then. It was a terrible thing.

"Then, when Chris was born, Steve didn't even have the money to get Bonnie out of the hospital. He had money for a motorcycle, but not to bring his wife and firstborn home. He had to come and ask me for the money."

After the trauma of that first discovery of her young husband's infidelity, Bonnie's reaction to further evidence that her marriage was failing was total denial.

This continued even after Steve had left her, in summer of 1972, when Chris was just over three and a half years old and Angela was almost two. Her approach had been to seal the wound tight, so no one would see how much it hurt. At first, she told no one. Only weeks later did she confide to her father what had happened. And even then she would say only, "Steve is gone, *and I don't want anybody talking about him.*"

By then, in Jean Spaulding's view, Bonnie's posture of denial when confronted by emotional upheaval had already had a profound effect on Chris, in whom the same reaction had already been cemented.

"Frequently," Dr. Spaulding said, "with children who are about two years old, you will find them mirroring their parents' behavior. That's one of the ways they incorporate and learn new behaviors. It's pretty age-specific. It's usually gone by three.

"If a child is mirroring a parent's denial, you wonder what happens to fantasy life. Here, in Chris's case, we would assume—and we are speculating—that by the time he's four or five, he's got this thick layer of denial: 'This is how you deal with the real world, or any trauma.'

"But underneath, he has to have some sort of fantasy life. And you wonder whether that has been stifled by the denial only to come out later in Dungeons and Dragons. And—this is also speculation—if a child's fantasy life has been dampened by this layer, a brick wall, essentially, of denial, and this fantasy life is down there trying to have some expression, it would be like an abscess. It would just grow and grow and grow. And once it was allowed expression, there would probably be an absolute outpouring."

When I began to talk to Chris, he told me that as far as he could tell, Dr. Spaulding was absolutely right.

I met him for the first time on Mother's Day of 1990, in a prison in Goldsboro, southeast of Raleigh, where he was in the midst of a drug and alcohol rehabilitation program. We talked for two hours in a room thick with cigarette smoke in which metal tables had been bolted into the floor approximately six inches from one another.

Terribly nervous, he chain-smoked cigarettes with trembling hands. His legs shook so hard the whole time we talked that his knees jiggled the surface of the metal table.

Chris was trying to grow a beard and he'd just submitted to some sort of radical haircut from an inmate barber. To anyone who had seen only his high school yearbook picture, he would have been unrecognizable.

"I'm secure now," he told me. "I know where my life is." He said he felt better being in prison than he'd felt at NC State in the weeks that led up to the murder.

"There was not a single twenty-four-hour period when I was not drunk or stoned or tripping. From first thing in the morning until the time I went to sleep. I felt the need to escape that badly."

"To escape from what?"

"Myself, I guess. But reality was indistinguishable from fantasy at that point. Our game characters were more important than real life."

He said they'd go to Wildflour for pizza and beer and Moog would shout, "Five thousand experience points to anyone who beats on the table with his mug and yells, 'Serving wench, bring us more ale!'" Moog would give them experience points for all sorts of things, such as stealing. The more expensive the object you stole, the more experience points you would get from the Dungeon Master.

"The whole point was, for doing something daring in real life, you'd be given points for your character. With the points, the character would accumulate wealth and power and advance to a higher level. And your character would do things a real person would never do. The game was a way of acting out your impulses without having to regret it later. At least that was the way it was supposed to work.

"The trouble was, with all the drugs, the distinction got kind of blurred. I just remember—as we were planning the murders—I wasn't thinking so much about the money, I was wondering how many experience points I would get."

He said he realized only afterward how much his character, Dimson the Wanderer, had in common with himself.

441

"She was a loner, her family was dead, she was cut off from herself, just like me. I always made it a point to not let any one person know everything. Never let anyone get the full picture. See, I have a basic distrust of everyone, and if they don't have the full picture, they can't get to me. The trouble was, I don't think I've ever been 'me.' I feel like I'm not *allowed* to be what I want to be. Nobody can see it, but I've built an invisible wall around me, brick by brick. I still feel one hundred percent alone. Even if I was in a room with a thousand people, I'd be by myself. And I know I'll feel alone forever."

In subsequent visits—he was eventually assigned to a prison called Craggy, just north of Asheville—we talked more about his feelings of alienation: of his sense that he'd never had a true home.

"The way it was with Lieth," he said, "when we were good, we were 'his kids.' But whenever we did something wrong, he would holler at Mom about it. I didn't like to hear him holler at Mom. In fact, that bugged the shit out of me.

"They had problems. Don't let anybody tell you different. I can remember lots of times. I remember once when my mom called my aunt Ramona on the phone, crying, and saying she was ready to leave Lieth and all of us. That was when I was in high school, a long time before anybody could start blaming things on the fact that Lieth's parents were sick.

"After a while, he started drinking all the time. You heard about the time he came after me in the living room, swinging at me. But that wasn't much. The second time, it really killed me. He was drunk, he tried to beat my ass, he was yelling, 'I hate you! I hate you! I hate you!' He tried to kick me and I wound up having to use my oriental martial arts. Tai-kwan-do. He thumped me in the face and said, 'Let's take it outside.' My mom and Angela were yelling, 'Stop it! Stop it!' Finally, I just ran. My escape, like it always is, was to just jump in my car and get away, drive like a complete maniac for a while."

Chris said things had been bad ever since they'd moved to Little Washington. "I guess I didn't like living in that house. It was the exact opposite of when I was younger and the family was there for me. But my mom never knew. I never told her about any of the problems I was having, about any of the bad feelings I had. I didn't talk to anyone in the family. I don't know why. I think it's an inherited trait.

"But maybe there was, for some reason, a deep-seated lack of trust of my mother. Like, when I was little, I was always afraid she'd leave me the way Steve Pritchard had. When she wouldn't come home from work on time, I'd sit at the day care or at my grandma's and just bawl and bawl until she finally came in the door.

"In Washington, my mom tried, but I had the feeling I just wasn't understood. I never felt I was understood by anyone. The reason I went to State instead of ECU in Greenville was not because it was a better school but because I wanted to get as far away from that house as I could. Home was not a place I was close to. Home, to me, was not a home."

We began to talk about feelings, and about his inability to express them in nondestructive ways.

"I have removed my emotions from the thought process," he said. "Man, I push them suckers all the way down to the bottoms of my feet. I would push them clear out the bottoms if I could. I learned that from somewhere, maybe from my mother. That's where escapism comes in. It was only in a fantasy that I could really let myself feel. My approach is to get up high, above my emotions. Compartmentalize. I want to get myself on a different, higher level than my emotions.

"At the same time, I *want* to be open. I *want* people to know me. The fact that I'm not open, I trace that back to my mother. That tells me where I got it from. My mom and I talked very, very seldom."

Once, I said that the way he described his family life made it sound like a connect-the-dot picture in which none of the dots were connected.

"Not dots," he said quickly. "Because at least dots have *something* in common. At least dots have the same shape.

This was worse. This was more like a tetrahedron, a square, a circle, and a polygon. Four different people living under the same roof, trying to lead separate lives.

"The conflict between us was always there, but most of the time it was like a ghost—not quite tangible. We all knew we weren't okay, but we felt we had to pretend. There was something out there that nobody knew how to deal with, or wanted to try to.

"It came down to the feeling, well, we have to live together, but that doesn't mean we have to like it. Everybody was always on edge. We'd go to restaurants and Lieth would raise hell and complain, but he'd raise hell and complain at home, too.

"And it really wasn't the same with Lieth after Chocowinity. He could just never let that go. So, after that, whenever I could, I just cleared out. When I could be gone, I was gone. Somewhere else. Anywhere else. It didn't matter. And whenever I could be, I'd be drinking. I remember coming home one time totally blitzed. Mom was there, I called her a bitch, then I went out to her car and threw up in it.

"But why did I want them dead? I can't blame it all on the drugs. These feelings had to have been there before. It was just the drugs that brought them out, and the game that gave me a way to do it."

"Why *did* you want them dead?" I asked. "So they'd never be able to reject you?"

There was a long pause. Then he said, "No. I think I wanted to kill them because if they were dead, I couldn't disappoint them anymore."

42

I also spent time in Little Washington. The best place to eat, incidentally, isn't Wendy's or Hardee's or even the Stage House, where Angela delivered the place mat to John Taylor. The best place to eat in Little Washington is Bill's Hot Dogs on Gladden Street, right next to A. P. Gerard and Son—Feed, Seed, Lawn and Garden Supplies, and just up the street from the First Presbyterian Church.

What you order at Bill's is an All-the-Way, which comes with chili that they make right there in the kitchen; and with mustard, and with most anything else you might want to put on it. You have to order two because, as they say at Bill's, "they're small in size but big in taste." The preferred drink is Pepsi-Cola, an original North Carolina product. At lunchtime, Bill's is one of the busiest places in town.

As Keith Mason had told Bonnie at the end of the trial, many people in Washington still believed that both she and her daughter were involved in the murder of Lieth.

I had one long conversation with Mitchell Norton during which, after several hours, and after he'd smoked innumerable Salem Lights, he mentioned what he called his Plan B, which he might have implemented if Chris had been a defendant.

This consisted, in essence, of putting Bonnie on trial for the murder: of suggesting that even though she hadn't been charged, much suggested that she had masterminded the plot in order to collect the money that would come to her when Lieth was dead.

Norton conceded that no physical evidence linked Bonnie to the crime, but none had linked Upchurch either. And Bonnie had a far better motive: a $2 million motive.

His goal, he said, would not have been to convict her—after all, she hadn't even been indicted—but to cause the jury to view her with suspicion and thereby to disregard anything she might say in support of her son.

To imply that she'd been involved, he would have referred to the undigested rice, the letters to Lieth from the woman in California, and the blood-spattered pages from *A Rose in Winter*. He would also have made an issue of Bonnie's demeanor: how she had not displayed grief or sorrow at appropriate times, in appropriate ways. And he would have dragged in Angela, too, as Upchurch's lawyers had tried to do.

The rice remained an unresolved question. More than a year after the trial, Page Hudson was still troubled by its implications.

"Rice is pretty easily digestible," he said in an interview. "Cooked chicken is pretty easily digestible. But the rice had undergone very little change. The chicken had undergone very little change. The longer in the stomach, the more frayed-looking the particles become. These didn't look frayed at all. If they'd told me he had eaten ten or fifteen minutes before, I would have said okay. But when they said *four or five hours* . . .

"I would have expected him to have had an empty stomach, or close to an empty stomach within a couple of hours. By midnight, I would have thought he would have had an empty stomach. Or that the material in it would at least have been practically unrecognizable.

"Look, most everything in life I've found an exception to, so I won't say it's impossible. I'll just say I'm astounded. In many cases, there's an item or two that doesn't seem to fit with everything else. So you sort of go along with the total mass of evidence. I'm not going to get up on a soapbox and say, 'Hey, justice wasn't carried out here because the rice wasn't digested.' But I'm still terribly surprised. I still have a great deal of difficulty believing that I was looking at five or six hours of digestion.

"You know, you develop over a period of time a spectrum of what can or will happen, and when something falls outside that spectrum, you say, 'Hey, wait a minute. I'm not willing to accept those facts.' I got very much that feeling with the Von Stein case, and I still have it. If I had the chance to see the great instant replays of all cases—if they said, 'Hey, you can pick a half dozen and go back and see the replay, to see what really happened'—this would be one of my six.

"Something is not quite right about this case. There's something missing here. There's another card yet to be dealt."

Dr. Hudson's feeling was shared by both of James Upchurch's public defenders.

"My feeling," Frank Johnston said, "is if the truth were told, there would be other people involved. I think there was involvement by those we've heard about that hasn't come to light."

He said he based his view primarily on two factors: the undigested rice and the attitude of Bonnie and her children during trial. "I detected a coldness from Bonnie, Chris, and Angela that shocked me. Bonnie just never showed—and maybe she's an emotionless person—but she never showed any real emotion, whether she was talking about her son or her husband. She's the most controlled individual I have ever seen."

Asked if he questioned her story, Johnston replied, "I definitely do. When you put in this problem with the time factor and the food not digested and her saying it happened at four or five in the morning, I just think there are things that could have happened that none of us would ever know. It looked to me like the medical evidence completely overruled what the State was saying. The time interval, medically, can't exist. So, either the medical science is not as precise as we think it is, or she's hiding something."

Wayland Sermons did not go quite so far, but agreed that "Bonnie was very unusual, personality-wise," and that Dr. Hudson's findings "pointed in an entirely different direction" from the story told by Bonnie, Chris, and Neal Henderson.

"The testimony that the death occurred in the neighborhood of twelve to one to two o'clock showed that Henderson and Pritchard were telling a tale they had manufactured," he said. And Sermons pointed to "tremendous discrepancies," even between their two stories, in regard to such matters as how far in advance the planning for the murder had begun, and as to where—the bathroom closet or beneath the cushion of a chair—Chris's car keys had been returned.

Also, in his statement to police Chris had said he didn't care when the murders were done, as long as his car was back before dawn. Yet, according to Henderson, it had not been. As the sun began to rise over Greenville, Henderson had been driving the white Mustang through a car wash.

And even in the absence of the undigested rice, there was the fact that Lieth had gone to bed—as was his custom—at nine-thirty P.M. By four-thirty, he would already have had seven hours' sleep and might have been awakened far more easily than if he'd been attacked at midnight.

"That is what still makes me wonder," Sermons said. "There were so many things that didn't add up. I think, at some point, someone's going to find there was someone else in the room."

For Sermons to have said "someone *else*" suggested an implicit admission that his client had been there, too, but that was not the point he wanted to make.

"I think the someone would probably be Henderson," he said. "Or Henderson and somebody else. There was just too much going on, too quickly, for one person to do." This point drew the support of both Page Hudson and Tom Brereton, not to mention of Bonnie herself.

"Henderson had a year to get his story straight," Sermons said. "And I don't believe for a minute that what he said on the stand is the truth, the whole truth."

Regarding Chris, he said, "By and large, I think everyone came away from the trial with the impression that poor Chris didn't know the truth. Or maybe he knew it but didn't know how to tell it. Or just that the truth wasn't in him."

As to his own opinion about what had happened, Sermons said only, "I'd rather not get into my personal beliefs." He added, however, in regard to Bonnie, "The thing that kept on with me was, 'Was she involved?' " And he emphasized that his colleague, Frank Johnston, was "incredulous that Bonnie could survive an attack with the superficial injuries she had."

Even Lewis Young admitted that for some time, even after she'd passed her polygraph test so handily, he continued to have doubts about Bonnie. "I felt like for the most part, all along, she was not a part of this. But I never ruled out that there was a lot of money at stake here, and she was the first to gain by having survived.

"But I have a hard time thinking that somebody would subject themselves to the injuries she received just to be that convincing. Even though they ultimately ended up being more superficial than life threatening, that bat could have just hit in the wrong place; that knife could have gone just a little bit deeper. And how do you control that?"

To Jean Spaulding, who examined Bonnie's medical records, there was nothing superficial about the injuries. "Her wounds were severe. They were not wounds you would inflict on yourself, or that you would want inflicted on you."

Indeed, Dr. Spaulding considered any suggestion that Bonnie herself might have arranged or participated in the murder to be ridiculous. "Having known Bonnie very well as her psychiatrist, I do not feel she has the capacity to have taken part in or to have planned anything like this. Not a murder in general, and certainly not the murder of Lieth, who was so important to her on so many levels.

"Every time Bonnie would go back to Lieth, in conversation, that's where I could see the warmth. That's where I could see so much humanity from her. The meaning of Lieth for Bonnie was bigger than life."

But even Bill Osteen, for a time, had his doubts. For Osteen, the problem was not Bonnie's seeming detachment or unusual degree of self-control, but something much more concrete.

"I think Bonnie really was trying to do well," he said. "I think she was trying to stand by her children. And I think Bonnie is—my guess is that she is a good person. But I'll tell you something I've never mentioned before.

"I think," he said, well after his involvement in the case had ended, "if you go back, you will find a couple of letters that were found in Lieth's office drawer. And I think those letters could be interpreted as giving rise to the possibility of a relationship with a lady in California. And I always wondered, during all that time, could this possibly be a plot which was beyond all of us here, that these people know about?

"I've discarded that. I really have. But I looked at those letters and said, 'Am I missing something? Is this more than it appears to be?' And that's a tough thing to say because, good gracious, if Bonnie has had the strength and fortitude to do the things she's done, if she's been able to withstand the heartache, then it's terrible to think, 'Well, at one time I had to consider you a suspect, too.' "

That left, of the items on Mitchell Norton's dirty-laundry list, only the four blood-specked pages from *A Rose in Winter*. In the chaos of the crime scene, no one recalled when or where the book itself was found. John Taylor remembered that at one point he was holding it in his hand, but does not know how he came to have it.

As to the pages, however, Lewis Young's recollection—supported by Taylor's crime-scene photographs—was quite specific. They *were* stacked neatly on top of the typewriter stand. And they had been spattered with blood. A T-shirt of Bonnie's, hanging on a chair just beyond them, was also blood flecked. To Young, this indicated that the pages were on the typewriter before the blood had been shed.

Also, it seemed unlikely to him—given the disregard they'd shown for other potential evidence—that an EMT or Washington patrolman would have carefully gathered the pages from the floor and stacked them neatly, in proper numerical order.

Yet Bonnie had testified at trial, "When I went to bed, there weren't any books that were torn apart or disassembled or had pages out of them."

Asked if she'd read this particular book, these pages of which bore such an insidiously close resemblance to what had occurred in the room where they'd been found, she had replied, "I don't remember the story. I read it several years ago."

And that was where the matter rested. No one seemed able to take it any further. At least not until Angela said in an interview, on June 14 of this year, 1991, that she knew the book well.

"Yeah," she said, "I've probably read it three times." An intriguing comment, given the nature of the book and the fact that Angela did not have a widespread reputation as a voracious reader, and that in March 1989, she'd told SBI investigators Newell and Sturgell she did not remember the book.

But in June 1991, she acknowledged that she knew what action occurred in those particular pages. She said the way she figured it, the book could have been open by the bed because she thought her mother was reading it at the time.

By June 1991, Chris's ex-roommate Vince Hamrick was also able to remember some intriguing details and to offer some provocative opinions.

First, in addition to his baseball bat, James Upchurch had kept a Japanese martial-arts weapon in his dorm room. This, made of two pieces of bamboo strapped together and bound at the handle, was a powerful weapon, not some sort of flimsy reed. The kind of weapon that—while it might not fracture a skull as easily as a baseball bat would—could certainly inflict damage to a forehead, especially if swung by someone standing over a woman who was lying on a floor. The thing he most remembered about the weapon, Hamrick said, was that it made a whistling sound when it was swung hard.

Second, for two weeks after the murder of Lieth, while Chris was away from the campus, James Upchurch had moved into the room and had slept in Chris's bed, becoming Vince's temporary roommate. At the time, Vince had seen nothing strange about it since they all were hanging around together so much anyway, and Moog had never discussed the crime, but in retrospect Vince found it odd indeed.

He recalled Upchurch as "incredibly unathletic." Once, Vince had taken him to lift weights, and Upchurch had been unable to lift them.

Henderson, a bigger man, was also "very devious." In D&D games, "he was the magic user. He would find magic items and lie to everyone that they weren't worth anything. Then he would go back and keep them for himself."

In Vince's opinion, Upchurch was too small and weak to have carried off the attack by himself. Based on Bonnie's description of her attacker, as well as Henderson's personality and size, Vince was convinced that Henderson had participated in the attack. So convinced that even in casual conversation he referred to how "they" did it, and what "they" were thinking. Vince's opinion was that Upchurch had done the stabbing, but that Henderson had wielded the club—whether it had been a bat or a bamboo rod.

If all he'd been was a last-minute driver, he wouldn't have been involved at all, Vince said. "Why would they ask him? He didn't really even hang out with our group."

Hamrick also recalled clearly the particular Dungeons & Dragons scenario that, at Moog's direction, the players had been enacting in the days leading up to the murder.

Moog had entitled it "The Rescue of Lady Carlyle," and he had invented it himself. They'd been playing it almost every night for at least two weeks before July 25, 1988. In essence, the characters had to rescue Lady Carlyle, an attractive young woman, from the castle where an evil baron was holding her captive. The baron did not have a last name.

Once rescued, Lady Carlyle would reward them handsomely with a part of the fortune her father possessed, and she would also bestow sexual favors upon them.

It was strange, Vince said, that at a time when the real murder plot had already begun to develop—in fact, just before the murder of Lieth (whom Chris, when he was younger, had called "Lieth Von Frankenstein")—Moog, as Dungeon Master, had advanced the scenario to the point where they were able to carry out the rescue by breaking into the castle in the middle of the night while Lady Carlyle lay asleep in her chamber.

What Neal Henderson told me was also unsettling. Henderson was imprisoned in Harnett County, not far from Fayetteville and Fort Bragg.

On two separate occasions in the spring of 1990, I talked with Neal Henderson for two hours, uninterrupted by prison personnel. He could have been telling me the truth, or he could have been lying with every word. He was perfectly willing to look me in the eye, but I had no idea what I was seeing when he did. It might still have been one big Dungeons & Dragons game, and I was simply a new element in the scenario.

But I can report this: he has a bulky upper body—quite distinctive, really—and a thick, short neck that makes it appear as if his head sits almost directly on his shoulders. Everything about him—his physical movements, his speech, his whole personality—seemed cautious and slow, restrained and controlled.

We talked about the improbability of his having moved the car to a different location. "It was taking him too long," Henderson said. "I just got scared, so I went looking for him."

While parked on the Airport Road, he said, he'd heard "the sound of someone running." When I asked how Upchurch could have spotted him that far down the Airport Road, he said, "I must have had the brake pedal depressed without knowing it, because when he got in the car, the first thing he said was, 'You know, your brake lights are on.' " Then Henderson added a line of dialogue not heard at the trial. "He said, 'Someone made a very loud noise. I had to hit the guy to make him be quiet. I'm surprised the whole neighborhood didn't wake up.' "

Despite the faith placed in it by Norton, Mason, Crone, Taylor, and Young—all of whom struck me as capable, honest men acting in good faith, but all of whom, it must be said, had every reason to *want* to believe Henderson (and none of whom ever subjected him to a polygraph test)—I had problems with Henderson's account of his own limited role.

There was, first, the power of Bonnie's impression, the validity of which Jean Spaulding had recently reiterated to me. "It was an internal, instinctive, overwhelming reaction," she said. "Not the sort Bonnie was accustomed to having, because she is very logical, and—not in a negative way—just so detached emotionally. Her insides, her viscera, had to be remembering something, and when she just *felt* his presence, she knew this was the man. She had a very strong total-body reaction. This was not something that seemed to start on a cognitive level, but was more or less an 'emotional memory.' And I take that very seriously, given my knowledge of Bonnie, because she is very logical and does not get overwhelmed by emotions at all."

Beyond that, there was the unlikelihood—emphasized by both Page Hudson and Tom Brereton—of one person, armed only with bat and knife, entering a house he'd never been in before, in which he knew at least three adults slept upstairs, intending to murder them all.

Dr. Hudson had said, "Given the wounds Mrs. Von Stein had and Mr. Von Stein had, it's easier for me to picture two people as attackers. I just have difficulty imagining how one attacker could have taken care of both of them."

Brereton, with his twenty years of FBI experience—some of which had been earned on Indian reservations, investigating more homicides by stabbing than he could count—felt even more strongly. "You would never assign one person to go in and kill three," he said. "How could you expect to kill the second, much less the first, without waking the third?"

Chris had said he'd drawn a second map—one presumably destroyed in the fire—that showed the location of the upstairs bedrooms. Thus, Upchurch would have known where Angela slept. But Chris had never said he'd told Upchurch Angela did not have a phone in her room. In fact, she did, and—if awake and frightened—could easily have used it to call for help.

Even with the downstairs telephone cord disconnected—and if one wanted to assure that no one upstairs could use a phone to call for help, why not simply take the downstairs receiver off the hook, rather than unplug the cord?—there was no reason to believe that an unaware Angela would not be awakened by the noise of a beating and stabbing in the bedroom right next to hers, and would not, when awakened, reach for her phone and immediately call the police, before either hiding in her closet or under her bed, or fleeing downstairs and running out the front door for her life, screaming as loud as she could.

Unless, of course, she was already awake, or had gone to sleep knowing that she would not be harmed.

Or knowing nothing in advance, she might have been awakened by the sounds of Lieth's screaming, and the thumping and the pounding, to discover not only a stranger—Neal Henderson—in her house, trying, with some success, to murder her mother and stepfather, but a stranger accompanied by James Upchurch, a young man she knew well, and liked, and who she knew was fond of her.

Chris had said in his formal statement that he did not know if James Upchurch had even met his sister. But Mitchell Norton had told me that Henderson had told him that Angela "had had intercourse with Upchurch on several occasions."

Now, sitting under a hot June sun at a small concrete table in the yard of the Harnett County Correctional Institution, with guards armed with rifles standing in towers just beyond a nearby high fence topped with razor wire, Henderson elaborated on what he said was his understanding of the relationship.

He told me that Moog had been infatuated with Angela Pritchard, even commenting, "Finally, I've met a girl I'd like to marry."

Henderson said, "I'd never heard James talk about a girl like that before. He *really* liked her. He said she was very pretty, intelligent, and of course, her parents had millions of dollars. It was so unusual for him to be talking like this that I remember it real well. It really floored me. And this was before any talk of the plot. I said to myself at the time, 'James Upchurch is saying this to *me?*' It made me feel kind of good that he would confide in me that way. It wasn't something he ordinarily did.''

As I was preparing to leave at the end of this visit, Henderson added that it was, of course, a standard Dungeons & Dragons scenario to kill the reigning royalty, marry the princess, and thus inherit the keys to the kingdom and all its wealth.

And Angela, who never expressed emotion, who slept through it all, who had not used her phone to call for help, and who had read *A Rose in Winter* three times, had cried when Moog had been sentenced to death.

43

''At some point,'' Jean Spaulding said to me in the spring of 1990, ''Bonnie needs to have one of those straightforward, eye-to-eye conversations with Chris. It would be brief, it would be nonemotional, but I think she needs to confront him with 'You planned to kill me.' Not even 'Did you plan?' but 'You planned to kill me and I need an explanation of that.' Then I think she could take that and she could work with that and she would process that and I think she could then lay it to rest.

''I could see it staying sealed over for a fair number of years, but I think, on an emotional level, she needs, at some point, to get that done. It will take some work and preparation, and we're not working on that currently.

''She has still not even come in and said to me anything like 'Chris tried to murder me.' Or 'Chris murdered Lieth.' Or 'Chris is responsible for this.' It has never come out directly.''

"So you think," I asked, "that she hasn't been able to fully accept that he tried to kill her, or have her killed? Of course, it's a hard thing."

"A very hard thing," Jean Spaulding said. "The only thing harder, I think, would be if Angela had some involvement."

This was a problem. There was no hard evidence, but in *all* quarters, from prosecutors to defense attorneys to family members to Dr. Spaulding herself, there were qualms about Angela's claim of total uninvolvement.

At trial, Frank Johnston had hinted that Angela might have played a role. Asked later if that role had been more active than passive, he said, "I *feel* that it was. I do not believe, and will not believe, that somebody could sleep through this type of thing. I don't think most people could sleep through screams in their own house." And, he pointed out that, like Chris and Bonnie, "Angela had a lot to gain financially."

And Angela's deportment—however much it was beyond her control, however much it might have been an involuntary response learned from her mother or bred into her genes—added to this whiff of suspicion.

There were friends of Angela's, and family members, and Angela herself, who told stories of her legendary ability to sleep through earthquakes, tornadoes, and volcanoes.

Yet combined with her apparent indifference to what she found once she was awake—an attitude that, when it persisted for a year and a half, could not easily be attributed to temporary emotional shock—her tale of deep sleep was greeted with skepticism even from those who would have been far more comfortable believing her.

More than one of Chris's closest friends, not wishing to speak for attribution, wondered aloud whether—as one phrased it—"she might not have known more than she's let on." These were people who had been in the house on Lawson Road. They knew how sound carried, and how tightly the upstairs rooms were clustered.

Within Bonnie's family, doubts were expressed with varying degrees of bluntness.

Her sister Kitty would say nothing.

Her sister Sylvia vaguely remembers someone—she's not sure who—asking, "Do you reckon those kids had anything to do with it?"

Her aunt Bib—her father's sister—says, "That question was floating around."

Her sister Ramona said flatly, "If Chris knew, Angela knew."

And her brother, George, who had felt so conflicted about ever speaking to Lewis Young that almost three years passed before he would even acknowledge that he'd done it, said, "Exactly what I am thinking is that she may have known something and didn't say."

His wife, Peggy, added, "I wasn't sure about Angela then, and I'm still not."

But as recently as June of this year, 1991, the question bothered them and kept them talking.

"There ain't no way in the world someone could sleep through that," George said.

"I could almost accept Angela sleeping through the murder, but I was having a real hard time with the police and ambulance coming down the street, and *up to your front door*," Peggy said.

"And them waking her up," George said. And it wasn't as if the noise had been confined to the master bedroom, though the noise of a grown man screaming as loudly as he could, repeatedly, while fighting vainly for his life, should have woken even the soundest of sleepers. But Bonnie—he'd learned later—had said she'd heard thumping noises from the hallway, even after her door was closed. That would put loud noise even closer to Angela's room.

"We went through the 'in shock' theory," Peggy recalled. "That would have been great if the kids had stayed home the night after the murder, away from people. But you're not in shock if you're okay to go out and party."

"It was like," George recalled, " 'I don't understand. Why aren't these kids in tears? Why aren't they sitting up at that hospital protecting their mother?' I would be there day and night!"

And it wasn't just that first day and night. It was the next three years.

Even Bonnie's mother said to me one hot summer evening, with a terrible sadness in her voice, "Angela—you never know *what* she's thinking or feeling. My son asked me, 'Does Angela have any feelings at all?' "

And as recently as Father's Day, 1991, Steve Pritchard, who quite unexpectedly had received a phone call from Angela that day, voiced concern to me, but would not be specific as to why. He said only, "What's done is done. Nothing can change it. There's no hard evidence. I personally have chosen not to pursue it any further."

It was, ironically, the person Bonnie feared most in the world who provided, at least indirectly, what some considered the strongest support for belief in Angela's uninvolvement and unawareness.

As Lewis Young put it, "With all that Neal Henderson told us, I don't see any way he wouldn't have given us Angela if he'd known she had anything at all to do with this. After giving up Chris and giving up Moog, Neal would have no reason to protect her. Now, maybe they never told *him*—look, the further this goes, the stranger it gets—but I have a hard time buying that Chris and Angela and Moog were all in this together and for some reason Neal never found out about her."

Jean Spaulding, however, from her perspective, responded to further questions.

"A policeman walks into her room and he says, 'Excuse me, miss,' and she's not, like, shrieking! She was seventeen at the time? I don't know of too many seventeen-year-old girls who are just going to sit up and adopt a conversational tone if a policeman appears in their room in the middle of the night. Not at the front door, but in their room! That doesn't seem to ring true. Maybe she was in shock from the moment she saw the policeman, but I would expect something different.

"And her door is close to their door? And she didn't, like, immediately run into her mother's room? That's amazing. Either she very much needs some help, or she knew what was going on, I would venture to say.

"Where did she fall apart? Where did she break down? Where did she cry? What did she say?"

Dr. Spaulding also found it peculiar that Angela would have dressed in the presence of a young police officer she knew and did not like.

"She got out of bed and put her blue jeans on while he was standing there? That's a little striking, too. She's seventeen years of age and she's dressed in panties and a shirt? And she gets out of bed and pulls her blue jeans on in front of him? I don't know of many seventeen-year-olds who, in any sort of normal state, would do that. And maybe that's the issue: maybe she wasn't in a normal state of mind."

When informed that the only time Angela was known to have cried in public was at the sentencing of James Upchurch, Dr. Spaulding seemed almost amazed.

"That's striking to me," she said, "because if we're going to postulate that we don't see emotion from her because she's a Bates—if we're going to give her that degree of credit—then why is she weeping for this person that she supposedly barely knew?

"This man is being sentenced because he killed her stepfather. That's one aspect. But I think even more important is that this is the man who supposedly almost murdered her mother. Her mother has scars on her face to this day because of that assault. So how can you weep, if you're a Bates, at the sentencing of the murderer? That doesn't fit."

Not only had Chris said, in his December 27, 1989, statement to authorities, that he did not know whether Angela had ever met James Upchurch, he also made it a point, on six separate occasions, to emphasize either that she was not considered in his planning, or that he didn't care if she lived or died.

In Lewis Young's report, these comments read as follows: "There was not any discussion about Angela. . . . Pritchard stated he never thought about Angela at all during these discussions [with Upchurch]. . . . He had not thought about Angela." Then, as the plot moved closer to execution, "Upchurch said he would be making some noises and he would have to get Angela as well. Chris stated he told Upchurch it was okay to go ahead and kill Angela as well. . . . Pritchard stated it was determined by him and Upchurch that Angela would be killed so Pritchard would get all the money. . . . He pointed out on the map of the house where Angela's bedroom was located.''

But Jean Spaulding, for one, found it hard to accept that Chris could have been so callous in regard to his sister.

At my request, she had met with Bonnie in July 1990 to review numerous photographs of Bonnie, Chris, and Angela taken over the children's entire life span. Dr. Spaulding had said she'd found this technique an invaluable aid in developing insight into the nature of family relationships.

In August, she wrote me a letter that said in part:

One of the most striking issues that I would like to raise with you for your consideration is the large number of photographs of Chris and Angela engaged in an embrace or some other manifestation of physical closeness. I have over the many years of practice reviewed many family albums and many, many pictures of brothers and sisters. I was struck by the apparent warmth and closeness demonstrated in these pictures over such a prolonged period of time of Chris's and Angela's lives. There are pictures of them hugging from earliest childhood all the way up to the latency years. Additionally, most of the photographs during the adolescent years that are of a casual basis demonstrate an apparent warmth and camaraderie between Chris and Angela. One would wonder at Chris's ability to participate in a plot that would harm the one person with whom, by documentation in these pictures, he appeared to have a warm and normal bond.

Even Bill Osteen, who'd long since overcome his doubts about Bonnie, continued to harbor uneasiness about Angela. When asked if he found *her* lack of affect, as opposed to Bonnie's, to be suspicious, he answered, ''Very much so. I still—I always wondered if there wasn't something somewhere that we were missing. I always have felt that there was something between Upchurch and Angela that I don't know about. I would love to have a video of Upchurch out at that little shack on the day he waited there. I always had some question about whether Angela knew he was there."

I met Angela for the first time in the spring of 1990, in the same small living room where I'd been spending so many hours with her mother. Her hair was brownish blond, with a hint of red. Her skin was clear. She wore no makeup, just a T-shirt and shorts. If not stunningly beautiful, she certainly was pleasant looking.

But what surprised me—since I'd been led to expect some sort of zombie or department-store mannequin—was how lively and agreeable she turned out to be. She was cordial, talkative, and with one exception, did not seem at all self-conscious. She had at least two things in common with her mother: she did not strain to make an impression, and no question asked seemed to upset her.

First of all, she wanted to say there had been absolutely no problems at all in the Von Stein house. She had loved Lieth and he had been good to her. He had never given her a hard time about anything, and she'd never had a bad word to say either to him or about him. He and Bonnie had gotten along splendidly, and so had he and Chris. "He cared about us very much," Angela said. "And Chris and Lieth didn't hate each other. I know, because I saw it from inside."

Only when I asked about Moog did she get what I would call a schoolgirl smile on her face. She looked away briefly, and if she didn't quite blush, she came close. "I'm drawing a total blank," she said. "I may have seen him at the beach or in Washington. And maybe in Chris's dorm."

The more we talked, however, the clearer her recollection seemed to grow. Before the day was over, she was able to say, "Moog stands out vividly in my mind. He was drunk the first time I met him. I think this was when Chris was still rooming with Will Lang, which would have had to be his freshman year."

The first meeting, in fact, had "probably" been the night

of a campus concert given by a group named Def Leppard, which would have put it in the last week of January, almost five months before Chris says he first made Upchurch's acquaintance. That recollection was bolstered by a comment from her best friend, Donna Brady, that she seemed to remember meeting Upchurch "during the year." Donna, in fact, appeared almost shocked upon hearing that Chris said he hadn't met Moog until summer session.

"I remember him skating into Chris's room on a skateboard," Angela said. "His hairdo is what sticks out in my mind. Weird, very weird. Just a strange-type person all around. Basically your wired-type, off-the-wall person." When asked directly, she did say, "I guess you could consider him cute."

She said she saw him "many times" during the semester when she would drive up to State to visit Chris. These trips, she said, would occur every "two to three weeks." In contrast, Bonnie, at trial, had said Angela visited the NC State campus "very infrequently."

Despite the shy smiles, Angela would not admit to any particular affection for him, much less intimacy (she later told her mother she'd been a virgin the whole time she knew him), but said she did recall John Taylor telling her in Elizabeth City during the trial that Moog had told Henderson he'd wanted to marry her.

And though Angela said she did not recall it, Donna Brady had said, "I think I remember someone saying Moog told Chris he was going to marry his sister, or something like that. I can't remember if it was Chris, or maybe Angela's mom, that was kidding around about it one day. It may have been Chris."

"I was in shock when he was arrested," Angela said. "He doesn't strike me as a violent-type person. Never has, never will. And I know him. I mean, I've seen him high, I've seen him on acid, and I've seen him drunk. And he was never a violent-type person. I don't know Neal Henderson, but I definitely can't see Moog doing it. I just can't really—I don't believe Moog actually did it. I don't, to this day. I just can't. I can't." Saying this, she became more animated than at any other time during the talk.

So strong was this belief, that, yes, it was true, as I'd heard elsewhere, Angela—the girl who never shows emotion—had cried in the Elizabeth City courtroom when Upchurch had been sentenced to death.

But then she said, "I didn't know him well. I had seen him a couple of times in Chris's room." Not only had she not slept with him, or thought of him as a prospective husband, she said, "Mmm mm," shaking her head to mean no, when asked if she'd even kissed him.

She said, in fact, she had no recollection of ever even seeing him alone. "I don't remember having any private conversations with Moog. I really don't. It was just a bunch of people going out together."

As for Chris, she told me, in an absolutely flat, affectless tone, that she was angry at him not so much for what he'd tried to do to her—have her murdered in her bed so he could have more money for drugs—but mostly "because he hid it so long and put Mom through so much hell. He knew he was guilty, but he still made Mom pay all that money for his defense. It was pointless. He could have made a deal in the beginning instead of dragging it on and on."

Like her mother, Angela had never spoken to Chris about the murder in detail. "I'm afraid that if I did, I'd get really mad at him and end up hating him. And I don't want to hate him. So, I've never sat down and discussed it and I probably never will. I wanted to talk to him when he first confessed. I wanted answers, but I was afraid of what he might say. Sometimes, it's like I want to know, but I don't really want to *know*. So I just accepted what happened. It was over, in the past, and there was nothing I could do to change it. There was no point in going back to relive the whole thing again.

"Look, he can discuss it with his psychologist. It's easier for me not to have to sit down and talk about it. Why or how it happened, I really don't want to hear. There's nothing he could say or do to change it, so what's the point?"

She said, "Probably the reason I didn't react more in Vosburgh's office was that the night before, Chris took me aside and said, 'I'm gonna tell you something tomorrow that's gonna shock you, but please don't hate me.' And I said, 'Nothing you could say would make me hate you. You're my brother.' But I knew then for sure that he was guilty and that he would tell us the next day.

"Until that night, I would have laid my hand on a Bible and said he had nothing to do with it. In Vosburgh's office, as Chris was talking, I just kept thinking, 'I don't believe this.' I was just like, 'No way.' I was mad. I was shocked. Because for a year I had said, 'No, Chris had nothing to do with it. That wasn't my brother. That wasn't the brother I'd known all my life.' When I'd look over at my mom, I was wondering what she was thinking and what was going through her mind. But we never really talked about it. Not then, or ever. There really wasn't anything we could say.

"And I've never talked about it to Chris, either. That first night, driving to Greenville, I remember *not* talking about it. I didn't want to. I just remember talking about my friend Steve Tripp. Chris was hungry, but all I wanted to do in Greenville was see Steve. Chris did ask what Mom had said, and I said, 'Nothing,' because she hadn't really said anything to me."

The one time she had wanted to know more was during the period surrounding Chris's arrest and hospitalization. "I was sort of left out in the dark. I would have liked to have had more answers then, but the way the lawyers and everyone treated me, I was just the third member of the family, and I didn't want to disturb Mom or Chris.

"I've learned to control my feelings the same way my mom has. If I'm upset, I'll go to the barn and cry on my pony. I did let it get to me, but no one ever saw it."

If people were disturbed by her apparent lack of reaction, that was their problem, not hers, she said with no apparent resentment.

"My first thought when Edwards opened my door and woke me up was," she said, " 'What the hell is Danny the Dickhead doing in my house?' " She said she wasn't frightened, she was angry.

There could well have been unmelted ice in her glass. There probably was. First of all, the house was cold. Lieth liked the house very cold. And second, she had her fan on.

If John Taylor later thought he needed to turn up the air-conditioning, that was probably because the doors had been opened a lot, with people running in and out and up and down.

"After that, people say I didn't react, but I walked to that door and looked in and saw Lieth on the bed, and that's why—I went into shock then and there. I knew he was dead. It's just like you really go ice-cold. It feels like your heart just stops. And you're like, 'Oh, my God.' It's not, 'Well, is he okay?' It's, 'Oh, my God, he's dead.' So I was very calm. I was in shock. I wasn't in hysterics. I was calm."

When asked why she didn't go straight to the hospital, even riding in the ambulance with her badly injured mother, who appeared, at the time, to be near death, she replied, "I remember feeling like I needed to be at the house. I didn't think I should walk out of the house with ten million people there. You know, my parents were always like, 'We don't want anybody in the house when we're not here.' "

It might have been answers like that that caused people to question her role. But Angela had no apologies to make for her behavior.

"I just don't like to show emotion," she said. "The way I look at it is, my emotions are nobody else's business, unless it is a close friend. I want people to think I can take care of myself. It's like, 'Don't worry about me, I'm fine.' That's the reason I don't want to talk to a shrink. Because I don't like to talk to someone I don't know. I don't like to show emotions in front of people I don't know."

Returning one more time to her conduct on the morning of the murder and in the following days, she said, "I was seventeen years old. I don't know how to handle it. I figured my best bet, in order not to totally lose it, was to go out with people I knew. To surround myself with my friends. Because I mean, really, except for my mom, I'm not that close to my family. My friends were more like a family. That's who I wanted to be around, rather than hearing Ramona and Kitty bitch about Peggy being there, because she's not really part of the family. I didn't need to hear that. I didn't want to be around it. And I wasn't worried about what everyone else was thinking at the time, or whether they wanted to see me or not."

Leaving her that day, and seeing her on a couple of other occasions during the summer, I found myself liking Angela. She did not strike me as cold. But I wasn't so sure she was fine. Gliding along on the surface of life, she seemed passive, unstimulated, and more than a little bit lost.

But she had read *A Rose in Winter* three times.

And there had been blood on four neatly stacked pages by the side of the bed. Pages that contained references to blood-darkened daggers, villainous lords of the manor, a victorious hero named Christopher, and a heroine who softly sobbed out her relief.

Tom Brereton had been struck by her apparent anger over the fact that Lieth's inheritance had made no significant difference in her life. From someone normally as blasé as Angela, this would have been a surprising show of feeling in front of a stranger.

Chris had said, "I don't know if James had ever met Angela."

But Angela herself said she'd met him in Chris's room, months before Chris admitted to knowing him.

And, whenever they'd met, Moog had become his best friend, mentor, LSD source, coconspirator, and Dungeon Master. And he'd known about the money and, according to Henderson, had said he was so attracted to Angela he might even want to marry her.

Even Bill Osteen felt there was "something" between Moog and Angela.

And she'd cried when Moog was sentenced to death.

44

The truth, Bonnie had said, was what she wanted. However it turned out. And Wade had said there was no way I could hurt her: that she was a person with nothing left to lose.

But there are problems.

Chris said he came home on the Friday night before the murder to go out with friends. But the friends did not go out with him. Then he said he couldn't remember why he'd gone home. Finally, he said he'd gone home to steal the key to the back door so either he and Moog, or Moog alone, could enter the house silently. This, he had specified very clearly in his December 27 statement to investigators, was the key to the *new* back door, the *outer* back door.

The problem is, that is not the key he took. The key marked "back door" that hung on a rack in the kitchen was the key to what had been the back door before the porch had been enclosed. That was now an inner door, which Bonnie did not even lock at night.

To the new back door, there were only two keys. Bonnie kept one on her key ring at all times, and that key ring was found inside the house after the murder. There was no indication that any key had been removed from it, and no one had ever said he'd done so.

The other key to the outer back door was with a woman who lived elsewhere, a woman who came to take care of the pets when Bonnie and Lieth were away. That key had remained in her possession, undisturbed. Neither Chris nor Angela had a key to the outer back door. Not even Lieth had a key to that door.

So the key that Chris had stolen—whatever he thought it might have done—would not have opened the new back door, which Bonnie distinctly remembers locking that night. And one might surmise that Chris, having lived in the house for seven years, would have realized to his dismay that Friday night that the key he had come for was not a key he could obtain.

Angela's friend and next-door neighbor, Stephanie Mercer, remembers Angela sleeping over at her house that Friday night. She also remembers Chris coming to the back door of her house Saturday morning to speak to Angela privately.

Later in the morning, despite the fact it was raining, Angela and Donna Brady drove two hours to the beach. Angela purchased a peach-colored shirt at a Benetton store, paying with a credit card and obtaining a receipt. In the miasma of forgetfulness and blurred memory that surrounded so many events on this weekend, both Angela and Donna—and Bonnie herself—have a remarkably clear recollection of that.

Chris, by then, was back in Raleigh, picking up Moog and depositing him in a little shack behind the airport, about a mile from his house. There, from three until at least eight P.M., Moog waited, presumably alone, although Bill Osteen has his doubts about that.

Meanwhile, Chris was preparing the hamburgers that were supposed to put everyone to sleep. Preparing them all by himself—unless one goes back to his statement of August 1, 1988, when he told Lewis Young he and Angela had made the hamburgers together; or to either of the two statements Bonnie made saying the same thing. Only after it was disclosed that the hamburgers were part of an aborted murder plot did recollections that Chris and Chris alone had prepared them lock into place.

In any event, nothing happened Saturday night. Chris picked up Moog and went back to Raleigh at some point. Angela, back from the beach, was in and out of the house, but not sure where or when or with whom.

On Sunday night, Angela breaks a date with a boyfriend. ("I was supposed to go out with David. I cannot remember his last name to save my life." When the last name was given to her, she said, "Yeah, that's the one. I was supposed to go out with him and I didn't want to. So I told him Lieth wouldn't let me go out.") Instead, she goes out with Donna Brady. She isn't sure where. One time, she seems to remember it was the mall. Another time, she thinks it was down by the river. It might have been both. Wherever it was, it was boring, there was nothing to do, so she comes home early, well before her curfew, an almost unprecedented occurrence.

And for some reason, Donna Brady, who had been planning to spend the night at Angela's house, goes home instead. Donna says she doesn't remember why she didn't sleep over. Angela says only, "For some reason, she did not."

Lieth is already asleep. Angela goes upstairs to read and to listen to music. Bonnie watches the Ted Bundy miniseries with her rooster, then goes to bed.

And Neal Henderson and Moog cruise past the house, checking it out.

Moog has his knife and his bat and his flashlight—and maybe a hollow bamboo rod that "whooshes"—but no key to the new back door.

The key to the old back door also opens the front door, but nothing suggests that Moog would know this. Nowhere, in any of Chris's statements, has he said he told Moog he was not able to steal a key to the new back door, but not to worry because the key he *did* take would open the front door. In fact, Chris has made it a point to say something very different: that the key he took *was* the key to the new, outer back door. But that key can't open that door.

The new back door is directly under the master bedroom where, by four A.M., Lieth had already been sleeping almost seven hours. There is glass on the new back door, but it might be Plexiglas, hard to shatter. There is also a large, double-paned glass window farther from the door. To shatter this with a baseball bat would make a noise. There are many men, and women, too, who, upon hearing a large pane of glass shattered just beneath their bedroom window at four A.M., might wake up.

In any event, John Taylor, Lewis Young, and even Tom

Brereton are in agreement on one point: the scene resembled a staged break-in, done after the fact, not a real one.

So one is left to consider this question: If Moog had no key, and if he did not break in, how did he enter the house?

And then one might ask: Just how did the Dungeon Master, who may have wanted to marry the sleeping princess, gain entrance to the castle of the evil overlord?

Was there even the slightest possibility that someone already inside had gone downstairs before his arrival, unlocked the door, and then carried a glass of ice water back upstairs?

As Jean Spaulding once said, "There is a lot yet in this story that's untold."

"If there's a metaphor for Bonnie," Dr. Spaulding said on another occasion, "I see her as a tree where the roots are planted very deep in the soil of her family. And it is as though she can weather many storms. She has a quiet strength, a quiet serenity, but I would hate to see her take many more blows.

"One of the dominant features of Bonnie is her true love for her children. Yes, her true love for her husband was there, but without him at this point, and then going back to before he came into her life, these children are so important to her.

"That she's not demonstrative doesn't mean she doesn't love them. You cannot connect those two. Her role model for how to deal in these close relationships is her father, who doesn't cry, who doesn't have mood swings. He's busy out there in the woods by himself, carving all the trees. That seemed to be his outlet for his emotions. And so, dealing as a mother, she would tend to emulate the way her father dealt with her. She's really kind of tucked her father in there psychologically. It would be his manner of parenting that she would reflect in her style.

"But now there have been so many losses. I cannot imagine, in one lifetime, having to experience the losses that she has. She's lost her husband because he's dead. Then to lose her father right at that time, especially because he was such a source of strength. And though Chris is not dead, it's still a loss. Their relationship will never be the same. And yet she doesn't get knocked over, she just keeps right on.

"Bonnie is very involved with Chris, but with respect to Angela there's another sort of involvement. Chris has to live out x number of years in prison, but Angela is still out in the real world. So, on a different level, Angela is Bonnie's raison d'être. I would hate for anything to happen to Angela in any shape or form. There are all these things that would make one wonder, but I would certainly hope that nothing happens that would lead one to conclude that Angela is guilty of anything.

"Bonnie's primary mechanism is denial, and she's going to hold tenaciously to it, especially if something's going around on the fringes of her brain to bring up doubt. Is someone guilty or are they innocent? If you have doubt, then internally you're going to be in conflict. You counter your conflicts by holding on to your defense mechanisms. And with Bonnie, if we strip her of her defenses, I don't know what's there. And I don't think I want to know. That's all she has.

"She's already lost a lot of herself. And if somehow Angela were taken away from her, not by misfortune, death, or accident or something—but by some complicity in this whole thing—that, I think, might be more than Bonnie could endure. That might be the last little domino. Should that topple, then we'd have a very different sort of situation, I fear."

45

On Friday, June 14, 1991, at the Craggy Correctional Institute just north of Asheville, it was suggested to Chris that perhaps his sister had been told that on that Sunday night Moog was coming down just to play a prank. This would be fun, she might have been told. He was going to sneak into the house in the middle of the night and steal a few things, maybe the VCR, the stereo, the TV. Lieth would be really pissed when he woke up, but back at State they could all have a good laugh about it.

The thing was, Chris hadn't been able to find a key to the new back door. So what Angela should do, after Bonnie went to bed, was go downstairs and turn that little handle inside the knob, unlocking the door from the inside, so Moog would be able to get in.

Just an innocent prank, that's all it would be. And maybe Angela, a good sport, and eager to share in an adventure with Moog, had gone along.

Only then—to her stark, absolute, and forever-traumatizing horror—she had been awakened by the sounds of Lieth screaming, and by both him and her mother being beaten and stabbed.

That was the kind of shock, it was suggested to Chris, that could, for very sound psychological and even legal reasons, cause a person in the position Angela would have been in—had she, in all innocence, done such a thing—to withdraw deep inside herself and never come out, saying only that she didn't know anything about anything, that she'd slept through the whole thing.

At first, Chris seemed confused. "I have no idea how they got in," he said. "If Angela knew, it was not from me." Then he said, "I have to have a cigarette, do you mind?"

A moment later, he said, "It's horseshit. I did not tell Angela. If she knew, then it has her so messed up she doesn't remember."

When asked about speaking to Angela on Saturday morning at the rear of Stephanie Mercer's house, Chris got tears in his eyes. He said, "I don't remember. . . . I have no idea about that. . . . There's no way I would have told her. . . . I don't remember going by Stephanie's house."

Asked more about Moog's possible relationship with his sister, he responded in a way quite different from earlier statements. He said he remembers Moog having a crush on Angela, and saying once, "Man, your sister is good-looking."

As the conversation continued to focus on Angela, Chris seemed increasingly disturbed and upset, almost angry. He kept saying, "I don't know." He never jumped up from his chair, but he kept fidgeting in it, his legs bouncing.

"All these points are valid," he said, "but they're not true." He then added, "I'm not going to believe any of this."

Later, somewhat calmer, he said, "You got me rattled. . . . I don't want to believe it. . . . You wouldn't bring these things up without knowing something. . . . Maybe she'll talk to me. . . . I have questions, too, I want to ask her. I want to know for myself. My family is so destroyed now, but I don't want it any worse."

He continued to insist that he had not met Upchurch for the first time until summer session, and that "there's no way Moog was with us at the Def Leppard concert."

But if he didn't push back the date on which he'd first made Moog's acquaintance, he did admit that the relationship continued far beyond any point to which he'd ever before admitted. He said, contradicting all earlier statements, "We played D and D together until 1989." But never, he insisted, except on that one bad, acid-filled night in August, had they ever even mentioned the crime.

* * *

Also on June 14, two hours away, in the off-campus house she shared with college classmates, Angela responded to further questions. On this hot, sticky night a fan was blowing in her upstairs room. She seemed more alert than in earlier conversations, and her answers were more deliberate. At three separate points, she cried.

She said she and Stephanie Mercer were good friends and she slept over at Stephanie's house often, but "I just don't remember being there that night. I won't sit here and say I remember sleeping in my bed, but I do not remember sleeping at Stephanie's house. Not at all."

As for Saturday, she said first, "I went out with Donna. I probably went out to the barn." When told that Donna recalled that they had instead gone to the beach, she remembered and added, "I remember us coming back from the beach to eat dinner. Me and Donna made french fries. Chris made hamburgers."

By now, Bonnie was saying that *she* had made the french fries and couldn't even remember if Angela was present in the kitchen. But given all that happened in subsequent hours, such confusion may be free of unpleasant implication.

Though she didn't recall his being at Stephanie Mercer's back door, Angela said, "I knew Chris was going to be home that night because I saw him that morning. He asked me to be back for dinner. He said something about him making it."

About Sunday night, her statements were much more direct.

"I didn't open the door," she said. "I can tell you that much. I didn't open that door. It was probably unlocked."

She listened carefully to the explanation of how an observer could grow curious about Moog's means of entrance into the house and did not shy away from the obvious implication.

"I know," she said. "But I mean, I didn't do it. And really, the only thing I can say to any of that is go ask Neal and go ask Moog. And go ask Chris.

"But I know Chris doesn't know. And obviously Moog's not going to say anything. And Neal doesn't know me from a hole in the ground."

But as for her deliberately unlocking the door, however innocently, she was insistent. "No way. No way."

Asked if there was anything that could have led people to think she and Moog had had a closer relationship than she said they did, Angela replied, "No. I mean, I'm a very outgoing, friendly person anyway. It's nothing for me to hug someone. I may or may not have hugged him, I don't remember."

Why, then, had she cried when he was sentenced? Her answer came without hesitation.

"Because he got the death penalty. He was sentenced to die. And at that point in time, like I told you before, I still had some doubts about whether he actually did it. Because, like I said, I just don't—I mean, I knew him. I had seen him drunk before, I had seen him high before, but I just don't remember him—he wasn't the violent type. I just didn't believe he was guilty, and I couldn't believe he'd been given the death penalty.

"I just can't picture little scrawny Moog doing that. And from what Mom had said about the figure she saw being big, it just didn't fit together in my mind and it still doesn't. And it never will until he says, 'Okay, I did it,' or, 'No, I had nothing to do with it and this is what happened.' And I don't see that happening."

What then, if any, was his involvement?

"That he was there. That he, he may have been in the house. I don't know. But I just don't think that he actually did it."

A few minutes later, the questions shifted to her relationship with Lieth. This was when tears welled in her eyes.

"My relationship with Lieth was great," she said. "We had our problems, our minor disputes. Every father-daughter . . . no big deal. We had a great relationship. I loved him. I would not do anything in the world to hurt him. If I knew it was going to happen before, I would have done everything in my power to stop it. I would have told them. Just because I would never do anything to hurt Lieth or my mom. Lieth was the only dad I ever knew.'"

When asked if it bothered her that so many people were

still suspicious of her, Angela's voice took on its first trace of genuine anger.

"Yeah, it does," she said. "The only thing that pisses me off is the people that knew me before. The people who didn't know me, I could care less."

The continuing suspicions of attorneys and investigators did upset her, however.

"That pisses me off because they're the ones who talked to Chris and Neal and Moog. They're the ones who got the story before any of us knew about it. And they can sit there and have the facts laid out in front of them and still suspect an innocent party. That's what pisses me off. I had faith in, you know, you're innocent until proven guilty. I never realized there was such a thing as you're guilty anyway, whether you're innocent or not. Also, it pisses me off that Moog won't say anything."

"Why?"

"He's the one who can say why nothing happened to me. He's the one who can actually—and Chris, too. Chris can say if I had something to do with it or not. It was his plan. It was his idea. And he knows I had nothing to do with it."

Then she said, "I'd like to go under hypnosis. I'd like to do that. I would do that to see if there's anything there that I know. Because I don't remember any of it. If there's anything there, I don't know it."

And then, as the conversation shifted to Bonnie, Angela became very subdued. Her voice was soft and sad. She spoke more slowly.

"If there's one person in this world I would do anything for, it's my mom. I would not let anyone hurt her. She's my life, and I don't know what I'd do without her, honestly. If she would have died, I would be in a mental hospital somewhere.

"I had nothing to do with it. And I'm glad that she's the one person that believes me. That honestly believes me. That has no doubt. And she may, but she hides it very well if she does."

As the talk ended, focusing on the subject of Chris, Angela's voice became shaky and tears came again.

"The reason I haven't talked to him about it is because *I don't want to*. I don't want to because after I do, I'll hate him. There's no doubt in my mind. He killed my dad. He almost killed my mom. He's my brother and I want to love him because he's my brother, but I just can't. So I just don't want to talk to him about it."

Actually sniffling now, Angela said, "I love him because he admitted it, but I hate him because he did it."

And then she said that in the year and a half since he'd been in prison, and even though he was now only two hours away, she'd never once been to visit him alone.

"I just never have," she said, "because I'm afraid it's going to come to talking about it, and I just don't want to talk about it."

The road back to Asheville from the house where Angela was living—in a small town where northeast Tennessee meets southwest Virginia—starts out like any other highway. It's four lanes at the outskirts of Johnson City, Tennessee. Then, looking ahead, you get your first glimpse of the always hazy, misty Blue Ridge Mountains rising to the south and west.

The road narrows to two lanes and then begins a thirty-mile climb up a mountain. There's no passing here. The road winds through small crevices. Sometimes, there's the illusion that the road will slam you right into the side of the mountain, but then it will gently groan around a curve and shoot you off toward another pass.

Eventually, it takes you up and over the ridge and deposits you back in North Carolina. It's a beautiful road, a great road for thinking.

And one of the thoughts that comes to mind is how ironic it is that these two sad, forlorn children, once so close to each other, and so cut off from all else that they'd hug silently for hours on end, are now separated not only by such a mountain, but by the indelible horror of July 25, 1988.

Unless, at some dark, subterranean level, that horror has drawn them closer together.

Chris wrote to me on June 21, 1991, in response to further questions about Angela: "The questions you have are legitimate and they deserve legitimate answers. But your point about my sister's involvement is wrong. It is valid, but wrong. I wasn't at the house during the murder, but I do know my sister. While in high school, little short of throwing water on her or bodily removing her from bed would wake her up. It is thus possible for me to believe that she slept through it all. She had no prior knowledge of what happened."

Later in the letter, he wrote, "I got so sick of lying during the period following my dad's murder, I vowed to never lie again. I would not actively or consciously lie, even if my life depended on it. I can say that with assurance."

But just before closing, he added, "In all honesty, if my sister had been involved and I knew about it, I wouldn't tell you."

46

Three months earlier Chris had written in response to my asking if he spent much time thinking about why it was that he was in prison.

He replied:

Do I think about what happened to put me here? Yes and no. Let me explain. At first, all I did was think about everything that happened during the previous two years. Most of the things that came to mind severely depressed and disgusted me. My first two or three weeks in prison left me unable to hold down any food. During this time, suicide was still an option. I was receiving Serentil during this period and I had been collecting it in my cell, under the nose of the nurse who "supervised" me while I took it. Before my imprisonment, I had researched this medication to see what an overdose would do. The book I used said it would put me into a coma just before I died. As you know, I did not go through with it.

The guilt I had been hiding for the previous year and a half had been exposed in full. My family and friends knew everything and they loved and supported me anyway. In my first two months, I got over 150 letters and cards from them. I averaged seven letters a day from them after the first three weeks. This overwhelmed me emotionally. It was inconceivable to me, at the time, that *anyone* could love me. My self-esteem had never been high and was at its lowest point. The guilt I felt was unbearable.

My thoughts ran along these lines: *I* killed my father and ruined my family and friends' lives. My life had been handed to me on a gold plate and I rejected it. To add insult, I spat upon what was handed me. Every time my mom came to visit, all I could see was her lying in intensive care. The only good thing I could see was that I was no longer out there to further injure, emotionally, those that I loved. It seemed I only brought misery to those who tried to love me.

No matter how much my family showed me their love . . . for a long time I simply could not forgive myself. I felt I deserved to die. My mom kept coming to see me and I eventually snapped out of my depression. I saw that my family and friends had forgiven me. My next step was to forgive myself.

I have to do that all the time. Whenever I think back at the damage I did, I get depressed. After I let those thoughts torture me awhile, I get to thinking about how everyone who matters treats me. God has forgiven me and so have my family and friends. Therefore, I must forgive myself.

I still struggle with my past, though not as often. My insane past made me sane. Everything is much different for me now. I don't worry about things anymore—I think about them. No longer am I a confused, insecure, emotional child. I can feel free to let my emotions show, although that opportunity doesn't arise very often here.

I deserve to be punished and will accept the punishment I have, but damn it, no one will benefit from my imprisonment! I can do very little from here to teach other people how to avoid this place. I'm not whining about my time, nor do I stay depressed about it. I miss a lot of things about society, most of all being with my family and friends.

There is a flip side to this prison coin, however. Had I not come here, I probably wouldn't have discovered my family and friends. Their love was ever before me—as was God's—but I had to come here to find it. In a sense I am more free now than I was when I was out in the world. I have plenty of time to search my soul. I'm finding out who I really am, deep beyond the surface. I like what I find. Prison has, in fact, set me free.

From certain quarters, however, forgiveness has been slow to come. There is, of course, Angela. But there are also Bonnie's two sisters, Kitty and Sylvia, who do not wish to see Chris.

Sylvia says she admires Bonnie for being able to visit him, but she herself cannot. She simply cannot forgive him for what he's done. This has even caused her to stop teaching Sunday school at the Methodist church in Welcome.

"I cannot stand in front of a group of people and teach forgiveness if I myself cannot forgive."

This is not something about which she's been able to talk to Bonnie, she said, because "Bonnie is a very private person."

And then there is Bonnie's brother, George, who, this past June, reflected on all that has happened since the murder.

"I've been in touch with Bonnie a lot more," he said. "For the simple fact that I know I almost lost her. And that if I had lost her"—here, already, he paused, his eyes filling with tears—"I never would be able to just pick up the phone and call her again."

He can still vividly recall going from his early-morning meeting with Lewis Young, where he first pointed the finger of suspicion at Chris, to the hospital where he looked down upon Bonnie in her bed.

"Boy," he said, shaking his head at the memory. "It was like, 'Sis, I hope . . . I hope . . . I hope what we're thinking or feeling is not true. And I hope you won't think bad of us. I don't want to be the heavy. I don't want to be the one who says, "Look, your son did it," or, "I squealed on your son," or, "I even had something to do with putting the police on your son." I don't want to be the bad one here.'

"But I did it because I did not want anything to happen to my sister. My first concern was for her. I was thinking, 'I hope this is not true. But I've got to say how I feel, what I see, for your safety. I hope it's not true.' But at this point you can't leave any stone unturned, any suspicions. You cannot take any chances.

"I didn't care what anybody else thought. When it came to her safety, I could not take that chance. I would rather be an outcast and have her hate me for the rest of my life, not speak to me, knowing that she's going to live. And they're not going to get to her again.

"And to this day," he said, tears overflowing his eyes, *"I'm not sure it won't happen again."*

After a pause, he was asked why.

"Because," he said, "I've seen the bullshit letters from Chris. And I worry that the strict father-figure is no longer there. 'There's no one to tell me no. I can get around Mom.' It's almost like, 'So, I'll cool my heels and I'll be out in a while and I'll go back and I'll get everything. No matter what.' "

He said he had not yet shared this misgiving with Bonnie because he did not want to upset her further. Besides, it was a hard thing to talk about.

But he said he'd neither written to Chris nor visited him. "My mother does," he said. "Mom is just like Bonnie. She believes that he realizes he's done wrong and has mended his ways. That he's going to follow the right path. I'm sorry. I will not. I just cannot. I'm from the old school. I just don't believe that. I have not written him. I have not seen him since the trial. It's something I cannot condone. To try to kill your own mother—that's probably the worst possible thing someone can do."

His comment reminded me of a rhetorical question Jean Spaulding had once asked. "If he had gotten away with it, would he have any sense of remorse?"

And even Bonnie's mother—little four-foot-nine-inch, sixty-eight-year-old Polly Bates—said forgiveness had come hard for her.

"I probably spent more time with Chris in those first couple of years after Steve left than she did," Bonnie's mother told me one evening in Welcome.

"What I remember most is how he would just lie right there on the floor, screaming and crying. There was just no way to make him stop. I'd tell him over and over again that his mommy was coming home, but there was nothing you could do to calm him down. Angela, she'd never say a word. Just sit there silent as a ghost. And when Chris wasn't crying, and Bonnie was late getting home, the two of them would just sit there on the hearth for hours, all huddled up together, neither one of them saying a word, just hugging each other. And I'd always tell them, 'Don't worry, your mom will be here soon.'

"Everywhere we'd take those kids, Angela would sit as still and quiet as a statue, but Chris, he'd walk up to complete strangers—just somebody filling our tank at a gas station—and he'd say, 'My daddy left me.' If I heard it once, I heard the poor boy say it a hundred times, every time he met somebody new—'My daddy left me'—those would be the first words out of his mouth.

"I think George and I were the only stability that poor boy had growing up. He loved his granddaddy so much. They'd plant watermelon seeds, and he'd be so proud when his watermelon came up better than his granddaddy's. Then, of course, they'd go fishing in the creek. George had

a very special love for that boy, which is what made it all
the harder for him to contend with what happened.

"This was why we were so happy when Lieth came into
Bonnie's life. She'd tried so hard, and it seemed she'd had
such little happiness. But Lieth was wonderful to her. And
to me, too. When I was sick in the hospital, he'd call me
two times a week, asking if there was anything I needed.
He would tell me he loved me, and I really believe that he
meant it.

"But Bonnie? Believe me, he was the light of her life.
So, I tell Chris I love him, but it's hard. Because I have too
much to forget. I can't blame anyone for turning away."

And then Bonnie's mother, like her brother and like
Angela, began to cry.

"We went to see Lieth before he was cremated," she
said. "And every night, when I go to sleep, that's the
image I still see: poor Lieth, his head split open in three
places.

"So I write to Chris, and I tell him I love him. But every
time I say those words, I see Lieth lying there with his
head split."

She was crying harder now, but had one more thing she
wanted to say.

"All I know is I feel so bad for Bonnie I could die."

And Wade Smith, who'd brought me into all this, had
one last summation he wanted to give concerning Bonnie.

"If you could attach colors to grief," he said, "Bonnie's
grief would be a different color, a far more intense color,
a deeper pain. She *began* with the grief of a loved one
killed violently, and it went downhill from there. And it
continued to go downhill to the end, when she suffered a
kind of ultimate numbness over the realization that her own
flesh and blood had killed her husband.

"At that point, there was no place to which she could
retreat. All her options were gone. She could either die or
she could somehow manage to live through it. And she
chose to just keep on going.

"And in that process I came to admire her and respect

her and like her. And to believe that she was a human being of enormous worth, of tremendous personal strength.

"She didn't whine. She didn't come in and sit and weep for hours. She simply quietly took it with what I perceive to be a real dignity. So I see her as a very sympathetic figure. A woman who has suffered just about as much as a human being can tolerate.

"Are you going to hold it against a person who reaches inside for strength, and who bears this burden with great dignity and with real courage? No one I know of ever had a harder, heavier cross to bear than Bonnie did. This cross Bonnie was bearing, it had twists to it that were just unbelievable. The twists jerked her all over the place, jerked her emotions from side to side. Yanked in one direction loving her husband; yanked in another direction loving her son; yanked in *another* direction with Bonnie herself at first a suspect and having to be polygraphed; yanked in another direction when her father died; yanked in another direction when she had to pay for the defense of her son. It put her in a place where she had to choose to believe her son when he said he didn't do it. She had to gradually learn the truth. It might have been easier for her had she learned it all at once. But we let her learn it over a period of time.

"It's possible in her heart she knew. But I never held it against her for refusing as long as she could to believe that her son would do this to her husband, and to her. I thought that was natural and logical. And that even if she held out longer in that belief than we would think, upon reflection, was wise, we can forgive her for that.

"We *should* forgive her for that. This boy was her son and she had a right to wait as long as she could before she yielded to the evidence and started to believe that maybe he did it.

"When I think of Bonnie," Wade said, "I always picture the gods as having, for their entertainment, conceived this remarkable scenario in which they could test her. Test the limits of her endurance. Of anyone's endurance.

"The gods get bored because they have everything they want and can do anything they want. And when they get bored, they are the most dangerous to us. Because then they make up games and they play games with us.

"They got bored and used Bonnie. I can picture them devising this very complicated, convoluted, weird situation which would test her: where they could enjoy watching her skitter across the hot landscape, watch her dance, see how much she can take.

"And when, at the end, it appeared that she just might be making it, the gods said, 'This won't do,' and they introduced a new wrinkle, which was to take her father in an ironic way. To not let him die of a heart attack or in peace, but to let him be killed by a tree. To add a bizarre twist to hurt her even more.

"I will always think of Bonnie as a little droplet of water skittering across a hot skillet that had been devised by the gods. And the gods were dancing."

47

Until June of 1991, when she had her phone number changed, Bonnie kept Chris's voice on the answering machine. So that almost three years after he'd tried to have her killed, and almost eighteen months after he'd started serving his prison term, you could still hear his voice by calling Bonnie.

"I'm not there yet," she told me in June, "but I can see that the road to recovery is open. I know I've still got a lot of anger. Anger towards Chris. And I know that someday I will have to deal with it. But I'm not ready to do it yet. I know it's there but I'm not ready to deal with it. It's a lot easier to lay down new linoleum, or stay up until three in the morning, putting a fresh coat of paint in the kitchen. But I do know, now, that that day must come.

"It's something I'm working on. Just like with Angela. I'd like to have her start to see Dr. Spaulding. I think Dr. Spaulding would be able to draw Angela out in a way that no one else ever has. I think that might do Angela a lot of good. She doesn't need this weighing her down for years to come."

Bonnie was well aware of how many people, in and out of her family, still had qualms about Angela's role. But Bonnie herself had no doubts. As Angela sensed, Bonnie believed in her and trusted her and wanted only to find a way to help her heal.

In one late-night conversation with me, Bonnie asked suddenly, her voice faltering, "Why did Lieth get stabbed in the back? He'd been sitting straight up, facing his attacker head-on, fighting for his life. Why did he get stabbed in the back?"

She paused and sighed, and I could tell she was as close to real tears as she'd ever been when speaking to me.

"It was," she said, "because he had thrown himself across me, trying to cover me up, trying to protect me, trying to somehow save my life. Lieth died trying to make sure I would live.

"And if he could do that for me, I guess what I can do for him is just persevere and get on with it and try to still find something worthwhile in my life.

"It's been a long time since I've been able to think like that, much less say it, but I think I might be getting ready to begin."

And that brought back to mind one warm Saturday morning the previous spring when I'd gotten out of the Winston-Salem house with her, down to Welcome, to her real home.

It had been by far the most enjoyable time I'd ever spent with her. She drove me all over the town, stopping at her mother's house so I could admire the quilts and orchids, and so I could see the attic dormitory where she and her sisters had grown up.

We'd gone on into Lexington and she'd showed me the

very drive-in (long since shut down) where she'd pulled up next to Steve Pritchard's car.

Then she took me to Finch Park, where she and Lieth and her two little children would come on Saturday mornings—just like this one—when he was down from Cincinnati. This was after she'd overcome her fear that he would forget her once he moved.

Bonnie's step was lighter that morning, as was her mood. There was a flicker of something almost approaching joy that I'd not seen before. It seemed to come just from being, however briefly, and however different the circumstances, back in a place where she'd once felt hope.

There were swans in a large pond, there was a bandstand, there were shade trees, open, grassy fields, a path around the edge of the pond, playground equipment for the children.

This was where she had first seen it. This was where she had first sensed that her future might still hold some measure of happiness: with this man, whose head she cradled in her lap, as together they watched her young children play on the swings.

About the Author

JOE McGINNISS is the author of five previous nonfiction works—*The Selling of the President, Heroes, Going to Extremes, Fatal Vision,* and *Blind Faith*—and one novel, *The Dream Team.*